100 Greatest Science Inventions of All Time

DISCARD

100 Greatest Science Inventions of All Time

Kendall Haven

A Member of the Greenwood Publishing Group

Westport, Connecticut • London

Library of Congress Cataloging-in-Publication Data

Haven, Kendall F.
   100 greatest science inventions of all time / by Kendall Haven.
     p. cm.
   Includes bibliographical references and index.
   ISBN 1-59158-264-4 (pbk : alk. paper)
   1. Inventions–History. I. Title. II. Title: One hundred greatest science inventions of all time.
   T15.H38 2006
   609–dc22   2005030805

British Library Cataloguing in Publication Data is available.

Library of Congress Catalog Card Number: 2005030805
ISBN: 1-59158-264-4

First published in 2006

Libraries Unlimited, 88 Post Road West, Westport, CT 06881
A Member of the Greenwood Publishing Group, Inc.
www.lu.com

Printed in the United States of America

The paper used in this book complies with the
Permanent Paper Standard issued by the National
Information Standards Organization (Z39.48-1984).

10 9 8 7 6 5 4 3 2

This book is dedicated to
two awe-inspiring groups:
first, the scientists, engineers, and others
whose drive, passion, insight, and creative flashes of genius
have given us the endless array of inventions
that ease our every moment and every day;
and second,
the dedicated teachers
who bring the world of science into thrilling,
vivid life for their students.

Contents

Acknowledgments

This book would not have been possible without the help, guidance, and support of many people. In particular, I owe thanks to the library staffs at the Sonoma County Library System and the Sonoma State University library for their help in locating and obtaining the reference material for these inventions. Barbara Ittner, the editor for this and many of my other Libraries Unlimited books, provided guidance, vision, and wisdom in great abundance that helped to give focus and shape to this work. Finally, my greatest debt of thanks goes to Roni Berg, the love of my life, who critiqued and refined each page of the book.

Introduction

Invention! The mere word stirs the blood and quickens the pulse. Inventions are exciting, even thrilling. An invention feels as exciting as finding buried treasure. It is the creation of something useful where nothing existed before. Invention is a sure expression of practical genius. The world is a fuller, richer place because of an invention.

Why study inventions? Studying inventions is an effective way to track the progress and development of societies. Inventions form a roadmap of the history of human development. They are the physical manifestation of the best human ingenuity and cleverness. Inventions form the leading edge of development and technology in each age and culture. It is impossible to study the history of human science and development without turning to inventions.

In this book I present the 100 greatest of all science inventions. In each entry I describe the process of, and effect of, each of these major inventions. This book will be a useful tool for teachers and students to learn about inventions and their critical role in human development. These stories introduce the process of inventions and the most important inventions.

I had four purposes in mind as I wrote this book:

1. I want to present the nature and scope of past great inventions and show their importance to our modern lives.

2. I want to place each of these specific inventions within the continuum of technological development. I want to show what came before and what came after each great invention.

3. I want to clearly show students that the world around them is created by, and defined by, these master inventions that are woven into the fabric of our daily existence.

4. I want to show the role of science and of the scientific process in the process of invention.

But what is an invention? Where does *invention* stop and *discovery* start? Is there a dividing line between the two? When I was a seventh grader, I remember thinking that Isaac Newton *invented* gravity. And I wondered how people held onto the earth and how far they could throw a baseball before Newton invented gravity.

Then I learned that he didn't *invent* gravity. It existed long before Newton or any other human set foot on the earth. You can't *invent* something that already exists.

Then did Newton *discover* gravity? No again. Scientists had known about gravity for hundreds of years before Newton was born. To discover something, you have to be the first one to detect or become aware of the thing being discovered.

So, what *did* Newton do for gravity? Why do we associate his name with gravity? Newton invented mathematical expressions that accurately described gravity, and he invented a whole new system of math (calculus) that allowed people to make calculations involving gravity.

Nothing like calculus existed before Newton created (invented) it. Like any good invention, Newton's calculus (and his equations) let people easily do things that they needed to do and that they could not do before. To be an invention, it had to be a tangible thing, not just an idea.

Frederick Banting discovered insulin in 1921. That was a discovery. After two additional years of work, he created (invented) synthetic insulin (a specific product that took advantage of his previous discovery). Not all discoveries lead directly to practical invention, and not all inventions follow on the heels of a specific discovery. Still, that is a common pattern as discoveries and inventions twirl through their improvisational dance toward progress and advancement.

Beyond the idea for an invention, and the science knowledge to support that idea, inventions need money and the ability to create the necessary materials. Charles Babbage conceived of a mechanical computer a hundred years before the first digital computer was built. But he couldn't build his computer because no metal shop of his time could fabricate the precision parts he needed.

Alexander Graham Bell invented a photophone, a version of the telephone that transmitted its signal over a beam of light. It was a predecessor of fiber optics. In 1878 when Bell invented it, no one cared. It didn't satisfy any existing need. If flopped. One hundred years later, fiber optics became a huge communications industry. In 1978 people were ready to use a communication system that transmitted signals over light.

If the knowledge, materials, funding, and need all exist at the same time, then the glories of invention await only an inventor and his or her idea—the spark of inventive genius that sees how to create the thing that needs to be invented—and the determination and work to bring that vision into physical being.

This is a book about the 100 greatest science inventions of all time. But what do I mean by "great science inventions?" Several brief definitions will help:

- An *invention* (as we have seen above) is a created device or product that includes significantly new technology or application to mark this thing as distinctively different from all previous products.

- *Great* means beyond the ordinary, especially important and powerful or significant in history. Great inventions change the human world, alter human direction, or redefine human life. Color TV is an important and much-used invention. However, it is really just a refinement of a previous invention—television. The invention of television changed the world. It is a great invention, whereas color television is not.

- *Science* is a branch of study concerned with facts, principles, and methods; a series of specific disciplines divided into the physical sciences, earth sciences, and life sciences.

A *great science invention,* then, is a created device or product based on knowledge derived from one of the branches of science that transcends the ordinary invention, that alters human history in an important and powerful way, that reshapes or redirects the progress of human society.

The inventions described in this book are the greatest of the great science inventions. Great inventions gain widespread use. They become a central part of life and of their culture. They redirect the structure and development of science and of societies and cultures.

There are many more than 100 great science inventions, and many times that number of great inventions if we expand beyond the science fields to consider *all* inventions. Here are the questions I used to evaluate and rank the many hundreds of inventions to arrive at the 100 greatest:

1. Is this invention something new, or just an improvement on or refinement of an existing product? Did its invention change the course of (or at least affect) human development?

2. Dos this invention fall within a recognized field of science? Did the inventor use tools and processes of science for its invention?

3. How much of our daily lives is affected by this invention?

4. How much of our income, time, and energy are spent on it?

5. What percentage of the population owns or uses the invention?

6. What would be the effect on society of losing this invention?

7. How many people are employed in jobs related to this invention?

Many worthy inventions and inventors are not here because they do not qualify as *science* inventions. This list includes language, the alphabet, money, table manners, civility, sports and games, chocolate, clothes, art, music, towns, worship, law, hospitals, credit cards, universities, libraries, etc. They qualify as great inventions that have touched many of our lives, but not as great *science* inventions, and so are excluded from this book.

Likewise, many important inventors are not included. Just because a person's invention is not on the top 100 list doesn't mean that person hasn't made major contributions to human development and doesn't deserve our study and praise. Hypatia, Madam CJ Walker, Benjamin Franklin, Emmett Chappella, Elijah McCoy (the "real McCoy") , Granville Woods, George Washington Carver, Benjamin Bannaker, Nolan Bushnell, and hundreds of others were all important inventors, but not the inventors of one of the top 100 science inventions.

Many of science's greatest heroes are also not included in this book. Isaac Newton, Albert Einstein, Copernicus, Gregor Mendel, Robert Boyle, Charles Darwin, and a host of others aren't here because they are responsible for great discoveries, not inventions.

This book can be used as a read-aloud or to enhance a unit introduction for either inventions or technology in general. Students can use these entries as a reference to support their research on inventors and inventions. Finally, these inventions and the process of their development make for fascinating leisure reading.

The bulk of this book is a chronological listing of the 100 greatest science inventions. Each entry contains several subsections. The entries begin with the year that item was invented, a definition of what it is, and who invented it. Then I explain why this is one of the greatest of the great inventions and show how it has affected human development and life. In presenting the process used for creating each invention, I include a section describing what people did before this invention and another describing what has happened since it was invented in order to place it within the continuum of inventive development. Finally, I include a few of the many available references for these inventors and inventions.

Several entries feature two separate inventions that were integral parts of a single greater development. For example, development of skyscrapers depended on two inventions: steel skeletal construction and elevators. Those two fit so tightly hand-in-hand that I combined them into one entry. Similarly, sailing ships' ability to navigate by calculating longitude depended on two inventions: a seaworthy clock and an improved sextant. They, too, are grouped into one entry.

Several entries include two inventions because, collectively, they qualify as a great invention even though individually they do not. Velcro and the zipper are a good example. They qualify collectively as "Fast Fasteners." Individually—although important inventions—they would not make the top 100 list.

I have included several appendixes in the back of the book. Appendix A is an alphabetical list of inventors featured in the book, appendix B is a list of the inventions grouped into their areas of invention, and appendix C is a list of the next 40 inventions. These are 40 great science inventions that *almost* made it into the top 100 list. I suggest that these inventions and inventors are excellent research topics to explore. Finally, appendix D contains references on the general topics of inventions, inventors, and inventing.

Enjoy the list of included inventions and the idea of great inventions. Ponder which inventions you would have included and which you think are great. Marvel at the dedication and perseverance of these inventors. (Thomas Edison often said that invention is 1 percent inspiration and 99 percent perspiration.) Relish their ingenuity. Marvel at their variety of backgrounds, education, age, purposes, and paths.

Then, perhaps, begin to search for the thing you have always wanted to invent!

Inventions That Predate History

Why Are *These* Included in the List of Greatest Science Inventions?

A few important inventions were in use so long ago that they predate written records. We don't know how they were invented or who invented them, or even if they had a true, single inventor.

However, the following nine inventions are so basic to human and scientific beginnings that they must be mentioned. Take these away, and our civilized world falls apart. They form the first cornerstones of human progress.

Prehistory Critical Science Inventions

Balance Scale

A balance scale is a way to compare two weights. A teeter-totter is an example of a balance scale. Metal scales dating to 5000 B.C. have been found in archeological digs. Balance scales were in use by 4000 B.C. in both Egypt and China. Egyptians were able to accurately measure to a small fraction of an ounce by 1500 B.C.

The ability to compare two weights led to units of weight (tons, ounces, grams, pounds, etc.) and to number scales. Commerce evolved because balance scales gave merchants the ability to measure weights of product and payment and to measure their gains and losses.

Bow and Arrow

The first humanoids used bows and arrows for hunting sometime before 30,000 B.C. Those early bows were little more than a vine stretched across a bent sapling branch. The first arrows were most likely sharpened sticks

We do not know how, when, or why, some clever human decided that short spears (arrows) would go farther, harder, and faster and be more deadly if he used the spring and power of a thin branch and a vine to propel them. But someone did, and the bow and arrow was born.

Over time, humans improved the flexibility, strength, spring, and resiliency of their bows. Surely bow makers conducted thousands of experiments, testing and comparing different types of wood and of building and layering a bow. Creating better hunting weapons helped early man learn how to conduct experiments, tests, and scientific investigations.

High-powered crossbows first appeared in Europe around A.D. 1000. The famed English longbow first appeared about 200 years later. These two versions of the bow were the world's first long-range weapons as well as being a great boon to hunting and to food production. In its various forms the bow was also the most powerful and dominant weapon on Earth for almost a thousand years—until gunpowder made muskets more lethal.

Dam

Nature's logjams created the first partial dams. Humans undoubtedly saw such dams and understood the value of creating artificial ponds and lakes behind thick barriers. However, it was the Egyptians who built the first known dams some 5,000 years ago.

Once the concept of dams took hold in human communities, ponds created by dams became the basic supply of water for sustained agriculture and irrigation in the arid and semiarid parts of the world. (*Irrigation* comes from the Latin for "to water inward.") A solid dam plus irrigation ditches guaranteed steady, good harvests and allowed communities to settle and to grow.

But dams themselves were large-scale engineering and construction projects and a massive investment in the infrastructure of the community. Dams were one of the first collective actions and a building block of community and government. Dams helped lead to the creation of city-states.

Knife

The first knives were probably sharpened rocks—most likely obsidian or one of the sedimentary rocks that layers easily (such as flint). Or perhaps jagged bones served as the first knives, and ground and polished rocks came second. What a great leap forward it was to be able to cut things at will! Rope, bread, meat, fur for clothes—humans have always needed to cut and reshape a thousand daily things.

The knife quickly became a hunting tool, a weapon, a basic tool of commerce to seize and deliver a precise amount of a product, an eating utensil, and an indispensable domestic tool. The knife was also one of the first and most basic tools of early doctors. Knives cut and divide, both basic steps for much research and science. It is impossible to imagine human development or modern civilization without knives.

Lever

A lever is a rigid bar that rotates around a fixed point (the fulcrum) and is generally used to lift a weight placed on one end. Some early human figured out that a boulder was easier to move if he wedged a solid branch under it and pushed down on one end of the branch in order to lift the stone with the other.

Levers were first mathematically described by Archimedes in 230 B.C. He is often mistakenly called the inventor of the lever. The lever is many thousands of years older. Archimedes gave us mathematical ways to understand what happened with a lever.

Scissors, pump handles, sheers, tongs, pliers, seesaws, nutcrackers, all use the principle of a lever. A lever is one of the most basic construction concepts. Few buildings, bridges, and other large projects could be built without making use of a lever.

Pulley

In its simplest form, a pulley consists of a rope thrown over a horizontal tree branch or pole. You pull down on one end of the rope to lift something attached to the other. That kind of pulley predates all records.

However, a pulley only became a specific mechanical device when the pulley's rope was looped not over a branch, but over a wheel that was free to turn. That meant that the wheel had to be mounted on an axle, and the axle was then suspended from some secure beam, bar, or branch above. By 3000 B.C., such pulleys with grooved wheels (so that the rope wouldn't slip off) existed in Egypt and Syria.

The Greek mathematician and inventor Archimedes gets credit for inventing the *compound* pulley in about 230 B.C. In a compound pulley, not one, but a number of wheels and ropes combine to lift a single object. Compound pulleys multiply the lifting power of a person. Modern block and tackle systems are examples of compound pulleys.

Rope

The first ropes were undoubtedly vines—nature's ropes—hanging from trees in thick forests. Stripped of leaves, they served to tie objects and packs together and could be woven into thick bundles used as nets for hunting or for building footbridges over streams and gullies. The use of these vine ropes likely dates back 30,000 years or more.

Manufactured rope from hemp and from the stringy fibers of Nile River reeds and plants dates to around 5000 B.C. Ropes held together early construction projects. Ropes connected great blocks of stone to the lines of humans and animals used to pull them into place. Ropes raised the sails on ships and hold those sails in place to catch the wind. They fastened heavy loads onto mules and oxen and into early wagons. Ropes secured tents. Western lassos were made of rope.

Soap

Soap is the basic cleaning agent for humans. We wash ourselves, our clothes, our hair, our dishes, and our cars with soap. Soap is the most basic weapon in the war to protect our health and to fight disease-causing germs.

Soaps have been found that date to 3000 B.C. However, soap itself was in use long before that time. Early soaps were a mixture of melted animal fat and ash. Legend says that soap was discovered clumped along the shore downstream from places where animals were sacrificed and burned. Fat from the animal and ash from the fire landed in streams, mixed, and solidified into soap. But no one knows for sure. Further, those legends do not record who the clever person was who first saw that lumpy, slippery mass along the shore and realized she could clean something with it.

For centuries, soap makers boiled slabs of animal fat in bubbling pots and added a strong alkali (ash, caustic soda, or potash). By the sixteenth century, scents, moisturizing oils, and perfumes were added to encourage sales. After 1916, chemically created detergents replaced animal fat.

Wheel

Cars, scooters, wagons, and bikes have wheels. Manufacturing plants and machines are loaded with wheels. Clocks have internal wheels. Even chairs often have wheels. Nearly every machine created in the past 2,000 years has used some form of wheel. The value and importance of the wheel cannot be overstated.

From the best that researchers can determine, it appears that wheels did not begin as rolling devices, but as potters' wheels—wheels mounted horizontally at table level that spun as a potter worked her clay into shape. Potters' wheels have been found in archeological digs at ancient Mesopotamian sites that date to earlier than 4000 B.C.

Rolling wooden wheels suddenly appeared in Sumeria (Southwest Asia) around 3500 B.C. The axle connecting two wheels first appeared in Egypt around 2000 B.C.

100

Greatest Science Inventions of All Time

Roads

Year of Invention: 250 B.C.

> **What Is It?** A reinforced, smooth surface over which large vehicles and wagons can easily travel.
>
> **Who Invented It?** Roman engineers (in Italy)

Why Is *This* Invention One of the 100 Greatest?

Nothing is more basic or essential to our transportation system than roads. Truck, cars and motorcycles need roads. Commuters, vacationers, and shoppers depend on roads. Roads connect groups and cities. Roads have allowed the development of commerce and trade.

History of the Invention

What Did People Do Before?

Early humans followed animal paths through the forest, jungle, and meadow. Paths were widened for carts. Dirt cart paths were usually little more than two parallel ruts replacing the single rut that had been a foot path.

It was difficult—almost impossible—to move a large mass of men (such as an army) and a large amount of supplies and equipment (such as an army's baggage train) along these bumpy, muddy, low-grade dirt roads. Wagons placed a greater load on the road surface and turned it into an impassible quagmire.

How Was the Road Invented?

By 270 B.C. a lack of reliable roads to move armies and supply trains across the Roman Empire had become a major concern. Engineers were assigned to fix it. They watched as roads disintegrated into potholes, mud, and ruts. They experimented to find the root causes and to test a variety of possible fixes.

The first thing these engineers discovered was that, over time, roads were trampled into depressions in the ground—often many inches lower than the surrounding landscape. Roads became natural pooling places for water. Pooled water turned quickly to mud. Roman principle number one: roads needed to be raised and built to provide proper drainage.

By 260 B.C. this principle had come to mean that every road needed a porous—but solid—foundation. Next, Roman engineers studied ways to handle the massive weight of the four-wheeled baggage carts that trailed behind a marching Roman army. They decided that a series of layers designed to spread the force of heavy wheels would protect and preserve the smooth top surface of their roads. They experimented with different top surfaces, searching for ones that were durable, stable, strong, and easily available.

By 250 B.C., Roman engineers had developed a road-building manual that would not be equaled for another 2,000 years. Roman roads were carefully surveyed and carefully built in four layers. The names for these layers can still be found in the words we use to describe roads today.

First, laborers would dig and smooth the *pavimentum*—a trench for the road, lined with edging stones and made of smoothed, rammed earth. Next, a layer called the *rudus* would be laid on top of this hard dirt surface. The *rudus* was made of concrete mixed with broken stones and tile. Its job was to provide drainage and to evenly spread any weight passing along the road onto the ground below.

Above the *rudus*, laborers laid the *nucleus*, a layer of slag or lime, chalk, tile, etc. The *nucleus* acted as a cushion to absorb most of the stress of marching feet and loaded wagon wheels. Finally, the top layer, the *summum dorsum* of fitted flagstones, would be laid into place. This was the actual surface that people marched on and wagons rolled over.

Roman engineers constructed 372 major roads across their empire, including more than 53,000 miles of developed roadway that stretched from Africa to Scotland, from Spain to Greece. Masses of slave labor from conquered lands were used to cut and haul rock and other materials to road construction sites as well as to dig, smooth, and lay the road layers. The work was brutal. But the resulting roads were magnificent and were not duplicated for another 2,000 years.

What's Happened Since Then?

As Rome's empire collapsed, road construction in Europe reverted to undeveloped dirt. France was the first country to reinstate a systematic approach to road building under the direction of engineer Ipierre Tresaguet beginning in the 1730s. By 1740, England had begun to develop a few major road thoroughfares.

In 1765, "Blind Jack" Metcalfe began building roads in England under contract with the government. He was the first person (since the ancient Roman engineers) to identify the importance of roadway drainage and foundation. By 1790, Metcalfe had completed 300 miles of roads—the first roads as good as the Roman roads build almost 2,000 years earlier.

It wasn't until 1824 that an entire town's roads were systematically paved. Thomas Telford undertook that effort for a wealthy suburb of London. Beginning in 1905, the popularity of motorcars created a demand for smoother road surfaces. Macadam and tarmac emerged as the best surfaces for "black top" roads. Blacktop spread across America and Europe, connecting cities and towns with shimmering ribbons of black.

The first road built exclusively for cars opened on Long Island, New York, in 1914. The first American freeway connected Pasadena to Los Angeles, beginning in 1953.

Fun Fact: The world's *lowest* road runs along the Israeli shore of the Dead Sea. In spots it hits 1,289 feet below sea level.

More to Explore

Crump, Donald J., ed. *Builders of the Ancient World: Marvels of Engineering.* Washington, DC: National Geographic Society, 1996.

Hennessy, B. G. *Road Builders.* New York: Puffin Books, 1996.

Hill, Lee. *Roads Take Us Home.* Minneapolis, MN: Lerner Publications, 1997.

McNeil, Ian. *An Encyclopedia of the History of Technology.* New York: Routledge, 1996.

Nardo, Don. *Roman Roads and Aqueducts.* New York: Lucent Books, 2000.

Norman, Donald. *The Designs of Everyday Things.* New York: Basic Books, 2002.

van Dulken, Stephen. *Inventing the 20th Century.* New York: New York University Press, 2000.

Woods, Michael B. *Ancient Construction: From Tents to Towers.* Minneapolis, MN: Lerner Publications, 2000.

The Screw

What Is It? Any inclined surface wrapped around a central post or pillar. A screw is commonly thought of as a spiral and threaded pin or a dowel used in construction.

Who Invented It? Archimedes (in Syracuse, Sicily)

Why Is *This* Invention One of the 100 Greatest?

The screw is one of the six basic mechanical devices on which virtually all machines and construction depend. Archimedes's screw is the basis for modern screws, drills, bolts, worm gears, augers, water lifts, and ship propellers. Screws lock and secure construction projects.

Screws multiply mechanical force just like moving the fulcrum on a lever. That mechanical advantage makes them powerful and versatile workhorses. Giant augers with blades eight feet in diameter drill their way down mine shafts. Some—so small they cannot be clearly seen with the unaided eye—are key to the operation of fine Swiss watches. Such tiny augers cost far more than their weight in gold.

History of the Invention

What Did People Do Before?

Before screws, people fastened things with nails, ropes, hammered pegs and pins, and cement. Before Archimedes's screw, people lifted water in buckets.

How Was the Screw Invented?

By the age of 42 (around 235 B.C.), Archimedes was the most famous inventor and mathematician in Sicily and a revered treasure of his hometown, Syracuse. He had already deduced a number of mathematical concepts that became famous, including the principles of a lever, the value of π, and the concepts of specific gravity and buoyancy. He also invented several lethal weapons based on these mathematical principles that had been successfully used to defend Syracuse against Roman naval assaults.

In 235 B.C. a new problem was plopped into Archimedes's lap during a trip to Egypt. Irrigation water was being raised from ditches into fields by hand-lifted buckets. That method of crop irrigation was too slow and labor intensive. Could Archimedes find a better way to raise a continuous stream of water from a ditch into a field?

It seemed a simple but intriguing question to Archimedes. As always, he approached the problem mathematically. First, from observing water, he noted that water always flowed downhill. Certainly, this was not a new discovery. However, Archimedes concluded that he might be able to use this fundamental concept to lift water.

Next, Archimedes began to sift through various geometric shapes. He knew that lifting along an inclined ramp is easier than a straight vertical lift and therefore focused on various shapes and forms of inclines. Among these is a spiral—an incline wrapped around a central cylinder.

No historian recorded the specific thought process or physical experiments Archimedes used to develop this idea. At some point, he decided to focus on a spiral enclosed within a cylindrical tube so that the spiral's edges brushed against the inside wall of the tube. Through experiments, he realized that if he laid the tube (with a turning spiral inside it) at an angle, then he could use that spiral screw as a water pump.

As long as the tube was angled enough so that the *lowest* point of each turn of the spiral screw was lower than the *highest* point of the turn just below it, then water could never flow back down the spiral to the ditch from whence it came. As he turned the spiral with a hand crank, water was lifted up the tube while it tried to flow back downhill.

Archimedes's water screw continuously lifted water without straining the operator. *Archimedes's screw* was celebrated as a miraculous invention and was widely used throughout the Mediterranean region.

What's Happened Since Then?

Generally, water screws were long ago replaced by waterwheels, windmills, and then powered pumps (first steam, then electric, and then internal combustion engine).

It was the *principle* of the screw Archimedes invented that had lasting value. However, as important as the screw is, no one extended the concept of Archimedes's screw to modern screws and drills until some time around the year A.D. 1400, when images of augers and drills began to appear in paintings in Western Europe. Hand drills and screws were in use by 1600. The first power drill press was invented by French engineer Jacques de Vaucanson in 1728. The first handheld power drill (steam powered) was invented in England in 1864. German engineer Wilhelm Fein invented the first electric drill in 1894.

Now advanced, super-strength glues and cements have replaced many applications formerly reserved for nails and screws. It is likely that this trend will continue. However, though diminished by space age super glues, the descendents of Archimedes's screw will enjoy a prominent place in our society for decades to come.

 Fun Fact: Ice augers are big screws. At the 2005 Minnesota Ice Fest, the winner bored his auger through 18 inches of ice in 16 seconds.

More to Explore

Adler, Robert. *Science Firsts.* New York: John Wiley & Sons, 2002.

Bendick, Jeanne. *Archimedes and the Door of Science.* New York: Franklin Watts, 1995.

Clark, Donald. *Encyclopedia of Great Inventors and Discoveries.* London: Marshall Cavendish Books, 1991.

Forbs, R. J. *Studies in Ancient Technology.* Camden, NJ: Brill Academic Publishers, 1998.

Haven, Kendall. *Marvels of Science.* Englewood, CO: Libraries Unlimited, 1994.

Keating, Susan K. *Archimedes: Ancient Greek Mathematician.* Atlanta, GA: Mason Crest Publishers, 2002.

Stein, Sherman. *Archimedes: What Did He Do Beside Cry Eureka?* New York: Mathematical Association of America, 1999.

Woods, Michael B. *Ancient Construction: From Tents to Towers.* Minneapolis, MN: Lerner Publications, 2000.

Yenne, Bill. *100 Inventions That Shaped World History.* New York: Bluewood Books, 1993.

Zannos, Susan. *The Life and Times of Archimedes.* New York: Mitchell Lane Publishers, 2004.

Glass

Year of Invention: 100 B.C.

> **What Is It?** A transparent, rigid liquid made by fusing (with heat) sand, soda ash, and lime combined with a variety of trace components.
>
> **Who Invented It?** Syrian glassmakers (in Syria)

Why Is *This* Invention One of the 100 Greatest?

Windows, windshields, eyeglasses, magnifying glasses, mirrors, and lenses for telescopes, microscopes, and periscopes are all made of glass. So are the glasses we drink from and the beakers and other lab-ware scientists use to conduct laboratory experiments. We have designed houses, schools, and offices around glass.

Glass is one of the truly unique substances on Earth. Glass is technically a liquid because its molecules don't align into regular patterns, as do the molecules of all solids. Glass flows—albeit very slowly—so that every window eventually grows thicker at the bottom than at the top. Glass is the only liquid that can cut you. It is the only liquid that can break.

History of the Invention

What Did People Do Before?

Glass occurs naturally. Obsidian is black glass created in the fiery heat of a volcano. When lightning strikes sand it can fuse silica sand into flowing sculptures of glass. Roman historian Pliny reported that Phoenician sailors accidentally discovered the formula for making glass around 3500 B.C. While boiling fish stews on the beach, they balanced cook pots over the fire on blocks of saltpeter because the beach had no suitable rocks. After the embers died, those sailors discovered that the saltpeter and sand had fused into lumpy rings of crude glass.

Buildings had few windows. Light streamed inside when doors were left open. Those windows that existed were simply small open spaces in a wall that were often covered with a blanket to block out the cold and rain.

How Was Glass Invented?

Egyptian craftsmen had learned the techniques of rudimentary glass-making by 1500 B.C. Craftsmen made a glass jar by first making a clay pottery jar. The craftsman then smeared molten glass over the outside surface of this clay jar and smoothed the glass before it cooled. After the glass cooled, a worker used a metal scraping tool (much like an over-sized dental hygienist's scraping pick) to reach inside and scrape away the original clay jar. With the clay removed, the craftsman was left with a smooth glass jar of the same size and shape. Egyptian craftsmen spent centuries developing softer clays that would be easier and faster to scrape out as well as more precisely shaped scraping tools.

This process was both slow and expensive. It took days to produce each glass jar, since that process required the craftsman to gather the ingredients for, design, and finally produce two jars (one clay and one glass). Glass jars were considered a luxury item, not a staple of ordinary daily life.

Around 100 B.C., an unknown Syrian craftsman was struck with a glorious idea and made the technological breakthrough that forever changed the world of glass. The Iron Age was at hand. Sturdy, dependable iron had become the metal of choice for axles, spears, swords, pots, and any other product that required metal. Glassmakers used iron rods and pokers to stir and to carry molten glass.

Glass melted at around 1,200 degrees Fahrenheit. Iron stayed firm to over 2,000 degrees and so could be used to hold, stir, and spread glass without danger of melting the iron. Then that unknown glass man had his brilliant idea. Instead of using an iron *rod* to lift a blob of molten glass from the fire and smear it across a clay pot, he used an iron *tube*—a thin iron pipe.

With a blob of gooey glass on the end of his tube, he blew into the tube and found that he could blow the glass into the round shape of a jar. The time- and labor-consuming step of making a clay pot became obsolete.

Glass blowing made glass practical, fast, and cheap. Modern glassmakers still use the same process and same ingredients (silica sand, calcium oxides, soda ash, and magnesium) used by those first Syrian glassblowers.

What's Happened Since Then?

Blown glass jars, glasses, and vases became standard fare by the first century A.D. The next major development in glass technology was the invention of clear (transparent) glass in 1290 by Venetian craftsmen on the Italian Island of Murano. In 1675, George Ravenscroft in England added lead oxide to his glass ingredients and invented crystal.

In 1688 the process of producing flat plate glass for mirrors first appeared in Germany, then in France. By 1720, glass windows had become common and affordable.

In 1902, American Irving W Colburn invented and patented a "sheet glass drawing machine" that made mass production of window glass possible. In 1904, American Michael Owen invented a "glass shaping machine" to make the mass production of glass bottles and jars possible.

In 1959, Sir Alastair Pilkington in London invented the "float glass" process. Rather spreading molten glass over a metal surface, Pilkington poured streams of it onto a bath of liquid tin. The glass and tin did not adhere to each other, did not mix, and, miraculously, the surface between them always stayed perfectly flat and smooth. Over 95 percent of all glass is now produced in float glass factories.

 Fun Fact: Each year, U.S. glassmakers produce almost six million tons of float glass—enough to cover seven billion square feet. That much glass could make a window 1,000 feet high and over 1,000 miles long!

More to Explore

Asimov, Isaac. *Asimov's Chronology of Science and Discovery*. New York: Harper & Row, 1989.

Dyson, James. *A History of Great Inventions*. New York: Carroll & Graf Publishers, 2001.

Ellis, William. *Glass from the First Mirror to Fiber Optics*. Phoenix, AZ: Sagebrush Corp., 1999.

Kassinger, Ruth. *The Story of Glass*. Minneapolis, MN: Lerner Publications Group, 2003.

McNeil, Ian. *An Encyclopedia of the History of Technology*. New York: Routledge, 1996.

Oxlade, Chris. *How We Use Glass*. Chicago: Raintree Library, 2004.

Waterwheel

Year of Invention: 25 B.C.

What Is It? A wheel fitted with paddles that converts water (stream) current into mechanical circular motion to drive some industrial activity.

Who Invented It? Vitruvius (in Rome, Italy)

Why Is *This* Invention One of the 100 Greatest?

Waterwheels were the first human machine in which a natural force was controlled and converted into mechanical motion to power human land-based activity.

Waterpower, converted into mechanical energy by waterwheels, was the primary power source for grain mills, saw mills, leather works, textile mills and even blast furnaces for more than 1,500 years. Waterwheels provided the major source of civic and industrial power until the invention of the steam engine in the late 1700s.

History of the Invention

What Did People Do Before?

The power to grind grain, saw wood, spin lathes or turn potters' wheels always came from human and animal labor—as did the power needed for any industrial or production process.

Wind power helped moved ships at sea. But even ships relied far more on oars and human power than on wind, until the ninth or tenth centuries.

As villages expanded into towns and cities, the demand for mechanical power increased. However, until the waterwheel was invented, no alternatives to human and animal power existed.

How Was the Waterwheel Invented?

The waterwheel emerged to meet two vital needs of early societies: grind grain and lift water for irrigation. In 100 B.C., grain grinding was by far the more pressing need.

Grain was ground between stones. Handfuls of grain were dropped into a large, concave stone and ground into flour with a second handheld stone. By 150 B.C., Greek millers had flattened and enlarged both stones. Workers pushed the top, moving the stone back and forth across the stationary bottom stone to grind the grains trapped between.

12

Sometime before 100 B.C., most Greek millers converted from large, square stones to circular grinding stones. Now the upper stone could be turned while lying on top of the stationary lower stone to grind grain. A vertical shaft and handles extended from the upper grinding stone. A worker used these handles to push the stone in a circular motion.

Then, sometime between 95 B.C. and 85 B.C., some clever Greek realized that he could use the power of a flowing stream to turn the vertical shaft that spun his grinding stones. He had to build his mill directly over a stream. A wooden shaft extended out of the floor of the mill down to water level. On that shaft, he secured a horizontal wheel. Onto the wheel, he fixed a number of cup-shaped paddles.

When the open side of the paddles faced upstream, they caught the current like a sail catching wind. That forced the wheel to turn. On the other side of the wheel, the backside of each curved paddle had to rotate back upstream. However, the curved backside created much less resistance in the water than did the open, cup-like side of the paddle. So the stream always forced the wheel to turn in one direction. True, the horizontal waterwheel lost some power because the backside of each paddle had to rotate back against the current. But the wheel still produced plenty of power to run a small mill.

Waterwheel technology quickly migrated to Rome. Roman millers and engineers made two significant improvements. First, they learned to dam a stream above a mill and channel water in a roaring torrent over the dam and down past their waterwheels. This greatly magnified the power their waterwheels produced.

Second, they realized that they could eliminate drag on their waterwheel by turning it on its side to create a *vertical waterwheel*. The engineer and author Vitruvius is given credit for this invention, and he described it in detail in one of his engineering design books, *De Architectura* dated to 25 B.C.

Now each paddle entered the water and was swept powerfully downstream. Then it lifted out of the water before it began its rotation back upstream. Resistance was eliminated and the waterwheel's power was again multiplied. This Vitruvian waterwheel mill was the first efficient, powerful, general-purpose waterwheel design.

What's Happened Since Then?

Vitruvian (vertical) waterwheels were soon adapted to power lumber saws and to drive early spinning and weaving machines. This waterwheel was still the primary source of power 1,700 years later when waterwheels powered the drive belts and conveyors of the early mills and factories of the Industrial Revolution. In America, many textile and cloth mills as well as grain mills were driven by waterwheels through the eighteenth century.

The Roman waterwheel at Bouches-du-Rhone (near Asrles in France) was built around A.D. 285 and is the greatest example of a Vitruvian waterwheel mill. Engineers built an aqueduct to divert the natural stream to a holding pond just above a steep slope. Two parallel channels were dug down the face of this slope. The mill complex sat on land between the two channels. Sixteen Vitruvian waterwheels (eight on each channel) were placed one above the other and frantically whirred to power the largest mill in the Roman Empire. The millers used a complex set of gears to allow shafts to turn at different speeds for different milling operations.

However, the inventions of the steam engine pushed water power out of major industrial uses. Steam engines produced more power and could be located anywhere. Waterwheels disappeared from industrial operations.

Waterwheels reemerged as a source of electricity. The first hydroelectric plant was built in Germany in 1891. Hydroelectric plants use a waterwheel (called a *turbine*) to create electricity instead of mechanical work. Now almost 8 percent of U.S. electric power comes from hydroelectric plants.

 Fun Fact: The Laxey waterwheel on the Isle of Mann (in the Irish Sea) is the largest working waterwheel in the world. Built in 1854 to pump water from lead mines, it stands 72 feet in diameter (eight stories high).

More to Explore

Asimov, Isaac. *Asimov's Chronology of Science and Discovery*. New York: Harper & Row, 1989.

Beshore, George W. *Science in Ancient China*. New York: Scholastic Library Publishing, 1998.

Forbs, R. J. *Studies in Ancient Technology*. Camden, NJ: Brill Academic Publishers, 1998.

Gies, Frances. *Cathedral, Forge, and Waterwheel: Technology and Invention in the Middle Ages*. New York: HarperCollins Publishers, 1995.

McNeil, Ian. *An Encyclopedia of the History of Technology*. New York: Routledge, 1996.

Reynolds, Terry. *Stronger Than a Hundred Men: A History of the Vertical Water Wheel*. Baltimore, MD: Johns Hopkins University Press, 2003.

Smith, Thomas. *Vitruvius on Architecture*. New York: Monacelli Press, 2001.

Woods, Michael. *Ancient Machines: From Wedges to Waterwheels*. Minneapolis, MN: Lerner Publishing Group, 1999.

Yenne, Bill. *100 Inventions That Shaped World History*. New York: Bluewood Books, 1993.

The Magnetic Compass

Year of Invention: A.D. 83

> **What Is It?** A device that aligns with the earth's magnetic field and indicates direction by always pointing north-south.
>
> **Who Invented It?** Unknown (in China)

Why Is *This* Invention One of the 100 Greatest?

The compass revolutionized open water sailing by allowing accurate, all-weather open sea navigation. It opened the world to exploration.

Beginning in the thirteenth century, virtually every ship that left port had a compass. Almost every airplane ever built has had a compass. Many cars now feature built-in compasses. Every explorer, and almost every mountain hiker, has relied on a compass for direction and navigation.

For over 2,000 years the simple magnetic compass has been the most used and most successful direction-finding tool on Earth.

History of the Invention

What Did People Do Before?

Before the invention of the compass, travelers walked from one landmark to the next. Sailors hugged coastlines—even for long voyages—using coastal features as markers. Some ventured into the open oceans using the polestar (North Star) by night and the sun by day as navigational guides. However, these markers were useless during periods of cloud cover, and many ships strayed far off course to their doom while waiting for the clouds to clear.

The principle of the compass was discovered first in China sometime around the fourth century B.C. There are also references to the magnetic property of certain stones in early Greek and Egyptian writings, but no indication that either group made significant use of compasses.

The Chinese discovered that thin chips of loadstone, a naturally occurring magnetic ore, would spin when suspended in water and always point south. Once discovered, this ability of loadstone was not used for navigation, but for *feng shui*. Chinese used the first compasses to align buildings, rooms, windows and furniture with nature according to the principles of *feng shui*.

It would be another five centuries before anyone realized the value of a compass for navigation.

How Was the Compass Invented?

Some time during the Han Dynasty some clever person figured out that the loadstone chips used for *feng shui* and fortune telling could also provide essential directional information for travelers. Written reference is first made in A.D. 83 to a "south pointer" being used to guide jade collectors on their journeys. That first compass was made of loadstone in the shape of a tiny spoon and floated in a bowl of water. Chinese travelers soon took to calling compasses "floating fish."

Sometime around A.D. 600, another inspired Chinese person discovered that iron, brushed repeatedly against loadstone, worked as well as the original loadstone. Magnetized iron faithfully pointed south, and slivers of iron lasted longer than fragile loadstone. Around that same time someone invented the idea of using a small block of wood instead of straw on which to float the iron needle. Wood didn't get waterlogged as easily.

By A.D. 800, floating iron compasses were common on Chinese ships and led to their bold, open-ocean exploration as far as India. The compass placed Chinese exploration and ship navigation centuries ahead of European and Arab counterparts.

Around this same time, an unknown Chinese ship captain invented the idea of floating his compass needle in oil instead of water. Iron needles floated more easily on the denser oil. Soon after that, another clever sailor decided that his compass would work better if it were in a closed container. The oil wouldn't slosh out as it did from a bowl during stormy weather.

That clever fellow enclosed oil, wood chip, and iron needle in a ceramic jar with a glass top. The modern compass had finally been invented.

What's Happened Since Then?

The first compass reached Europe sometime after A.D. 1150. In 1190, Englishman Alexander Neckam wrote about using one to guide his ship. Someone in France invented the pivot needle compass around A.D. 1240. Instead of suspending his compass needle in a liquid, he balanced it on a needlepoint so that the iron compass needle wobbled back and forth through the air. He called it a floating needle.

It was the Italians who invented the name "compass," around 1250. The word comes from the Italian word "*compassare*," literally "to stride around," figuratively, "to measure or guide."

Only minor improvements have been made to magnetic compasses since A.D. 1400. What *has* changed is our understanding of the earth's magnetic field and of magnetic forces.

Satellite global positioning systems (GPS) have gained in both popularity and use during the past 20 years. However, a GPS readout only tells you were you are, not which direction to go from here. For that, even the most high-tech expedition still relies on a simple compass.

 Fun Fact: Near either the north or south magnetic pole, a compass is useless. Its needle will wander in aimless circles and point to nowhere.

More to Explore

Banerjee. *History of the Magnetic Compass and the Discovery of Magnetism.* London: Oxford University Press, 2005.

Beshore, George. *Science in Ancient China.* New York: Franklin Watts, 1993.

Gurney, Alan. *Compass: A Story of Exploration and Innovation.* New York: Norton, 2004.

Jonkers, A. R. *Earth: Magnetism in the Age of Sail.* New Brusnwick, NJ: Johns Hopkins University Press, 2003.

Pumfrey, Stephen. *Latitude and the Magnetic Earth.* London: Icon Books, Ltd., 2004.

Schomp, Virginia. *The Ancient Chinese.* New York: Scholastic Library Publishing, 2004.

Temple, Robert. *The Genius of China: 3,000 Years of Science, Discovery, and Invention.* New York: Simon & Schuster, 2000.

Yenne, Bill. *100 Inventions That Shaped World History.* New York: Bluewood Books, 1993.

The Metal Plow

Year of Invention: A.D. 100

What Is It? A metal device to dig furrows in the earth and to turn the top soil in order to speed planting of a crop.

Who Invented It? Roman farmers (in Northern Italy)

Why Is *This* Invention One of the 100 Greatest?

The metal plow transformed the world's landscape and made mass agriculture possible. The rise of great cultures and empires was based on plentiful food supply, and that was based on the plow. Wheat, oats, rye, barley, and other grains could not have been successfully grown without a plow.

The plow changed the face of the world and the habitat for many of the world's animal species. It was the plow that allowed agriculture to spread across fertile flat lands and push wolves, bears, tigers, and other wild beasts out to the wild and woolliest fringe places of the world.

Finally, the plow forever changed farming. For the first time a piece of farm equipment became a major investment, often shared cooperatively by three or four farm families. Because of the metal plow, the economics of farming shifted toward efficient use of capital equipment.

History of the Invention

What Did People Do Before?

The first plows were forked sticks early farmers dragged through the dirt. The Sumerians were using simple wooden, handheld plows by 5000 B.C. Such a simple device worked well enough in the dry, sandy soil of Middle Eastern countries. But it failed miserably in the heavier, wetter soils of central and northern Europe.

How Was the Plow Invented?

The Romans were avid students of agriculture. By 200 B.C. Roman farmers had advanced from sharpened wood stakes to sharpened wood blades as plows. A strap holding the blades was slung over the farmer's shoulder. His legs provided the forward power to drive this plow through the rocky soil. His arms were the force that drove the plow blade

18

down into the earth. This man-powered blade, however, was only slightly better than Egyptian designs. It was still just a heavy stick that scraped a V-shaped furrow for planting and exhausted the farmer after only an acre of plowing.

Over the next several decades, plows grew bigger and heavier. A heavier wooden blade worked better but put more strain on the farmer's back. Writings by the famed Roman scholar, Pliny the Elder, show that by A.D. 50, a single wheel was appearing on plows in the heavier, richer soil of northern Italy and in the northern provinces conquered by the Roman army. With a wheel to carry much of the plow's weight, farmers were free to make their plowshare heavier by adding a metal (iron) cap onto the wooden plow blade. The metal facing added years to the life span of a plow and helped drive the blade deeper into the soil. This Roman wheeled plow was called a *carruca*.

Pliny wrote that, by A.D. 100, all-metal blades were common in the richer farm areas. Three new features made these plows noteworthy and—for the first time—capable of sustaining large-scale agricultural fields. First, the sword-sharp, all-metal blade was designed to cut deep into even the heaviest of soils. Second, a horizontal plowshare was designed to cut and lift slices of soil on either side of the blade. Finally, a curved moldboard—a curved upper part of the plow blade—turned the soil as the plowshare cut and lifted it. The plow actually flipped the top eight or nine inches of dirt upside down as each furrow was made.

This version of the *carruca* proved to be amazingly effective. However, it was also amazingly difficult for even two men to pull. Farmers turned to oxen to pull their plows and to convert acres of unused land into neat, plantable rows. Roman agriculture provided the first mass-produced, export crops the world had ever seen.

What's Happened Since Then?

In the sixth century A.D., a bigger, more powerful plow and moldboard appeared in the Slavic countries and spread across Europe. Because of its size, the plow had to be pulled by teams of up to six oxen. Oxen (and later horses) tended to strangle themselves in the rope harnesses. They also pulled hard enough for the straps to rub their neck and shoulder skin raw and to actually grind through the skin, leaving long gashes and painful welts.

Around A.D. 900, padded collars and harnesses first appeared in France. Teams could pull harder, faster, and more safely wearing these bulky pads that spread the strain of a plow's pulling straps. Plowing speeds more than doubled. In the 1600s steel plow blades replaced iron. In the 1800s, American farmers developed multiple plows to cut five or six furrows at one time, pulled by massed teams of as many as 20 horses. The invention of motorized tractors allowed farmers to increase to 20 plows mounted in a single frame.

 Fun Fact: Water buffaloes are the classic "tractors" of Asia. Even today, they provide almost half of the power to pull plows in Southeast Asia.

More to Explore

Brockman, John. *The Greatest Inventions of the Past 2,000 Years*. New York: Simon & Schuster, 2000.

Dyson, James. *A History of Great Inventions*. New York: Carroll & Graf Publishers, 2001.

Long, Catherine. *Agricultural Revolution*. Toronto: Thompson Gale, 2004.

McNeil, Ian. *An Encyclopedia of the History of Technology*. New York: Routledge, 1996.

Wilkes, Angela. *Farming through Time*. New York: DK Publishing, 2001.

Woods, Michael. *Ancient Agriculture*. Minneapolis, MN: Lerner Publishing, 1999.

Paper

Year of Invention: A.D. 105

> **What Is It?** A smooth, flexible surface made from cellulose (plant-based) fiber used to write and draw on.
>
> **Who Invented It?** Ts'ai Lun (in China)

Why Is *This* Invention One of the 100 Greatest?

How many pieces of paper do you touch, read, or look at in a day? How many paper bags, paper plates, paper napkins, paper towels, pieces of toilet paper, cardboard containers, or corrugated containers do you use? Cheap, plentiful paper made writing and art practical and possible as part of daily life.

The availability of paper made written language possible. Paper has shaped and molded the way we communicate and the way we organize our societies. Paper has defined the way we store, safeguard, and share our history and information. Amazingly, 19 of the other 99 of these 100 greatest science inventions directly depend on paper, and 48 of them indirectly depend on paper.

History of the Invention

What Did People Do Before?

People wrote on clay tablets and on dried sheepskins long before paper existed. But these were not available to ordinary people, and writing was the privilege of official scholars. By 3000 B.C., Egyptians were making writing scrolls from the peeled and pressed fibers of papyrus plants. By this same time, the Chinese were making a writing material called *tapa* from the peeled, dried, and pounded inner bark of mulberry, fig, or daphne (a kind of laurel) trees. Both the Chinese and the Egyptian writing surfaces were reasonably smooth, flexible, strong, and durable. However, like sheepskin parchment and vellum, they were available only in a limited supply and were too expensive for common use.

How Was Paper Invented?

Ts'ai Lun was a councilor in the royal court of Chinese emperor Ho Ti during the Han Dynasty. He was also a scientist. In the year A.D. 104 the emperor dumped a problem into Ts'ai Lun's lap. Tapa making was a slow, labor intensive process. Bark supplies were limited. The emperor ordered Ts'ai Lun to create better, more plentiful paper.

Ts'ai Lun first searched for new sources of fiber. He experimented with other kinds of tree bark. Some were brittle and shattered. Some produced off-colored tapa; some were too difficult to work with. Some pulverized instead of thinning into fibrous strands.

Walking through a market square one day, Ts'ai Lun noticed a discarded pile of rags—flax, hemp, silk, and linen. Surely these waste rags were made from natural fibers. Why couldn't they supply the fiber he needed to make paper? He scooped up an armful and took them to his workshop.

Little is recorded about the details of his experiments. At some point he came upon the idea of smashing, crushing, shredding, and macerating his various sources of fiber and of then stirring them in a large vat of water to separate each individual fiber. He dipped a screen of splintered bamboo fibers into the vat and lifted it up through the water, trapping a layer of the fibers on its surface. Once dried, this layer of interwoven fibers was to be his new writing paper.

To serve his needs, Ts'ai Lun's new paper had to be thin, smooth, clean, even, and strong, and it had to hold the writing ink without smearing or bleeding. His first attempts failed.

He experimented both with his new process and with his raw materials. How finely should he shred the rags? How long should he stir this mix of fiber soup? When he dipped his bamboo sieve too soon, the fibers had not separated fully and the tapa turned out lumpy. If he stirred too long, his fibers absorbed too much water and bloated. The tapa was slow to dry and never held together well. Too much pounding crushed the fibers. The tapa turned out too thin and flimsy.

Over time, he developed his skill and consistency with the process. In the spring of A.D. 105, he settled on a mix of mulberry bark with flax and hemp (from rags) and a bit of crushed bamboo. With this mix of fibers he created an exceptionally fine paper—far better than any he had created before. Each page was even, smooth, and uniform. This new tapa dried evenly and quickly and had good strength and flexibility. The rag fibers absorbed ink well and didn't allow it to seep across the page. Best of all, much of this paper's fiber came from readily-available rags that were thrown out in great heaps in every city.

Ts'ai Lun's tapa would not pick up the name "paper" for 1,000 years. When his tapa-making process finally reached Europe (around A.D. 1100), Europeans mistakenly thought that it came from Egyptian papyrus and called it "*paper*." Even after it was known that paper and papyrus come from different plants and were made by different processes, the name stuck.

What's Happened Since Then?

Ts'ai Lun's process for papermaking had spread to Korea and Japan by 600 and into the Arab world shortly thereafter. When the Moors invaded Spain, they brought papermaking to Europe. By 1300, paper mills dotted the European landscape—all still using Ts'ai Lun's process. A well-trained team of one master and five assistants could produce 2,500 sheets of paper a day.

Rags became valuable commodities since they were an essential ingredient of paper. Once printing presses existed, the need for paper grew rapidly, and a rag shortage threatened to collapse the entire industry. Ragmen stole clothes off clotheslines and new fabric from mills to make more rags.

In the late 1700s, German papermakers devised a process for pulverizing wood pulp as the source of fiber for paper. Within a century, wood from trees, not bark and rags, became the primary material in paper.

Nicholas Low Robert invented the first automatic papermaking machine in 1798. In 1870 Margaret Knight invented the paper bag, with its rectangular bottom. In 1794, Thomas Edison invented wax paper.

The use of e-mail, online research, PCs, palm pilots, and a drive toward "paperless offices" point toward a future reduction in our dependence on paper. Paper's 2,000-year reign as the focal point of human information storage and transfer is probably drawing to an end.

 Fun Fact: Americans consume over 97-million tons of paper annually. That translates to 2.3 pounds of paper per-person, per-day!

More to Explore:

Asimov, Isaac. *How Is Paper Made?* New York: Gareth Stevens, 1992.

Brockman, John. *The Greatest Inventions of the Past 2,000 Years*. New York: Simon & Schuster, 2000.

Compestine, Ying Chang. *The Story of Paper*. New York: Holiday House, 2003.

Cosner, Sharon. *Paper Through the Ages*. Minneapolis, MN: Lerner Publishing Group, 1997.

Cottwell, Arthur. *Eyewitness: Ancient China*. New York: DK Publishing, 2000.

Dyson, James. *A History of Great Inventions*. New York: Carroll & Graf Publishers, 2001.

Llewellyn, Clair. *Paper*. New York: Scholastic Library Publishing, 2001.

Schomp, Virginia. *The Ancient Chinese*. New York: Scholastic Library Services, 2004.

Cement

> **What Is It?** The component of concrete that acts as the binding and hardening agent, locking sand and gravel into a solid mass.
>
> **Who Invented It?** Roman engineers (in Pozzuoli, Italy)

Why Is *This* Invention One of the 100 Greatest?

Cement, and its construction form—concrete—have been the primary building material for cities, bridges, cathedrals, massive hydroelectric dams, skyscrapers, aqueducts, sewers, highways and roads, etc., for 2,000 years.

Launch pads for every rocket blasted into space have been made of concrete. Every major European cathedral, the great building wonder of the Middle Ages, was built of concrete. Roman bridges and aqueducts that have survived for over 2,000 years were built of concrete.

History of the Invention

What Did People Do Before?

The idea of mixing gravel and sand with some binder is at least 7,000 years old. Crude concrete-like floor slabs have been found in huts along the Danube River dating to 5000 B.C. The Egyptians had developed a cement-like material to use as a binder for concrete construction by 3000 B.C. But Egyptian cement lacked the strength and hardness to be durable. They used a mix of lime and gypsum (a calcium rich mineral) as their binder. It produced concrete with low strength and a nasty tendency to crack and crumble after only a few years.

The word *cement* comes from the Latin word *caementum,* meaning rough stones and rubble. Cement originally referred to any mixture of broken stone held loosely together by a binding material of lime, clay, gypsum, and sand. It was the Romans who shifted the word *cement* to mean only the binding material, They then invented the word *concrete* to refer to the entire mixture of sand, gravel, water, and the binding agent—cement.

How Was Cement Invented?

Early Roman engineers (around 300 B.C.) copied their cement and concrete techniques from Greek and Egyptian builders, using the proportions of cement, sand, gravel, and water that were common in these two countries. Limestone was burned in ovens and then ground into a powder to create cement. Some buildings lasted. Some cracked and needed repair after only a few years. By A.D. 100 Roman leaders had recognized this inconsistency as a major problem.

Records show that in 285 Roman engineers first experimented with volcanic earth near Pozzuoli, Italy, on the slopes of Mount Vesuvius. They found large areas covered with a granular, sand-like soil, colored a deep reddish-brown instead of sand's usual tan or light brown.

Builders were surprised to find that this concrete had exceptional strength and hardness. Engineers suspected that the extra strength came from the Pozzuoli sand they had used. They conducted experiments with this sand and learned that it was not ordinary sand at all, but rather volcanic ash and ground volcanic cinders that contained high levels of alumina (a form of aluminum) and silica. Further experiments showed that when ground silica and alumina were mixed with limestone (the common source of lime) before the limestone was burned and ground to form cement, the resulting cement was far superior to standard cement.

The Romans called this combination of silica and alumina with limestone *Pozzuoli-cement*. Engineers sought other sources of silica and alumina and experimented with their proportions. The final formula, though it no longer required Pozzuoli sand, was still named after the town where it was first discovered.

What's Happened Since Then?

With the collapse of the Roman Empire, much of the accumulated Roman knowledge and technology was lost, including their knowledge of cement making. For 1,200 years Europe struggled to build with concrete using low-grade, pre-Roman cement-making technology. In 1568, French construction engineer Philbert de l'Orme rediscovered the Roman cement principles and became the best-known builder of his age, returning concrete construction to a strength and quality it hadn't seen for 1,200 years.

In 1824, English bricklayer Thomas Aspdin decided to save money and make his own mortar (cement). He accidentally overcooked a three-to-one mix of limestone and clay. (He cooked it too hot and too long according to the wisdom of the day.) When he mixed that cement with water, this new concrete proved to be incredibly hard. Aspdin named it Portland cement after the name of a nearby town. To this day, Portland cement is the standard cement used by builders and do-it-yourselfers alike.

In 1867, Frenchman Joseph Monier realized that there was a way to compensate for concrete's one construction weakness. Concrete could withstand tremendous compressive loads (loads that wanted to squeeze the concrete), but was dismally poor under tensile loads (loads that pulled on a concrete column). Chains, rope, and rods are all good for tensile strength but fail under compressive loads. Monier combined the two. He placed metal rods in his columns as he poured the concrete and invented the first reinforced concrete.

Recently, cement prices have climbed sharply as Portland cement shortages threaten to slow the worldwide construction trade. This may spur the search for new construction binders. But as of modern times, no substitute for this ancient Roman invention has been found.

Fun Fact: The 185-storey, reinforced concrete CN Tower in Toronto, Canada, is the world's tallest tower. Built between 1973 and 1975, it used over 130,000 tons of concrete.

More to Explore

Dyson, James. *A History of Great Inventions.* New York: Carroll & Graf Publishers, 2001.

Llewellyn, Claire. *Concrete.* New York: Scholastic Library Publishing, 2001.

McNeil, Ian. *An Encyclopedia of the History of Technology.* New York: Routledge, 1996.

Nelson, Robin. *From Cement to Bridge.* Minneapolis, MN: Lerner Publications, 2004.

Williams, Linda. *Concrete Mixers.* Mankato, MN: Capstone Press, 2004.

Zero

Year of Invention: 810

> **What Is It?** The number for "none of the thing being counted," the number that links positive and negative number lines.
>
> **Who Invented It?** Muhammad ibn Al-Khwarizmi (in Baghdad, Iraq)

Why Is *This* Invention One of the 100 Greatest?

Numbers and math form the essential language of science. Numbers are also the only universal language, used by and understood by all cultures and countries on Earth. The Arabic number system of 10 digits and the corresponding methods for writing numbers and for doing basic math and algebra have made modern science and commerce possible.

Zero was the last cog in that system to exist, invented more than 300 years after the rest of the Arabic number system was in use. No one had thought of having a number for zero. Not the Greeks. Not the Egyptians, not the Romans, not Aristotle or Euclid or Archimedes or Pythagoras. The invention of zero as a real and working number completed the Arabic number system. Zero was the invention that made complex math possible.

Today there is scarcely any aspect of life that does not depend on our ability to handle numbers effectively and accurately. Computers, building construction, directions, making change, and telling time all depend on using numbers and math. They depend on the number zero.

History of the Invention

What Did People Do Before?

Hindu mathematicians in India around A.D. 500 created the numerals 1 through 9 that we now use. They also created the system for writing numbers and for adding and multiplying that we still use. In so doing, they found that they needed to invent a space holder to mark a place where there was no number. They created *sifr* (0), meaning "the absence of a number" as a placeholder. Now everyone could tell that 570 was different from 507 or 5700 or 5007.

Sifr was not a number, just a placeholder to keep the real numbers in the proper columns. Around A.D. 750, this number and math system (the most advanced math system on Earth) migrated west into the Arab world.

27

How Was Zero Invented?

In A.D. 810, Baghdad was the capital of the Arab world. The grand palace in Baghdad was called "The House of Wisdom" and drew Arab mathematicians and scientists to it. The most famous of these was Muhammad ibn Musa known as Al-Khwarizmi, the mathematician. In the spring of that year, while the desert wind whispered outside and juicy dates ripened on the palm trees, a great debate raged inside the Caliph's (ruler's) chambers.

Three men took part in the debate: the Caliph, himself, Al-Khwarizmi, and the palace mathematician, Ahmahd ibn Aziz. They argued about *sifr*, "the empty place," what we call zero. Years before, Al-Khwarizmi had helped convince the court that the Hindu number system was superior and should be adopted. Now he had come to court to convince the Caliph to change one central element of that system—the role of *sifr*.

Al-Khwarizmi reasoned that *sifr* had to be an actual number. Aziz countered that zero had always been just a placeholder, not a real number, and couldn't be changed now. The Caliph decided that if Al-Khwarizmi could show that *sifr* acted like a number and could perform all of the functions that numbers performed, then—and only then—he would decree that *sifr was* a number.

That meant that Al-Khwarizmi had to show that *sifr* (zero) could add and subtract, multiply and divide, be used as an algebraic exponent, and—like all numbers—be either odd or even.

Addition and subtraction was easy to show. 7 plus 0 equals 7. If you can do the addition, then zero must be a number. Numbers can only be added to other numbers.

Multiplication and division were harder for Al-Khwarizmi to explain. He used piles of coins to demonstrate. To multiply one pile by four, he had to lay down four piles of coins. To multiply by two, he had to lay down only two piles. To multiply by zero, he had to lay down exactly *no* piles. Any number times zero is zero.

Al-Khwarizmi used the same piles of coins to demonstrate division by zero and using zero as an exponent (raising some number to the power of zero). At the end of two days of questioning by the Caliph and by Aziz, Al-Khwarizmi had won. He had convinced the Caliph, who declared that *sifr* was a true number. The basic number system we still use and depend upon was complete.

What's Happened Since Then?

The word *algebra* was invented by Al-Khwarizmi from the Arabic words for "the math." Around 200 years after zero became a working number, "Arabic" numbers migrated into Europe, landing first in Italy, the math and science center of medieval Europe. Since the numbers had reached Europe from Arabia, Europeans called them "Arabic" numbers even though Hindu mathematicians in India had created them.

The number line and math systems continued to grow as needed. Imaginary numbers were created in 1545 in Italy by Rafael Bombelli. Calculus was invented in the 1660s and is generally credited to Isaac Newton (though other European mathematicians can claim at least part of the credit for calculus's invention).

The most recent addition to our number system is Surreal Numbers, used for counting the infinitely large and the infinitesimally small, created in 1992 by John Conway and Martin Kruskal at Princeton University. While our math systems will continue to evolve, the simple power of "nothing" will continue to be the cornerstone of all math.

Fun Fact: How many zeroes are there in a centrillion (the biggest recognized number)? Answer: 303. A google has 100 zeroes, a trillion has twelve, a billion has nine.

More to Explore

Asimov, Isaac. *Asimov's Chronology of Science and Discovery*. New York: Harper & Row, 1989.

Baker, Lawrence W. *Math and Mathematicians: The History of Math Discoveries Around the World*. New York: Thomson Gale, 1999.

Brockman, John. *The Greatest Inventions of the Past 2,000 Years*. New York: Simon & Schuster, 2000.

Downey, Tika. *How the Arabs Invented Algebra: The History of the Concept of Variables*. Chicago: PowerKids Press, 2004.

Haven, Kendall. *Marvels of Math*. Englewood, CO: Libraries Unlimited, 1998.

Loprest, Angeline. *The Place for Zero: A Math Adventure*. Watertown, MA: Charlesbridge Publishing, 2003.

Smith, Sanderson M. *Agnesi to Zeno: Over 100 Vignettes from the History of Math*. New York: Springer-Verlag, 2001.

Suplee, Curt. *Milestones of Science*. Washington, DC: National Geographic Society, 2000.

Gunpowder

Year of Invention: 1261

What Is It? An explosive mixture of three powdered ingredients: saltpeter, charcoal, and sulfur.

Who Invented It? Roger Bacon (in Paris, France)

Why Is *This* Invention One of the 100 Greatest?

Gunpowder revolutionized warfare and military thinking. Canons, muskets, rockets, and bombs powered by black gunpowder swept away all weapons and forces that existed before them.

But gunpowder was more than just a weapon. Gunpowder was a tremendous boon to civil engineering. Quarrying, cathedral foundations, and roadways were developed easier and faster. Gunpowder fundamentally changed the way engineers thought about major earth-moving construction.

History of the Invention

What Did People Do Before?

Before gunpowder, warfare relied on four weapons: sword, shield, lance, and bow. Before gunpowder, construction projects relied on brute physical force and labor. Large civil engineering works (roads, mines, dams, etc.) required the dedicated use of hundreds—if not thousands—of workers (usually slaves).

How Was Gunpowder Invented?

Gunpowder was first invented and used by the Chinese sometime between A.D. 850 and 1000. Nothing is recorded about who first created it or about the process of development used. In 1261, English-born scientist Roger Bacon developed and tested the formula on his own. And we *do* know how Bacon invented this explosive cocktail of chemicals.

In 1237, and at the tender age of only 17, Roger Bacon was appointed regent master at a Paris monastery, teaching arts and sciences. A brilliant thinker of his era, Bacon predicted and described with amazing accuracy steamships, automobiles, and airplanes 500 to 700 years before their existence and 300 years before Galileo described them. He invented the magnifying glass and conducted advanced optic studies. By 1260, he was often called *"Doctor Mirabilis"* (Doctor Wonderful).

Above all, Bacon considered himself an alchemist. Alchemy was the study of the properties of natural elements and of combinations of those elements.

During the summer of 1261, 47-year-old balding friar Roger Bacon began a series of experiments with saltpeter. Saltpeter (the chemical potassium nitrate) comes from decaying organic matter and is a major ingredient of many fertilizers.

As an alchemist, Bacon believed that his job was to combine the right elements of nature in the right way so that they could become more than the mere sum of those ingredients. Along one wall of his suite of rooms at the monastery Bacon had a long row of jars, vials, and sacks filled with his collection of natural ingredients.

One steamy morning that summer, Bacon lifted a jar of saltpeter and a bag of common charcoal onto his table. The day before he had combined these two ingredients in several different ways and proportions. But nothing happened. Today he had decided to add a third ingredient in an attempt to *activate* the reaction.

Bacon measured out a small pile of granular saltpeter and added an equal amount of granulated charcoal. Then he turned and studied the rows of bags and jars. Ah! Sulfur. Sulfur was known to be a good activating ingredient.

Bacon added a small amount of bright-yellow powdered sulfur to the gray-black pile and stirred.

Nothing happened.

This was not unusual. Many reactions required not only an activating ingredient, but also a *catalyst* to begin the reaction. Bacon slid the table next to his window. Alchemists knew that sunlight could act as a catalyst for many reactions.

Nothing happened.

From alchemy textbooks, Bacon knew that when light alone won't start a reaction, it may mean the ingredients are too cold. He let the mound of powdered ingredients warm in the sunlight.

Nothing happened.

When light and warmth fail, maybe fire is the correct catalyst.

Bacon brought a candle from the hallway and touched its flame to the pile on his table.

In a scorching flash of white-hot light the table exploded. A reverberating blast rattled teeth and rumbled across the monastery like thunder. Bacon was blown back against a wall. The small table disintegrated into splinters of wood, flung across the room. The wall around Bacon's window was blackened. Outside the friars and townspeople fearfully looked up into the clear morning sky. Thunder with no clouds?

Bacon was stunned. His eyebrows had been singed off by the blast, and his ears still rang. His eyes stung from the acid smoke still swirling in his room. He had certainly gotten his ingredients to react.

But that didn't end the experiments. It began them. Future experiments would determine the optimal mix of his three ingredients and the range of conditions under which they would explode. They would also reveal whether the order in which he mixed the ingredients was important or if other aspects of his procedure were critical.

Ten minutes later a second blast belched sparks and smoke out of Bacon's window. A second mighty clap of thunder rattled windows half a mile away.

What's Happened Since Then?

Roger Bacon was a curious scientist, not a practical inventor. He developed the formula for gunpowder (75 percent saltpeter, 10 percent sulfur, 15 percent carbon), then moved on to other experiments. It took the vision of German friar Berthold Schwartz, almost a century later, to see that Bacon's explosion could be used as a weapon.

Gunpowder remained the one available explosive until 1846, when Italian chemistry professor Ascanio Sobrero invented nitroglycerine. In 1866, Alfred Nobel improved on Sobrero's creation by inventing dynamite. By 1868, Nobel's mixture was commonly called TNT and had become the standard for explosives. Even nuclear and atomic bombs are measured and rated by the number of tons of TNT required to produce an equivalent explosion.

 Fun Fact: The Chinese first used gunpowder in fireworks with the hope that the noise would scare evil spirits away.

More to Explore

Clark, Donald. *Encyclopedia of Great Inventors and Discoveries*. London: Marshall Cavendish Books, 1991.

Clegg, Brian. *The First Scientist: A Life of Roger Bacon*. New York: Avalon Publishing Group, 2004.

Dyson, James. *A History of Great Inventions*. New York: Carroll & Graf Publishers, 2001.

Hakim, Joy. *The Story of Science: Aristotle Leads the Way*. Washington, DC: Smithsonian Books, 2004.

Hall, Bert. *Weapons and Warfare in Renaissance Europe: Gunpowder, Technology, and Tactics*. Baltimore, MD: Johns Hopkins University Press, 2002.

Haven, Kendall. *Marvels of Science*. Englewood, CO: Libraries Unlimited, 1994.

Kelly, Jack. *Gunpowder: Alchemy, Bombards, and Pyrotechnics: The History of the Explosive That Changed the World*. New York: Basic Books, 2004.

Redgrove, H. Stanley. *Roger Bacon: The Father of Experimental Science and Medieval Occultism*. New York: Kessinger Publishing Co., 2003.

Yenne, Bill. *100 Inventions That Shaped World History*. New York: Bluewood Books, 1993.

Eyeglasses

Year of Invention: 1280

> **What Is It?** Ground, clear lenses used to correct defects in human vision.
>
> **Who Invented It?** Alessandro della Spina (in Florence, Italy)

Why Is *This* Invention One of the 100 Greatest?

As a boy, future U.S. president Theodore Roosevelt looked through his first pair of glasses and was awed at "suddenly having the world come into focus." He said it was one of the most profound and memorable moments of his life.

Glasses create a clear, focused, and essential view of our ordinary world. They have made it possible for billions of people to read, become educated, enjoy life, and safely navigate our environments. As the need for clear, detailed vision increases in our modern world, so also does the importance of glasses.

History of the Invention

What Did People Do Before?

No one mentioned eyeglasses until 1250, though there must have been plenty of people with vision problems before then. In 1249, English scientist and inventor Roger Bacon wrote about "lenses to improve vision." That's the first recorded mention of using lenses to correct human vision. But there is no evidence that Bacon either had or made any. As early as A.D. 1000, people in China and parts of the Arab world are thought to have used polished concave surfaces to enlarge images and possibly to have used clear quartz lenses to look through as we would a magnifying glass.

In the mid-1200s, Venetian craftsmen (in Venice, Italy) gained exquisite skill in grinding and polishing lenses (mostly of clear quartz). Suddenly, magnifying lenses that did not distort an image were available (but expensive) for scientists to use. All glass was still colored (tinted by impurities and by the chemicals used in the glass-making process), often had tiny bubbles or blemishes, and was difficult to make smooth and nondistorting.

How Were Eyeglasses Invented?

Beginning in 1275, Dominican friar Alessandro della Spina worked with physicist Salvino delgi Armati on a variety of scientific experiments—many of them concerning the nature of light—in their hometown of Florence, Italy.

While experimenting with light refraction (the bending of light through various materials—water, quartz, glass, etc.) in 1276, Alessandro severely injured his eyes. His vision became blurred. He couldn't focus clearly on objects in his hands, on written records, or on the refracted light beams that formed his experiments.

Alessandro found it impossible to continue his work and retreated into the private world of the monastery. In 1278, Armati visited Alessandro carrying a set of clear quartz lenses he had purchased on a recent trip to Venice. Alessandro noticed that his vision improved dramatically when he looked through the *convex* lenses in Armati's set. Objects appeared bigger and clearer.

Alessandro was intrigued and, hoping to regain enough vision to return to his light experiments, began to test the lenses' effects. He traveled to Venice and worked with quartz grinders to vary the shape and degree of each lens's convex curve. He experimented with the outside shape (oval, round, or square) and with the size of the lens to see which gave him the least distorted view of the world.

Alessandro learned to grind and polish his own lenses and began to design frames for the lenses so he could hold them against his eyes. In 1280 he completed his design (called spectacles)—the world's first glasses. He had made two ground quartz convex lenses (custom designed for his eyes to best correct his specific vision problems) and had mounted them in a leather and metal frame. His spectacles had no nose grips and no earpieces. He had to hold a metal strip at the top of the spectacles against his eyebrows and forehead to keep them in front of his eyes. But Alessandro could see again.

What's Happened Since Then?

By 1300, nose pincers had been added so users didn't have to hold their spectacles. By 1310, spectacles were a fashion symbol in Florence. Everyone wanted a pair—even if they didn't need them. In 1340 concave (nearsighted) spectacles first appeared. Their inventor is unknown.

Around 1650 the first "sunglasses" (smoky tinted glasses) appeared in Germany. Soon colored glasses of every shade were available and popular. In 1727 Edward Scarlett (in London) invented earpieces to hold the glasses in place without having to pinch his nose. He called them "temple spectacles." The Thomin Company of Paris was the first to mass-produce glasses with earpieces beginning in 1746. In 1755 famed American inventor Benjamin Franklin tired of having to change back and forth between reading and distance glasses. He cut each lens in half (reading half on bottom and distance half on top), glued them together, and created the world's first bifocals.

Leonardo da Vinci sketched and described contact lenses in 1508. Rene Descartes (famed philosopher and mathematician) suggested them in 1632. Eugene Fick (Swiss) and Edouard Kalt (French) designed and used the world's first contacts in 1888. In 1936, William Fernblown, a New York optometrist, created the first American-made contacts and the world's first plastic contacts. In 1950, George Butterfield (in Oregon) designed the shape of modern hard contacts. Soft contacts were introduced in 1971, the creation of Otto Wickterle.

New laser surgery techniques are already reducing people's dependence on glasses. Near-sightedness and far-sightedness (the two most common vision problems) can both be corrected by new laser procedures. Eyeglasses may eventually become a relic of the dusty past.

Fun Fact: The Lion's Eyeglass Recycling Centers collect over 6.5 million pairs of old glasses each year to distribute to 3.5 million needy people in developing nations.

More to Explore

Brockman, John. *The Greatest Inventions of the Past 2,000 Years*. New York: Simon & Schuster, 2000.

Goldstein, Margaret. *Eyeglasses*. Minneapolis, MN: Lerner Publishing Group, 1997.

Sherrow, Victoria. *Benjamin Franklin*. New York: Friedman, Michael Publishing Group, 2001.

Struble, Steve. *To See or Not to See*. New York: Steck-Vaughn Publishers, 1997.

Yenne, Bill. *100 Inventions That Shaped World History*. New York: Bluewood Books, 1993.

Windmill

Year of Invention: 1280

What Is It? A device for harnessing wind power and turning it into mechanical power.

Who Invented It? Unknown (in Belgium and Holland)

Why Is *This* Invention One of the 100 Greatest?

Windmills first replaced waterwheels as the primary means of grinding grain. Windmills next were used as water pumps in arid regions and to pump excess water out of flooded, low-lying regions. Windmills made large-scale settlement of, and agricultural development of, the American plains and West possible by pumping water to the surface from underground aquifers (bodies of water).

Finally, windmills have become an important renewable source of electric energy. Versatile, nonpolluting, and dependable, windmills have served as an important source of power for 1,000 years.

History of the Invention

What Did People Do Before?

Sailing ships were using wind power to drive their ships by 3,000 B.C. However, thousands of years passed before it occurred to anyone to harness the wind for other purposes.

Communities in Persia were the first to harness the wind on land. As early as A.D. 600, people there were mounting small sails of reed mats, woven palm fronds, and occasionally slats of wood onto vertical shafts extending through the roofs of buildings. The sails spun horizontally, turning the vertical shaft to provide grinding power below.

However, horizontal windmills don't work well in places with variable or erratic winds and so they never spread into Africa or Europe.

How Was the Windmill Invented?

Around A.D. 1100, the "Mediterranean" windmill began to appear in Italy. Massive, two-story stone buildings were mounted with vertical sails set like a ship's jib sail (front, triangular sail). These sails were turned at right angles to the wind so that the wind hit not the front, but the side or edge, of the pinwheel of sails. The sails connected to a vertical shaft that drove the mill grinding stone below.

However, Mediterranean windmills only worked when the wind blew from the correct direction and when it blew within the correct range of velocities. Much of the time, these mills were closed because conditions weren't right.

The first practical windmill emerged sometime around 1250. This design was called a *post mill*. Evidence suggests that post mills were first developed in the low countries and spread very quickly to England. No one knows who first added the features that made the post mill so superior to all previous designs. With these added features the post mill could operate all year, in virtually any wind. For the first time, windmills became more reliable and more desirable than waterwheels.

Post mills contained seven remarkable developments that accounted for their superior performance. First, post mills featured a rotating top. The entire top of the stone tower rotated on wooden rails so that the mill's sails always pointed into the wind. Second, those sail fingers of the windmill faced *into* the wind—like propeller blades—so that they caught a larger area of wind and generated more power.

Third, post mills featured a tail—very much like an airplane tail—that shifted with the wind to keep the windmill's blades pointed into the wind. This tail could also be manually turned to align the windmill blades.

The sails themselves (either wood or canvass) dipped close to the ground at the bottom of their rotation, making it easy for the miller to change or to re-rig the sails so he could run the mill in extremely light wind and in storm-strong winds.

Inside, the post mill contained three important new features. It was the first wind-driven mill with a clutch to allow the miller to disengage the grinding stones from the windmill blades. An extensive wooden cog gearing system meant that the miller could control the speed of the rotating grinding stones and thus the quality of the grinding and the coarseness of the flour produced. Finally, post mills featured multiple vertical beams and supports, making it far more sturdy and stable than any previous windmill.

Post mills spread like weeds across Europe. Even where ideal streams flowed, many communities converted to wind since rivers froze in winter or dwindled to a trickle during dry spells and brought the mill to a halt. For 600 years wind was king.

What's Happened Since Then?

The first post mills didn't appear in America until the mid-eighteenth century. American colonists preferred waterwheels to power grinding and light industrial factories.

In the mid-eighteenth century, tower windmills became popular. Simple frame towers holding wooden slat veins, tower windmills pumped water. In lowlands prone to flooding, they pumped water off the land and into drainage canals. As American families migrated into the western prairies, tower windmills pumped water to the surface to support orchards, cattle, farms, and settlers' needs. Tower windmills made American western expansion possible and helped convert rolling plains of grass into dense fields of grain.

By the early nineteenth century, steam engines had begun to replace windmills as the preferred power source for grinding and for industrial uses. By the late nineteenth century, electric motors and internal combustion engines had spread across the land and replaced most windmills. There are still a few windmills in use on the American plains. But their number, like the number of surviving buffalo, is a tiny fraction of their peak glory.

Now wind has found a new use: generating electric power. A dozen major "wind farms" exist in the United States, looking like fields of giant airplane propellers mounted on steel telephone poles. Collectively, they provide a significant portion of the 12 percent of the country's electricity produced by renewable fuels.

 Fun Fact: When, in 1846, the tiny Caribbean island of Barbados built its 506th windmill, it had more windmills per square mile than any country on Earth. By 1849, the number of active windmills had declined and Barbados dropped back to second place, behind Holland.

More to Explore

Forbs, R. J. *Studies in Ancient Technology*. Camden, NJ: Brill Academic Publishers, 1998.

Hills, Richard. *Power from Wind*. New York: Cambridge University Press, 1998.

Kealy, Edward. *Harvesting the Air*. Berkeley, CA: University of California Press, 1997.

McNeil, Ian. *An Encyclopedia of the History of Technology*. New York: Routledge, 1996.

Righter, Robert. *Wind Energy in America*. Norman, OK: University of Oklahoma Press, 1996.

Yenne, Bill. *100 Inventions That Shaped World History*. New York: Bluewood Books, 1993.

Glass Mirror

Year of Invention: 1291

> **What Is It?** A smooth, clear, or polished surface that reflects light to create an accurate, undistorted image of the thing being reflected.
>
> **Who Invented It?** Craftsmen (in Venice, Italy)

Why Is *This* Invention One of the 100 Greatest?

You know what you look like because you've looked at yourself in mirrors. Mirrors have created a universal awareness of the concept of "looks." Until mirrors became common and affordable, most people had only a vague idea of their physical appearance and rarely thought about their outward "looks." From mirrors sprang fashion, makeup, and glamour.

Science depends on mirrors for laser projectors, telescopes, and many scientific instruments that let us see, record, and measure essential phenomena our eyes cannot detect. Mirrors on automobiles and bicycles and at blind alleys make life safer and save countless lives. But most frequently we use mirrors to study our outer appearance. We spend billions of dollars each year on beauty products. We spend hours each day studying our looks, preening and adjusting our looks, and worrying about our looks—all because of mirrors.

History of the Invention

What Did People Do Before?

The ancient Roman historian Pliny claimed that handheld mirrors made of hammered gold existed by 4000 B.C. in the Lebanese city of Sidon. However, no such mirror has ever been found by archeologists.

Polished obsidian (a naturally occurring black volcanic glass) mirrors date to 2000 B.C. They were the property and privilege of royalty. Polished bronze mirrors in China date to 500 B.C. They appeared in Rome about the same time. These, however, were small, handheld mirrors and frightfully expensive. The first full-body mirror (a Roman bronze, wall-mounted mirror) dates to A.D. 100.

How Were Mirrors Invented?

In the first half of the thirteenth century glass-making became a specialty of craftsmen in the Italian city of Venice. In 1286, the doge (ruler) of the Venetian city-state ordered the glassmakers and their shops moved to the guarded island of Murano in the bay to protect the secrets they had developed. He ordered that anyone carrying glass-making secrets off the island was to be both severely punished and banished from Venice. Venetian glass-making became an ever more closely guarded secret as Venetian glass itself became increasingly prized for its quality.

The work of these craftsmen focused on three areas: decorative glass (mostly blown glass) of exquisite beauty, flat pieces (plates) of clear glass, and mirror making. The Venetian craftsmen conducted experiments for more than 30 years, adding different amounts of different chemicals to their glass recipe trying to create clear glass. Glassmakers of that period couldn't refine and purify their ingredients as we can today. The trace minerals and metal impurities created colored hues and tints in the glass that left the glass opaque and smoky.

In late 1290 or early 1291 the Venetian craftsmen found the right formula and produced the world's first completely clear glass. That formula was rated as their most-prized glass-making secret.

A year or two before, they had perfected a method for spreading and smoothing a blob of fiery-hot, molten glass into a thin, smooth sheet. Molten blobs of glass had always been stuck on the end of long iron tubes and literally blown into shape before they cooled. Venetians developed a method for rolling their glass into sheets that eliminated virtually every blemish, bubble, and wave from the glass. The finished plates of glass were as clear and smooth as our modern windows.

Other craftsmen on the island experimented with different backings for mirrors to create a reflective surface. Metal backings had to be thin, pliable, highly reflective, and easy to adhere to a piece of glass. Gold and silver worked but were too expensive for large-scale production. During the early part of that same year, 1291, these craftsmen settled on a mixture of tin and mercury for their mirror backing. This combination was easy to work into thin, smooth sheets; adhered well to glass; was highly reflective; and was plentiful and inexpensive compared to gold.

Sometime during the year 1291, these separate developments came together to produce the first modern, practical, clear-glass mirrors.

What's Happened Since Then?

By 1300, Venice had become the glass and mirror center for all Europe. The rulers of Venice tried to keep their glass process a carefully guarded secret. However, valuable secrets are hard to protect. By 1350, the process had leaked out and other cities were copying Venice's glass technology—if not the skill of the Venetian craftsmen. Mirror frames (first metal and later wood) first appeared in 1390 on German-made mirrors and, by 1600, wall-mounted mirrors were the decorating rage of Europe.

In 1835, Justus von Liebig invented a new process for chemically coating a silver backing directly onto his mirrors and produced the first mirror made with the general methods still used today. Five years later, new glass production techniques made German mirrors cheaper and more available for all classes in European society to enjoy.

Clear plastics and acrylics have reduced our total dependence on glass for mirrors. Some mirrors are now made of polished metal. However, our use of mirrors has—if anything—actually increased over the past 50 years. Houses, stores, and offices use mirrors as wall treatments more than ever before. Houses typically have more mirrors than did the houses of our grandparents.

 Fun Fact: The Biami tribe of New Guinea had never seen a mirror or an accurate reflection of their appearance until the mid-1970s. Their initial reaction to seeing their reflections in a mirror was terror. However, within days they got used to their looks and began to demand mirrors for grooming.

More to Explore

Asimov, Isaac. *Asimov's Chronology of Science and Discovery*. New York: Harper & Row, 1989.

Brockman, John. *The Greatest Inventions of the Past 2,000 Years*. New York: Simon & Schuster, 2000.

Ellis, William. *Glass from the First Mirror to Fiber Optics*. Phoenix, AZ: Sagebrush Corp., 1999.

Kassinger, Ruth. *The Story of Glass*. Minneapolis, MN: Lerner Publications Group, 2003.

Oxlade, Chris. *How We Use Glass*. Chicago: Raintree Library, 2004.

Blast Furnace

Year of Invention: 1350

> **What Is It?** A furnace capable of blasting a stream of hot air through burning metal ore to improve the purity of the finished metal.
>
> **Who Invented It?** Monks at the Rievaulz Abbey (in Yorkshire, England)

Why Is *This* Invention One of the 100 Greatest?

The blast furnace turned iron into the greatest construction material on Earth. Iron instantly became the favored medium for the construction of bridges, towers, and buildings. The Industrial Revolution was built on iron. Iron withstood both tension (pulling) and compressive (pushing) loads. It was strong and easy to work. The availability of masses of cheap iron changed the way weapons (canon barrels) and construction were thought of. Iron changed the landscape of cities and war. Giant iron blast furnaces belching flame and shimmering heat provided the iron to build the Industrial Revolution.

History of the Invention

What Did People Do Before?

Blacksmiths using small, fireplace-sized hearths traditionally created any metal pieces that were needed. But their coal and wood fires didn't burn hot enough to fully melt iron ore, so blacksmiths used hand-powered bellows to force air through the fire to make it hotter. Raw metal ore was crushed and melted in small batches, then poured into stone molds. After reheating it in the glowing coals of the fire, blacksmiths pounded the softened metal into shape with hammers and grinders.

These craftsman's skills worked well on small pieces of iron or other metal. But construction beams and girders could not be created this way, and so construction engineers relied on concrete, wood, and stone.

How Was the Blast Furnace Invented?

In the Middle Ages, European monasteries were the major economic enterprises and centers of wealth as well as of learning. Cistercian monks at the Rievaulz Monastery in North Yorkshire, England, were typical. The monks owned 1,400 sheep, grain fields, gardens, beehives, orchards, hop presses, herds of pigs and cattle, vast land holdings, and a sizeable metal works. They hired peasants to do the manual labor while most of the monks labored over manuscripts.

Some of the Cistercian monks, however, spent their lives experimenting with the production of iron. They produced their own plows and sheers, metal axles for wagons and rims for wheels. They were contracted to produce swords and shields. Though their ironwork was renowned throughout England, the monks searched for ways to improve the quality of their iron and to vastly increase the quantity of their production. The abbot wrote, "Iron is more useful to man than gold."

Around 1348, the monks discovered that they could separate pure iron from the other elements and impurities in the ore if they forced their forge to reach temperatures at which iron ore would melt into a boiling liquid. Bellows that forced air through burning wood or charcoal increased the fire's temperature, but not enough. The monks searched for ways to force not puffs of air, but great and constant blasts of air, through their fire, hoping this would produce the temperatures they needed.

In 1350, the monks moved their iron furnace next to the bank of a small river. They built a waterwheel, driven by the river's current, and attached the waterwheel to gears that drove powerful bellows. Wind howled through the iron furnace from these blasts of air. Temperatures inside their thick brick furnace soared.

But not enough. These blasts of cold outside air held down the furnace temperature. The monks decided to preheat their air by circulating it through pipes above the furnace exhaust before blasting it through the furnace bellows.

Raw iron ore from the mines was mixed with fuel (charcoal) and poured into the furnace. Hot air roared through from the bellows. Temperatures inside their furnace approached 3,000 degrees F, more than hot enough to turn iron ore into a bubbling mass of lava-hot, bright yellow-red liquid. Molten metal ran out through a tap trough. Impurities rose as a dark slag to the surface where they could easily be skimmed off. Pure iron was heavier and flowed along the bottom, where it ran through channels cut in stone and poured into stone or brick molds that cast the iron into a desired shape, size, and form.

The monks steadily increased the size of their blast furnace until it could produce over a ton of cast iron each day. The age of iron construction was born.

What's Happened Since Then?

By the mid-1600s, the surrounding forests had been stripped of suitable wood for charcoal and the Rievaulz Iron Works was closed. However, blast furnaces modeled after the Rievaulz furnace spread across England and then Europe.

In 1709, English engineer James Darby invented the coke-fueled blast furnace. Coke (a form of coal) produced a hotter, more efficient fire than did the wood charcoal. In 1856, Sir Henry Bessemer invented his Bessemer process for making steel in a multistaged blast furnace.

Although fuels have changed over the years, furnace sizes have grown to monstrous, cavern-sized giants, and electric motors now power blasts of air through a furnace, modern blast furnaces still follow the principles first invented by Cistercian monks over 650 years ago.

Fun Fact: Modern giant blast furnaces produce over 60,000 tons of iron in a week's work. That's enough iron and steel to make a car every 15 seconds.

More to Explore

Dyson, James. *A History of Great Inventions*. New York: Carroll & Graf Publishers, 2001.

McNeil, Ian. *An Encyclopedia of the History of Technology*. New York: Routledge, 1996.

Mitgutsch, Ali. *From Ore to Spoon*. Minneapolis, MN: Lerner Publishing, 2001.

Ricketts, John. *The History of Iron Making*. Pittsburg, PA: Iron and Steel Society, 2000.

Whitney, Elspeth. *Medieval Science and Technology*. Westport, CT: Greenwood Publishing Group, 2004.

Williams, Alan. *Kings and the Blast Furnace*. New York: Brill Academic Publications, 2003.

Caravel (Sailing Ship)

Year of Invention: 1410

> **What Is It?** The first long-distance, transoceanic sailing ship.
>
> **Who Invented It?** Prince Henry (in Lisbon, Portugal)

Why Is *This* Invention One of the 100 Greatest?

The first Portuguese Caravel set sail thousands of years after the first ship equipped with a sail. But the Portuguese-built Caravel redefined the world as no other ship had done. It expanded Europe's reach across the globe.

The Caravel made global ship navigation possible. Like the *Apollo* capsules were in space, the Caravel was an explorer built to venture into seas and parts of the world no other European had been able to reach. The Caravel opened Africa to European exploration (and exploitation).

A Caravel was the first ship to round Cape Bojador (the tip of West Africa). Using Caravels, the Portuguese discovered the Islands of Madeira and the Azores, both in the open Atlantic Ocean. Columbus sailed three Caravels to discover the New World. A Caravel was the first ship to round Cape Horn at the southern tip of Africa and venture into Indian Ocean waters. The Caravel set the stage for Europe's ocean trade and colonization across Africa, India, and the Americas.

History of the Invention

What Did People Do Before?

Few early ships relied exclusively on the wind. Cargo and military boats were designed with long rows of oars that propelled the boats when winds and currents did not flow the right way. War galleys—the most advanced ship designs—were rigged with a single mast and square sail to travel with the wind and as many as three rows of oars to power and maneuver the ship during battle. As late as 1571, Christian and Turkish fleets were rowed to war for the Battle of Lepanto. Ship captains used wind when it was handy and the backs and sweat of their sailors (and slaves) when it was not.

How Was the Caravel Invented?

As the fourteenth century drew to a close, Portugal sat at the forefront of European exploration and territorial expansion. The great exception was the spice trade with Asia. Using overland routes, Portuguese traders had to travel a thousand miles farther than Greek or Italian caravans, which started out much farther east. Though only 16 years old in 1410 when he assumed power, Portuguese Prince Henry (later called Henry the Navigator) was determined to maintain his country's dominance in European exploration and expansion. He was also convinced that it was possible to sail south around Africa and establish an ocean route to the Asian spice trade, slicing thousands of miles and several months of dangerous walking off the overland routes.

Prince Henry realized that the problem lay in the ship designs Europeans used. He decided to combine the best of Arab and European features with some original ideas of his own. Beginning with ship improvements first launched in 1410 and continuing over the next decade, Prince Henry invented nine improvements in ship design and operation. The improved ships he invented were called Caravels.

First he designed his new ships with triangular sails (like modern racing yachts) that were hung from a sloping cross beam. This design allowed the ship to sail much closer into the wind and eliminated time-consuming tacking (sailing back and forth at an angle to be able to sail into the wind). He built his first Caravels with two masts, but soon shifted to three masts and later to four in order to catch more wind power.

Prince Henry built his ships small—only 60 to 100 feet long. He hung the rudder from an axle and built the Caravels with a shallow draft (the bottom of a Caravel was less than eight feet under the ocean's surface) so that they would be more maneuverable. Caravels were the sailing equivalent of a space probe—small, compact, speedy, and built for long-range exploration. Caravels carried only enough storage room for food and supplies to support the voyage and precious little cargo space.

Henry changed from traditional ropes to stronger hemp ropes and to sails of expensive cotton or linen canvas. This shift simplified the rigging and allowed his sails to function efficiently over a wider range of wind conditions. There were fewer ropes for the crew to pull, and they had to pull them less often. Thus, the Caravel could get by with a smaller crew (as few as 25) and could sail farther and longer between necessary stops to resupply.

Henry squared the stern of his small ships so that there would be more room to accommodate the crew. He also built smaller hatches and tightly sealed the deck, slathering it with pitch to improve watertightness.

Portuguese carpenters who worked on Henry's Caravels were forbidden (on pain of death) to explain or reveal how they built the Caravel, to sell ships to foreigners, and to build ships for foreigners.

Prince Henry's last invention had a profound impact on European navigation. He realized that his Caravels could out-sail existing navigation charts and knowledge. He established a School of Navigation at Sagres, along the southwest tip of Portugal, to study currents, wind, and stars where the polestar (North Star) was not visible. This school developed a system of latitude tables based on the sun, which could be used anywhere on any ocean to determine how far north or south of the equator one was.

What's Happened Since Then?

By 1450, Portuguese Caravels had sailed around Africa and into the Indian Ocean. They had also ventured into the mid-Atlantic and discovered the islands of Madeira and the Azores. Caravels opened the door for European trade with distant Africa and India.

However, Prince Henry's Caravels, like the Apollo space program, were frightfully expensive. Portuguese exploration drove Prince Henry and Portugal to the brink of bankruptcy. The Portuguese empire collapsed. Portuguese Caravels were idled or scuttled (intentionally sunk) to keep them out of the hands of Portugal's enemies. There are no surviving examples or detailed diagrams of Caravels—only rough sketches and many stories.

Other nations soon copied and improved on Prince Henry's designs. By 1600, much larger three-masted ships, hanging square (rectangular) sails, had replaced Caravels. But during their brief dominance on the open seas, Caravels literally changed the political and economic reality of the world. Thanks to Prince Henry's Caravels, European fleets controlled the world's oceans for the next 300 years.

 Fun Fact: The largest sailing ship ever built was the steel-hull, five- masted *France II*, launched at Bordeaux, France, in 1911. At 418 feet in length, it was over four times as long as the average Caravel.

More to Explore

Brockman, John. *The Greatest Inventions of the Past 2,000 Years*. New York: Simon & Schuster, 2000.

Cipolla, Carlos. *Guns, Sails and Europe*. New York: Abrams, 1998.

Jacobs, David. *Master Builders of the Middle Ages*. New York: HarperCollins Children's Books, 1998.

Macaulay, David. *Ship*. New York: Houghton-Mifflin, 1996.

McNeil, Ian. *An Encyclopedia of the History of Technology*. New York: Routledge, 1996.

Stark, Rita. *The Four Caravels of Christopher Columbus*. New York: Xlibris Corp., 2004.

Unger, Richard. *Cogs, Caravels and Galleons*. Annapolis, MD: Naval Institute Press, 1998.

Printing Press

Year of Invention: 1454

What Is It? A device to make multiple identical copies of a document using movable type characters and letters.

Who Invented It? Johannes Gutenberg (in Mainz, Germany)

Why Is *This* Invention One of the 100 Greatest?

Many have called the printing press the greatest single invention in the last 2,000 years. The printing press could print more copies in a few weeks than formerly could have been produced in lifetimes of work by hand. The printing press made mass literacy and education possible.

The scientific revolution depended on scientists being able to record and share their findings. The printing press made it possible for scientists to read what others had discovered. The printing press changed the fundamental structure of human society, thought, and activity.

History of the Invention

What Did People Do Before?

Copies of documents had always been made by hand—most commonly by monks. Books were frightfully slow to produce and outrageously expensive. Worse, hand copying produced errors. Each new generation of copies compounded the errors.

The answer to these problems was printing. Printing started in China. In 1040, Pi Sheng invented printing using movable clay pottery characters as his type. Pi Sheng is the true inventor of movable type printing. More impressive, while the western alphabet requires printers to work with 26 letters, Pi Sheng had to make multiple clay copies of over 5,000 Chinese characters for his printing.

In 1403, King Htai Tjong of Korea invented movable metal type—much sturdier and more practical than Pi Sheng's clay type. But he did not develop an entire printing system to use with his type.

How Was the Printing Press Invented?

It is unclear how much Johannes Gutenberg invented and how much he assembled from other, existing inventions. Historians believe that he was unaware of printing developments elsewhere in the world and believed that he was inventing an entirely new technology.

Gutenberg was born in the picturesque town of Mainz, Germany. Sometime around 1440, nearing the age of 50, he began developing his ideas about a printing press. He took the next decade to solve three basic needs.

First, he needed a press. Gutenberg modeled his press after the heavy presses used to crush olives. He modified and reinforced the press so that it would press down evenly across an entire page at the same instant.

Second, he needed ink. Monks and block printers used water-based inks. Gutenberg consulted with well-known painters (including Van Dyke) and decided to switch to the new oil-based inks painters favored and to the new colored pigments with which painters were experimenting. With this new ink Gutenberg got sharper lines and bolder print than water-based inks could produce.

Finally, Gutenberg needed movable metal type. His metal type is Gutenberg's biggest contribution to printing. He spent years experimenting with different metal alloys, searching for one that had a low melting point so that forming letters in his molds would be easy, but that was strong enough to resist the pressure and wear of thousands of pressings and squeezings during printing. By 1450, he had settled on a mix of lead and tin with a dash of antimony.

Sometime around 1452, Gutenberg's press was ready to go to work. He borrowed 800 guilders to buy the paper, ink pigments, oils, lead, tin, antimony, and other supplies he would need and began his first book—the great 42-line Gutenberg Bible (42-line refers to the number of lines of text on each page). He set his text one letter at a time in rows in a wooden tray using metal spacing bars between rows and metal wedges to hold the letters tightly in place. Once the first page was laid out and test printed to make sure that the letters were all even and that the ink was the correct thickness on the type, he printed 300 copies of that page.

First page done. Gutenberg then disassembled the 3,000 to 4,000 letters from that page and cleaned and restored each in the appropriate letter bin. Now he was ready to start work on the second page. This process was repeated 1,282 times and consumed three years to print every page of 300 copies of his bible. By hand, the copying would have taken over 1,200 years of labor.

What's Happened Since Then?

Gutenberg's Bible not only was the first book printed in Europe with movable metal type, it was a magnificent job of printing—as good as could be produced today. Gutenberg's process survived unchanged and unimproved for three and a half centuries. It is a testimonial to the quality and soundness of Gutenberg's work.

Before Gutenberg completed his Bible, he lost his shop and all its equipment to his financial backer, Johannes Fust, because Gutenberg couldn't make payments on a 2,000-guilder debt. Gutenberg died in 1467, impoverished, forgotten, and ignored by his society. Still, Gutenberg's invention changed a world hungry for information and reading.

Over the next 45 years, more than 500 publishers created Gutenberg-like presses and printed over one million books!

Now hand-set movable type has been replaced by computers, computer-driven presses, and photocopying technology. The technology Gutenberg invented is only a distant memory.

 Fun Fact: The original Gutenberg Bible is still the most valued and valuable book in the world. A surviving copy recently sold for almost $2 million.

More to Explore

Brockman, John. *The Greatest Inventions of the Past 2,000 Years*. New York: Simon & Schuster, 2000.

Burch, Joann. *Fine Print*. Minneapolis, MN: Lerner Publications, 1999.

Clark, Donald. *Encyclopedia of Great Inventors and Discoveries*. London: Marshall Cavendish Books, 1991.

Dyson, James. *A History of Great Inventions*. New York: Carroll & Graf Publishers, 2001.

Fisher, Leonard. *Gutenberg*. New York: Simon & Schuster Children's Books, 1998.

Koscielniah, Bruce. *Johann Gutenberg and the Amazing Printing Press*. New York: Houghton Mifflin, 2003.

Lomask, Milton. *Invention and Technology Great Lives*. New York: Charles Scribner's Sons, 1994.

McNeil, Ian. *An Encyclopedia of the History of Technology*. New York: Routledge, 1996.

Yenne, Bill. *100 Inventions That Shaped World History*. New York: Bluewood Books, 1993.

Projection Maps

Year of Invention: 1569

> **What Is It?** An accurate projection of the three-dimensional globe onto a flat (two-dimensional) map.
>
> **Who Invented It?** Gerard Mercator (in Duisburg, Germany)

Why Is *This* Invention One of the 100 Greatest?

Street maps, world maps, resource maps, population maps: We rely on maps to tell us where we are and to show us where we want to go. Maps show us the spatial relationship of places and geographic features.

Long voyage navigation was dangerous and uncertain until maps accurately showed voyagers how to get where they were going. Accurate maps—for the first time—created an understanding of the world around us. With Mercator's maps, ancient Greek geography ended and modern geography began.

History of the Invention

What Did People Do Before?

Historically, maps were hand-drawn sketches, often drawn from memory or from interviews with those who were there. Such maps included gross errors of distance and proportion. Mapmakers typically made no effort to keep their maps in any scale. A distance of 50 miles might be represented as *one* inch on one side of a map and as *five* inches on the other side, with no indication of any scale change. Most travelers relied first on landmarks, second on the sun and Pole Star (North Star), and used maps only as backup.

Arab mapmakers (cartographers) maintained more accuracy and science in their maps during the third through twelfth centuries (the European Dark Ages) than did Europeans. By the early 1300s European cartographers were copying from Arab maps. By the mid-1300s, generally accurate maps (called "portolans") based on compass readings and shore landmarks directed merchants from port to port within the Mediterranean. Outside the Mediterranean, however, maps were horribly inaccurate. When Magellan reached the Philippines in 1521, he miscalculated his position by over 3,000 miles.

How Were Projection Maps Invented?

European governments began to apply great pressure on cartographers to create reliable, accurate maps. The biggest problem cartographers faced was Earth's curvature, its roundness. Undetectable to human eyes or to a sailor at sea, the fact that the earth was a three-dimensional sphere played havoc with two-dimensional, flat maps.

Cartographers wanted to maintain correct land relationships. But if mapmakers accurately held land shapes and land relationships as they flattened the three-dimensional world onto a piece of paper, the shape of the seas became warped. As a result, straight lines at sea (a straight compass course) appeared as a curved line on the map. The map would show that a ship should regularly change compass headings. But if they did, they'd wind up thousands of miles off course.

In 1552, Flemish cartographer Gerard Mercator moved to Duisburg, Germany, and started a mapmaking center. In 1568, he was commissioned to prepare a set of "the best" world maps. He had, to that point, specialized in making maps of the North Sea and Danish coast. This would be his first try to improve world map design.

A year later (1569) he was still floundering, unable to reconcile the problems of representing a global planet on a flat piece of paper. He decided he would have to solve this age-old mapmaking problem if he was ever going to complete his commission.

Over a three-month period, Mercator studied existing maps and interviewed sea captains and ship navigators. He was struck with a brilliantly simple image. In this image, he saw the world as a globe, a round ball, with a piece of paper wrapped into a cylinder around it so that the paper touched the globe at the equator. Next he imagined a light shining out from inside the globe, projecting the earth's surface features onto the paper. If he then unfolded that paper, he would have a new world map.

On this projection map, longitude (vertical) and latitude (horizontal) lines would form a rectangular grid that could be used to direct ships. Compass direction lines (azimuth lines) would show on the map as straight lines across the oceans. A navigator would plot a straight-line course on the map, and then set that compass heading and go.

It *was* true that land features grew increasingly distorted moving away from the equator. (Greenland appears bigger than Africa on a Mercator projection map even though Africa is actually almost 14 times bigger than Greenland.) But that problem didn't bother Mercator. This new map would be used primarily by ship navigators for ocean voyages.

What's Happened Since Then?

The Mercator projection map was not an instant success. Only as transoceanic shipping became more common and as known ports existed farther and farther from Europe did sailors recognize the advantage of Mercator's projection system and begin to demand and buy his maps.

By 1580, Mercator had prepared books of his various maps and placed an image of the Greek titan, Atlas, holding the world on his shoulders, on the cover of each book. The books were soon called *atlases*. "Atlas" became the general name for any book of maps.

For the past 500 years, Mercator projection maps have been the most popular and common of all world maps. In this age of computers and satellite imagery, no mapping system has yet stepped forward to replace or to challenge Mercator's simple projections.

Fun Fact: Before Mercator, Europeans most commonly used maps that were reproductions of charts by the ancient Greek, Ptolemy. A 1492 replica of his *Cosmographia* (world map) recently sold for $1,925,000 in a New York auction.

More to Explore

Aberg, Rebecca. *Latitude and Longitude.* New York: Children's Press, 2003.

Asimov, Isaac. *Asimov's Chronology of Science and Discovery.* New York: Harper & Row, 1989.

Bredeson, Carmen. *Looking at Maps and Globes.* New York: Scholastic Library Publishing, 2001.

Chambers, Catherine. *All About Maps.* New York: Scholastic Library Publishing, 1998.

Johnson, Sylvia. *Mapping the World.* New York: Simon and Schuster, 1999.

McNeil, Ian. *An Encyclopedia of the History of Technology.* New York: Routledge, 1996.

Suplee, Curt. *Milestones of Science.* Washington, DC: National Geographic Society, 2000.

William, Brian. *Latitude and Longitude.* New York: Smart Apple Media, 2003.

Microscope

Year of Invention: 1590

> **What Is It?** An optical device that magnifies small objects and allows humans to see objects too small to be seen with the naked eye.
>
> **Who Invented It?** Hans and Zacharias Janssen (in Middleburg, Holland) and Anton van Leeuwenhoek (in Delft, Holland)

Why Is *This* Invention One of the 100 Greatest?

Microscopes revolutionized science. Studies of cells, microscopic organisms, blood, molecules, and atoms would never have been possible without microscopes. The fields of medicine, engineering, anatomy, biology, zoology, and chemistry all depend on, and were made possible by, microscopes.

Microscopes opened the human mind to the possibilities of other worlds and of universes too small for our eyes to register and our minds to imagine. Microscopes are a profound source of knowledge and understanding and have taught us more about ourselves and the natural world than has any other single invention.

History of the Invention

What Did People Do Before?

Surely even the earliest humans were aware of the concept of magnification. Dewdrops on a leaf magnify the features of the leaf. But no one pursued the idea of artificially creating that magnification for thousands of years.

By 1290, craftsmen in Venice, Italy, had developed the ability to grind and polish high-quality transparent glass lenses. Over the next hundred years, lens making for spectacles (eyeglasses) swept through Europe. Glasses became a fashion statement. Most of these spectacle lenses magnified images—but only to a slight degree.

In 1558, Swiss naturalist Konrad Gesner had a more powerful (more curved) convex lens made and mounted into a metal frame. He used this magnifying glass to examine snail shells. This was the first recorded use of a lens for optic magnification and scientific study.

How Was the Microscope Invented?

Hans Jannssen and his son, Zacharias, were spectacle makers in Middleburg, Holland. They knew that any convex lens magnified the objects in front of it. In early 1590 it occurred to Zacharias that two lenses might magnify even more. He placed a convex lens at each end of a tube and found that he couldn't focus on anything in front of his lenses and that mostly what he saw was the tube itself.

For a time Zacharias set the idea aside. Then his father—Hans—wondered how much magnification two lenses could produce and began more earnest experiments. Holding one lens in each hand, he tried to find the specific distance between the two lenses, between the front lens and an object, and between the rear lens and his eye that would produce the biggest and clearest image. He repeated the experiment with a variety of different strength lenses, repeatedly regrinding and adjusting the two lenses.

Finally, father and son built a metal tube to hold the two lenses with which they had achieved the greatest success. This was the world's first microscope and was between nine and ten power (*power* identifying the number of times the microscope magnified an object in front of it).

The Janssens had invented a microscope but had no real idea of what to do with it. For 50 years, microscopes were considered frivolous novelties and sold mostly at fairs.

In 1652, Dutch cloth merchant Anton van Leeuwenhoek took up where the Janssens left off. Twenty-eight-year-old Leeuwenhoek lived in Delft, Holland, and had become an avid amateur scientist and glass lens grinder. As a young apprentice to a cloth merchant, he had been fascinated by the strong magnifying glasses inspectors used to count individual threads and determine the quality of a piece of cloth. That fascination had driven him into science.

Leeuwenhoek decided to put the microscope to practical use for scientific discovery. First, he ground and polished much stronger (more curved) lenses than spectacle maker Janssen ever considered making. Within months, Leeuwenhoek built a 250-power microscope. However, this new power brought with it new problems. Only a tiny sliver of space in front of his lenses stayed in sharp focus. Any hand jiggle as he held an object to study (and there always was some movement) was magnified to the point of giving Leeuwenhoek terrible headaches and eyestrain.

Leeuwenhoek spent the summer of 1652 devising a holder for objects he wanted to study through his microscope. By fall, he had added screw adjustments on this platform to move an object laterally and vertically so that he could obtain and maintain proper focus. This was the world's first practical microscope.

What's Happened Since Then?

By 1660, Leeuwenhoek was one of Europe's most famed scientists because of the series of startling discoveries he had made with his microscope, including—among many other things—the existence of microscopic organisms, the existence of such organisms in drops of ordinary water, the nature of blood, and the nature of bacteria. Leeuwenhoek's microscope opened new worlds for science to study.

Famed English engineer and scientist Robert Hooke picked up microscope studies beginning in 1665. Many of his most famous discoveries can be credited to his microscope, an improved version of Leeuwenhoek's original model.

In 1889, Swiss scientist August Kohler invented a microscope with a built-in light source and focusing mirrors for the light so that objects to be viewed would be brightly illuminated and clearer. In 1884, American inventor Charles Spencer invented a compound (multiple lens) light microscope that offered the viewer an amazing 1,250-power magnification! Science journals claimed that it would never be surpassed.

Forty years later (in 1926), German scientist Hans Busch invented the electron microscope, which was over 1,000 times more powerful than Spencer's. In 1933, Max Knoll built the first practical electron microscope in Berlin. This microscope was capable of seeing objects as small as one-one-millionth of a millimeter!

 Fun Fact: Electron microscopes look at objects so small that ordinary rulers can't be used to measure them. Specialty, miniature rulers have been invented to serve this need. How small are they? The smallest division on these rulers is only 18 atoms thick. Ten whole rulers stacked end to end would not equal the diameter of a single human hair.

More to Explore

Baker, Henry. *The Microscope Made Easy*. New York: Science Heritage, 1997.

Dyson, James. *A History of Great Inventions*. New York: Carroll & Graf Publishers, 2001.

Headstrom, Richard. *Adventures with a Microscope*. Mineola, NY: Dover Publications, 1997.

Marton, L. *Early History of the Electron Microscope*. San Francisco: San Francisco Press, 1992.

Oxlade, Chris. *The World of Microscopes*. New York: Usborne Books, 1999.

Suplee, Curt. *Milestones of Science*. Washington, DC: National Geographic Society, 2000.

Yenne, Bill. *100 Inventions That Shaped World History*. New York: Bluewood Books, 1993.

Telescope

Year of Invention: 1608 and 1609

What Is It? An optical device that uses concave and convex lenses to allow the viewing of distant objects.

Who Invented It? Hans Lippershey (in the Netherlands) and Galileo Galilei (in Florence, Italy)

Why Is *This* Invention One of the 100 Greatest?

The telescope brought the solar system, the galaxy, and the greater universe within our grasp. It radically changed who we, as a species, thought we were. The telescope shrank space and has forever changed our perspective of the size of our world, the space around it, and our place and purpose in the cosmos.

The telescope also helped give birth to modern science and made the field of astronomy possible. Telescopes turned specks in the night sky into spherical objects—into *places* rather than pinpricks of light.

History of the Invention

What Did People Do Before?

The general idea of using curved, transparent lenses to magnify distant objects was known by the eleventh century. Turkish and Moorish armies used simple telescopic devices during the late Crusades.

The necessary technology to build a telescope was readily available long before anyone thought of inventing one. High-quality, clear lenses were developed as early as 1290 by artisans in Venice, Italy. Eyeglasses (spectacles) soon followed, and spectacle makers became a common feature of every city by 1500. The microscope was invented in 1590. That device uses curved (convex) glass lenses to magnify close-up views of objects.

How Was the Telescope Invented?

Business was slow for Hans Lippershey, Dutch spectacle maker, in the spring of 1608. The Netherlands was in the midst of a prolonged rebellion against Spain. The Spanish navy blockaded Dutch ports. Merchandise and business had slowed to a trickle.

During an idle moment one afternoon that spring, one of Lippershey's assistants played with the lenses Lippershey had ground for a customer's eyeglasses. The apprentice noticed that if he held two lenses in front of the same eye—one at a distance from the other—and looked through both, a distant church steeple seemed to be much closer than it really was.

Over the next several days, that apprentice shared his discovery, and the game of "spying" on distant townsfolk, with several friends, before being caught in the act by Lippershey. Lippershey instantly realized the value of his apprentice's casual discovery. He hastily conducted experiments to identify the distance between the two lenses that produced the clearest and largest image of a distant object. Then Lippershey built a metal tube to hold the lenses in those positions and created the first modern telescope. Lippershey named it a *telescope,* from the Greek words meaning "to see far."

Lippershey's telescope was somewhere between five and seven power (magnified objects five to seven times bigger than they would appear to the naked eye). Rather than attempting to refine his invention. Lippershey filed for a patent and offered his telescope to the Dutch army. The army tried to keep it a secret. However, within months word leaked out and copies of the telescope were being manufactured all over Europe.

Galileo Galilie saw his first copy of a Lippershey telescope in late 1608 and instantly recognized that a better telescope could be the answer to the prayers of every astronomer and a way to add precision to astronomy while reducing eyestrain.

Galileo began to experiment. He varied lens shape and spacing within the telescope. He varied the number of elements that he used in his telescope. In early 1609, Galileo produced a 40-power, two-lens telescope. That 1609 telescope was the first practical telescope for scientific use.

What's Happened Since Then?

In 1610, Galileo discovered four moons circling Jupiter. These were the first observed moons other than our own. Later that same year he was able to see and study the rings of Saturn. Suddenly the heavens seemed filled with wondrous spectacles instead of orderly, uniform dots of light.

Sixty years later (1670), Sir Isaac Newton made the only fundamental improvement that has ever been made to Lippershey and Galileo's basic design. Newton invented the *reflecting* telescope. The optic lenses of Newton's telescope focused on a concave mirror that reflected and focused the image to be viewed onto a flat plate or eyepiece. This system allowed Newton to substantially increase the power of his telescope and to eliminate most of the distortion inherent in Lippershey's design.

Binoculars were invented by Frenchman J. P. Lemiere in 1825. Italian Ignatio Porris was the first to build a working pair of binoculars based on Lemiere's work.

The last inventive advance in telescope technology was the radio telescope. This telescope is not an optic telescope at all. Instead, it is a radio receiver that is focused to detect radio signals beaming from one tiny cone of space at a time—just as an optic telescope only receives light from a narrow cone.

Karl Jansky invented the radio telescope in 1949 while working at the Bell Telephone Lab in New Jersey. English astronomer Jordell Bank built the first working radio telescope in 1957.

Fun Fact: The amazing Hubble space telescope has provided our greatest images of the universe because it never has to deal with atmospheric distortions. However, when first launched, flaws in the grinding of its mirrors *did* blur its vision and forced NASA to create and launch a series of corrective lenses. The Hubble telescope now wears glasses and sees perfectly.

More to Explore

Asimov, Isaac. *Ancient Astronomy*. New York: Random House, 1994.

Boekhoff, P. M. *Galileo*. Chicago: Thomas Gale, 2003.

Clark, Donald. *Encyclopedia of Great Inventors and Discoveries*. London: Marshall Cavendish Books, 1991.

Doah, Robin. *Galileo*. Deerfield Beech, FL: Compass Point Books, 2005.

Lampton, Christopher. *Astronomy from Copernicus to the Space Telescope*. New York: Franklin Watts, 1997.

Lomask, Milton. *Invention and Technology Great Lives*. New York: Charles Scribner's Sons, 1994.

Sis, Peter. *Starry Messenger: Galileo Galilei*. New York: Farrar, Straus & Giroux, 2000.

Suplee, Curt. *Milestones of Science*. Washington, DC: National Geographic Society, 2000.

Yenne, Bill. *100 Inventions That Shaped World History*. New York: Bluewood Books, 1993.

Barometer

What Is It? A device to measure atmospheric pressure.

Who Invented It? Evangelista Torricelli (in Florence, Italy)

Why Is *This* Invention One of the 100 Greatest?

The barometer is an incredibly simple device—no moving parts, no gears, no buttons to push. Still, the barometer allowed scientists to understand atmospheric pressure and the nature of the atmosphere. It made prediction and understanding of the weather available to common people.

The barometer also allowed scientists to discover that there is an upper limit to the atmosphere. This shattered the idea that our atmosphere rises up to the stars and introduced the idea of open space.

History of the Invention

What Did People Do Before?

No one proposed or considered that the atmosphere had weight and that the atmosphere pushed down on every person and object on Earth. The thought simply had not occurred to anyone. No one studied the air column that rose from Earth's surface up to the edge of space. It hadn't occurred to anyone that there was anything there to study.

How Was the Barometer Invented?

It had long troubled mining engineers that their hand-driven suction pumps could not lift water more than 33 feet (9.7 meters). In 1620, the problem was turned over to famed scientist Galileo Galilee. Galileo conducted a few experiments but had little success. He conducted the last of these experiments in the mid-1630s at a Florence, Italy, public well assisted by Evangelista Torricelli. Torricelli, the son of a wealthy merchant, was an aspiring scientist.

In this experiment, Galileo looped a tube over a bar raised 40 feet (12 meters) above a public well. One end of the tube reached into the well's water. The other connected to the suction pump that Torricelli and another volunteer would operate. The two men pumped until sweat dribbled down their faces and their arms ached. But they could not pump water any higher than 9.7 meters above the level of the water in the well.

Galileo proposed that—somehow—the weight of the water column made it collapse back to that height.

Galileo died several years later. In 1643, Torricelli returned to the problem of the suction pump. If Galileo were correct, and any liquid column could only support a fixed amount of weight, then a heavier liquid should collapse at a lower height. Liquid mercury weighted 13.5 times as much as water. If Galileo were correct, a column of mercury should never rise any higher than 1/13.5th the height of a 9.7-meter water column, or about 30 inches (0.72 meter).

Torricelli filled a six-foot glass tube with liquid mercury and shoved a cork stopper into the open end. Then he inverted the tube and submerged the corked end in a tub of mercury before he pulled out the stopper. As he expected, mercury flowed out of the tube and into the tub. But not *all* of the mercury ran out.

Torricelli measured the height of the remaining mercury column—30 inches, just as expected.

But Galileo's explanation still felt wrong to Torricelli. He suspected that the true answer had something to do with the vacuum he had created above his column of mercury.

The next day, with wind and a cold rain lashing at the windows, Torricelli repeated his experiment, planning to focus not on the mercury column in his glass tube, but on the vacuum he would create above the mercury. However, on this day the mercury column only rose to a height of 29 inches in his glass tube. Now Torricelli was perplexed. He had expected the mercury to rise to the exact same height as yesterday. What was different? Rain beat on the windows as Torricelli pondered this new wrinkle.

Then, in a brilliant flash of insight, Torricelli understood. What was different was the atmosphere, the weather. Torricelli realized that the atmosphere pushed down on the mercury in the tub. That weight of air forced some mercury up into the tube. The weight of the mercury in the *tube* had to be exactly equal to the weight of the atmosphere pushing down on the mercury in the *tub*.

When the atmosphere changed and became either more dense or less dense, it would push down either a little bit more or a little bit less on the mercury in the tub and drive the column of mercury in the tube either a little higher or a little lower. Torricelli had invented a device to measure the pressure of the atmosphere, a barometer.

What's Happened Since Then?

The scientific community instantly applauded Torricelli's barometer. In 1647 French philosopher and scientist Rene Descartes realized that changes in Torricelli's barometer reading were linked to, and could predict, changes in the weather.

In 1648, another French scientist, Blaise Pascal, used a barometer to prove that there was less air pushing down at the top of a mountain than there was at its base. Extending this idea, Pascal realized that the higher one climbed, the less air sat above him, and that there must be some height at which one would reach the *top* of the atmosphere.

This was a revolutionary idea. Everyone had always thought that the atmosphere rose forever. Using Torricelli's barometer, Pascal proved that there was an upper limit to the atmosphere and that above that height lay empty space.

The mercury barometer has remained unchanged for 460 years and is still the standard for measuring barometric pressure. Modern electronic substitutes are beginning to replace the mercury barometer for scientific use. But they are much more expensive and only marginally more precise than Torricelli's original.

 Fun Fact: The greatest atmospheric pressure drop ever measured was 100 millibars (over three inches of mercury). The pressure drop was recorded inside an F4 tornado near Manchester, South Dakota, on June 24, 2003.

More to Explore

Asimov, Isaac. *Asimov's Chronology of Science and Discovery*. New York: Harper & Row, 1989.

Clark, Donald. *Encyclopedia of Great Inventors and Discoveries*. London: Marshall Cavendish Books, 1991.

Haven, Kendall. *Marvels of Science*. Englewood, CO: Libraries Unlimited, 1994.

Middleton, W. E. *The History of the Barometer*. Baltimore: Johns Hopkins University Press, 2003.

The Mechanical Clock

Year of Invention: 1657

What Is It? A mechanical device that will accurately measure time.

Who Invented It? Christian Huygens (in the Netherlands)

Why Is *This* Invention One of the 100 Greatest?

Clocks changed human concepts of time. Without clocks there can be no hours, minutes, or seconds. There is only the passing of day and night, of seasons, and of lifetimes.

The dependable precision of clocks made scientific measurement possible. They made possible the development of natural laws by such scientific giants as Newton, Descartes, and Leibniz.

Clocks also dictate our schedules and our lives. Clocks tell us when to go to bed, when to get up, when to eat, when to work, and when to play. Because the clock has made time so important, we often measure distance not in miles, but by how much time it will take to cover that distance.

The clock was created to serve the human need to define time, and now that same clock controls the masters it was created to serve.

History of the Invention

What Did People Do Before?

The first humans measured time by the sun (dawn, noon, and sunset). At some point, some clever humans stuck a stick in the ground and realized that they could mark the position of the sun's shadow at different times of the day around that stick. The device was called a sundial. By 3500 B.C., sundials were common in both China and Egypt. The Greek inventor, Anaximander, built the first Greek metal sundial in about 600 B.C.

Candles that burned a set number of inches in a fixed amount of time first appeared around 1500 B.C. as a way to keep track of time's passing. So did the hourglass, in which fine sand dripped from an upper chamber into a lower. Water clocks had also become popular by 1000 B.C. In a water clock, water dripped from one chamber into another at a known rate. In 800 B.C., several major Egyptian temples featured 24-hour (one day) water clocks.

In A.D. 725 and after almost 30 years of development, Chinese courtier Yi Xing built a magnificent and complex water clock to track the movement of the planets and stars. That clock was expanded by Buddhist monk Su Sung in 1092. A model of Su Sung's clock is on display in Beijing, the most elaborate water clock ever created.

How Was the Mechanical Clock Invented?

By 1100, mechanical clocks had begun to appear as an alternative to water clocks. Mechanical clocks relied on weights, pulleys, and balance bars instead of on the flow of water or sand to mark the regular passage of time. French Benedictine monk Gerbert d' Aurillac (who later became Pope Sylvester II) made a clock with a "system of gears and counterweights" in 999. Town records for Citeaux, France, in 1120 claim that they had a tower clock that struck a bell every hour throughout the day. The word *clock* is derived from the French word for bell.

In 1335 the Viscount of Milan built the first known public clock. Its bell struck the correct number of times to indicate the hour. Other cities soon followed with fancier and fancier town clocks: Padua, Italy, in 1364 and the St. Albans cathedral in Wallingford, England, in 1368.

This generation of mechanical clocks was more convenient than water clocks, but no more accurate. It was common for them to lose or gain up to 30 minutes a day. Such clocks were fine for deciding when to go home for lunch but were unacceptable for science.

Galileo made the discovery that made accurate clocks possible. In 1594 Galileo was a 21-year-old mathematics professor at the University of Pisa, Italy. Galileo often sat in a local cathedral when some nagging problem weighed on his mind. Lamps gently swung on long chains to illuminate the cathedral. One day in the summer of 1594, Galileo realized that those lamps always swung at the same speed.

He decided to time them. He used his neck's pulse beat to measure the period of each swing of one of the lamps. He borrowed one of the long tapers alter boys used to light the lamps and swung one lamp more vigorously. Again he timed it. Over many days he timed the lamps and found that the lamp always took exactly the same amount of time to travel through one complete arc. It didn't matter how big the arc was. The lamp traveled faster through big swings and slower through small ones.

When he shortened the chain holding a lamp, then its period of oscillation (the time required to complete one arc) grew shorter. When he lengthened the chain, the period grew longer. But the size of the arc (the distance the lamp traveled through one arc) didn't affect the time required to complete that arc at all!

Galileo was fascinated. Four years later, he used this discovery to disprove Aristotle's Law of Falling Objects. But he did not use it to build a better clock.

Dutch scientist Christian Huygens was the first to realize what Galileo's discovery could do for clocks. In 1657, Huygens decided to use a pendulum to finally create an accurate clock. He used a weighted metal rod for his pendulum and repeated Galileo's basic experiment.

He replaced the balance bar of a large clock with a pendulum whose weight could be adjusted up and down along the pendulum's rod so that the pendulum would swing through the correct number of arcs to accurately count out one hour. While old-style mechanical clocks often lost 20 or 30 *minutes* a day, Huygens's clock never lost more than 15 *seconds* a day. The world finally had a dependable, accurate clock.

What's Happened Since Then?

Within three years, over 100 clockmakers across Europe churned out pendulum clocks. Every city, fashionable home, and business felt it needed one of Huygens's inventions.

The first pocket watch was invented by German locksmith Peter Henlein. Henlein's pocket clock picked up the name *watch* from sailors. Sailors replaced the hourglass they had used for timing the length of each of their *watches* (four-hour duty shifts) with Henlein's pocket clock. Soon the clock itself was called a *watch*, and the name has stuck ever since.

The first electric (battery-driven) clock was invented in 1840 by Scotsman Alexander Bain. French clockmaker Antoine Redier built the first alarm clock in 1847. Frenchman Louis Cartier invented the first wristwatch specifically for his Brazilian aviator friend Alberto Santos-Dumont. It was first worn during Alberto's speed-record flight in Alexander Graham Bell's plane on November 27, 1907.

In 1949, American physicists Harold Lyons and William Libby invented the first atomic clock for the National Bureau of Standards. Their clock used the vibration of atoms as their oscillator and was accurate to within 1/1,000,000 of a second per year. The general public neither needs nor understands this level of accuracy, but many scientific experiments do.

The first electronic digital watch, developed by Time Computer Corporation of America in 1971, was called The Pulsar and cost $2,000. Similar ones now cost less than $15.

 Fun Fact: Time used to be measured by the passing of the sun. Now one second is officially defined as 9,192,631,770 vibrational periods of a cesium 133 atom at room temperature.

More to Explore

Brockman, John. *The Greatest Inventions of the Past 2,000 Years*. New York: Simon & Schuster, 2000.

Burton, Eric. *The History of Clocks and Watches*. Minneapolis, MN: Chartwell Books, 2004.

Dyson, James. *A History of Great Inventions*. New York: Carroll & Graf Publishers, 2001.

McNeil, Ian. *An Encyclopedia of the History of Technology*. New York: Routledge, 1996.

Roberts, Derek. *Precision Pendulum Clocks*. Las Vegas, NV: Schiffer Publishing, 2004.

Tait, Hugh. *Clocks and Watches*. Cambridge, MA: Harvard University Press, 1995.

Van Rossum, Gerhard. *History of the Hour*. Chicago: University of Chicago Press, 1996.

Williams, Brian. *Measuring Time*. Philadelphia: Smart Apple Media, 2003.

Yenne, Bill. *100 Inventions That Shaped World History*. New York: Bluewood Books, 1993.

Thermometer

Year of Invention: 1714

> **What Is It?** A device to accurately, quantitatively measure the temperature of another object.
>
> **Who Invented It?** Daniel Fahrenheit (in Amsterdam, Netherlands)

Why Is *This* Invention One of the 100 Greatest?

Whenever you're sick, you take your temperature—with a thermometer. To decide what to wear, you check the temperature outdoors—on a thermometer. When baking, you use a thermometer to check the temperature of your oven. Our daily life depends on knowing the temperature. Temperature depends on thermometers.

Science depends on precise temperature measurement even more than the general public does. Accurate measurement of heat and temperature has been essential to the development of medical science, thermodynamics, physics, astronomy, chemistry, and meteorology.

History of the Invention

What Did People Do Before?

Ancient people had no way to measure temperature other than by touch. However, humidity and wind both affect how hot a given temperature feels. There existed no reliable, accurate way to measure and compare temperatures.

In 1581, Galileo was the first to create a crude thermometer. From previous work, he knew that gasses (air) expanded when hot and contracted when cooled and planned to use expanding air as a way to measure temperature. He invented the word *thermometer* from the Greek words meaning "to measure heat."

However, Galileo's thermometer was monstrously inaccurate. Changes in air pressure (or in the water vapor trapped in the bulb's air) changed the thermometer's reading. It was unacceptable for scientific work.

How Was the Thermometer Invented?

Thirty-four-year-old Daniel Fahrenheit moved to Amsterdam from his native Germany to set up a plant to manufacture meteorological instruments. Fahrenheit regularly felt frustrated by the lack of a decent thermometer and, by 1713, had decided to create one on his own.

In early 1714 he made the first, and greatest, of his two innovations that led to his working thermometer. He decided a thermometer would be more accurate if he shifted from *gas* (air) to *liquid*. After several months of searching, he settled on liquid mercury as the best possible liquid for his thermometer. It had a low freezing point (-38 degrees C) and a high boiling point (over 380 degrees C). Mercury also expanded at the same rate at all temperatures, it didn't vaporize, and its silver color made it easy to see as it rose or fell in a thermometer.

In the summer of 1714, Fahrenheit perfected a way to purify (clean) liquid mercury so that it would not stick to the sides of a thin glass tube. Thus, he was able to use small amounts of mercury and build a practical (small) thermometer. Thick glass sides on the neck of his thermometer magnified the width of a capillary-thin column of mercury and made it easier for scientists to read.

Fahrenheit's second innovation was a workable temperature scale to mark on his thermometer. Isaac Newton had proposed in 1701 that the difference between the freezing point of water and body temperature should be divided into 12 divisions that would create a starting point for a temperature scale. Fahrenheit decided to use Newton's concept, but wanted to avoid negative numbers on his thermometer. (Temperatures on cold days fell well below the freezing temperature of water.)

Fahrenheit added salt and ammonium chloride to water and cooled that mixture until it froze to obtain a zero degree point on his temperature scale. Fahrenheit decided that the distance between this zero degree point and body temperature was too great for just twelve divisions. He split each of Newton's twelve divisions into eight smaller parts he called *degrees*. Thus, body temperature became 96 degrees on Fahrenheit's scale (12 X 8).

By that fall, Fahrenheit decided to adjust his scale so that there would be an even 180 degrees between the boiling and freezing points of water. This shifted normal body temperature to 98.6 degrees on his adjusted scale.

Fahrenheit's thermometer and temperature scale were instant hits and were quickly adopted all across Europe and America.

What's Happened Since Then?

Fahrenheit's temperature scale thrived for only 26 years. In 1741 Swedish clockmaker Anders Celsius proposed that there should be an even 100 divisions (degrees) between water's boiling and freezing points and created the Celsius temperature scale. It was called the centigrade scale because *centi* is Latin for 100. All Europe (except England) quickly adopted the centigrade scale. England finally shifted to centigrade early in the twentieth century. Only America has held onto the Fahrenheit scale, though the United States is slowly converting to Celsius, or centigrade.

In 1866, British physician Thomas Allbut was the first to use one of Fahrenheit's mercury thermometers to record a patient's temperature. It took five minutes of the mercury bulb's resting under the patient's tongue to register a temperature but was hailed as one of the greatest medical advancements of the century.

New electronic digital thermometers have recently replaced mercury ones in hospitals and are beginning to do so for home use. Soon Fahrenheit's thermometer, like his temperature scale, will have faded into history. However, the world has relied on them for almost 300 years.

 Fun Fact: Scientists at Kassel University in Germany invented a thermometer using nano-wires (wires less than one-thousandth the diameter of a human hair) that can accurately measure temperature changes of only one-thousandth of a degree centigrade.

More to Explore

Chang, Hasok. *Inventing Temperature.* New York: Oxford University Press, 2004.

Coleman, George. *The Addison-Wesley Science Handbook.* New York: Addison Wesley, 1996.

Cork, James. *Heat.* Philadelphia: Textbook Publications, 2001.

Dyson, James. *A History of Great Inventions.* New York: Carroll & Graf Publishers, 2001.

Gratzer, Walter. *Eurekas and Euphorias.* New York: Oxford University Press, 2004.

Middleton, W. E. *The History of the Thermometer.* Baltimore, MD: Johns Hopkins University Press, 2003.

Yenne, Bill. *100 Inventions That Shaped World History.* New York: Bluewood Books, 1993.

Accurate Ship Navigation
(Portable Clock and Sextant)

Year of Invention: 1759

What Is It? Two devices that, when combined, accurately determined longitude (the distance east or west that a ship has sailed from its home port).

Who Invented It? Clock: John Harrison (in Lincolnshire, England). Sextant: John Campbell (British naval officer at sea)

Why Is *This* Invention One of the 100 Greatest?

In 1676, the English government declared that navigation was the greatest scientific problem of the age. European countries were poised to expand into global trade and conquest. But they couldn't do it if their ships had no way to accurately know their position when out of sight of land.

History of the Invention

What Did People Do Before?

Early sailors hugged coastlines and used landmarks for navigation. In 1100 B.C. the Phoenicians, were the first to cross the Mediterranean Sea using the Pole Star (North Star) as their navigational guide.

Navigation had improved only slightly by the late 1600s. Latitude (the distance north or south from the equator) was easy to measure with a device called a *quadrant* that measured the height of the sun at noon and the height of the Pole Star at night. From either of those measurements, a navigator could calculate how far north or south his ship had sailed.

However, longitude (the distance east or west of some home port) was virtually impossible to even guess. Without a way to measure longitude, a ship on the open ocean would always be lost. Shifting currents and winds might carry a ship hundreds of miles off course without the crew ever detecting it or their compass needle ever showing the problem.

How Were the Portable Clock and Sextant Invented?

In order to calculate a ship's position, the navigator used a *quadrant* to determine noon (the moment when the sun was at its highest). This time was compared to the local time at the ship's home port. The difference in hours between these two times told the navigator how far east or west of that home port the ship had sailed.

There was, however, a problem. No clock existed that could keep accurate home port time onboard a pitching ship. Pendulum clocks were worthless on the swaying deck of a ship. Pocket watches existed, but they often lost or gained 20 minutes a day. Within a week, such a watch could be off by an hour or more. And that translated into longitude errors of a thousand miles!

In 1714, the British government offered a reward of £20,000 (an incredible fortune) to anyone who would "devise a method of determining a ship's longitude."

To win the prize, a clock—at sea on a swaying ship—had to be accurate to within 2.8 seconds a day. *Minute* hands had only recently been added to fancy clocks. Now this sea clock had to be accurate to within a few *seconds* every day—all the while absorbing the pounding of rolling, turbulent sea voyages!

In 1728, English clockmaker John Harrison took up the challenge. The son of a carpenter and with no formal education, Harrison was fascinated by clocks from childhood. As a young man (age 25) he built several all-wood pendulum clocks that compensated for changes in temperature and humidity, required no oil, and were accurate to within a few minutes each month—a phenomenal achievement for the day.

Harrison studied ships and ship motion and completed his first model, H1, in 1735. That pendulum clock adjusted for temperature shifts and ship motion. In 1736, the H1 was mounted in a British navy ship to be tested on a trip to Lisbon, Portugal and back.

The H1 gained less than eight seconds a day. Good, but not good enough to win the prize. Harrison completed his H2 in 1741. H2 performed no better than H1 had during trials on a trip from London into the Mediterranean and back.

In 1749, Harrison completed his H3. He built into this model a temperature sensitive, bimetallic strip (still used in thermostats today) for his pendulum to compensate for temperature shifts, a caged roller race (forerunner of ball bearings and gyroscope) to prevent clock sway, and a mechanism to keep the clock going while it was being wound.

The H3 proved to be more accurate at *sea* than any other clock was on *land*. It lost an average of just under two second a day. At the end of a 45-day voyage, it accurately predicted the ship's position within 10 miles of its actual location.

H3 qualified for the prize. But Parliament refused to pay and demanded further improvements.

Dejected and frustrated, Harrison went back to work. Sometime around 1757 he got the idea to abandon pendulum clocks and make his next try an improved, spring-driven pocket watch. He completed H4 late in 1760. The H4 was tested on two voyages from England to the West Indies, one in 1761, the other in 1764. On both voyages the H4 proved accurate to within five seconds over three months! It was an achievement equivalent to landing a space probe on Neptune within a few feet of the original target.

However, Parliament *still* balked at paying the £20,000. They said that they needed to consider other systems. Actually, they hoped that new improvements in the sextant would keep them from having to pay at all.

In 1757, Naval officer John Campbell redesigned the *quadrant* to create the *sextant*, a vast improvement in calculating both latitude and local time. Campbell proposed using the Royal Observatory's lunar and star tables to then calculate longitude.

If Campbell's sextant worked, Campbell was a naval officer and wouldn't have to be paid at all. Parliament would save £20,000 and still be able to equip British ships with a working navigational system.

Ship captains, however, recognized immediately the superiority of Harrison's H4 pocket watch to tell home port time and the sextant to calculate local time. The H4 was much more accurate then were the Royal Observatory's charts. Parliament finally relented and paid Harrison in March 1776, on his eighty-third birthday.

What's Happened Since Then?

Of all of the hundreds of new clock and watch designs created between 1760 and 1970, none significantly improved on the accuracy and dependability of Harrison's H4. Computers, radar, and satellite location guidance systems finally made sextants obsolete in the 1970s.

 Fun Fact: The Global Positioning System (GPS) consists of 24 satellites that each orbit the earth once every 12 hours. From 120 to 500 miles up, these satellites can locate your exact position within two feet.

More to Explore

Aberg, Rebecca. *Latitude and Longitude.* New York: Children's Press, 2003.

Andrews, William. *Illustrated Longitude.* New York: Walker & Company, 2003.

Borden, Louise. *Sea Clocks.* New York: Simon & Schuster Children's Books, 2004.

Dyson, James. *A History of Great Inventions.* New York: Carroll & Graf Publishers, 2001.

Lasky, Kathryn. *The Man Who Made Time Travel.* New York: Farrar, Straus & Giroux, 2003.

McNeil, Ian. *An Encyclopedia of the History of Technology.* New York: Routledge, 1996.

Sobel, Dava. *Longitude.* New York: Penguin Books, 1996.

Suplee, Curt. *Milestones of Science.* Washington, DC: National Geographic Society, 2000.

The Spinning Jenny

Year of Invention: 1764

What Is It? The first mechanical device to spin multiple threads of raw flax, wool, or cotton at the same time.

Who Invented It? James Hargraves (in Lancashire, England)

Why Is *This* Invention One of the 100 Greatest?

You can't make clothes without first making thread to weave into cloth to sew into clothes. The slowest part of the entire cloth-making process was spinning thread from raw cotton, wool, flax, or silk. Spinsters spun by hand—one thread at a time. It was slow and tedious work.

Then James Hargraves invented a machine that could spin eight threads at once. The spinning jenny allowed for the mass production of thread, cloth, and clothes. It slashed the price of clothes and made them affordable for ordinary working families.

The jenny created the industrial technology that triggered the beginning of the Industrial Revolution. For the first time, people went to factories and mills to work. Hargraves's spinning jenny changed the world.

History of the Invention

What Did People Do Before?

Spinning and weaving were standard parts of farm life in the evenings. Typically, three women (spinsters) spun thread on large, vertical spinning wheels while one man (weaver) wove cloth. Selling this cloth to clothes mills was a large part of many farm families' income.

In 1733 Englishman John Kay upset the balance between spinsters and weavers by inventing a device called the flying shuttle, which more than tripled the speed of weavers. Suddenly each weaver needed 10 to 15 spinsters. Weavers wove fast enough to run out of thread. The lack of thread threw the weaving industry into crisis. The London Society of the Arts offered a reward of £50 for a spinning machine that could spin at least six threads at a time.

72

How Was the Spinning Jenny Invented?

Born in 1720, James Hargraves was raised on an English farm. Spinning and weaving were part of his upbringing. In 1760, a neighbor asked James to create a better carding machine. Carding was another labor-intensive step in the thread-making process that had to be completed before spinning. Carding removed tangles, knots, and debris so that the wool fibers would be smooth and ready for spinning.

Hargraves experimented with levers, pulleys, and springs to emulate the motion of a carder's wrists, elbows, and arms. In less than three months he had built a carding machine that doubled the speed of that process. This success (and the London Society's prize) spurred James on to investigate the next step—spinning. He toyed with different designs, devices, ideas, and schemes for three years with no success.

In early 1763, an accident gave him the answer. His daughter was spinning one evening in their Lancashire home and accidentally knocked over her spinning wheel. The wheel continued to spin as it lay on its side even while the spindle (the wooden dowel that held the already spun yarn) continued to spin vertically in its mount on the spinning wheel frame. Hargraves claimed that the complete design for a spinning machine flashed into his head as soon as he saw that horizontally spinning wheel.

In less than 60 days Hargraves built the first spinning jenny ("jenny" being local slang for "engine"). The jenny simultaneously produced eight threads faster than a spinster could produce one. In four months he built one that produced 20 threads at a time! One spinster could now supply more than enough thread for one weaver. Within a year, a jenny was built that spun 120 simultaneous threads. One lone machine operator could now supply seven or eight weavers—putting 100 spinsters out of work.

Unfortunately, Hargraves's spinning jenny stirred up bitter riots. Many rural families feared their women would be cheated out of work by the contraption. An angry mob smashed its way into Hargraves's home and workshop and destroyed every shred of equipment and every tool he owned. Hargraves fled to Northampton, England.

What's Happened Since Then?

Hargraves didn't patent his invention until 1770—seven years after its invention. By then it was too late. Others had copied his design, and he was unable to enforce his patent. He died disappointed and relatively poor.

England's Richard Archwright benefited most from Hargraves's invention. In 1769, Archwright built a larger version of the jenny powered by a waterwheel. This design gave his machine more power. Power allowed him to create a tighter weave to his threads, producing thinner threads with greater strength and versatility.

Samuel Crompton, another Englishman, combined the best of both designs into his spinning mule, patented in 1779. This spinning machine became the standard of the vast English and American fabric and clothes factories—immense, dingy, dust-choked mills that served as models for the urban Industrial Revolution spanning the next hundred-plus years.

Computer brains now control and direct thread making, cloth making, clothes making, and sewing machines. However, the basic process—making thread from some natural or synthetic fiber, weaving cloth, cutting out and sewing up clothes—has not changed from the day Hargraves first invented the jenny.

Fun Fact: In 2002 U.S. mills converted 833.5 million pounds of wool into yarn and 40,000 bales of cotton into thread.

More to Explore

Clark, Donald. *Encyclopedia of Great Inventors and Discoveries*. London: Marshall Cavendish Books, 1991.

Connolly, Sean. *The Industrial Revolution*. Portsmouth, NH: Heinemann Library, 2003.

Dyson, James. *A History of Great Inventions*. New York: Carroll & Graf Publishers, 2001.

Harris, Jennifer, ed. *5000 Years of Textiles*. Washington, DC: Smithsonian Institute Press, 2004.

Lomask, Milton. *Invention and Technology Great Lives*. New York: Charles Scribner's Sons, 1994.

McNeil, Ian. *An Encyclopedia of the History of Technology*. New York: Routledge, 1996.

Schoeser, Mary. *World Textiles*. New York: Thames and Hudson, 2003.

Smith, Nigel. *The Industrial Revolution*. New York: Raintree Publications, 2003.

Yenne, Bill. *100 Inventions That Shaped World History*. New York: Bluewood Books, 1993.

Lighter-Than-Air Flight

Year of Invention: 1783

What Is It? Flight in ships that rise by being lighter than the surrounding air.

Who Invented It? Joseph and Etienne Montgolfier (in Paris, France)

Why Is *This* Invention One of the 100 Greatest?

Flight has forever thrilled the human imagination. Lighter-than-air flight was the first successful human flight. The first time a human was able to rise above the ground and shed the bonds of gravity was in a hot air balloon. The second human flight used a hydrogen-filled balloon. Flight went on to airplanes, rockets, and space travel. But it began with lighter-than-air balloons.

History of the Invention

What Did People Do Before?

All early attempts at flight mimicked birds. People built wing-like devices that were strapped onto human arms and flapped—always into failure. Even the great Galileo designed his aeroplane with bird-like wings and mechanical gears to flap the monstrous and feathered appendages. Scientists assumed that, if wings made birds fly, then wings were also what should be used to make people fly.

It is both odd and fascinating that, throughout 5,000 years of recorded history, no one thought of hot air balloon flight. The technology to build an adequate balloon and to produce hot air had been around for millennia. Certainly people were aware that hot gasses rose from a fire and lifted into the air. It seems that, for thousands of years, the idea simply never occurred to anyone.

How Was Lighter-Than-Air Flight Invented?

In 1766, English scientist Henry Cavendish isolated a new colorless, gaseous element: hydrogen. He said hydrogen had "negative weight" since it rose up into the air and proposed that it could be used to lift objects from the earth. But he never pursued the idea.

Joseph and Etienne Montgolfier (sons of a wealthy paper merchant) lived on the outskirts of Paris. In 1782 the brothers read about Cavendish's work and hypothesized that whatever Cavendish found in his hydrogen must also be present in the smoky air rising from a fire. That smoky air surely had "negative weight" and carried ashes up into the sky.

The Montgolfier brothers decided to use the negative weight of smoky air to make a human fly. By early summer 1783 they had built a paper-lined cloth (linen) bag 30 meters in diameter. On June 4, they took it to the market square in Annonay, France, and lit a bonfire under it. As the fire's wood began to crackle, both Montgolfiers tossed wool, hay, and old shoes into the flames to increase the smoke since they thought that "negative weight" came from the smoke. Thick, black smoke billowed into and around the balloon, driving the crowd back and obscuring their view of the balloon as it puffed and filled. Joseph Montgolfier held the release rope and had to cover his nose and mouth with a handkerchief. His eyes stung and ran.

Joseph released the tether and the Montgolfiers watched with an amazed crowd of several hundred as their balloon rose 300 meters into the air. The red-painted, undulating ball drifted off, landing over two kilometers away after a 10-minute flight. The brothers were stunned and delighted at their success—far greater than anything they had dreamed of.

The brothers scheduled their next demonstration for September 9 and built a balloon bag twice the size of their first. They also added a basket that carried a duck, a rooster, and a sheep 800 meters into the air for a 19-minute flight. A cheering crowd of 300,000 watched, including American Benjamin Franklin. That flight was also watched by King Louis XVI and Marie Antoinette. Their applause made the brothers Montgolfier instantly famous.

The Montgolfiers scheduled their first manned flight for November 21, in Paris. Piatre de Rozier and the Marquis d'Arlandes would ride in this bigger-than-ever balloon—the first humans to fly. (The Montgolfier brothers preferred to stay on the ground.) This flight lasted over 30 minutes and rose to a height of over 8,000 feet (2,500 meters). All of France was electrified by this achievement. The French word for hot air balloon is still *la montgolfiere.*

Meanwhile, French scientist Jacques Charles decided to follow Cavendish's experiment and use hydrogen for a flying balloon. Through quick experiments, he determined that hydrogen had three times as much lifting power as did hot air. A smaller hydrogen balloon could fly longer and higher than could any hot-air balloon.

Throughout the summer of 1783, Charles raced to design a balloon lining capable of trapping and holding gaseous hydrogen. However, Charles was not able to construct a balloon for a demonstration flight until December 1—10 days after the Montgolfiers' manned flight. Charles filled his new balloon with hydrogen gas, rose over two miles (3,500 meters) into the air, and covered almost 50 kilometers during his 90-minute flight.

What's Happened Since Then?

On June 4, 1784, Elizabeth Thible became the first woman to fly, ascending over the town of Lyon, France. James Satler made the first British balloon flight in his hot air balloon on October 4, 1784. Nine years would pass before the first balloon flight in America (in 1793).

The French army formed the world's first air force in 1794, using four observation balloons against Austrian forces in the Battle of Fleurus. In 1804, Swiss scientist Joseph Gay-Lussac made the first scientific use of hot-air balloons to study air chemistry and composition over the Alps mountains.

In 1906 the first flight using the gas helium was made. While hydrogen offered greater lift, it was also dangerously explosive. By the time the first shots of World War I rang out, helium had replaced hydrogen for most lighter-than-air flights.

Fun Fact: In March1999, Bertrand Piccard and Brian Jones became the first humans to circumnavigate the earth in a balloon. Their trip lasted over 477 hours. In 2002, Steve Fossett became the first to do it solo.

More to Explore

Asimov, Isaac. *Asimov's Chronology of Science and Discovery*. New York: Harper & Row, 1989.

Charles, Rodney. *Lighter Than Air*. Miami, FL: Sunstar Publishing, 1996.

Dyson, James. *A History of Great Inventions*. New York: Carroll & Graf Publishers, 2001.

Freeman, Tony. *Hot Air Balloons*. New York: Children's Press, 1996.

Hallion, Richard. *Taking Flight*. New York: Oxford University Press, 2003.

McNeil, Ian. *An Encyclopedia of the History of Technology*. New York: Routledge, 1996.

Nakun, Andrew. *Flying Machines*. New York: DK Publishing, 2004.

Owen, David. *Lighter Than Air*. New York: DIANE Publishing, 2004.

Yenne, Bill. *100 Inventions That Shaped World History*. New York: Bluewood Books, 1993.

Cotton Gin

Year of Invention: 1793

> **What Is It?** A machine that separates cotton fibers from seeds.
>
> **Who Invented It?** Eli Whitney and Catherine Greene (in Mulbury Grove, Georgia)

Why Is *This* Invention One of the 100 Greatest?

The cotton gin revolutionized cotton production and saved the Southern economy. It saved Southern plantation agriculture and helped to preserve the institution of Southern slavery for at least three generations. The cotton gin raised cotton to king and made the South rich.

History of the Invention

What Did People Do Before?

By the time of the Revolutionary War, giant English spinning mills were eagerly gobbling up every ounce of cotton Southern plantations could produce. Growing cotton was easy in the warm Southern climate.

The problem came during harvesting. Picking each boll (cotton pod) by hand left the picker's hands raw and bloody. Worse, separating cotton fibers from seeds (*ginning*) was slow, hard work that consumed tremendous amounts of time. Ginning kept most slaves out of the field for much of the day. Picking slowed to a crawl, and much of each year's cotton crop was left to rot in the fields unpicked. Plantations often made no profit on their vast fields of cotton.

How Was the Cotton Gin Invented?

By age 27, Massachusetts born Eli Whitney had tried law, teaching, and running his own metal works forge making nails and pins. But nothing lasted. Early in 1792, he was invited to visit the Georgia plantation of Revolutionary War hero General Nathanael Greene. Greene died shortly after the war and left the Mulbury Grove plantation to his capable wife, Catherine Greene.

Mrs. Greene was impressed when Whitney made a series of repairs and mechanical improvements around the plantation and built a new embroidery frame that was the envy of Catherine's friends.

In late 1792, Catherine Greene described to Whitney the problem plantation owners faced with cotton ginning. Mrs. Greene said that whoever created a machine that removed human labor from this process would become instantly famous and wealthy.

Whitney agreed to take on the challenge and retired to Greene's basement workshop. Most agree that Catherine gave Whitney at least a general outline of a ginning machine as a starting place. Whitney, however, still struggled for six months developing his design, picking seeds out of hundreds of cotton bolls to better understand the problem and its possible solutions.

The idea of his design was simple. Cotton would be dumped into a hopper from a picker's long, over-the-shoulder bag. Teeth on a rotating cylinder at the bottom of this bin would grab the cotton fibers and pull them through a series of narrow metal slots—slots too narrow to allow seeds to pass. A set of brushes would lift the ginned cotton off these rotating teeth and guide it to bagging.

However, his simple design was beset by problems. Cotton fibers were gnarled, sticky, and tough and often clogged the gears and wooden cogs. Many cotton seeds were deeply knotted into the fibers and would not pull free as his rotating teeth turned through the machine's metal slots. If he made the slots wider, too many seeds slipped through. If he made the slots narrower, cotton fibers balled up and jammed the slots.

In the spring of 1793, Catherine suggested that metal wires would work better for his teeth than the wooden pegs Whitney had been using. At first Whitney scoffed at the idea. But his continued failures led him to try her idea. The revised machine worked wonderfully.

Even a small, hand-cranked version of Whitney's machine could gin cotton as fast as 50 workers. Bigger cotton gins could replace over a hundred.

What's Happened Since Then?

Neither Whitney nor Greene became rich off their invention. They stalled in patenting the device for a year. By then it was too late. The idea had been pirated across the South. Hundreds of gins already sat ready to speed the 1794 harvest through ginning. Whitney, a bad businessman, did become famous, but he went broke trying to manufacture and sell his cotton gins.

Cotton gins spread cotton fields across the South, replacing indigo as the biggest cash crop of the region. Whitney's and Greene's cotton gin design survived until first electric, and then gasoline, motors allowed cotton planters to change the basic design of the machines they used.

 Fun Fact: Modern cotton balers compress cotton with over 800,000 pounds of force to stuff it into bales.

More to Explore

Clark, Donald. *Encyclopedia of Great Inventors and Discoveries*. London: Marshall Cavendish Books, 1991.

Jeffries, Michael, and Gary Lewis. *Inventors and Inventions*. New York: Smithmark, 1997.

Hale, Margaret. *Eli Whitney.* Portsmouth, NH: Heinemann, 2004.

Lomask, Milton. *Invention and Technology Great Lives.* New York: Charles Scribner's Sons, 1994.

Meltzer, Milton. *The Cotton Gin.* New York: Marshall Cavendish, 2003.

Vare, Ethlie Ann, and Greg Ptacek. *Mothers of Invention.* New York: William Morrow, 1994.

————. *Patently Female: Stories of Women Inventors.* New York: John Wiley & Sons, 2002.

Vaccinations

Year of Invention: 1796

What Is It? An injection designed to produce immunity to a particular disease.

Who Invented It? Lady Mary Wortley Montagu (in London, England) and Edward Jenner (in Gloucester, England)

Why Is *This* Invention One of the 100 Greatest?

Have you had small pox? Polio? Typhoid? Probably not. Smallpox killed over 100,000 people a year for a century and left millions horribly scarred and disfigured. The influenza epidemic of 1918 killed over 25 million worldwide. Polio killed countless thousands in the early twentieth century and left millions paralyzed.

One simple invention not only stopped the spread of these diseases, it virtually eradicated them. That idea was vaccinations. Vaccinations have saved countless millions of lives and have prevented unimaginable amounts of misery and suffering.

History of the Invention

What Did People Do Before?

Infectious diseases have always plagued humankind. In fact, the word *plague* comes from one the first of these killer diseases—the plague. Over the course of repeated epidemic outbreaks through the fourteenth and fifteenth centuries, the plague killed nearly half of the population of Europe.

By the dawn of the eighteenth century, smallpox replaced the plague as the greatest terror on Earth. England alone lost 45,000 a year to smallpox and many times that number during major outbreaks. Benjamin Franklin's son was killed by smallpox during an outbreak in America in the 1750s. Europeans were desperate for a way to escape from this horrid disease that seemed to lurk in every corner and village.

How Were Vaccinations Invented?

Vaccinations were invented in two steps.

Twenty-four-year-old Lady Mary Wortley Montagu, a well-known English poet, traveled to Turkey with her husband in 1712 when he became the British ambassador there. Lady Mary soon noticed that Turkey suffered from little or no smallpox, the dread disease that regularly decimated England and that had left her disfigured and pockmarked.

The Turkish freedom from the terror of smallpox sparked Mary's curiosity. She soon learned that each autumn old women performed what was called "ingrafting." Previous British travelers had dismissed the practice as a meaningless tribal ritual. But Mary saw that this annual event held the secret to their immunity from smallpox.

Village families would decide if anyone in the family should have smallpox that year. An old woman would arrive carrying a nutshell full of infected liquid. She would open one of the volunteer's veins with a needle dipped in the liquid as the family sang and chanted. The infected person stayed in bed for two to three days. That person was then as well as before, never got a serious case of smallpox, and had no disfiguring scars.

Upon her return to England in 1713, Lady Montagu began ingrafting convicts and orphans (with the approval of Caroline, Princess of Wales). She collected the puss from smallpox blisters of sick patients and injected small amounts of the deadly liquid into her test subjects. Death rates for those she inoculated were less than one-third that for the general public and five times as many of her subjects got mild, nonscarring cases.

The English population had grown so desperate for protection from smallpox that many jumped at the chance to have their children inoculated with Lady Mary's ingrafting. However, there was a problem with ingrafting. Inoculations with live smallpox viruses were dangerous and unpredictable. Some patients died from the smallpox injections that were supposed to protect them.

Enter Edward Jenner, a young English surgeon, in 1794,. He decided to find a way to vaccinate without risk to the patient. Living in a rural community, Jenner soon noticed that milkmaids almost never got smallpox.

Jenner found that virtually all milkmaids *did* get cowpox, a disease that caused mild blistering on the hands. Jenner theorized that cowpox must be in the same family as smallpox and that getting mild, safe cowpox made a person immune to the deadly smallpox.

He tested his theory by injecting 20 children with liquid taken from the blisters of a milkmaid with cowpox. Each infected child got cowpox. Painful blisters formed on their hands and arms, lasting several days.

Two months later, Jenner injected live smallpox into each of his test children. If Jenner's theory was wrong, many of these children would die. However, none of his test children showed any sign of smallpox.

Jenner invented the term "vaccination" to describe his process when he announced his results in 1798. *Vacca* is the Latin word for cow; *vaccinia* is Latin for cowpox.

What's Happened Since Then?

The early twentieth century brought the next great epidemic that seemed right for the development of vaccinations. In the midst of the horrors of World War I, an influenza (flu) epidemic spread across the world. Twenty-five million died from it in alone. Hundreds of researchers scrambled to create a vaccine. Ever since, annual flu shots have been offered as a precaution against new strains of this potentially deadly disease.

Shortly thereafter, polio spread across the globe, attacking infants' and young children's central nervous systems. Thousands died. Millions were left paralyzed in its wake.

Two men get the credit for creating the polio vaccine. The first was American microbiologist Edward Salk, who sought ways to kill the polio virus that would make the dead virus incapable of causing polio but leave it strong enough to force the immune system of healthy people to create antibodies against polio (create immunity).

Salk conducted tests and trials between 1950 and 1954 before his vaccine was declared both safe and effective. By 1961, American polio cases had diminished by 95 percent.

The second man, American microbiologist Albert Sabin, feared that Salk's dead virus vaccine was too weak to create *permanent* immunity. In 1957, Salk developed a live strain of polio that (like cowpox for smallpox) was too weak to cause the disease but, as a live virus, would trigger a stronger immune response in patients and thus guarantee permanent immunity. Between these two vaccines, polio has virtually disappeared from the world.

 Fun Fact: Children are now regularly vaccinated for as many as 15 diseases, including polio, measles, mumps, rubella, diphtheria, typhus, whooping cough, typhoid, tetanus, hepatitis A & B, chicken pox (varicella), pertussis (whooping cough), and flu.

More to Explore

Asimov, Isaac. *Asimov's Chronology of Science and Discovery*. New York: Harper & Row, 1989.

Clark, Donald. *Encyclopedia of Great Inventors and Discoveries*. London: Marshall Cavendish Books, 1991.

Dyson, James. *A History of Great Inventions*. New York: Carroll & Graf Publishers, 2001.

Haven, Kendall, and Donna Clark. *100 Most Popular Scientists for Young Adults*. Englewood, CO: Libraries Unlimited, 1999.

Vare, Ethlie Ann, and Greg Ptacek. *Mothers of Invention*. New York: William Morrow, 1989.

Yenne, Bill. *100 Inventions That Shaped World History*. New York: Bluewood Books, 1993.

Steam Engine

Year of Invention: 1798

What Is It? An engine that creates mechanical power by boiling water to create steam.

Who Invented It? James Watt (in Birmingham, England)

Why Is *This* Invention One of the 100 Greatest?

Steam powered the Industrial Revolution. Steam powered England into world economic dominance in the eighteenth and nineteenth centuries and provided the energy to run industry, pumps, trains, and ships for 150 years. The Industrial Revolution, powered by steam, built on blast furnace iron and steel, radically changed the direction of human evolution. Without steam, it couldn't have happened.

History of the Invention

What Did People Do Before?

The idea of the steam engine goes as far back as A.D. 200. Hero of Alexandria observed that expanding water vapor could provide energy to make objects move or turn. But no one could imagine anything practical to do with it, and the idea was dropped for 1,500 years.

European coal mines had the nasty habit of flooding. Miners were desperate for pumps that could keep their mines dry. Several Englishmen invented steam engines to power mine pumps. Most barely produced enough energy to run themselves, much less pump water. In 1712, Thomas Newcomen invented the best of this generation of steam pumps, but even this engine was temperamental and notoriously weak.

How Was the Steam Engine Invented?

In 1792, English engineer and businessman Mathew Boulton hired 35-year-old Scottish engineer James Watt to create a new (and better) steam engine.

Steam was created in a boiler and escaped through a nozzle into the bottom of a large cylinder. There, increasing steam pressure drove a piston up. The piston rod connected to one end of an overhead rocker arm. Pushing the rocker arm up and down operated a pump, which was the point of the engine.

However, steam pumps were frightfully slow and weak. When the piston reached the cylinder's top, a valve closed, shutting off the flow of steam. Water sprayed into the cylinder to cool the steam inside, and as it cooled, gravity pulled the piston back down.

In late 1793, Watt studied the physics of heat and energy and quickly found two gross inefficiencies in the existing design. First, boiler rooms were stifling hot because steam boilers weren't insulated. Watt wrapped his boiler in layers of insulation.

Second, Watt realized that it was a waste of both time and energy to re-condense steam inside the engine's cylinder. He built a second condenser chamber. Once his piston reached the top of its stroke, a new valve opened at the bottom of the cylinder. Steam gushed into a condenser chamber, where water sprays cooled and condensed it back to water. This way, Watt's cylinder stayed hot and ran much more efficiently.

Watt's 1794 steam engine tripled the output of any existing steam engine.

That was good for simple water pumps, but not good enough to power factories. Watt and Boulton realized two things. First, each stroke of a steam engine had to produce considerably more power. Second, factories and mills didn't need the up and down motion of a pump. They needed to turn shafts, lathes, and conveyors. They needed *rotary* motion.

Watt envisioned a two-stroke engine. Steam would hiss into his cylinder alternately from both ends, thus powering the piston back and forth and gaining work from each direction of its motion. He struggled for over a year to design the timing belt that would open and close the appropriate valves at the correct instant to direct steam into and out of each end of a closed cylinder. Watt quit in disgust dozens of times. Boulton and Watt's wife, Ann, always talked him into trying again.

In 1798, Watt completed the design of a gear system by means of which any desired speed of rotary motion could be produced by his steam engine. Watt's 1798 steam engine revolutionized fabric mills and industrial plants across England. It was practical and powerful.

What's Happened Since Then?

Watt's steam engine provided the mechanical power to launch the Industrial Revolution. Soon after, steam engines were adapted to work on trains and ships.

In 1820, Jacob Leupold, working in Leipzig, Germany, designed a high-pressure steam engine. His engine allowed steam pressures of up to 30 psi (pounds of pressure per square inch). By 1850, better designs allowed pressures to rise to hundreds of psi.

A continuous stream of improvements and refinements to Watt's basic design peppered the decades of the nineteenth century—improved power output, improved speed of the engine, improved energy efficiency.

But these were all just refinements of Watt's original design. For 150 years, the world ran on steam. By then the electric motor existed. Electric motors became more popular for factories. The internal combustion engine also emerged in the late nineteenth century. By the early twentieth century, the gasoline engine had pushed steam out of all transportation systems. Watt's engine was but a memory. But before it faded into history, that engine changed the world.

Fun Fact: The world's most powerful working steam engine is on a locomotive called the American No. 700, built in 1916. It can pull with a force of over 166,000 pounds!

More to Explore

Clark, Donald. *Encyclopedia of Great Inventors and Discoveries*. London: Marshall Cavendish Books, 1991.

Crane, William. *The Man Who Transformed the World: James Watt*. New York: Messner, 1993.

Dickinson, H. W. *A Short History of the Steam Engine*. 4th ed. London: Cass, 1990.

Haven, Kendall. *Marvels of Science*. Englewood, CO: Libraries Unlimited, 1994.

Lomask, Milton. *Invention and Technology Great Lives*. New York: Charles Scribner's Sons, 1994.

McNeil, Ian. *An Encyclopedia of the History of Technology*. New York: Routledge, 1996.

Nahan, Andrew. *James Watt and the Power of Steam*. Sussex, England: Wayland & Hove, 1994.

Electric Battery

Year of Invention: 1799

> **What Is It?** A device that stores electric energy and produces a constant flow of electric current from that store.
>
> **Who Invented It?** Alessandro Volta (in Padua, Italy)

Why Is *This* Invention One of the 100 Greatest?

Batteries are essential elements of virtually every electronic, and many electric, device that exists in our modern world. Your watch, flashlight, iPod®, radio, car, camera, clock, cell phone, cordless drill, laptop computer, and thousands of other devices all depend on batteries.

Batteries were also the first portable energy source. Batteries became an essential element for the development of the fields of physics, electromagnetism, and chemistry.

History of the Invention

What Did People Do Before?

In 1663, Otto von Guericke, mayor of the Prussian town of Magdeburg, invented the first electric generator. He built a cage with a spinning ball of sulfur to create a static electricity charge. That started interest in electricity.

Electricity became a prime focus of eighteenth-century science. By 1720, static electricity was well established as a popular party game in Europe and America. Partygoers held hands as they shuffled across a thick carpet before the end person touched a metal doorknob to shock them all.

In 1745, Pieter van Musschenbroek, a professor at the University of Leyden in Holland, invented the Leyden jar. This was a glass jar, partly filled with water and sealed with a cork. A long nail pierced the cork and reached down to water level. Leyden jars became the rage of European and American society. Leyden jars were the first device capable of storing an electric charge. (Now a device that does what a Leyden jar did is called a *capacitor*.)

By 1752, American Benjamin Franklin had conducted numerous experiments with Leyden jars and had vastly improved their capacity. Franklin's Leyden jars were potentially deadly things. Franklin suspected that the two known forms of electricity (static and lightning) were just two forms of the same thing. To prove it, he flew a kite into storm clouds to collect static electricity from the clouds—his famous kite experiment. Two months later, two French scientists tried to repeat Franklin's experiment and were killed when their kite was actually struck by lightning.

Leyden jars could store electrical energy. But they couldn't *create* it.

How Was the Battery Invented?

In 1775, 30-year-old Alessandro Volta was appointed professor of physics at the Italian Royal School of Cuomo in Padua, Italy. Electricity first pricked Volta's interest when he read English scientist Joseph Priestly's *History of Electricity*.

After reading about Luigi Galvani's 1793 experiments, Volta began to wonder if an electric current could be created just by the presence of two different metals. He began a series of experiments to see if he could force an electric current to flow between strips of two different metals. He laid them next to each other. Nothing happened. He laid them across each other. Nothing happened. He changed metals. Nothing happened. He submerged them in water. Nothing happened.

However, when he submerged the metal strips in a strong acid, he found that he created a steady, strong electrical current flowing between the metal strips. He experimented with different metals and found that copper and zinc worked best.

Each time he created an electrical current, however, it soon dwindled and ceased. Volta noted scaly deposits on one of his two metal strips and suspected that these somehow blocked the electrical flow. Volta, however, was unable to identify the deposits or to prevent them from forming and throttling his electric current.

Volta wrote papers describing these 1795 experiments and put forth the idea that electrical currents were created whenever two different metals were exposed to the same acid solution. After a few additional experiments over the next two years, Volta came to the conclusion that chemical reactions involving strips of two different metals were what created an electric current. The metals and acid solution created a chemical reaction that freed a flow of electricity. He began to call the acid solution an *electrolyte*, since it freed electricity from the metal strips placed in it.

In 1800, Volta decided to build a battery using metal strips to prove his theory. He filled a series of bowls with acidic brines and connected the bowls with strips of copper and zinc. He was able to show that this arrangement created a steady current for almost an hour before it faded and trickled to a stop.

What's Happened Since Then?

In 1801 the French emperor, Napoleon, summoned Volta to demonstrate his battery. Napoleon was so impressed that he bestowed the Legion of Honor on Volta and made him a count. William Cruickshank of England was the first to take advantage of Volta's invention. He mass-produced Volta batteries beginning in 1805 and made a fortune.

In 1859, French physicist Gaston Plante invented the rechargeable battery. By designing a lead-acid battery, he was able to force a current through it backwards and recharge the battery. (Modern car batteries are lead-acid batteries.) In 1866, French chemist Georges Leclanche invented the dry cell battery. His battery was made of carbon and zinc electrodes in an ammonium chloride solution with a mixture of carbon grains and manganese dioxide to soak up any hydrogen produced at the electrodes. The common (modern) alkaline battery was invented in 1914 by Thomas Edison. (He called it an alkaline battery because he used powdered alkaline for the electrolyte.)

When Volta died in 1827, the scientific community decided to honor him by using his name for the unit that measures electric potential—the volt.

 Fun Fact: Japanese scientists have invented a new kind of battery. It uses seawater as its electrolyte. The batteries are manufactured and stored dry. Whenever you need battery power, just add sea water!

More to Explore

Bevilacqua, Fabio. *Nuova Voltiana: Studies on Volta and His Times*. Rome: Hoepli, 1996.

Bodanis, David. *Electric Universe: The Shocking True Story of Electricity*. New York: Crown Publishing Group, 2005.

Clark, Donald. *Encyclopedia of Great Inventors and Discoveries*. London: Marshall Cavendish Books, 1991.

Dyson, James. *A History of Great Inventions*. New York: Carroll & Graf Publishers, 2001.

Marcello, Pera. *The Ambiguous Frog: The Galvani-Volta Controversy on Animal Electricity*. Princeton, NJ: Princeton University Press, 1997.

McNeil, Ian. *An Encyclopedia of the History of Technology*. New York: Routledge, 1996.

Pancaldi, Giuliano. *Volta: Science and Culture in the Age of Enlightenment*. Princeton, NJ: Princeton University Press, 2005.

Seven Hills Book Distributors, ed. *Alessandro Volta*. New York: Seven Hills Book Distributor, 1997.

Yenne, Bill. *100 Inventions That Shaped World History*. New York: Bluewood Books, 1993.

Railroad

Year of Invention: 1804

> **What Is It?** A transportation system that carries heavy loads along tracks of metal rails.
>
> **Who Invented It?** Richard Trevithick (in Coalbrookdale, Wales)

Why Is *This* Invention One of the 100 Greatest?

Railroads were the first efficient transportation system capable of moving large quantities of material (coal, cattle, grain, iron ore, etc.). Using low-friction steel wheels on steel rails, trains could move great weights of cargo using a tiny fraction of the power that would be needed to move that cargo along a road by horse and wagon.

Railroads made it practical to mine vast quantities of raw materials and to transport them to distant markets. They made it possible to concentrate great herds of cattle in the Western United States and gave rise to the era of the cowboy.

The railroads were responsible for creating the four standardized time zones in the contiguous United States (Eastern, Central, Mountain, and Pacific). They opened the American West and, for a century, were the most important and advanced form of land transportation.

History of the Invention

What Did People Do Before?

Bulk goods were moved by horse-drawn wagon to a waterway and then by boat to a destination. Inland waterways used horse-drawn barges because winds could not be depended upon to drive a boat up- or downriver. Cities developed along the major rivers and coasts because those were the only places where masses of goods could be gathered, processed, and distributed. Many commodities were simply not developed because transportation costs were too high.

How Was the Railroad Invented?

Richard Trevithick was an established British inventor who, by 1796, specialized in developing compact high-pressure steam engines. Most of Trevithick's engines were used to pump water from mines—a constant and serious problem.

90

One afternoon in the summer of 1798, Trevithick was inspecting the pumps he had installed in a coal mine in Coalbrookdale, Wales. He happened to see a group of six miners struggling to push a loaded coal cart up the winding iron tracks of their mineshaft. It struck Trevithick as a terrible waste of time and energy.

He began to wonder if he couldn't mount one of his steam engines on a coal car and make it self-propelled. Even Trevithick's compact steam engines were far too big to fit on a coal car, so he decided to start by mounting a steam engine on a wagon. It didn't work. The engine didn't produce enough power to drive the wagon over the ruts, rocks, and rough bumps of the dirt road.

Trevithick made three decisions. First, he would build iron tracks for his locomotive to run along. Second, he would need to get more power out of his engine. Third, he would have to make the engine more compact.

After six months of experiments, Trevithick learned that he could increase steam pressure and thus engine power if he eliminated the condenser (part of Watt's steam engine) and vented steam directly into the atmosphere. As a side benefit, this would let him reduce the size of his boiler and engine.

Trevithick sought backing for his new locomotive. However, no one believed that smooth metal wheels would gain sufficient traction on a smooth metal rail to pull a heavy load, and certainly 'not while traveling uphill. It was one thing for a horse with hooves on solid ground. But—they said—it was folly to think that the train could do it.

In 1802, Trevithick demonstrated his next model. This engine was marginally successful. It moved itself but didn't develop enough power to pull a train. Trevithick increased the size of his engine, increased its steam pressure again, and shifted to double pistons instead of a single piston. He also added gearing.

He fired up this new model on February 20, 1804, and ran it over a nine-mile track from Penydarren to Merthyr using a bin of coal as his fuel. Just to make sure that his skeptics paid attention, he pulled a five-car train loaded with ten tons of coal and 70 men. A crowd gathered along the length of the tracks and cheered as Trevithick roared by at the blinding speed of 10 miles an hour, billows of steam and smoke hissing into the morning sky.

In 1805, Trevithick redesigned the rails that the train ran on to the now common upside down "T" shape, which was more stable and easier to secure to wooden cross-ties. With those final improvements, Trevithick's trains began to roll across the coal district of England.

What's Happened Since Then?

Between 1810 and 1814 the Napoleonic Wars (wars between France and England) drove the price of horses and feed so high that steam trains became economical. Haulers of other commodities suddenly clamored for their own rail lines.

In 1829, Englishman Robert Stevenson built the *Rocket*, the first "high-speed" train. It chugged along at 16n mph while pulling a 40-ton train, and at over 36 mph when uncoupled. The *Rocket* was the first man-made object to outrun a horse.

The first passenger locomotive service started in 1829 in America. Peter Cooper built passenger cars for the Baltimore & Ohio Railroad line. That first train engine was called *Tom Thumb*.

The first diesel engine (modern trains are all diesels) was built in Switzerland in 1912, but it was never developed because it appeared to be less efficient than steam. The first practical diesel, the streamlined *Flying Hamburger*, built in Germany, went into service in 1932. The first diesel service in the United States, the *Pioneer Zephyr* made the 1,015-mile run between Chicago and Denver, averaging 77.6 mph on May 26, 1934, to the wonder of all and disbelief of many.

 Fun Fact: The largest steam locomotives ever built were the 4-8-8-4 Big Boys, built by American Locomotive between 1941 and 1944. Each stood 131 feet long and weighed over 500 tons.

More to Explore

Chant, Christopher, ed. *The World's Railroads: History and Development of Rail Transportation.* New York: Book Sales, Inc., 2000.

Dyson, James. *A History of Great Inventions.* New York: Carroll & Graf Publishers, 2001.

Garratt, Colin. *Illustrated Book of Steam and Rail.* New York: Barnes & Noble Books, 2003.

Ierley, Merritt. *Wondrous Contrivances.* New York: Clarkson Potter, 2002.

Lomask, Milton. *Invention and Technology Great Lives.* New York: Charles Scribner's Sons, 1994.

McNeil, Ian. *An Encyclopedia of the History of Technology.* New York: Routledge, 1996.

Yenne, Bill. *100 Inventions That Shaped World History.* New York: Bluewood Books, 1993.

Steamship

Year of Invention: 1807

What Is It? A ship propelled by steam.

Who Invented It? Robert Fulton (in New York City)

Why Is *This* Invention One of the 100 Greatest?

Steamships finally freed ocean travel from the whims of current and wind. They freed river traffic to sail at any time, in any weather. Commerce flourished. Inland farms and factories blossomed, knowing that the rivers and steam power could reliably get their products to coastal ports.

Steam power freed ship builders from the rigid weight and design limits imposed by the need for masts and sails and from the need to design ships so that they could operate in light, irregular winds.

History of the Invention

What Did People Do Before?

Before steam engines, river and canal traffic was usually horse drawn. The barges were really little more than floating wagons. River traffic moved at a crawl of 2 mph upstream and swept by as fast as the current would carry it when traveling downstream.

Open ocean travel moved as fast as wind and current would allow. Arrival times were always general estimates, plus or minus a couple of weeks depending on the wind.

How Was the Steamship Invented?

Frenchman Marquis Joffroy D'abans was the first to try to build a steamship. He made his first steam launch in 1776 along the banks of the River Seine in Paris. D'abans lowered a small, wood-fired steam engine onto a riverboat. The engine's rocker arms connected to paddles that looked like flopping duck's feet. The rocker arms dipped back and forth. The duck-feet paddles thrashed comically, but the ship never moved.

The Marquis's second try was in 1779. He used a bigger steam engine this time. However, with the engine heaped on its deck, this boat was too heavy and sank as it was launched. D'abans made his final try in 1783 along the River Saone in Lyons, France. His new ship, the *Peryscaphe*, hissed, wheezed, and puttered slower than a man could walk.

Still, it lumbered in a cloud of smoke and steam upstream for 15 minutes before it shook itself apart and sank. The *Peryscaphe* used a small, side paddlewheel for power, and that established the paddlewheel as the way to drive a steamship.

As a young man, Robert Fulton supported himself as a portrait painter and, in 1887, he traveled to England to study under painter Benjamin West. By 1793, his interest had turned to ships, and he moved to Paris to study shipping by river and canal.

By 1796, Fulton had fallen in love with submarines and actually built one that successfully sat on the bottom of the Seine for 24 hours before he steered it back to the surface and to the dock.

While urging the French government to buy his submarine design as a weapon to use against the British, Fulton met Robert Livingston, U.S. ambassador to France. Even though Fulton's heart belonged to submarines, Livingston convinced him to at least *study* steamships. From that study in the archives, shipyards, and libraries of Paris, Fulton learned that in all previous steamship designs the engine had been too big and heavy for the ship. He would need to make the ship wider and shallower. Fulton also experimented with different oar and paddle designs and concluded that twin sidewheel paddles were the most effective.

In 1804, Fulton traveled back to England, hoping to sell his submarine to the British as a weapon they could use against the growing French fleet. The English were not interested in submarines and, discouraged, Fulton sailed back to New York City in 1806 to try to sell the idea to the United States. After dabbling with submarine designs for another six months, he had an unexplained about face and decided to build a steamboat.

Fulton ordered an advanced Boulton and Watt steam engine from England and went to work rebuilding a 133-foot ship based on his Paris research to accommodate this engine, at the Greenwich Village docks of Manhattan. He hired an iron works company to construct two 15-foot-high paddlewheels. Seven months later (in the spring of 1807), the *Clermont* was ready for river trials. The ship belched puffs of thick, black smoke and billows of snow-white steam as it splashed easily around upper New York harbor.

A week later, Fulton guided the *Clermont* on its maiden voyage—a 132-mile run upriver to Albany. Crowds lined the riverbank to cheer. The *Clermont* completed the run in a record setting time of 32 hours—over 4 mph *against* the current! It made headline news. The ship returned downstream to New York in just under 12 hours.

What's Happened Since Then?

Within a year, an entire fleet of paddlewheel steamships was plowing up and down the Hudson. The design was soon copied on other rivers. As ships grew bigger and steam engines more powerful, the size of the paddlewheels grew, until Mississippi River steamers of the mid-nineteenth century sported paddlewheels often four stories high.

The first oceangoing steamer was built by Scotsman Henry Bell in 1812. The first transatlantic steamship crossing was made by the American ship *Savannah* in 1819. However, the *Savannah* was technically a hybrid since it carried sails and used them for part of the crossing. The *Great Western* made the first all steam-powered crossing in 1837.

The invention of the modern ship's propeller was claimed by several inventors, all clustered around the years 1828 to 1832. The two men generally credited are English engineer Robert Wilson and Swedish-born American engineer and inventor John Ericsson. Paddlewheel construction was finally abandoned by 1880 in favor of propellers.

Steam engines were abandoned as ship power plants by the early twentieth century. Gasoline engines, diesels, and later nuclear power were more compact, lighter, and more reliable. Steamships are now only found as an occasional amusement park novelty. But 100 years ago, they opened the seas and rivers of the world to new possibilities for travel and commerce.

 Fun Fact: Author Samuel Clemens worked for years as a riverboat captain. He adopted the pen name "Mark Twain" because *mark* was a signal for measuring river depth (measured in fathoms—six feet) and *twain* was slang for 12. Twelve fathoms was an ideal water depth for riverboats and was used as riverboat slang for "all's well!"

More to Explore

Clark, Donald. *Encyclopedia of Great Inventors and Discoveries*. London: Marshall Cavendish Books, 1991.

Ford, Carin T. *Robert Fulton: The Steamboat Man*. Berkeley Heights, NJ: Enslow Publishers, 2004.

Gillis, Jennifer. *Robert Fulton*. Portsmouth, NH: Heinemann, 2004.

Kroll, Steven. *Robert Fulton: From Submarine to Steamboat*. New York: Holiday House, 1999.

Lomask, Milton. *Invention and Technology Great Lives*. New York: Charles Scribner's Sons, 1994.

McNeil, Ian. *An Encyclopedia of the History of Technology*. New York: Routledge, 1996.

Parks, Peggy J. *Robert Fulton*. Seattle, WA: Blackbirch Press, 2003.

Pierce, Morris A. *Robert Fulton and the Development of the Steamboat*. New York: PowerKids Press, 2003.

Shagena, Jack L. *Who Really Invented the Steamboat?: Fulton's Clermont Coup*. Amherst, NY: Prometheus Books, 2004.

Stethoscope

Year of Invention: 1816

> **What Is It?** A device that allows doctors to clearly hear sounds within the body.
>
> **Who Invented It?** Rene Laennec (in Paris, France)

Why Is *This* Invention One of the 100 Greatest?

A simple stethoscope is the most basic, cost-effective diagnostic tool available to a doctor. It reveals precise and valuable information about the working of lungs, heart, voice, blood, stomach, and other internal organs. Amazingly complex and sophisticated high-tech tools have been added to a doctor's diagnostic bag of tricks (X-rays, MRI, cat scan, endoscope, etc.). Yet it is still the stethoscope doctors grab first. It is the simple stethoscope you see doctors carry wrapped around their necks. A stethoscope is as basic and essential for a doctor as a calculator is for an engineer or accountant.

History of the Invention

What Did People Do Before?

Even the earliest physicians in ancient Mesopotamia and Egypt knew that listening to the sounds of the body was an important diagnostic step. The physician's ear was pressed against the patient's chest, side, or back so that the doctor could hear the sounds made by heart and lungs.

How Was the Stethoscope Invented?

In 1816, 38-year-old Rene Laennec was already a well-established Paris doctor and a well-respected diagnostician of breathing, lung, pulmonary, and other chest and abdominal cavity disorders (bronchitis, emphysema, tuberculosis, cirrhosis, etc.).

In the summer of 1816, Laennec was asked by another physician to examine and diagnose a young woman with breathing difficulty. Laennec's normal procedure was to have the patient partially disrobe so that he could place his ear against a thin handkerchief covering bare skin in five spots: against the side under each arm, against each side of the upper back, and against the upper breast bone.

This young woman, however, was, first, a young woman. Second, she was exceedingly fat. And third, she was perspiring heavily from both her poor health and the stifling Paris summer heat. Laennec felt uncomfortable wedging his head into her clammy folds so that he could clearly hear the sounds he needed in order to make a diagnosis.

He hesitated. What should he do? At that moment of embarrassment and consternation, Laennec recalled an acoustic fact he had learned in college. Sound travels well through solid objects. Laennec grabbed 24 sheets of paper, rolled them tightly into a bundle, and secured them in shape with paste glue. He applied one end of this paper roll against the young woman's chest and the other to his ear.

Laennec was delighted to find that he heard her heart and the air flowing through her lung's bronchia better and more clearly than if his ear had been pressed against her chest. He shifted the position of the paper roll and found that he could actually hear the flow of blood through her arteries and veins.

Laennec was fascinated by the potential of so simple a device and began five months of experiments with different solid materials and different shapes of material. He tested bars and tubes of a dozen different metals. He tried wadded and pressed cotton and other fibers. To Laennec's surprise, none worked nearly as well as the rolled paper or a wooden dowel.

Watching the shape of musical horns at an evening concert, Laennec got the idea to flare one end of his tube into a funnel. Then he cut his listening post into two parts—the tube and the funnel, both for ease of carrying and for ease of production on his home lathe.

Laennec published articles describing the precise dimensions of this device he simply called "Le Cylindre" (the tube). Others tried to attach his name to the device. Laennec objected and, to prevent them from creating excessively grand names, he named the device a *stethoscope* from the Greek words for "I see" and "the chest."

What's Happened Since Then?

The medical profession did not readily embrace Laennec's stethoscope. In 1828, Adolphe Piorry, a Paris physician, added a "pleximeter" (a thin metal plate to amplify the sound from the body and send it into the stethoscope) to the front of his stethoscope, with amazing results. The clarity and crispness of the sounds shocked other doctors. That established the acceptance and popularity of the stethoscope.

In 1835, the first flexible interwoven cord was used as a tube on an English stethoscope. In 1870 the first stethoscopes with rubber cones at the end appeared in the United States. Twenty years later, flexible rubber tubes became common.

Dozens of other diagnostic tools—from X-rays, MRI, cat scan, and endoscope to radioactive dye tracers—have been invented over the past century. However, doctors still pull out their trusty stethoscopes first and probably will through the foreseeable future.

 Fun Fact: It's simple to make your own working stethoscope. Directions are available at www.rossonhousemuseum.org/stethoscope.

More to Explore

Asimov, Isaac. *Asimov's Chronology of Science and Discovery*. New York: Harper & Row, 1989.

Blaufox, Donald. *Ear to the Chest: The Evolution of the Stethoscope*. New York: CRC Press, 2001.

Casanellas, Antoni. *Great Discoveries and Inventions That Improved Human Health*. New York: Gareth Stevens, 2000.

Dowswell, Paul. *Medicine.* Portsmouth, NH: Heinemann Library Publishing, 2001.

Eyewitness Books Staff. *Medicine*. New York: DK Publishing, 2000.

Storring, Rob. *Doctor's Life: A Visual History of Doctors and Nurses through the Ages*. New York: Penguin Group, 1998.

Electric Motor

Year of Invention: 1831

What Is It? A machine that converts electrical energy into mechanical motion.

Who Invented It? Michael Faraday (in London, England)

Why Is *This* Invention One of the 100 Greatest?

Sewing machines, streetcars, blenders, fans, air conditioners, power saws and drills, washing machines, refrigerators, vacuum cleaners, hair dryers, and dishwashers all run on electric motors. Your family's car starts with an electric motor. Almost everything you own or use that has moving parts runs by an electric motor. Since the beginning of the twentieth century, most of the world's factory and household motors have been electric.

History of the Invention

What Did People Do Before?

Humans used manual labor, animal power, wind power, and water power to move equipment, run mills and machines, and power agriculture. They burned wood and coal to power forges and stoves and provide heat.

When James Watt invented the steam engine, industry and transportation shifted to steam. However, no engine existed for small uses—for motors inside the home, small appliances, or small work engines. Electricity was still a novelty in the early 1800s. Power stations and distribution lines did not exist.

How Was the Electric Motor Invented?

Michael Faraday was the son of a blacksmith and had no formal education. Apprenticed to a bookmaker at age 14 (in 1805), he was a self-taught science enthusiast. By the age of 18, his first love had settled on chemistry, and for all his life he called himself a chemist even though his fame came from his discoveries and inventions with electricity.

In 1820, Danish scientist Hans Christian Oersted discovered that there was a link between electricity and magnetism. In 1822, Faraday, now working as an assistant to famed English scientist Sir Humphry Davy, decided to use Oersted's amazing discovery to invent a device Faraday called the "rotator."

99

Faraday's rotator was a wire suspended over a strong magnet. When the wire was connected to a battery, the electric current generated an opposite magnetic field to that of the magnet. The magnet repulsed the wire, and the wire was forced to rotate around the magnet. It was really just a toy, and not even Faraday looked at it as a serious advancement.

In 1831, it struck Faraday that the reverse of his 1822 toy should also be true. An electric current should be created when a conductive metal (a wire or round disk) moved through a magnetic field. He created the name *electromagnetic induction* for this phenomenon since he was using a magnetic field to induce an electric current to flow through a wire. He wrapped two coils of wire around an iron ring, one on either side of the ring. He connected a battery to one of the wire coils. The current in that coil created a magnetic field in the iron ring that induced a current in the second coil of wire.

This experiment, however, produced only a momentary flash of current in the new coil. Faraday was disappointed. He had hoped to create a current in the second wire that would flow as long as the first wire was connected to a battery. After pondering the problem for several months, Faraday realized an electric current was induced by a *changing* magnetic field or by a *moving* piece of metal that cut across a magnetic field.

He changed the iron ring to copper, and, on October 29, 1831, suspended a metal disk above a horseshoe magnet. When he spun the disk, he measured a small—but continuous—electric current flowing through a wire attached to it. (Moving metal through a magnetic field creates an electric current.) This simple device was the world's first electric generator. Electric generators using Faraday's principal are all around us in our modern world.

Faraday then reversed the process. He wrapped a wire around a magnet and connected it to a battery. He attached a device to that wire that could change the direction of its current flow from one end of the magnet to the other. Each time the electric current flopped from one end of the magnet to the other, it reversed the direction of the magnetic field. That changing magnetic field forced the suspended disk to spin. (A changing magnetic field creates physical motion in metal objects placed in it.) This was the world's first electric motor. (An electric current created a changing magnetic field that created physical motion.)

What's Happened Since Then?

Once Faraday revealed the principles of electric motors and generators, progress toward large, practical versions of each was rapid. In 1832, Englishman William Sturgeon invented the commutator, a device to rapidly switch the direction of an electric current from a battery. The commutator made Faraday's electric motor practical and efficient.

In 1837, American Thomas Davenport built the first American electric motor. His was the first to resemble modern electric motors. Over 200 patents had been issued for electric motors by 1870. Chemistry Professor Sibrandus Stratingh of the Netherlands launched the first electric boat in 1840. In 1842, Scotsman Robert Davidson built the first electric carriage. The first permanent electric railway went into service in 1881 in Germany.

Refinements on electric motors and generators continue to this day. There appears to be no end in sight for our dependence on electricity to power our world. Electricity is still the most used form of energy; Faraday's electric motor is still the most common way to convert electricity into mechanical motion.

Fun Fact: Early electric motors were heavy and bulky. However, in 2003 the UC Berkeley Nanotechnology Department built an entire electric motor so small that it measures only 500 nanometers across. That's only 200-thousandths of an inch!

More to Explore

Clark, Donald. *Encyclopedia of Great Inventors and Discoveries*. London: Marshall Cavendish Books, 1991.

Dyson, James. *A History of Great Inventions*. New York: Carroll & Graf Publishers, 2001.

Fulick, Ann. *Michael Faraday*. Portsmouth, NH: Heinemann Library Publishing, 2000.

Lomask, Milton. *Invention and Technology Great Lives*. New York: Charles Scribner's Sons, 1994.

McNeil, Ian. *An Encyclopedia of the History of Technology*. New York: Routledge, 1996.

Ross, Stewart. *Michael Faraday*. New York: Raintree Publishing, 2003.

Russlee, Colin. *Michael Faraday*: *Physics and Faith*. New York: Oxford University Press, 2001.

Suplee, Curt. *Milestones of Science*. Washington, DC: National Geographic Society, 2000.

Williams, Brian. *Faraday: Pioneer of Electricity*. Hauppauge, NY: Barron's Educational Series, 2003.

Combine Harvester

Year of Invention: 1831

> **What Is It?** A machine to simultaneously cut, gather, separate, and bag a grain.
>
> **Who Invented It?** Cyrus McCormick (in the Shenandoah Valley of Virginia)

Why Is *This* Invention One of the 100 Greatest?

Endless miles of waving grain fields did not exist back when grain was harvested by hand. Cutting, gathering, threshing (separating grain from stalk), winnowing (separating grain from husk), and bagging consumed long hours and meant that farms could only plant and harvest enough grain for their own livestock.

Then Cyrus McCormick invented the combine harvester. That one machine revolutionized grain harvesting. What had consumed long weeks of hard work could be done in a day. The combine increased food production and shifted agriculture toward grains. It transformed farming from a low-intensity family affair into a capital-intensive big business.

History of the Invention

What Did People Do Before?

Harvest had always been a grueling, backbreaking, labor-intensive process. Wheat, rye, oats, and other grains were cut by hand with a scythe. A good man could cut several acres a day. Others raked up the cuttings into rows, where still others gathered them into sheaves (bunches of stalks—three to four feet in diameter—stood on end and tied). The sheaves were beaten by hand to shake off the grains, which then had to be separated from their husks. On a family farm, the entire family would slave from dawn to dusk to get the crop in before rain or snow ruined it.

How Was the Combine Harvester Invented?

In 1820, inventor and farmer Robert McCormick attempted to design and build an automatic, horse-drawn reaper (cutter) on his rolling farm in Virginia's Shenandoah Valley. Frustrated, he abandoned the project in 1829.

Just as his father quit this effort in disgust, Robert's 19-year-old son, Cyrus, became inspired to pick up the project himself. However, Cyrus dreamed of creating a single machine that would combine the tasks of cutting, reaping, and threshing into one automatic process.

Cyrus watched farmers up and down the valley at work in the fields, studying the mechanical, repetitive movements they made for each step in the harvesting process. In his father's barn workshop, Cyrus experimented with how to mechanically replicate each of the motions he had catalogued.

Based on these experiments, Cyrus mounted a paddlewheel above a reciprocating knife with metal blades to cut the grain. He built a wide wooden platform behind these blades to receive and hold the cut stalks. Cyrus mounted a second set of paddles on a rotating drum above this platform. These paddles beat (thresh) the cuttings to knock grain off the stalk. The grain fell through a metal mesh to a storage bin below. Cyrus hoped that this design would leave stalks ready to be baled into straw and the grain ready for bagging.

He quickly discovered that the straw tended to scatter across his wooden platform. He added a pair of mechanical rakes that moved back and forth to push the stalks back under his threshing paddles and to then gather the sheaves of straw for baling.

McCormick faced one final challenge. Each individual part of his reaper-thresher worked, but they also had to work in concert with each of the other parts. Paddles and blades had to rotate together but not interfere with each other. Rakes and paddles had to be timed.

He realized that every action of his combine could be linked to the speed of the wheels. The faster they turned, the faster the reaper moved forward, and the faster the cutting blades would have to turn. Cyrus built gears and pulley supports on the axle between the reaper's two wheels. He mounted drive belts through these links to power his various shafts and rotors.

Cyrus McCormick built his first production model combine on an eight-foot-wide platform and attached harnesses for a pair of horses to pull it. This combine sped through the fields faster than a team of 30 men.

What's Happened Since Then?

McCormick's combine harvesters sold as fast as they could be built. Each new year's model added extra width and new features. By 1870, giant combines pulled by 40 horses cut swaths 35 feet wide and included onboard balers.

Modern self-propelled, air-conditioned, computer-equipped, satellite GPS (Global Positioning System)-guided combines cost $400,000 or more, far more than the total cost of a large, well-equipped farm 80 years ago. And a combine is only one of the many pieces of expensive equipment a modern farm needs.

 Fun Fact: Combine harvester racing has become a popular part of alternative motor sports, along with tractor cross and tractor pulling.

More to Explore

Aldrich, Lisa. *Cyrus McCormick.* Greensboro, NC: Morgan Reynolds Publishing, 2002.

Brunfield, Kirby. *This Was Wheat Farming.* New York: Schiffer Publications, 1996.

Casanellas, Antonia. *Great Discoveries and Inventions That Advanced Industry and Technology.* New York: Gareth Stevens, 2000.

Casson, Herbert. *Cyrus Hall McCormick.* Stockton, CA: Beard Book, Inc., 2001.

Dyson, James. *A History of Great Inventions.* New York: Carroll & Graf Publishers, 2001.

Long, Catherine. *Agricultural Revolution.* Toronto: Thompson Gale, 2004.

McNeil, Ian. *An Encyclopedia of the History of Technology.* New York: Routledge, 1996.

Yenne, Bill. *100 Inventions That Shaped World History.* New York: Bluewood Books, 1993.

Telegraph

Year of Invention: 1838

What Is It? An electrical system for sending and receiving messages along an electrical wire. In Greek, *tele* means "far" and *graph* means "writing."

Who Invented It? Samuel Morse (in Massachusetts)

Why Is *This* Invention One of the 100 Greatest?

In an age when news traveled only as fast as a person could carry it, a telegraph that flashed messages across country at the speed of light was magic. The telegraph connected and united nations and the world in ways never imagined before.

Just two centuries ago, news took months to spread across the world. The telegraph changed all that. Morse's telegraph made possible real-time dialogue between distant countries. The telegraph saved lives and improved human communication a thousandfold.

History of the Invention

What Did People Do Before?

In 1774, Swiss scientist Georges Lesae invented a bulky, 26-wire pull system that could communicate over several miles. In 1832, Russian engineer Baron Paul Shilling created a five-wire electric telegraph capable of transmitting up to eight miles. An operator had to set five dials to send a single letter. The receiving operator sent a signal back confirming that he had received that letter and was ready for the next. The system was dismally slow.

In Munich, Germany, Karl van Steinheil invented an electric telegraph in 1834. His system featured a needle that swung from side to side as the electric current was either turned on or off. An operator was required to watch constantly. One blink could lose a letter.

How Was the Telegraph Invented?

By 1830, the telegraph needed a promoter and an idea man more than it needed a scientist. Samuel Morse seemed an unlikely promoter. His profession was painting. Born in Massachusetts in 1791, he wanted to paint landscapes. But Americans wanted to buy portraits. Morse reluctantly took up portraiture.

In 1832, Morse returned from Europe aboard the *Sully*. During the early days of the 12-day crossing, a group of men gathered on deck for a discussion of electricity, magnetism, and electric transmission. One demonstrated the simple electromagnetic equipment he had purchased in London.

Morse was fascinated—thrilled. He reasoned that, while electricity magically sped down a wire, it could certainly carry information with it as it went. Morse spent the last eight days of the crossing excitedly filling three notebooks with sketches, notes, and ideas.

Morse went to work on his telegraph in 1835. He purchased and assembled the equipment he thought he needed. And it didn't work. For 18 months he couldn't make it work. Failure felt particularly frustrating because the telegraph seemed so simple.

Morse realized he didn't know enough about electricity and electromagnetism to understand why his designs failed. He brought in Joseph Henry (a prominent American scientist and head of the new Smithsonian Institution), Leonard Gale (an established scientist and engineer), and electrical engineer Alfred Vail to assist in his efforts.

The team quickly found a series of problems. Morse's relays to open and close the circuit were too bulky and slow. Alfred Vail spent three months designing and building new ones—elegant, sleek, and quickly responsive to an operator's touch. Henry realized that a single wire couldn't create a complete electrical circuit and showed Morse how to use the ground itself to complete his circuit so that electricity would flow.

Morse's signal now traveled from terminal to terminal, but it didn't have enough power to drive the receiving electromagnets when the wire extended over half a mile in length. Joseph Henry ordered more powerful batteries. Ezra Cornell, a New York City engineer who knew Morse from his portrait-painting days, suggested that Morse should string the telegraph wire on poles, rather than lay it along the ground.

Henry designed a thick rubber coating to insulate the wire from weather and created glass insulators for each pole. He also designed new horseshoe-shaped magnets to boost the magnet's power to pull the spring-loaded receiver pen.

Morse designed a notched board to record incoming dashes and dots. It was slow, awkward, and prone to error. Leonard Gale invented a clock-driven, pen-and-ink paper recorder system that worked much better. Morse's notched-board design was abandoned.

The telegraph now worked wonderfully for about 12 miles. Then the signal weakened too much to accurately direct the pen's movement. Joseph Henry went to work again and designed battery-powered signal booster relays. With relays placed every 10 miles along the line, Morse's telegraph signal could now travel forever, as he had originally dreamed. News could travel a thousand miles as quickly as across the street.

What's Happened Since Then?

In 1843, Congress awarded Morse a $3,000 grant to demonstrate his telegraph. He built a 44-mile line from Baltimore to the basement of the Capitol in Washington, D.C. The Maryland road along which he strung his wire was renamed "Telegraph Road" and is still so called over much of its length.

Congress was impressed with Morse's May 24, 1844, demonstration of this telegraph system and line. They appropriated money to build a national telegraph system. By late 1846, 1,300 miles of telegraph lines stretched across the United States. The system worked perfectly but was outrageously expensive. In 1855, typical fees exceeded $1.00 for 20 words to travel 500 miles. A 500-word story telegraphed from New Orleans to New York could cost $130 (the equivalent of over $10,000 today).

The telegraph also created considerable confusion. People wondered if it was possible to be in two places at once. Some sat underneath the telegraph lines watching to see a letter go by. Many thought that they should be able to travel down the telegraph line with their letters.

In 1875, Elisha Gray in Chicago invented a system that allowed station operators to simultaneously transmit six telegraph messages on a single line. Prices dropped, and telegraph use climbed dramatically.

In 1865, an American company laid the first transatlantic telegraph cable. It worked "sputteringly" for a month, then died. The next year, Cyrus Field laid a 2,500-mile copper cable from Boston to England that worked for 20 years. The *New York Times* called it "One of the great achievements 'beyond the reaches of the soul.' "

Radio and telephone systems have replaced the telegraph. Though the telegraph may be an outcast technology of the past, it will live forever as the first communications system to unite the world.

 Fun Fact: One of the most famous telegraph messages ever sent was sent by the Wright brothers on December 17, 1903, to announce their successful flight. The brothers had to hike over four miles to the Kitty Hawk weather station to reach a telegraph station where they could announce their success.

More to Explore

Asimov, Isaac. *Asimov's Chronology of Science and Discovery.* New York: Harper & Row, 1989.

Hall, Margaret. *Samuel Morse.* Portsmouth, NH: Heinemann, 2004.

Haven, Kendall. *Marvels of Science.* Englewood, CO: Libraries Unlimited, 1994.

Ierley, Merritt. *Wondrous Contrivances.* New York: Clarkson Potter, 2002.

Lomask, Milton. *Invention and Technology Great Lives.* New York: Charles Scribner's Sons, 1994.

McCormick. *The Invention of the Telegraph and Telephone in American History.* Berkeley Heights, NJ: Enslow Publishers, 2004.

McNeil, Ian. *An Encyclopedia of the History of Technology.* New York: Routledge, 1996.

Tucker, Mary. *History Hands On! Telegraph and Telephone.* Carthage, IL: Teaching and Learning Company, 2004.

Yenne, Bill. *100 Inventions That Shaped World History.* New York: Bluewood Books, 1993.

Zannos, Mary. *Samuel Morse.* Bear, DE: Mitchell Lane Publishers, 2004.

Vulcanized Rubber

Year of Invention: 1839

What Is It? The first strong, useful rubber product.

Who Invented It? Charles Goodyear (in Philadelphia)

Why Is *This* Invention One of the 100 Greatest?

Rubber boots, rubber raincoats, rubber tires, rubber bands, elastic, rubber soles on tennis shoes, foam rubber, rubber gaskets that seal our plumbing, rubber tires, rubber seals for refrigerators, rubber insulation on electrical wires—rubber is one of the most important substances in our modern lives. Without rubber, no car, airplane, ship, elevator, or factory would run.

We depend on rubber in every location and activity of our daily lives—home, car, school, work, and play. During World War II, shortages of rubber threw the country into a panic. If the country ran out of rubber, officials feared that the national economy would grind to a halt.

History of the Invention

What Did People Do Before?

Rubber comes from the milky sap of rubber trees that grow most abundantly in the rain forests of South America. Spanish explorers found that Aztec and Mayan communities made extensive use of liquid rubber for waterproofing clothes and buildings and wrote that these native communities also played with rubber balls.

Those explorers brought rubber back to Europe. But rubber had two big problems. It became brittle when cold, tending to crack and break. It also grew sticky, oozy, and could melt when too warm. It had a narrow temperature range over which it behaved as it was supposed to.

Scientists went to work, experimenting to fix the problem, but made virtually no progress. In 1770, English scientist Joseph Priestly discovered that soft rubber would "rub" out pencil marks. He is the one who named it "rubber."

How Was Rubber Invented?

By 1830 American Charles Goodyear, a self-educated man, was one of the small—but growing—group of people fascinated by rubber. Rubber became his obsession. In 1832, he lost his hardware store because he spent too much time dreaming about rubber, reading about rubber, and attending lectures on rubber instead of minding his store. Goodyear could see a vast market for rubber clothes, boots, and hats. All he had to do was overcome rubber's intolerance to heat and cold. Many others had tried. Goodyear was convinced the answer was just past their fingertips and that—with a little more time and effort—he would surly find it.

In 1833, he quit all other work to begin serious rubber experiments. By 1835 he was virtually penniless and had a wife and three children to support. He had to scrounge and beg for both his few experimental supplies and part-time work (and slowly sold the family's jewels, china, and furniture) to keep food on his family's table. He conducted experiments in the kitchen, stinking up the house as he boiled each batch of rubber. All his time he devoted to reading about, and talking with scientists about, rubber.

In September 1837, Goodyear mixed rubber with turpentine to keep the rubber pliable, magnesium to make it strong, and lime to cure—or tan—the rubber as was done with hides to tan them into leather. He boiled the mixture for 20 minutes and let it cool. When he tested it for heat and cold tolerance, it passed, remaining firm and pliable at all temperatures.

Goodyear thought he had found the winning formula and opened a rubber clothes shop, using every cent he could borrow. Within a week, every item he had sold was returned. Even a drop of mild acid (like salad dressing) or a weak base (like dish soap) melted Goodyear's rubber.

Officially, Goodyear swore off rubber. But secretly he continued infrequent experiments when his wife and children were away. He began one such experiment in February 1839, when his wife unexpectedly returned home. Goodyear had added sulfur to his previous formula because a chemist had told him that sulfur might boost rubber's resistance to acids. To avoid being caught experimenting, Goodyear pitched his blob of rubber into the stove's firebox to hide it.

Fifteen minutes later, with his wife back outside, Goodyear retrieved his rubber, sure that it must be charred and ruined. However, it was neither burned nor destroyed. It was solid, pliable, elastic, and soft. That burned rubber passed every test. Sulfur and firing—instead of boiling—were the final keys to success. Goodyear named it vulcanized rubber, after the Roman god of fire.

What's Happened Since Then?

Goodyear was deeply in debt and so could not finance the development or marketing of his vulcanized rubber. He gave samples of his rubber to Thomas Hancock, an English scientist with whom Goodyear had corresponded. Hancock patented the manufacturing process in his own name and made a fortune. Goodyear died a pauper. But his invention created a craze for rubberized clothes. Brazil's annual rubber exports rose from 31 tons in 1827 to 39,000 tons by 1885.

In 1838, the clothes manufacturing company of Rattier and Guibel in Paris produced the first elastic fabric for belts and hose using vulcanized rubber to get the stretch into their fabric. Thomas Hancock invented the elastic (or rubber) band in 1852. In 1887 Jon Boyd

Dunlop created the world's first rubber tires in his English shop. They were springy, quiet, and an instant hit—especially with owners of the new-fangled automobile.

In 1941 the first synthetic rubber (created in a chemistry lab) appeared on the market. After 60 years of development, synthetic rubber sales represent only 8 percent of total rubber sales. Other products have nibbled at rubber's share of the market, but nothing yet invented can step up to take its place.

 Fun Fact: The Goodyear Rubber Company has recently invented a process to "de-vulcanize" rubber products (such as the 800 million scrap tires in this country) and reuse the original rubber for other products. The process's inventor said it is a lot like trying to get the original egg back out of a baked cake.

More to Explore

Editors of Time-Life Books. *Inventive Genius.* Alexandria, VA: Time-Life Books, 2001.

Haven, Kendall. *Marvels of Science.* Englewood, CO: Libraries Unlimited, 1994.

Korman, Richard. *Goodyear's Story.* Cincinnati, OH: Encounter Books, 2001.

Pierce, Bradford. *Trials of an Inventor: Life and Discoveries of Charles Goodyear.* Stockton, CA: University of the Pacific Press, 2003.

Quackenbush, Robert. *Oh, What an Awful Mess!* New York: Simon & Schuster Children's Books. 1991.

Richards, Norman. *Dreamers and Doers: Inventors Who Changed the World.* New York: Simon & Schuster Children's Books, 1998.

Stack, Charles. *A Noble Obsession.* New York: Hyperion, 2003.

Photography

Year of Invention: 1840

> **What Is It?** A camera system that records and fixes a visual image on a light-sensitive surface (film).
>
> **Who Invented It?** William Talbot (in England)

Why Is *This* Invention One of the 100 Greatest?

Only a photograph can capture a moment, freezing it for all time on a piece of paper in all its detail and candid glory. Photographs teach us about our world, our universe, and ourselves as words alone can never do. Photographs have swayed public opinion, driven public outrage, and created public sympathy. Photos have decided guilt or innocence in trials. Photographs have changed history.

Photographs form the core of most families' treasured memories. Photographs are often the first thing people grab when fleeing their homes in a disaster and are often the thing most miss when they are lost.

History of the Invention

What Did People Do Before?

Before photography, there existed no way for ordinary people to capture images and moments of their lives. People scheduled sessions with a painter for portraits. The process often took weeks and was so expensive that only the wealthy had their images preserved.

Only the most significant events were immortalized on canvas. However, even these historic events were not accurately presented in paintings. The painter "interpreted" the event, picturing the scene and the characters to achieve the impact that the artist desired.

How Was Photography Invented?

By the late 1700s many scientists had observed that silver salts (most commonly silver chloride) darkened when exposed to sunlight. In 1818, French amateur scientist and store clerk Joseph Niepce was the first to use this concept to create a photograph. He built, in effect, the first shoebox camera. At one end he punched a tiny hole and placed a metal plate coated with bitumen (an asphalt-like tar) laced with silver chloride against the other end. After a long (eight-hour) exposure time, an image was fixed on the metal plate.

However, Niepce couldn't preserve his images, and they quickly faded. Over the next 20 years, others tried but had similar results.

Two men watched these developments with keen interest. One was French showman, artist, and entrepreneur Louis Daguerre. The other was William Talbot, an English naturalist who was constantly frustrated by the fact that he couldn't draw. Talbot hoped that photography might relieve him of the necessity to draw the leaves, birds, insects, and landscapes he observed.

In 1835, Daguerre consulted with fellow Frenchman Joseph Niepce, and like Niepce, he decided to produce his images on metal plates. For several years, Daguerre experimented with different chemicals and chemical reactions, searching for a way to "fix" a photograph—that is, to keep the image from fading after the exposure was completed.

In late 1838, Daguerre hit upon a method that worked. He coated a copper plate with silver and (in his camera box) wafted iodine vapor over the silver to make it light sensitive. After removing the lens cover and exposing this copper plate to light, he fixed the image by treating it with mercury. The photographs he produced were called Daguerreotypes and were more brown and white than black and white. The biggest problem with Daguerre's system was the toxic—even poisonous—chemicals he had to use. Still, he triumphantly announced his invention at the 1939 Academy of Sciences meeting in Paris.

William Talbot's approach in no way resembled Daguerre's. Talbot drew on paper, so he planned to create his photographs on paper.

Talbot started by making contact prints of leaves (silhouettes) while he experimented with different solutions of light-sensitive silver brushed onto paper backing. By 1837, Talbot had discovered that he could "fix" the image after exposure by treating the photo with other strong salt solutions that rendered the remaining silver no longer sensitive to light.

The lacy images Talbot created were really negatives. Where light struck the paper, the silver turned dark. Where no light struck the paper (those areas corresponding to the dark areas of the scene in front of the camera), the silver didn't darken and the paper remained white.

In 1838, Talbot made the first of his two great discoveries. When he exposed a second sheet of light-sensitive paper that lay in contact with the first sheet (the negative), then the image on that second sheet became a positive image of whatever he had originally photographed. Talbot called his process *calotype*. This system was important because the photographer could make an unlimited number of prints once he had made a single negative.

However, Talbot's film required long (one-hour) exposure times and thus could not be used for events or portraits. Calotypes were only good for still life.

Talbot searched for a way to speed up his film. In 1840 he made his second momentous discovery. He discovered that even a brief exposure produced a "latent" image on his photographic negative paper that could be revealed and brought out through further chemical development in his photographic lab.

His exposure times dropped from over an hour to well under one minute. Talbot now exposed a light-sensitive piece of paper, developed that negative image, fixed it, and then used that negative to expose, develop, and fix as many positive image prints as he wanted. Talbot had invented every step and process of modern photography. Because his chemicals weren't dangerously toxic as Daguerre's were, anyone could now safely become a photographer. Talbot had discovered practical photography.

What's Happened Since Then?

Conceptually, photography didn't change from Talbot's 1840 system until the 1990s with the introduction of digital photography, in which computer codes completely eliminate film.

In 1878, George Eastman of New York invented a dry emulsion process so that photo plates could be prepared well ahead of time and stored dry until used. In 1889 Eastman invented long strips (rolls) of film that could be used in his Kodak camera to take a series of pictures before the film had to be turned in and developed.

The first color photograph was created by Frenchmen Auguste and Louis Lumiere in 1904. In 1947, Edwin Land invented the first "instant" photographic camera and film. Land's film used polarizing filters to block out light during the in-camera development process so that a finished positive emerged.

In that same year, Eastman released the first cheap, mass-produced camera, the Kodak Brownie. Suddenly, every family, even almost every child, could afford a camera and the film to shove into it.

Now digital cameras and computers have become part of photography. Film can be completely bypassed. Film—that part of the process Talbot and Daguerre worked so hard to develop—may soon be an obsolete memory.

 Fun Fact: For over a decade, the Japanese spy camera called the "Petal" was the world's smallest camera, with a diameter of 1.1 inches and a thickness of half-an-inch. Since it has been replaced by more versatile models smaller than a bottle top, the Petal has become a prized collector's item.

More to Explore

Dyson, James. *A History of Great Inventions*. New York: Carroll & Graf Publishers, 2001.

Fraser, Duncan. *Photography*. New York: Franklin Watts, 1997.

Jeffries, Michael, and Gary Lewis. *Inventors and Inventions*. New York: Smithmark, 1997.

McNeil, Ian. *An Encyclopedia of the History of Technology*. New York: Routledge, 1996.

Pflueger, Lynda. *George Eastman*. Berkeley Heights, NJ: Enslow Publishers, 2002.

Steffens, Bradley. *Photography*. San Diego: Lucent Books, 1998.

Yenne, Bill. *100 Inventions That Shaped World History*. New York: Bluewood Books, 1993.

Anesthesia

> **What Is It?** Drugs that block the sense of pain during medical operations.
>
> **Who Invented It?** William Morton (in Boston)

Why Is *This* Invention One of the 100 Greatest?

Anesthesia created safe surgery and made many operations practical and plausible. The trauma suffered by patients during operations was often so dangerous that it kept doctors from attempting many surgical procedures.

Anesthesia eliminated much of the pain, fear, anxiety, and suffering for medical and dental patients during most procedures and gave the medical profession a chance to develop and refine the procedures that would save countless millions of lives.

History of the Invention

What Did People Do Before?

The concept of anesthesia is millennia old. Doctors in ancient Chinese developed acupuncture techniques that blocked the transmission of pain sensations to the brain—effectively numbing parts of the body for surgery. Inca shamans chewed coca leaves and spit the juice (cocaine) into wounds and cuts to numb their patients' pain. European doctors issued gulps of brandy to dull their patients' senses before operating. By the sixteenth century, soldiers wounded in battle often gulped enough brandy while waiting for the "butcher's blade" (doctor's knives and saws) that they passed out and died from alcohol poisoning.

How Was Anesthesia Invented?

Three anesthesia drugs arrived in American and European hospitals within a few years of each other: nitrous oxide, chloroform, and ether. Two of them enjoyed brief popularity. One of them, ether, was commonly used for over a century.

Nitrous oxide (NOX) was the first to be developed and tested. English priest and chemist Joseph Priestly (the man who discovered and named oxygen) was also the first to chemically create NOX, in 1772. He noted its mind-dulling effects and moved on to other experiments.

In 1801, famed English scientist Humphry Davy experimented with Priestly's NOX by inhaling the stuff. Davy said that it made him lightheaded and giddy. He was the one who named it laughing gas. Within a few years, laughing gas was a popular English party craze.

By 1830, it had occurred to a number of English doctors that their patients might survive surgery more easily, and certainly more pleasantly, if they first sucked a few gulps of NOX. Unfortunately, NOX proved to be a troublesome anesthetic. Something about the trauma of surgery tended to amplify the side effects of the drug. Most awoke violently ill and with debilitating headaches, as if with a terrible hangover from a long drinking binge.

Doctors found that the appropriate dose varied too much from patient to patient and that the actual amount of the gas administered was too difficult to control. Far too many suffered organ damage from NOX that was lumped under the term "complications." NOX developed a reputation for causing cardiovascular collapse and death. Its popularity with surgeons was short lived.

Scottish obstetrician Sir Young Simpson was the first to experiment with chloroform. Chloroform came as a highly volatile liquid (one that would quickly evaporate at room temperature). He observed that patients who inhaled a few breaths of the gas (a wad of cotton soaked in chloroform was placed under their noses) quickly became relaxed and calm, and were soon unconscious. Upon waking they had no memory of events while they were out.

The two side effects Simpson noted were a dull headache upon waking and, if the dose was too strong, that nasal tissue could be burned and scarred by the fumes. He used the drug as part of his obstetrics practice, drawing virtually no attention until, in 1838, Queen Victoria asked for Simpson and his chloroform for the birth of her seventh child.

Chloroform became an instant fad with the English upper classes. However, it never gained general support from English doctors. Chloroform's greatest use came during the American Civil War. Southern cotton was often traded in England for medicines—including chloroform—which became a staple of battlefield operating tents for Southern doctors. After the war, chloroform continued to enjoy some popularity—especially in the South—until synthetic drugs were developed in the early twentieth century.

Ether was the third of these three to be developed and tested. It was by far the most successful, and the only one that gained widespread use as a general anesthetic. Georgia physician Crawford Long was the first to use ether during an operation, in 1842. He admitted to having extensive personal experience with "ether frolics" (a close cousin of the English laughing gas parties) and decided it might do for his patients what it did for most party guests at a frolic—leave them compliant and unable to act or feel pain.

Long first used ether that fall when he removed a neck tumor from James Venable, a local judge. The operation went perfectly. The patient was most pleased. But Crawford Long never bothered to publicize his success.

Two years later Boston dentist Horace Wells picked up the notion of using ether to dull operation pain. He scheduled a tooth extraction for one of the amphitheater rooms in Boston's Massachusetts General Hospital. The gallery was packed with doctors there to observe this new attempt at anesthesia.

Wells mistakenly turned off the gas too soon. His patient sat up and screamed. The crowd scoffed and departed, shaking their heads, calling Wells's claims about ether a hoax.

One year later (1845), Boston dentist William Morton decided to give ether another try. Morton scheduled a tooth extraction for the same amphitheater in the same hospital.

Afraid that no one would come to watch if he announced that he planned to use ether, Morton said he was experimenting with a new anesthesia that he called *letheon*. A large and skeptical crowd gathered. Morton's operation went flawlessly. The crowd of doctors was appreciative and interested, but still not convinced when Morton confessed that he had used ether.

Only after Morton's second successful public operation with ether, and only after he had published several articles touting the glories of ether, did doctors across America—and then Europe—turn to ether as their primary anesthetic.

What's Happened Since Then?

All anesthetics up until 1884 were used as general anesthetics. That is, they were used to induce unconsciousness in the patient. In 1884 cocaine was the first drug used as a local anesthetic. In 1904, novocaine was first produced and added to the local anesthetic options. In 1916, the first synthetic local anesthetic, barbital, appeared on the market.

Anesthesiology is now a major medical specialty and an important position in every operating room. While it is probable that new drugs and new types of anesthesia will be developed in the coming decades, the roll and function of this important aspect of medicine will be with us forever.

 Fun Fact: With its October 12, 2004, launch, Space Ship One became the first private spaceship. It was powered on that flight by a mixture of rubber and laughing gas—nitrous oxide, first developed as an anesthetic.

More to Explore

Asimov, Isaac. *Asimov's Chronology of Science and Discovery*. New York: Harper & Row, 1989.

Dyson, James. *A History of Great Inventions*. New York: Carroll & Graf Publishers, 2001.

Fradin, Dennis. *We Have Conquered Pain: The Discovery of Anesthesia*. New York: Simon & Schuster Children's Books, 1996.

Galas, Judith. *Anesthetics: Surgery without Pain*. New York: Thomson Gale, 1995.

Lace, William. *Anesthetics*. New York: Lucent Books, 2004.

Radford, Ruby. *Prelude to Fame: Crawford Long's Discovery of Anaesthesia*. Atlanta, GA: Geron-X, 1990.

Storring, Rob. *Doctor's Life: A Visual History of Doctors and Nurses through the Ages*. New York: Penguin Group, 1998.

Yenne, Bill. *100 Inventions That Shaped World History*. New York: Bluewood Books, 1993.

Antiseptics

Year of Invention: 1847

What Is It? A substance that inhibits the growth and action of microorganisms.

Who Invented It? Ignaz Semmelweiss (in Vienna, Austria)

Why Is *This* Invention One of the 100 Greatest?

Perhaps the single most important of all medical inventions, the seemingly simple idea of using antiseptics—of washing to kill germs and prevent their spread into open wounds during surgery—has saved countless millions of lives. Surgery used to be deadly dangerous— more so from post-operation infection than from the actual surgical procedure. The word *antiseptic* comes from the Greek words meaning "against rotting."

History of the Invention

What Did People Do Before?

Through the eighteenth century, far more soldiers died from post-operative infection than from enemy bullets or swords. Surgeries to remove a bullet, to sew up a gash, or even to remove a limb were simple and safe compared to the probability of infection, fever, and resulting death afterward. Surgeons were viewed as butchers. Surgery was an absolute last resort.

How Was Antiseptic Invented?

Doctor Ignaz Semmelweiss was more embarrassed than surprised, more incensed than curious. In 1847, Semmelweiss was a highly regarded Hungarian obstetrician at the Vienna General Hospital in Vienna, Austria. He was reading a study he had ordered of births in the hospital over the past year. In the wards where Semmelweiss and his trained medical staff examined expectant mothers and delivered their babies, one in five women died of puerperal fever. (*Puerperal* was a Latin word meaning "childbearing." In America it was commonly called *childbed fever*.)

But in the wards where midwives attended the women, only one in 30 died from the dreaded fever. How could untrained midwives be doing the same job that trained medical professionals were doing and saving six times as many women?!

117

Semmelweiss was outraged. Even worse, rumors claimed that somehow doctors themselves infected and killed their own patients. Semmelweiss knew that he had to identify and fix the problem fast or the entire medical system could collapse.

For several weeks he quietly studied hospital operations. Semmelweiss was a Hungarian doctor in charge of the medical staff of a hospital in Austria where anti-Hungarian sentiments ran high. He had to work carefully for fear of losing control of the Austrian doctors under him.

Semmelweiss noted that many of the midwives came and treated only one patient, then left. His doctors, however, treated five or six in succession during their rounds. He also noted that medical students arrived for obstetrics rounds after performing dissections on corpses during their anatomy studies—many still carrying dead tissue and blood on their hands and under their fingernails.

Semmelweiss suspected that these small amounts of dead tissue somehow caused the increased rates of fever and death. Then Semmelweiss attended the autopsy of a doctor friend, a pathologist, who had pricked himself while dissecting a corpse and died of fever a month later. Semmelweiss was struck by the similarity of the lesions on his friend's body to those on the women who died of puerperal fever.

In Semmelweiss's mind this confirmed his suspicions. Students must be carrying some lethal agent from corpses to his obstetrics wards. Semmelweiss ordered them to wash their hands in a dilute bleaching powder before examining women.

Death rates plummeted. Semmelweiss felt both vindicated and elated. However, over the course of the next four months, he noted that death rates did not drop for patients attended by senior doctors—even for his own patients. Perhaps it wasn't specifically corpse tissue, but, more generally, something doctors carried from patient to patient.

Semmelweiss ordered *all* doctors to wash before they entered the wards and in between attending each patient. At first the Austrian doctors refused. They resented the inference that they—skilled doctors—had been causing disease rather than curing it. They were also proud of the "hospital odor" of their hands. It was a badge of honor, a mark of a doctor, and they had no intention of washing it off.

Semmelweiss insisted. He ordered. He threatened. The doctors grudgingly agreed. Death rates dropped. Fewer than one woman in 60 contracted puerperal fever—half of the midwife rate and one-tenth what it had been before. Semmelweiss's invention of hand washing marks the birth of antiseptic surgery.

What's Happened Since Then?

In 1849, Hungary revolted against Austria. The Austrian doctors at the hospital seized the opportunity to throw Semmelweiss out. They stopped washing, and rates of puerperal fever jumped back to previous levels.

In 1865, English doctor Joseph Lister, who had read of Semmelweiss's work and Pasteur's writings on his germ theory, concluded that infections after operations might be the result of germs and that those germs might come from the doctors themselves or from their instruments. Semmelweiss had been right. He just hadn't known why washing was effective. It killed the germs Pasteur had identified.

Lister began the practice of washing hands and all instruments with phenol solutions (a harsh detergent) before each patient. Post-operation death rates dropped at once. By 1880, a range of better, less-irritating cleaning agents had been invented for doctors to use, and modern antiseptic medicine had been born.

 Fun Fact: How long should you wash your hand to kill germs? Wash long enough to sing the "Happy Birthday" song twice.

More to Explore

Asimov, Isaac. *Asimov's Chronology of Science and Discovery.* New York: Harper & Row, 1989.

Bankston, John. *Joseph Lister and the Story of Antiseptics.* New York: Mitchell Lane, 2004.

Dyson, James. *A History of Great Inventions.* New York: Carroll & Graf Publishers, 2001.

Pickstone, John, ed. *Medical Innovations in Historical Perspective.* New York: Palgrave Macmillan, 1993.

Williams, Guy. *The Age of Miracles: Medicine and Surgery in the Nineteenth Century.* Chicago: Academy Chicago Publishers, 1997.

Elevator and Skyscraper

Year of Invention: 1852 (and 1885)

> **What Is It?** Elevator: A mechanical lift to raise people and material vertically through a building. Skyscraper: A building of 10 or more stories.
>
> **Who Invented It?** Elevator: Elisha Otis (in New York). Skyscraper: James Bogardus (in New York)

Why Is *This* Invention One of the 100 Greatest?

Elevators and skyscrapers go hand in hand. The elevator made taller buildings practical. Skyscrapers created a demand for elevators and made modern cities possible. Skyscrapers redefined how planners design urban areas and allowed for the creation of dense urban cores. Skyscrapers changed the way we live and work in cities and made dense urbanization possible. Before, higher floors brought cheaper and cheaper rents because tenants had to walk up stairs. Elevators reversed the priorities. Suddenly top floors and penthouses were all the rage and demanded by every fashionable person.

History of the Invention

What Did People Do Before?

Traditionally, buildings were limited to four or five floors. No one wanted to climb stairs to go any higher. Worse, each extra floors added weight to the building and meant that the lower floor masonry walls had to be thicker, thus shrinking prime first-floor space.

Cities could sprawl, but they couldn't pack into compact hubs around prime urban neighborhoods.

How Were the Elevator and Skyscraper Invented?

Elevator: Elisha Otis was 38 when, in 1849, he moved from his native New Hampshire to New York City to take a job as a mechanic in a New York bed factory that was expanding. His first job was to help move equipment and bed-making supplies into the new four-story warehouse. The owner assigned Otis to oversee the installation of machinery in the new building—especially the equipment that had to be lifted to the upper floors.

The new building had a mechanical lift and platform. But it shook and teetered as it lurched up and down. Otis had to tie down each load and could only pack the center of the platform without risking the loss of valuable equipment as the lift jerked its way to the

120

higher floors. On the second day of moving, one company employee was permanently disabled when the lift slipped and crashed. Two days later, the lift rope broke. The platform crashed three stories to the ground floor, destroying an expensive electric motor.

Otis was devastated by these mishaps and swore to invent a better lift. He identified three flaws that he must overcome. First, existing lifts wobbled and drifted side to side. Second, there was no emergency safety system to stop the lift's fall if its ropes broke. Third, things (and potentially people) fell off the open sides of the lift platform.

The first problem was easy to fix. Otis installed vertical metal poles on both sides of the elevator shaft to hold the lift platform in place as it rose or descended. However, the platform tended to scrape and screech along the metal poles. Otis installed wheels on the lift so that it would roll smoothly up and down against the poles.

The third problem was also easy. Otis built a waist-high metal cage railing along the outer edges of the lift's platform.

Designing a safety braking system became a bigger problem. Otis's breakthrough came when he realized that the ropes holding the lift up were always under tension (pressure) because they held the weight of the platform. The only way that tension could be released was for the lift ropes to break and let go of the platform.

Otis decided that the lift ropes could hold back a set of springs as well as hold up the platform. If the lift ropes broke, then the springs would snap forward and engage an emergency braking system.

First Otis tried rubber-lined metal pads that would clamp around each side pole when engaged. They *slowed* the lift, but wouldn't completely stop it. While touring other factories hoping for new ideas, Otis noticed a ratchet system and realized it could work well on his elevator.

Otis lined the side poles with ratchet teeth. He mounted metal jaws on the bottom of his elevator platform. When the springs were released, these jaws snapped forward to lock with the ratchet teeth and stop the lift's fall.

The Otis elevator had been invented. (He preferred the word *elevator,* which came from the verb *to elevate.*)

Skyscrapers: Taller buildings had always meant thicker outer walls to support the great weight of upper floors. It was impractical and too expensive to build higher than five stories.

The problem galled New York City engineer and architect James Bogardus, who dreamed of designing buildings that would reach "into the sky." One day in early 1848, Bogardus was struck with a revolutionary idea: *don't* have the outer walls carry the building's weight. He envisioned a rigid iron frame hidden inside the building with the walls hung onto it.

Thrilled by the potential of this idea, he built the Cast Iron Building (sometimes called the Flat Iron Building), a five-story factory in New York City—not a skyscraper, but the first building ever built with an iron skeletal frame. After the Chicago fire of 1871, Bogardus got his chance to build a skyscraper when the Home Insurance Company hired him to design its new 10-story office building. He finished building this towering structure, the world's first skyscraper, in 1885. And, of course, he designed two Otis elevators into this building.

What's Happened Since Then?

By the beginning of the twentieth century, cities across the globe were exploding with skyscrapers. Steel quickly replaced iron framing beams and girders, but skyscraper design has changed very little since Bogardus invented the metal framework.

Now virtually every office building and hotel—even many two-story buildings—come equipped with an elevator. Until space age transporters can "beam us up," elevators and skyscrapers are irreplaceable in the modern world.

 Fun Fact: There are now more than 6,500 skyscrapers in the world, 430 in New York City alone.

More to Explore

Brown, Henry. *507 Mechanical Movements*. Mendham, NJ: Astrogal Publishers, 1995.

Dupre, Judity. *Skyscrapers*. New York: Black Dog & Leventhal Publishers, 1998.

Dyson, James. *A History of Great Inventions*. New York: Carroll & Graf Publishers, 2001.

Goodwin, Jason. *Otis: Giving Rise to the Modern City*. Chicago: Ivan R. Dee Publishing, 2001.

Jeffries, Michael, and Gary Lewis. *Inventors and Inventions*. New York: Smithmark, 1997.

Terranova, Antonia. *Skyscraper*. New York: Barnes & Noble Publishing, 2003.

Yenne, Bill. *100 Inventions That Shaped World History*. New York: Bluewood Books, 1993.

Aspirin

Year of Invention: 1853

> **What Is It?** A general pain-relieving, nonaddictive drug.
>
> **Who Invented It?** Carl Gerhardt (in Paris, France)

Why Is *This* Invention One of the 100 Greatest?

Aspirin is the most basic and widely used pain reliever in history. Most people with either a headache or fever take aspirin first and call the doctor second. Hundreds of millions of people depend on aspirin above all other drugs for basic pain relief.

History of the Invention

What Did People Do Before?

By 1000 B.C., people living in countries with either willow or silver birch trees had learned that the ground bark of either tree relieved minor pain. People chewed on the bark or ground it into a pain-relieving tea. It worked, but relief came slowly.

How Was Aspirin Invented?

The tidy office of chemist Charles Gerhardt in Paris was filled with the pungent smells of stacked compounds and chemicals stored in boxes and bottles on the shelves lining the walls. In June 1851, a doctor and acquaintance, Maurice Duphan, entered with a problem. Ordering patients in pain to "chew on tree bark" sounded antiquated. A "modern" doctor needed a modern-sounding and stronger pain reliever to prescribe.

Gerhardt suggested straight salicylic acid (the active ingredient in willow bark).

Duphan scowled. "Awful stuff! Creates brutal mouth and stomach irritation that's worse than the original pain."

Gerhardt realized that there wasn't anything else to prescribe for minor pain. Intrigued, he decided to try to create a "strong, modern pain reliever," even though he had no idea of how to start his quest.

Two days later Gerhardt was jolted awake in the middle of the night by a beautifully simple idea: Start with what already worked, and make it better.

Chemists already knew that the substance in willow bark that actually blocked pain was an acid, salicylic acid. However, pure salicylic acid also created terrible mouth and stomach sores. Gerhardt decided to look for a way to block those side effects rather than to hunt for a new painkiller.

Gerhardt poured through every medical reference manual and technical paper he could find. They offered no help or guidance.

For two years he searched for a way to prevent (buffer) the brutal side effects of salicylic acid. He added and tested over 200 different compounds with the acid. None worked.

He traveled across France seeking fresh opinions and new ideas. He poured through every medical and scientific library in the country. Nothing seemed to block the acid's side effects without also blocking its pain-relieving benefits.

In early 1853, Gerhardt heard of a young English researcher who was experimenting with carbon chain molecules—creating them and adding them to existing compounds. He called the process *acetylation*. Gerhardt tried the process with salicylic acid.

The procedure was slow and delicate. Gerhardt failed the first several times he tried it. When he finally succeeded, he named the carbon chain molecule he had created acetylsalicylic acid (acetylized salicylic acid). This new compound was startlingly effective on headache pain, and Gerhardt's two test patients experienced none of salicylic acid's brutal side effects. Pain relief with no bad side effects.

However, Gerhardt realized that the process of creating acetylsalicylic acid was far too difficult and slow to make commercial production possible. He set acetylsalicylic acid aside and continued his search for a modern miracle painkiller. In 1864 Charles Gerhardt sadly abandoned his search, believing that the practical miracle painkiller he sought would never be discovered.

Exactly 30 years later, in 1894, German chemist Felix Hoffman's father lay in bed dying and in excruciating pain. Felix sought a painkiller to relieve his father's suffering. He stumbled upon a short paper by Charles Gerhardt describing his experiments with acetylsalicylic acid and tried to duplicate Gerhardt's earlier work.

By 1894, new processing techniques existed. The procedure that was nearly impossible for Charles Gerhardt was relatively simple for Felix Hoffman. He easily created a large batch of acetylsalicylic acid and successfully relieved his father's pain. Modern aspirin had finally arrived in the marketplace.

What's Happened Since Then?

The Bayer Chemical Company bought the production rights to acetylsalicylic acid from Felix Hoffman. Gerhardt received no profit from his invention because he never bothered to patent it. Bayer marketing executives created the name *aspirin* for this new wonder drug in 1896.

Even though Gerhardt's invention buffered the worst side effects of acetylsalicylic acid, aspirin has always tended to upset some people's stomachs. That problem opened the door to a flood of alternative (non-aspirin) pain relievers in the 1970s and 1980s. Aspirin's role in pain and fever treatment has been greatly reduced over the past 20 years.

However, aspirin has recently found a new medical niche. Aspirin's ability to reduce blood clotting and to maintain blood supply to the heart and brain has created a new market for aspirin. Many adults now take low doses of aspirin every day as an anticoagulant to reduce both the chances of, and the severity of, heart attacks and strokes. Recent studies also suggest that regular does of aspirin may protect against nerve damage, may help inhibit the AIDS virus from multiplying, and may inhibit bowel and colon cancer.

While its original role as a primary pain reliever has eroded, Charles Gerhardt's aspirin is finding new and valuable life as a medical preventative tool.

 Fun Fact: Doctors are working on an aspirin patch. Soon you'll be able to get pain relief through your skin without having to swallow a pill.

More to Explore

Dyson, James. *A History of Great Inventions*. New York: Carroll & Graf Publishers, 2001.

Haven, Kendall. *Marvels of Science*. Englewood, CO: Libraries Unlimited, 1994.

Jerreries, Diarmud. *Aspirin: The Remarkable Story of a Wonder Drug*. Princeton, NJ: Bloomburg Publishing, 2004.

Mann, Charles. *Aspirin Wars*. New York: McGraw-Hill, 1996.

van Dulken, Steven. *Inventing the 19th Century*. New York: New York University Press, 2001.

Yenne, Bill. *100 Inventions That Shaped World History*. New York: Bluewood Books, 1993.

Steel

Year of Invention: 1856

> **What Is It?** A hard compound made when carbon is mixed with iron.
>
> **Who Invented It?** Henry Bessemer (in Sheffield, England)

Why Is *This* Invention One of the 100 Greatest?

The modern world is built on steel. Steel made modern cities possible. Bridges, sky-scrapers, malls, schools, car and truck frames, and towers are automatically built on frames of steel. Dollar for dollar and pound for pound, there is no better construction material available.

History of the Invention

What Did People Do Before?

Steel was accidentally discovered (but not named *steel*) shortly after the rise of iron (around 200 B.C.). At that time, iron craftsmen occasionally produced what they called super-hard iron (steel). However, they did not understand what turned regular iron into steel, and they were unable to control the process of forging steel.

Steel was viewed as a rare and mysterious hit-or-miss thing. Up through the Middle Ages builders worked with iron or bronze. By the fourteenth century, craftsmen had learned how to "case harden" iron (make its surface harder). A forged iron sword (for example) would be reheated while packed in coal or charcoal. This process hardened the edge. (Actually this process created a thin steel coating over the blade.)

In 1740, Benjamin Huntsman (a Doncaster, England, clockmaker) stumbled onto a process for producing weak steel. He case hardened iron strips and then melted them in a clay crucible. He called it crucible steel. He could only create it in small batches and found that it was only slightly stronger than iron.

How Was Steel Invented?

By the beginning of the nineteenth century, engineers had learned how to make steel. The smelter mixed iron ore with charcoal in a small smelting furnace to produce *cast iron*. But cast iron was brittle because it had way too much carbon in it. Cast iron was then re-heated in a blast furnace to remove the carbon. This produced *wrought iron*. Wrought iron was malleable and decorative, but too soft for construction or armor.

If, however, the smelter then added back just the right amount of carbon, he produced steel. This three-step process was slow, expensive, and iffy at best.

Henry Bessemer was already a famed English inventor when he turned his attention to steel in 1855, having invented an improved lead pencil, new printer's type, bronze powder, embossing velvet, un-forgable government stamps, a method for making plate glass, and machinery for crushing sugar cane.

In 1854 he invented a new type of rifled gun and offered it to the British War Department. However, they turned him down when his iron gun barrels failed too often. Bessemer became obsessed with the need for high-quality (and cheap) steel for his gun barrels.

When Bessemer studied the steel-making process, it occurred to him that much time and effort was wasted by first removing carbon from cast iron and then adding some back. Why not combine the steps and remove just *some* of the carbon in the first place?

In his first attempt to create a more efficient process, Bessemer tried to burn the excess carbon out of his cast iron by continually supplying new oxygen into the molten cast iron mix. He provided new oxygen by adding a steady stream of new iron ore to his furnace. Bessemer found that this process was frightfully difficult to control. Worse, it was slow and therefore cost too much.

Bessemer next wondered if he could supply the needed oxygen with simple blasts of air. Common wisdom said "no." The air would cool the metal too much—a well-known danger of iron making. But Bessemer calculated that—if he *could* make it work—he would produce steel at a fraction of its going price.

Bessemer didn't even bother to heat the air. He simply installed high-pressure fans to blast a stream of air through his molten iron ore and charcoal mix as it cooked, hoping that this air would burn off the impurities and just enough carbon to leave him with perfect steel.

To his surprise, Bessemer found that carbon from the iron ore and oxygen from the air blasts chemically combined and actually *heated* the mix more and reduced his fuel costs. Bessemer experimented throughout the rest of 1855 to learn how to control the process so that he left just the right amount of carbon in his steel.

Next he needed to increase the capacity of his furnace so that he could produce large quantities of steel. By June 1856 he had enlarged his furnace into a monstrous vat shaped like a modern concrete mixer, capable of heating 40 tons of iron ore and charcoal. The vat tilted on its side to load, swung upright to heat, and titled again to pour molten steel into forming troughs. Bessemer designed special air ducts into the furnace vat that forced jets of air through his molten mix. He named his invention the Bessemer blast furnace.

On August 11, 1856, Bessemer made his first public demonstration. It was a failure. The steel was poor quality and brittle. Bessemer didn't know that his process required phosphorous-free iron ore, or that the batch he used for this demonstration had a high phosphorous content. After months of study, Bessemer realized the problem and also that most European iron ore contained phosphorous.

Bessemer moved his blast furnace operation to Sheffield, England, an iron-rich area whose iron was phosphorous free. The steel he produced was magnificent and quickly became the favorite steel of all Europe.

What's Happened Since Then?

In 1880, specialty alloy steels (steel made with trace additives to improve the sharpness of a razor blade, the steel's strength, or its corrosion resistance) began to appear. In 1915, Henry Brearley, working in Sheffield, England, added chromium and molybdenum (two metallic elements) to his steel and produced a strong steel highly resistant to corrosion. He named it *stainless steel.*

While hundreds of improvements have been made over the years in the steel industry, the basic Bessemer process and furnace are still the backbone of the worldwide steel industry. Many new space age metals are now on the market. But none has reduced the demand for steel.

 Fun Fact: The world's largest dental cap is made of surgical steel. This cap is 19 inches long, 5 inches in diameter, weighs 28 pounds, and was surgically fitted onto a tusk of Spike, a resident Asian elephant at the Calgary Zoo in Canada.

More to Explore

Bessemer, Henry. *Sir Henry Bessemer.* London: Institute for Materials, 1993.

Bodsworth, C., ed. *Sir Henry Bessemer: Father of the Steel Industry.* London: Maney Publications, 1998.

Clark, Donald. *Encyclopedia of Great Inventors and Discoveries.* London: Marshall Cavendish Books, 1991.

McNeil, Ian. *An Encyclopedia of the History of Technology.* New York: Routledge, 1996.

Parker, Steve. *How Things Are Made.* New York: Random House, 1996.

Suplee, Curt. *Milestones of Science.* Washington, DC: National Geographic Society, 2000.

Tweedale, Geoffrey. *Steel City.* London: Oxford University Press, 1996.

Pasteurization

Year of Invention: 1858

> **What Is It?** A process of killing bacteria in food by heating.
>
> **Who Invented It?** Louis Pasteur (in Paris, France)

Why Is *This* Invention One of the 100 Greatest?

Wine, beer, milk, yogurt, and other liquid foods naturally have a short shelf life. That is, they sour, curdle, and rot after only a short time.

Then Louis Pasteur invented the process of pasteurization. Pasteurization provided a safe food supply. The dairy, wine, and beer industries grew from small, local operations into giant, international concerns. Pasteurization has been called one of the most famous and useful industrial processes ever invented and has saved millions of lives by preventing the spread of micro-bacterial diseases.

History of the Invention

What Did People Do Before?

Cow's and goat's milk had always been drunk fresh. The consumer had to be near the animal because milk soured and spoiled in a day or two. Wine and beer making were also very uncertain processes, and the products soured into undrinkable waste more often than not. Wine was traditionally made at monasteries by monks. When the process worked, they produced wine. When it failed—as it often did—they produced bitter vinegar.

How Was Pasteurization Invented?

In 1856, 34-year-old Louis Pasteur began his fourth year as the Head of Sciences at the University of Lille in France. He was supposed to be down in his second-floor office preparing university budgets and program plans. But at heart Pasteur was a pure research chemist. He had found a small, abandoned room in the attic and commandeered it for a laboratory. To the university's dismay, he spent more time in that cramped attic nook than in his spacious, carpeted second-floor director's office.

In the fall of that year, Maurice D'Argineau, a local businessman, found Pasteur in his cramped corner lab. D'Argineau's consistent failure to make wine from his fields of sugar beets without it going sour was driving him to financial ruin. Could Pasteur please *do* something to save him?

Pasteur was particularly intrigued by this problem since it hinted at the involvement of one of his pet interests, and he readily agreed to study the matter.

In 1858, everyone "knew" that fermentation was a simple chemical reaction—just like mixing any other chemicals. If you mixed the necessary compounds and ingredients in the right way, you always got the same result. That was chemistry. But D'Argineau swore that he *was* doing the chemistry perfectly. He brought a detailed description of his process to prove it.

The popular theory was that, when molds did appear (as on a piece of meat left on the counter), it was because that mold "spontaneously materialized"—materialized out of nowhere. Pasteur, however, believed that unseen microscopic, living organisms were all around us—on surfaces and in the air—all the time. Molds came from these organisms He also suspected that these microorganisms were somehow involved in D'Argineau's dilemma.

Pasteur examined D'Argineau's failed fermentations under a microscope. He knew that the fermentation process could produce two mirror-image versions of the alcohol molecule, which he called left-handed and right-handed. From previous research, he knew that if fermentation was a simple chemical process, it should produce an equal number of left-handed and right-handed alcohol molecules. However, he found only left-handed alcohol molecules in D'Argineau's fermentation.

Pasteur suspected that this was the mark of a living organism at work instead of a purely chemical process. He studied other samples of fermenting liquids. He also studied samples of D'Argineau's yeast. Yeast was the active ingredient that caused beer and wine to ferment into alcohol, and Pasteur now suspected that yeast was (or contained) living microorganisms and was not just an inert chemical compound. He suspected that the action of some yeast cells must control the souring process.

Under the microscope Pasteur found that some yeast cells were spherical while others were elongated, and he proposed that different types of yeast cells produced different fermentation results or acted at different times during the fermentation process. If allowed to continue their metabolic work unchecked, these organisms caused beer and wine to sour.

The answer seemed simple: as soon as the yeast cells had completed their essential fermentation task, kill them all to stop them from souring the wine. That solution would only work, of course, if Pasteur was right and the yeast contained living microorganisms. However, while killing the culprit to prove his theory, he couldn't ruin the taste of the wine.

Pasteur began the search for simple ways to kill samples of D'Argineau's yeast. He soon found that heat was the surest and best way to do the job. But winemakers were horrified at the thought of cooking their wine. Pasteur experimented to find the minimum amount of heat required to kill the active bacteria in yeast and found that gently heating a fermented liquid to 57 degrees C (144 degrees F) killed all yeast organisms.

Pasteur directed the production of 20 bottles of wine—half heat treated after initial fermentation, half not. He conducted taste tests with these bottles and showed that heating had no effect on taste.

What's Happened Since Then?

In 1859, pasteurization spread from wine to beer and to dairy products. Late that same year, Pasteur completed work on his germ theory and started the field of microbiology by proving that organisms—invisible to human eyes because of their microscopic size—float in the air and are on virtually all surfaces.

Combined with sterilization techniques for containers and processing plants, pasteurization has become the primary process of the food industry. It is simple, easy, inexpensive, and always works. Like hand washing to prevent the spread of disease, pasteurization is here to stay.

 Fun Fact: In addition to being pasteurized, the food NASA astronauts eat has all been irradiated to sterilize it and prevent food borne bacteria from escaping into space.

More to Explore

Clark, Donald. *Encyclopedia of Great Inventors and Discoveries*. London: Marshall Cavendish Books, 1991.

Dyson, James. *A History of Great Inventions*. New York: Carroll & Graf Publishers, 2001.

Fullick, Ann. *Louis Pasteur*. Portsmouth, NH: Heinemann Library, 2000.

Gogerly, Liz. *Louis Pasteur*. New York: Raintree, 2002.

Silverthorne, Elizabeth. *Louis Pasteur*. New York: Thomson Gale, 2004.

Smith, Linda. *Louis Pasteur: Disease Fighter*. Berkeley Heights, NJ: Enslow Publishers, 2001.

Yount, Lisa. *Louis Pasteur*. New York: Thomson Gale, 1995.

Refrigeration

Year of Invention: 1859

What Is It? A machine to keep food at a constant cold temperature to prevent decay and rot.

Who Invented It? Ferdinand Carre (Paris, France)

Why Is *This* Invention One of the 100 Greatest?

Even in early twentieth-century America, practical, working refrigerators did not exist, and the fear of being poisoned by food purchased at the local market was an everyday concern. Essential items like eggs, chicken, fish, milk, and cheese that had been improperly stored killed hundreds every year and made thousands seriously ill.

Refrigeration for the home, store, factory, truck, and cargo ship solved this mounting crisis. Refrigeration inhibited the growth of bacteria, stalled rotting, and enabled people to ship perishable foods. Refrigeration saved countless lives and made it possible for cities to continue to grow.

History of the Invention

What Did People Do Before?

Ice was the only source of cold for many thousands of years. Blocks of ice were cut from ponds in the winter and stacked in underground pits lined with an insulator like straw. Early Greeks built such icehouses. In the 1300s, the Chinese discovered that evaporating salt brine created intense cold. This technology had spread to Italy by 1600 and was used to freeze the first ice skating rink in London.

In 1805 Oliver Evans invented a cooling machine using compressed ether in his Pennsylvania workshop. But it didn't cool enough to do much good.

In 1844, Dr. John Gorrie took advantage of the new electric motor (invented in 1831) and invented an expanding air-cooling machine. But it seemed better suited to cooling the humid air in his Florida home than his food.

Metal, insulated iceboxes for the home were invented in the 1830s, appearing almost simultaneously in Europe and America. A new industry was created to deliver blocks of ice door-to-door from ice wagons. People slid a block of ice into the ice compartment of their home icebox to keep food cold. Still, spoilage in iceboxes was a common and major problem.

132

How Was Refrigeration Invented?

Between 1834 and 1840, Jacob Perkins, a retired American inventor in his seventies and then living in London, began to experiment with the notion of mechanical refrigeration for food. Having invented a bathometer (for measuring water depth), an aquatic speedometer (for measuring boat speed through water), a steel-plate system for printing bank notes, and a new system for making steel nails, among others, Perkins was a well-known inventor by this time.

European scientists conducted countless studies on the nature and behavior of gasses during the first third of the nineteenth century. Oliver Evans had shown that when gasses expanded rapidly they absorbed heat from their surroundings and could even freeze the valves used to control the gas flow. When gasses were compressed, they gave off heat. Different gasses absorbed or emitted heat at different rates.

Perkins reasoned that he should be able to create a closed loop with some gas that would move heat from one place to another. Electric motors (invented in 1831) were available to drive gas compressors. The pieces seemed to be available to construct a working system in his modest London flat.

Perkins envisioned a system in which a compressed gas would expand through some kind of nozzle, absorbing heat from the space he wanted to cool. But the gas wouldn't be released into the air. It would—even as it expanded—still be in closed metal pipes. The gas would then be pumped away from the refrigeration area and compressed again. Compression would release heat—the very heat absorbed in the refrigeration area—into the outside air. The gas could then be pumped back to the refrigerator to begin the cycle again.

Perkins hired local mechanics to build his system because he was too old to do the work himself. In 1840, Perkins's system produced a small chunk of ice (it froze water), but age and ill health caused Perkins to drift away from the project.

In 1857, Frenchman Ferdinand Carre picked up Perkins's work. Carre was able to assemble the components of a closed-system heat engine for a refrigerator in a few months. However, he found that his system didn't work well with most available gasses. Some required too much energy to compress. Others compressed into liquids when he wanted them to stay gasses. Others didn't absorb enough heat when they expanded.

In 1859 he changed the gas in his refrigerator to ammonia and found that it worked wonderfully well. He had created a practical refrigerator.

What's Happened Since Then?

Because the demand at the time was for ice, Carre never considered using his refrigerator to directly cool food. He designed it to produce ice that would be carried to iceboxes that refrigerated food.

In 1873 Karl von Linde (in Munich) invented the first portable refrigerator, hoping to entice buyers to abandon the icebox. Because of its noisy electric generator and motor, van Linde's refrigerator never sold well. In 1877, Carre designed the first refrigerated ship for transoceanic food shipments. In 1913 John Domeler, in Chicago, invented the first in-home refrigerator. Electric utilities existed by this time, and his model was made without an electric generator of its own.

Domeler's design, however, was not a grand success. Like all refrigerators of the time, it couldn't control humidity. Cold circulating air sucked moisture as well as heat from meat, lettuces, and vegetables and spoiled them. Other foods grew damp and rotted when the refrigerator door closed and the rapid cooling of warm, moist air caused condensation that dripped onto the food and ruined it.

In 1913, Mary Engle Pennington solved the humidity problem. By adding an extra motor and fan to control air circulation inside the refrigerator, she was able to control moisture levels. The practical refrigerator was finally born. President Hoover awarded Mary Penington a Notable Service Medal because her refrigerator designs made it possible for America to successfully feed U.S. troops during World War I.

Kelvinator released their first home refrigerator design in 1918. Frigidaire followed in 1919. General Electric was next in 1920, but made its biggest hit with dual temperature control (one setting for the freezer and a different one for the refrigerator), which it premiered in 1939. By the mid-1950s the iceman and his ice wagon were a forgotten footnote of the past. In 2002, U.S. manufacturers sold 13.4 million refrigerators.

 Fun Fact: In 1973, the average refrigerator used over 2,000 kilowatt-hours of electricity. Modern efficient models use less than one-quarter of that energy. If every household in America used one of the new models, we would save enough electricity to eliminate 10 large power plants and all of their pollution.

More to Explore

Dyson, James. *A History of Great Inventions*. New York: Carroll & Graf Publishers, 2001.

Ford, Barbara. *Keeping Things Cool*. New York: Walker & Co., 1996.

McNeil, Ian. *An Encyclopedia of the History of Technology*. New York: Routledge, 1996.

Miller, Rex. *Refrigeration and Air Conditioning Technology*. New York: Glencoe/McGraw-Hill, 1997.

Stwertka, Eve. *How Things Cool*. New York: Silver Burdette Press, 2000.

van Dulken, Stephen. *Inventing the 20th Century*. New York: New York University Press, 2000.

Vare, Ethlie Ann, and Greg Ptacek. *Mothers of Invention*. New York: William Morrow, 1989.

Yenne, Bill. *100 Inventions That Shaped World History*. New York: Bluewood Books, 1993.

Oil Well

Year of Invention: 1859

> **What Is It?** A drilling system to pump buried pools of petroleum to the surface.
>
> **Who Invented It?** Edwin Drake (in Titusville, Pennsylvania)

Why Is *This* Invention One of the 100 Greatest?

Gasoline, jet fuel, kerosene, tar, asphalt, grease and other lubricants, and several synthetic fabrics all come from petroleum. Oil and natural gas power many of our nation's electrical plants. Without a massive petroleum industry, the twentieth century could not have developed as it did. The entire industry depends on oil wells, starting with a single well drilled in 1859.

History of the Invention

What Did People Do Before?

Tars and oil have been known for thousands of years. Natural surface seeps of oil, gas, and tars occur around the world. The famed La Brea tar pits in Los Angeles are a natural surface oil seep. Traditionally, oil was used as it naturally appeared at the surface—mostly for waterproofing, some for lamp oil. The word "petroleum" derives from Latin words meaning *rock oil*. People assumed that oil was somehow squeezed out of rocks.

How Was the Petroleum Industry Invented?

In 1857, 38-year-old Edwin Drake arrived in the impoverished village of Titusville, Pennsylvania, riding on the back of the twice-a-week mail wagon. Drake, born in Greenville, New York, was an ex-railroad construction worker and railway conductor and had invested in a small Pennsylvania firm that gathered oil for medicinal purposes from oil seeps in eastern Pennsylvania.

Drake was impatient with the slow pace at which his company collected and sold medicinal oil. Drake wondered if he couldn't find a way to speed production. He had read of places where miners drilled for saltwater brines trapped beneath the surface, and he wondered if he could similarly drill for oil and have a bigger supply than was being provided by slow surface seeps.

Since his company had only bought the rights to collect surface oil seepage, Drake spent over a year trying to buy first drilling rights, and then entire farms that contained natural oil seeps. During this time he read about saltwater drilling techniques and even spent eight weeks inspecting two such facilities.

By the time Drake purchased two side-by-side farms that shared a promising natural oil seep, he had also designed a drill derrick to mount over the seep. By mid-1858 he had built his tower and shipped in a steam engine to power the drill. He purchased drill bits from suppliers of the salt drilling companies and hired a dozen salt miners to operate his drill.

Through the first four months of operation, Drake faced nothing but problems and setbacks. The drill bits were too soft and broke apart in the dense, rock-laden soil of Pennsylvania. His salt miners didn't know how to work with these soil conditions. The piston and rocker arm in his steam engine broke repeatedly. Work ground to a halt.

Drake fired his entire crew, studied drilling methods more carefully, and redesigned his derrick. Drake also decided that, rather than simply drilling down into the rock, he would build a drilling system that acted more like a steam hammer. Drake's new drill would ram a sharp drill bit and metal shaft into the rock to pound it and smash it into small bits before the drill bit ground down to the next rock layer.

In early 1859, he hired blacksmith William Smith to design and build new drill bits. Smith studied Drake's drilling plans and the local rocks before constructing a large forge on one of Drake's farms.

Drilling began in late July. On Saturday, August 27, 1859, Smith's drill bit smashed through a rock ledge at a depth of 23 meters (75 feet). Then it slipped into a dirt crevice and drilled down another eight inches. The sun was setting by this time and work halted.

On Sunday morning Drake discovered a wide pool of oil covering the ground around his derrick, as if the derrick was rising from the middle of a quiet, black lake. By noon on Monday, every container he could find was filled with oil—tubs, empty whiskey barrels, troughs, and jugs.

Drake erected other drilling derricks to pump a steady flow of black oil. Daily wagon trains hauled barrels of oil down to East Coast cities. Other caravans of empty barrels returned uphill to be filled the next morning.

Heavier oils (tars, kerosene, and thick lubricating oils) were separated onsite, barreled, and shipped. The lighter components of oil (primarily gasoline) were considered dangerous and undesirable. Drake siphoned this light oil off into great metal vats to be burned. Soon a constant black pall of smoke rose over Titusville from these gasoline fires. With steam engines and drill rigs hammering deeper holes 24 hours a day, Titusville was soon more crowded, grimier, and noisier than central New York City.

What's Happened Since Then?

Drake started by selling thick oils as lubricants. However, kerosene (as lamp oil) quickly became his most popular and profitable product. By 1870, heating oil was a third major product, replacing coal and wood fireplaces for home heating. Gasoline did not emerge as a viable product until early in the twentieth century, when automobiles and their internal combustion engines began to sputter down American and European roads.

Robert Chesebrough, a young New Jersey chemist, discovered an unexpected product in the Titusville petroleum fields. He noticed what the miners and drillers called "rod-wax"—a colorless oil residue that caked around the drilling rods. Chesebrough found that miners slathered this waxy substance on burns and cuts and swore that it sped healing. He bought the exclusive rights to market rod wax, named it *Vaseline*, and created a first-aid staple still popular today.

As world oil reserves dwindle, scientists race to find alternatives to oil. But to date no suitable candidates have emerged to replace any of the major uses we daily depend on petroleum products for.

 Fun Fact: More than 150 products are made from oil. The list includes transparent tape, pajamas, crayons, paintbrushes, shampoo, contact lenses, toilet seats, pantyhose, tents, candles, insect repellent, shoe polish, roofing, antihistamines, and heart valves.

More to Explore

Asimov, Isaac. *Asimov's Chronology of Science and Discovery*. New York: Harper & Row, 1989.

Dyson, James. *A History of Great Inventions*. New York: Carroll & Graf Publishers, 2001.

Jeffries, Michael, and Gary Lewis. *Inventors and Inventions*. New York: Smithmark, 1997.

Pees, Samuel, ed. *The History of the Petroleum Industry*. New York: American Association of Petroleum Geologists, 1995.

Sherman, John. *Drake Well Museum and Park*. Mechanicsville, PA: Stackpole Books, 2002.

Stewart, Anne. *John Mather: The Legacy of Pennsylvania's Oil Region Photographer*. Harrisburg, PA: The Colonial Press, 1995.

Weber, David. *Around Titusville, Pennsylvania*. Greensboro, SC: Arcadia Publications, 2004.

Dynamite

Year of Invention: 1866

> **What Is It?** A highly explosive, but stable, form of nitroglycerine.
>
> **Who Invented It?** Alfred Nobel (in Sweden)

Why Is *This* Invention One of the 100 Greatest?

Dynamite is the world's most commonly used explosive. For over a century it was the standard for civil engineering projects—roads, canals, foundations, railroads, or mountain cuts. More powerful than gunpowder, far more stable than nitroglycerine, dynamite made many engineering projects feasible and saved thousands of lives during both manufacturing and use. The success of dynamite also produced a fortune for Alfred Nobel—a fortune that allowed him to create the annual Nobel prizes.

History of the Invention

What Did People Do Before?

Gunpowder first appeared in China around A.D. 1000. In 1261, alchemist Roger Bacon was the first European to discover this explosive mixture.

Gunpowder was fine for firing rockets and muskets. However, it wasn't powerful enough for many rock-blasting and earth-moving projects.

How Was Dynamite Invented?

The story of Alfred Nobel's 1866 invention of dynamite actually starts in Italy in 1846. Ascanio Sobrero was a chemistry professor at the University of Turin. During the fall term that year, Professor Sobrero conducted a series of chemical experiments. During one of these he slowly trickled glycerin into a mixture of sulfuric and nitric acids and created—in his own words—a nightmarish liquid: nitroglycerine.

Even the slightest shock caused the stuff to explode—viciously, savagely. Sobrero was severely injured by the first explosion. The second time he slid liquid glycerin into a vial of the two strong acids, the explosion destroyed much of his equipment.

Sobrero gave up after his few brief tests all ended in failure (and most in explosions). Horrified by his fiendish creation, he destroyed his notes and refused to pursue commercial production of nitroglycerine. But word had already leaked out, and the world quickly learned of the power and terror of nitroglycerine.

Alfred Nobel's father manufactured underwater bombs (sea mines) for the Russian military. He used gunpowder, but by 1860 he wanted to shift to nitroglycerine because of its greater explosive power.

The Nobel family converted their Swedish factory to produce nitroglycerine bombs, each armed with one of the blasting caps Alfred Nobel invented to make nitroglycerine safer to handle. Business was brisk until a factory explosion in 1864 killed five people, including Alfred's younger brother.

Alfred Nobel swore that he would find a way to make nitroglycerine safe to handle and still a powerful explosive. He moved his experiments onto a barge anchored in the middle of a Swedish lake so that no one other than himself would be at risk. Vials of nitroglycerine were packed in cases of soft lakeside sediment, called *kieselguhr,* to cushion the deadly explosives during transport to the barge and onboard storage.

Nobel started a series of cautious and careful experiments, searching for an additive that would create some physical stability for nitroglycerine. One day Nobel noticed that a vial was leaking. A trickle of nitroglycerine oozed across the table. Horrified of the guaranteed explosion if even one drop rolled over the edge and fell to the floor, Nobel grabbed a handful of *kieselguhr* from an open packing case. Without thinking, he rubbed *kieselguhr* across the table to soak up the spilled nitro. He created a smear of pasty goo, but no explosion.

At first Nobel felt thankful to still be alive. Then he felt surprised that his wild fumbling hadn't set off the nitroglycerine in the blinding flash of a deadly explosion. Finally he began to wonder if *kieselguhr* might have had something to do with it. Could it be that a simple dredged sediment could make nitroglycerine more stable?

After a few simple tests, Nobel found that a mix of at least 25 percent *kieselguhr* made nitroglycerine stable and safe to handle. But would it still explode? Nobel attached a blasting cap to a packed wad of his new mix and set it adrift in the lake on a piece of wood. It exploded beautifully. The resulting explosion wasn't quite as powerful as pure nitroglycerine, but it was much more powerful than gunpowder and just as safe.

Nobel named the stuff *dynamite* from *dynamis*, the Greek word for "power."

What's Happened Since Then?

J. Wilbrand in Sweden invented another explosive, TNT (trinitrotoluene), in 1859. But pure TNT wasn't nearly as powerful as nitroglycerine and so didn't catch on outside of Scandinavia.

In 1868, Nobel got the idea to mix nitroglycerine with TNT. The resulting mix was more powerful than either explosive alone and just as stable as Nobel's original dynamite. Nobel's mixture was thereafter commonly called TNT and became the standard for all explosives. Even nuclear and atomic bombs are rated by the number of tons of TNT required to produce an equivalent explosion.

In recent years, plastic explosives (another compound derivative of nitroglycerine) have gained popularity for military uses. However, dynamite and TNT are still the standard for demolition work, mining, and civil engineering projects. One hundred and forty years after Alfred Nobel invented them, no practical alternative has yet been developed.

Fun Fact: The most expensive movie explosion sequence ever filmed took place in the 2001 movie *Pearl Harbor*. The explosion cost $5.5 million; used 12 cameras, 700 sticks of dynamite, and 4,000 gallons of gasoline; blew up six ships; and took over a month to rig.

More to Explore

Binns, Tristan. *Alfred Nobel.* New York: Scholastic Library Publishing, 2004.

Capeci, Anne. *Danger: Dynamite!* Atlanta, GA: Peachtree Publishers, 2003.

Clark, Donald. *Encyclopedia of Great Inventors and Discoveries.* London: Marshall Cavendish Books, 1991.

Dyson, James. *A History of Great Inventions.* New York: Carroll & Graf Publishers, 2001.

Editors of Time-Life Books, eds. *Inventive Genius.* Alexandria, VA: Time-Life Books, 2001.

Gleasner, Diana C. *Dynamite.* New York: Walker & Co, 1998.

Jones, Charlotte. *Accidents May Happen: Fifty Inventions Discovered by Mistake.* New York: Random House Children's Books, 1998

Traub, Carol G. *Philanthropists and Their Legacies.* Minneapolis, MN: Oliver Press, 1997.

Yenne, Bill. *100 Inventions That Shaped World History.* New York: Bluewood Books, 1993.

Typewriter

Year of Invention: 1868

> **What Is It?** A machine operated by a keyboard that causes metal letters to strike a piece of paper through an inked ribbon.
>
> **Who Invented It?** Christopher Sholes (in Milwaukee, Wisconsin)

Why Is *This* Invention One of the 100 Greatest?

Typewriters revolutionized office structure and office procedure, and created a social revolution as well. By 1895, business executives considered the typewriter to be so important that they created a new kind of office position—typist. Most of the people hired for typing jobs were women. For the first time in history, large masses of women marched out of the house alongside their husbands each morning to go out to work. It represented a social revolution. Over 100,000 American women worked as typists by 1898—a position that hadn't existed a few years before.

In June 1892 *Education Magazine* called typewriters, "a necessity of modern civilization." By 1910, typewritten material was the one universally accepted form of business and government communication.

History of the Invention

What Did People Do Before?

Gutenberg's printing press (1454) allowed books, fliers, and documents to be printed. But commerce and social interactions were still written by hand. Italian Pellegrino Turri built the first typewriter-like machine in 1808 so that a blind friend could write legible letters. It was slower than handwriting, but it worked.

In 1829, Detroit engineer William Burt patented a machine he named the typographer. It was bulky and unreliable, and it flopped.

How Was the Typewriter Invented?

Newspaper journalist Christopher Sholes was an avid engineering tinkerer. He wrote for the *Milwaukee News* and dabbled in local politics. Beginning in 1863, Sholes tinkered in Kleinsteuber's Machine Shop with ideas for a machine to automatically number the pages of a book. He made little progress until 1865, when two separate ideas turned him toward the idea of a typewriter.

The first idea popped into his mind as he watched a friend play piano. Sholes realized that the keys of a piano did the same thing he would need the keys of a typing machine to do. The pianist pushed a key with a finger and a spring-loaded hammer struck a string. Change the string to a piece of paper and you had a typewriter. Typewriters ever after functioned generally like pianos.

Sholes found his second idea in a June 1865 *Scientific American* article about Englishman John Pratt's writing machine. (*Scientific American* invented the words *typewriter* and *typewriting* for that article.) Pratt had built a typing machine for the blind, but Sholes thought he could invent a typewriter—modeled after a piano—that would be faster than writing by hand and useful to the general public.

In the machine shop, Sholes welded printer's type for the 26 capital letters, 10 numbers, and 8 basic punctuation marks to thin metal rods. He designed a keyboard in two rows with the keys arranged alphabetically. He attached keys to spring-loaded rods so that the rod would snap up when a finger pushed down on the corresponding key. The letter would strike a piece of carbon paper (invented in 1808) sandwiched with stationery on a flat plate.

Several problems quickly became apparent. First, the bulky metal letters frequently jammed against each other. Second, it was a "blind typewriter." The hammer-like keys struck downward so that they printed on the bottom of the carriage. The typist couldn't see the typing. Third, Sholes's typewriter typed only capital letters.

Jams seemed like the easiest problem to correct. But Milwaukee was a frontier, backwoods town whose crude machine shops couldn't produce finely honed precision parts. Sholes decided to separate letters that were likely to be struck in succession (such as "th") so that they would be less likely to physically hit each other.

Sholes hired local math teacher Amos Densmore to study the frequency of letter use and to identify all frequently struck pairs (th, ly, etc.). Sholes then separated those pairs and also made sure that frequently used letters were evenly spaced around the keyboard so that their rods and typefaces would be less likely to catch on each other and jam.

Because of this study, Sholes changed his keyboard to three rows and created the QWERTY keyboard (the one we still use today—named for the first six letters on the left side of the top row of letters). Typewriter jams dropped almost to zero.

Sholes released his first typewriter in 1866 without fixing the other two problems. The public wasn't interested.

It took Sholes another year to create a rolling front cylinder to act as the carriage that held and moved the paper. Then he consumed eight more months tinkering to develop a workable ink ribbon. His first ribbon was too thick. The letters weren't crisp and the ink smeared. Then he made the ribbon too thin and it tore when the letter hammers struck. He tested over a hundred combinations of ribbon material, kind of ink, and the amount of ink to soak into his ribbon before he settled on a system that delivered crisp, clean lettering on the page.

Sholes's second typewriter met critical acclaim, but sales were as dismal as for his first model.

For his third model, invented in 1868, Sholes invented a shift key and put both capital and lowercase letters on each hammer. With this 1868 model, Sholes finally created a working typewriter.

What's Happened Since Then?

Sholes sold his invention to the Remington company (the famed rifle manufacturers) in 1874. Remington assigned typewriter production to the 30 people in its sewing machine shop. Remington typewriters used a sewing machine stand and base, featured painted flowers (like on Remington sewing machines), and had a sewing-machine foot pedal to activate the carriage return.

Sales were slow.

In 1878, D. L. Scott-Brone opened the world's first typing school at 737 Broadway in New York. In 1881, the YWCA began offering typing instruction for young women wanting professional office work. In 1883, Mark Twain became the first person to submit a book manuscript (for *Life on the Mississippi*) typed on a typewriter.

Thomas Edison invented the first electric typewriter in 1872. It was one of his few commercial flops. Electric typewriters didn't gain popularity until the 1950s. In 1895, the Underwood Company released its first typewriter. Underwoods became the worldwide standard by 1920. The Olivetti company invented the first electronic typewriter with a memory and put it on the market in 1978.

Personal computers replaced typewriters beginning in the mid-1980s. Now it is hard to find a typewriter outside of antique stores. Typewriters, the mainstay of worldwide business and correspondence for a century, are fast on their way to the dustbin of history. But the office revolution they created has not changed.

 Fun Fact: Lee Stewart of Australia spent 16 years typing the numbers 1 to 1,000,000 on 19,990 sheets of paper. Starting in 1982, he made the final keystroke on December 7, 1998.

More to Explore

Adler, Michael. *Antique Typewriters from Creed to Qwerty.* Ft. Lauderdale, FL: Schiffer Publications, 1997.

Dyson, James. *A History of Great Inventions.* New York: Carroll & Graf Publishers, 2001.

Ierley, Merritt. *Wondrous Contrivances.* New York: Clarkson Potter, 2002.

Jeffries, Michael, and Gary Lewis. *Inventors and Inventions.* New York: Smithmark, 1997.

Kittler, A. *Gramophone, Film and Typewriter.* Palo Alto, CA: Stanford University Press, 1999.

Linoff, Victor. *The Typewriter: An Illustrated History.* Mineola, NY: Dover Books, 2000.

Russo, Thomas. *The Mechanical Typewriter.* Ft. Lauderdale, FL: Schiffer Publications, 2002.

Yenne, Bill. *100 Inventions That Shaped World History.* New York: Bluewood Books, 1993.

Barbed Wire

Year of Invention: 1873

What Is It? Long, double strands of wire with periodic sharp metal barbs.

Who Invented It? Joseph Glidden (in DeKalb, Illinois)

Why Is *This* Invention One of the 100 Greatest?

Simple strands of barbed wire strung across the endless miles of open prairie did far more to tame the Wild West than did the famed Western Winchester rifles or Colt six shooters. Barbed wire redefined the landscape of the American West. It opened the West to farmers and settlers, giving them security and ensuring that cattle barons couldn't trample their fields and gardens with massive herds. Barbed wire, far more than guns or lawmen, closed the Western open ranges and ended the great cattle drives.

History of the Invention

What Did People Do Before?

From earliest times, humans have been building barriers to keep some things out and others in. Usually they made those walls and fences out of locally available materials—stone, mud, brick, wood, thorn bushes, etc.

When settlers reached the rolling prairie of the American Midwest, they faced a new problem: how do you fence vast, open stretches of land with no trees and few surface rocks to use? Wire seemed to be the only available answer. But cattle could push over wire fences. Wire marked boundaries well but did little to discourage determined animals.

How Was Barbed Wire Invented?

In 1853, W. H. Meriwether in Minnesota invented "snake wire," a stretched wire with a second looping strand running parallel to it. It didn't work. In 1867, Lucien Smith in Kansas invented the first barbed wire. He hand-wove short metal spikes into wire at regular intervals and named it "artificial thorn hedge." Smith's thorn hedge was hugely popular. But it was handmade, and Smith couldn't produce enough to meet local demand, much less export it across the prairies.

Joseph Glidden was a New Hampshire rancher who moved to DeKalb, Illinois, in 1843 and bought a farm. In the summer of 1872, Glidden, then 60, spent a day at the DeKalb county fair. There he paused at a booth set up by farmer Henry Rose. Rose had hand-twisted metal barbs onto a strand of wire and was showing off his invention to admiring onlookers. Like Lucien Smith's barbed wire, Rose's wire was effective, but slow and expensive to produce.

Glidden believed that he could find a way to easily manufacture miles of this stuff and sell it cheap. If the crowd at Rose's booth was any indication, Glidden's inexpensive barbed wire would be a huge hit.

Glidden decided to start small, testing different ideas around his own farm. His wife encouraged him—even nagged him—to develop his idea by fencing in her vegetable garden. Deer were eating more of the greenery she grew than were the Gliddens.

Glidden worked in the kitchen of his house and searched for a way to quickly and automatically twist wire into barbs. Scrounging about the house, he got the idea to use his hand-cranked coffee grinder to twist his barbs. He placed one pin at the center of the horizontal top surface of his grinder and a second pin a fraction of an inch away so that he could just slide a length of wire between the two pins. When he gave a quick crank to the grinder, the pins caught and twisted the wire into tight loops. He used metal sheers to create lethal points on each barb.

Encouraged by his initial success, Glidden moved his operation to the barn. As he snipped the ends of each twisted barb, he slid it onto a long strand of heavy gauge wire. He used a turning grindstone to twist this barbed strand with another strand of wire so that the barbs couldn't move or shift.

It took Glidden less than two hours to make several hundred feet of heavy, deadly, barbed wire. That afternoon, he fenced in his wife's garden. Amazingly, two strands of barbed wire kept every animal out of Mrs. Glidden's garden. Glidden began to imagine the machinery he would need and the process he would use if he were going to mass-produce barbed wire.

Later that year, Glidden bought a factory building in downtown DeKalb and assembled the machinery to create an automated production line using his design for barbs and wire twisting. Barbed wire rolled out of the plant in long spools, and the West was forever changed.

What's Happened Since Then?

As Glidden's barbed wire was eagerly scooped off store shelves and onto fence posts, reaction came swift and strong. Farmers loved it. Ranchers hated it since livestock were often injured on their first encounter with the barbed wire. Oddly, many civic and religious groups also cried out against barbed wire. Many preachers called barbed wire "the work of the devil."

Glidden decided that Texas was the place to market his barbed wire. If it sold in Texas where there was the greatest dominance of cattle ranching, then it would sell anywhere. Texas was already a hotbed of the range wars between homesteaders and open range cattlemen. Glidden's top Texas salesman won the state with two demonstrations. First he showed cattlemen how effectively barbed wire kept cattle penned *in* when ranchers wanted to keep them in. Ranchers began to buy more barbed wire than farmers. Second, he showed railroads that lines of barbed wire would keep cattle off their tracks (2,000 cattle a year were being killed by trains along tracks of the Missouri, Kansas & Texas Railroad alone).

Sales of Glidden's barbed wire totaled $2,800,000 in 1876 and rose to over $50 million by 1879. By 1890, more than 1,200 types of barbed wire spanned the open ranges of the American West.

Barbed wire had faded on the open range in favor of electric fences by 1920. This was partly because the military bought every inch of barbed wire it could for use during the trench warfare of World War I. Barbed wire and its successors, razor wire and concertina wire, are now used more for security than for range control. Prisons, military bases, etc., string long coils of the stuff.

It is likely that high-tech electronic systems will eventually replace simple barbed wire. But for almost 150 years, Glidden's barbed wire has served superbly in doing what no other kind of fence could do.

 Fun Fact: The largest barbed wire museum in the world is Devil's Rope Museum in McLean, Texas. It features over 3,000 barbed wire specimens.

More to Explore

Cole, David. *Encyclopedia of Modern Everyday Inventions*. Westport, CT: Greenwood, 2003.

Higgins, J. *Dekalb, Illinois*. Columbia, SC: Arcadia Publications, 2004.

Jeffries, Michael, and Gary Lewis. *Inventors and Inventions*. New York: Smithmark, 1997.

Lomask, Milton. *Invention and Technology Great Lives*. New York: Charles Scribner's Sons, 1994.

McGough, Roger. *Dotty Inventions: And Some Real Ones, Too*. New York: American Natural Hygiene Society, 2004.

McSwain, Ross. *Tales from Out Yonder*. New York: Worldware Publications, 2001.

City Sewers

Year of Invention: 1875

> **What Is It?** A system of underground pipes to collect liquid and solid waste and prevent it from contacting a city population or a city's drinking water supply.
>
> **Who Invented It?** Joseph Bazalgette (in London, England)

Why Is *This* Invention One of the 100 Greatest?

At the beginning of the eighteenth century, the whole concept of cities and civilization seemed to teeter on the edge of self-destruction as the overpowering stench and danger of sewage threatened human survival. The smell grew unbearable. Disease ran rampant—especially cholera and other fever-producing diseases. Rats and cockroaches ruled the streets and alleys. Every European city had grown into a smelly, filthy, horrid, disease-ridden death trap. Then sewers—like the cavalry in old Western movies—arrived just in the nick of time, saving both Western civilization and countless millions of lives.

History of the Invention

What Did People Do Before?

Rome built the first sewer—a single underground pipe several miles long. Part of it is still used today. However this sewer served only a small part of the city around the capital. Sewers were not built again until well into the Renaissance.

European cities built public latrines. London Bridge had two ten-seaters that dumped straight into the Thames River and served more than 150 houses. Wealthy families built their own privies (commonly called *jakes*). The middle and lower classes often settled for one per neighborhood. Inside houses, wealthy people strategically positioned chamber pots and night pots so they wouldn't have to trudge out back or down the road in the rain and the dark.

Each morning someone had to empty the contents of all those pots into area cesspools (deep pits for the collection of human waste) or—often—just out into the street. Over the years, contaminants from these putrid mountains of waste leached deep into the ground and contaminated city water wells. Disease struck from two directions: from open piles of waste and from contaminated drinking water.

Two changes set the stage for the development of true city sewers. The first was the development of flush toilets. Sir John Harrington invented the flush toilet in 1597. He built

147

only one. It was for Queen Elizabeth I, his godmother. She installed it in her Richmond castle. No one else was allowed to use it. The problem was that there was nowhere for a flush to go other than outside the wall, to splash into a ditch that ran into a nearby creek.

In 1775, Alexander Cummings (also British) invented an improved "water closet." An overhead tank was filled by hand. A pull chain opened the valve that released a flood of water, which swept through the bowl and down the pipe, which drained straight down from the bowl's center.

Three years later, London locksmith Joseph Bramah created the internal workings still used in modern toilets. His was the standard for over 100 years, until English civil engineer Thomas Crapper created a more compact design in an all-porcelain shell. American soldiers stationed in England during World War I took to calling the device by the stamped manufacturer's name—which is how that particular slang for a toilet found its way into the American vocabulary.

The second change was the gradual development of massive city-wide water supplies, made necessary because city populations grew too dense to be supported by private and neighborhood wells and because centuries of raw sewage had leeched into the groundwater and contaminated many of those wells.

How Were Sewers Invented?

The fall of 1866 was a great relief for Joseph Bazalgette. A cholera epidemic had spread from France across England that summer. But when it reached London, it stopped at East End. Central London was spared because of Bazalgette's sewer and, for the first time in a decade, folks smiled, nodded, and tipped their hats to Joseph Bazalgette.

Born in 1819 to French immigrant parents, Bazalgette schooled and apprenticed as an English civil engineer. In 1853–1854, a cholera epidemic swept through London and killed more than 10,000 people in central London alone. Bazalgette led the group of engineers who claimed that cholera was a waterborne disease and that improved sanitation was the only way to stop it. Most Londoners laughed at such a preposterous idea.

A prolonged heat wave settled over London in the summer of 1858. It was called the "Great Stink." The Thames River was little more than an open sewer by this time, bordered by reeking mud flats and completely devoid of fish or plant life. The heat wave of 1858 cooked the smelly sludge and created such an awful stench that Parliament was driven out of London. They created the London Metropolitan Board of Works, appointed Bazalgette to be its chief engineer, and ordered him to fix the problem.

Bazalgette designed a sweeping underground sewer system to serve all of the sprawling mass that was London. His sewer system featured 83 miles of giant brick-lined sewers and 1,100 miles of smaller street sewers that fed into the giant mains. Bazalgette's workers tore up virtually every street in London. Political cartoons ridiculed Bazalgette as a destructive mole tearing up the city. Many denounced him as being deranged when he diverted part of London's new water supply to continually flush his sewer mains and prevent the buildup of dams of hardened waste.

For the first eight years of construction Bazalgette could offer nothing other than promises to make amends for the disruptions of his work. In late 1865, the Prince of Wales officially opened the first section of Bazalgette's sewers. That summer, a cholera epidemic raced through England but did not touch the parts of Central London now served by sewers.

People cheered Bazalgette, thanked him, and gushed about how London had never smelled this sweet and fresh.

Bazalgette completed his sewer system over the course of the next 10 years. It became the model for every city in the Western world. Bazalgette died in 1891 at the age of 72. That same year, a cholera epidemic started in Hamburg and spread through Germany, France, and England. Not one case was recorded in London. When Bazalgette was made a knight, he was credited with saving more lives than any engineer in all of history.

What's Happened Since Then?

No one has improved on Bazalgette's concept or general sewer design. Bricks have been replaced by concrete. Pumps have been made smaller and more efficient. But our sewers still look like Bazalgette's sewers. The focus of sanitary engineers in the twentieth century has been to improve treatment of collected waste.

Space age innovations in waste treatment (UV bombardment, irradiation, IR treatment, etc.) will certainly change our approach to waste treatment, but not the concept of using sewers to collect the waste. Bazalgette's design is here to stay.

 Fun Fact: You can't have a sewer in space. So what do astronauts do? Solid wastes are compressed, stored on board, and removed after landing. Wastewater is vented into space, but will be scrubbed and recycled in the future.

More to Explore

Cadbury, Deborah. *Dreams of Iron and Steel: Building the London Sewers to the Panama Canal.* New York: HarperCollins, 2004.

Colman, Penny. *Toilets, Bathtubs, Sinks & Sewers.* New York: Simon & Schuster Children's Books, 1998.

Darlington, Ida. *The London Commission of Sewers and Their Records.* London: Phillimore & Co., 1995.

McNeil, Ian. *An Encyclopedia of the History of Technology.* New York: Routledge, 1996.

Smith, Stephen. *Underground London.* New York: Time Warner Books, 2005.

Telephone

Year of Invention: 1876

What Is It? An electrical device that converts sound waves into electrical signals and then back to audible sound waves.

Who Invented It? Alexander Graham Bell (in Boston)

Why Is *This* Invention One of the 100 Greatest?

The telephone was the first communications superhighway and started the idea of personal mass communication. For the first time in history people were able to communicate directly with someone not in their physical presence. If you could reach a phone, you could reach the world! That concept revolutionized human perceptions of space and community. Telephones provide safety, security, connection, and education as well as instant links to family and friends.

History of the Invention

What Did People Do Before?

Humans had always either talked face-to-face or written letters. Then, in 1832, Samuel Morse invented the telegraph. The telegraph changed the world by opening the possibility of instant, distance communication. Letters now took seconds to travel hundreds of miles, not weeks. Still, the telegraph was not a conversation. Morse's dots and dashes were just a rapidly transmitted letter.

How Was the Telephone Invented?

In 1874, 27-year-old Alexander Graham Bell lived in Boston, teaching the deaf to speak. He also struggled to invent two electrical machines: the *harmonic telegraph* (a machine to send many telegraph signals over the same wire) and the *phonautograph* (a machine that drew the shapes of sounds by tracing their vibrations with pens). By late 1874, Bell realized he could combine the two ideas and transmit *voice* electrically over telegraph wires—a telephone.

Early in 1875, Bell teamed with 20-year-old electrical engineer Thomas Watson to develop his telephone. By June 2, the pair (crammed into their small, poorly ventilated third-floor walk-up apartment at 5 Exeter Place, Boston) still couldn't send anything but "clicks" down an electrical line, and Morse had done that 30 years before with his telegraph.

Bell and Watson set up the living room as the transmitting, or sending, room. Here were stacked large batteries and the equipment they hoped would change speech into electrical currents. From the transmitting room wires ran down the hall to a bedroom that had become the "hearing," or "receiving," room. Here sat more bulky rectangular batteries, magnets, and banks of equipment Bell hoped would one day change electrical current back into air pressure waves of normal speech.

Left alone in the transmitting room on that stifling muggy afternoon, Watson half-heartedly toyed with a carbon-filled canister with a thin membrane cover that they had not yet tested. Lazily he wired it into the transmitting circuit. Then he sank back into his chair and began to idly pluck the musical reeds they used as part of a test transmitter for the harmonic telegraph.

Bell burst into the room, his face flushed red. He had heard notes through the receiver—*musical* notes—the notes that Watson had played instead of mere clicks.

The heat was instantly forgotten. Both men turned to the one magic change Watson had made—the new canister.

Bell recognized the canister as one they had filled with activated charcoal. Powdered charcoal! Charcoal was carbon. And compressed carbon could carry a weak electrical signal. When sound waves pushed the membrane inward, the carbon in the canister was squeezed, compressed. The tighter the carbon was compressed, the better electricity was able to flow through it, and the bigger the current would be. When the membrane was pulled outward, the carbon inside expanded and electric flow decreased.

Bell felt confident that they had finally found the missing piece to convert mechanical energy into electrical energy and make his telephone work. On the afternoon of June 2, 1875, it seemed so simple. Bell thought he was only days away from ultimate success.

In reality, nine months later he was still not able to transmit a single word. By early March 1876, the pressure on Bell was immense. Chicago inventor Elisha Gray was nearing completion of his telephone system, and Bell had already been issued a patent for his telephone. If Bell couldn't produce a working telephone soon, it would not only be a disaster, but a fraud—a serious crime.

On March 10, 1876, Bell tested a new acid-based liquid transmitter unit. Watson was down the hall. As Bell tightened the electrical connections to this unit, he spilled acid across his sleeve and arm. Smoke swirled as fabric and skin burned.

Without thinking, Bell pushed the transmit button and called, "Mr. Watson, come here. I want to see you."

Moments later Watson raced down the hall shouting, "I heard you! I heard you!"

The mild acid burn was forgotten. The men spent the rest of the day giddily talking from room to room using the new transmitter unit. Bell's telephone worked!

What's Happened Since Then?

Bell made the grand public debut of his telephone during the Centennial Exposition (celebrating 100 years since the signing of the Declaration of Independence) in Philadelphia. Alexander Bell won the Grand Prize at the fair.

Bell organized the Bell Telephone Company later that year. But the system's growth was initially slow. Phones had to be leased and were expensive: around $50 to $60 a year (equivalent to $1,000 now).

The first public switchboard was built in New Haven, Connecticut, in 1878. It started with only 47 customers. By the late 1890s, thick webs of telephone lines snaked above every major road in virtually every town as the cost of lines and telephones began to drop. Dozens of lines (sometimes hundreds) stretched overhead like the thick rigging of a ship to dim the sun.

The first direct dial service was established (for local calls only) in 1924 in Pittsburgh and in San Francisco. Direct dial reached the nation's capital in 1930. The first telephone call to be transmitted through a communications satellite beamed up and back in 1965. Also in 1965, female inventor Teri Pall invented the first cordless phone.

The Federal Communications Commission approved the concept of cell phones in 1982. But early cell phones were expensive and massively clunky. Jouko Tattari invented the first practical cell phone (small, compact, and affordable) in 1989 while working for the Nokia Corporation in Salo, Finland.

Voice communications (telephones) are now melding with video and text messaging and with computer Internet systems. It is likely that, within a few years, people will stop viewing telephones as separate devices. A general-purpose communicator (under some yet undefined name) will emerge that provides a wide variety of instant communications options. The telephone will retreat to museum cases and the pages of history. But still it was Bell's telephone that created the world of personal distance communication.

 Fun Fact: In 1882, the phone company invented a new word as a standard greeting for their switchboard operators to use each time they connected to a local line: "Hello." Operators were often called "Hello Girls."

More to Explore

Clark, Donald. *Encyclopedia of Great Inventors and Discoveries.* London: Marshall Cavendish Books, 1991.

Dyson, James. *A History of Great Inventions.* New York: Carroll & Graf Publishers, 2001.

Fisher, Leonard. *Alexander Graham Bell.* New York: Atheneum Books for Young Readers, 1999.

Gains, Ann. *Alexander Graham Bell.* Vero Beach, FL: Rourke Books, 2002.

Haven, Kendall. *Alexander Graham Bell: Inventor and Visionary.* New York: Franklin Watts, 2003.

———. *Marvels of Science.* Englewood, CO: Libraries Unlimited, 1994.

Ierley, Merritt. *Wondrous Contrivances.* New York: Clarkson Potter, 2002.

Lomask, Milton. *Invention and Technology Great Lives.* New York: Charles Scribner's Sons, 1994.

McLeod, Elizabeth. *Alexander Graham Bell: An Inventive Life.* Minneapolis, MN: Kids Can Press, 1999.

Schuman, Michael. *Alexander Graham Bell: Inventor and Teacher.* Springfield, NJ: Enslow Books, 1999.

Phonograph

Year of Invention: 1877

What Is It? A device to record, store, and play back (broadcast) a sound, especially a voice or music.

Who Invented It? Thomas Alva Edison (in Menlo Park, New Jersey)

Why Is This Invention One of the 100 Greatest?

The phonograph created the ability to freeze sound (record it) and to enjoy it any time. The idea seemed like magic when Edison first claimed that he could do it. Before the phonograph, the only way to hear a sound was to be there when it was made. It was as if time itself could now be conquered and controlled.

The phonograph launched the music industry and started the home entertainment industry. Voice recordings, records, answer machines, record players, radio stations, tape players, compact discs, and iPods® all trace their roots back to Edison's phonograph.

History of the Invention:

What Did People Do Before?

In 1855, Frenchman Leon Scott de Martinville used a horn and membrane attached to a stylus (metal needle) to draw sound waves on a spinning cylinder. His goal, however, was to use this device to study the nature of sound. He visually recorded sound, but never developed a way to play it back. All he could do was look at the squiggly wave-like lines his device had drawn. However, de Martinville's work was the first human attempt to record a sound.

How Was the Phonograph Invented?

From his invention of the ticker tape machine and telegraph improvements, Edison was rich by the age of 26 (1873) and built an "invention factory" in Menlo Park, New Jersey. Through early 1876, Edison raced against Alexander Graham Bell and Elisha Gray to invent a working telephone. Bell won. Edison was forced to settle for making voice quality improvements on Bell's design and for inventing an improved microphone and speaker.

In early 1877, at age 30, Edison began serious work on inventing a sound recording machine he called the "talking machine." From his work on telephones Edison knew how to convert sound waves into electrical pulses and how to convert those pulses back into the physical motion of a sound wave.

Edison planned to place a device between these two ends that would record and store a voice. He envisioned that his recording devices would rely on a vibrating metal stylus, since he knew he could create a vibrating stylus whose vibrations would match those of an incoming sound wave.

Edison tore apart the bulky earpiece of his telephone receiver. In that device, wires wrapped around a small metal bar. Electric current through those wires created a magnetic field that pulled on small magnets attached to a paper diaphragm that vibrated in and out.

Edison decided that he could replace the speaker diaphragm with a metal stylus needle. The needle would vibrate up and down as the magnetic field increased or decreased. That physical motion would represent the sound (speech) that originally created the electric current at a telephone's mouthpiece.

But how would Edison record and preserve the physical motion of the stylus? He experimented with over a hundred materials before deciding on strips of tin foil. Edison mounted the foil on a metal cylinder attached to a hand crank. As the cylinder turned and slowly advanced, the stylus needle would vibrate up and down, imprinting on the tin the speech pattern and volume.

The process would work in reverse for playback. A spring-loaded needle would be forced to follow the grooves recorded in a strip of tin foil. That physical motion could drive the mouthpiece end of a telephone circuit and convert physical motion into a varying electrical current.

In August 1877, Edison made his first voice recording "Hallo. Hallo," and his second: "Mary had a little lamb." He found that it was impossible to crank his cylinder at a constant speed. The sound warbled. So he added a motor drive.

The "talking machine" worked. The sound was scratchy and less than perfect, but it worked and Edison had invented the phonograph. He later claimed that it was his favorite invention. In 1878, Edison was quoted as saying that it would be "a useful office machine."

What's Happened Since Then?

In 1879, Edison replaced tin foil with brittle wax cylinders. They were easier to handle and produced a more pleasing sound. When the cylinder's motor ran at 90 rpm (revolutions per minute), one cylinder produced four minutes of scratchy voice. At 160 rpm, it produced two minutes of recognizable music.

Emile Berliner, a German born American inventor, was intent on improving Edison's design and stealing the phonograph limelight. He had already clashed with Edison over mouthpiece patent rights for the telephone. In 1887, Berliner invented the gramophone. The gramophone used a flat record made of brittle plastic shellac (cheap to press) and ran at a speed of 78 rpm. Berliner's stylus needle vibrated horizontally in grooves of constant depth.

The gramophone was the first commercial phonograph hit. It was the model record player for the next 80 years and started the mass music industry.

In 1948, Columbia Records introduced vinyl records and "long playing" 33a rpm albums. Tape recorders were first offered in 1952. By the mid-1960s eight-track tapes began to eat into record sales. In 1977, Masaru Ibuka, chairman of the Sony Corporation, announced the invention of the Sony Walkman (whose idea he had stolen from Italian Andreas Pavel in Rome).

Sony also invented the compact disc (1979) using newly invented computer laser technology. By 1982 tapes and CDs had taken over the music market. Digital computer technology entered the music recording market when Steven Jobs (Apple Corp.) invented the iPod® in 2001.

 Fun Fact: The first double-sided record discs (records) hit the market in 1904. By 1920 records had to be played at any of seven different speeds, depending on the manufacturer. In a 1926 meeting, industry representatives agreed to settle on a standard record speed of 78 rpm. That speed was universal until $33\frac{1}{3}$ rpm single-song records appeared in 1948.

More to Explore

Dyson, James. *A History of Great Inventions*. New York: Carroll & Graf Publishers, 2001.

Gathridge, Sue. *Thomas Alva Edison*. New York, Aladdin Books, 1996.

Kimpton, Diana. *Edison's Fantastic Phonograph*. New York: American Natural Hygiene Society, 2004.

Lomask, Milton. *Invention and Technology Great Lives*. New York: Charles Scribner's Sons, 1994.

Murray, Peter. *Perseverance! The Story of Thomas Alva Edison*. Chicago: Child's World, Inc, 1999.

Sullivan, George. *Thomas Edison*. New York: Scholastic, Inc., 2002.

van Dulken, Stephen. *Inventing the 20th Century*. New York: New York University Press, 2000.

Yenne, Bill. *100 Inventions That Shaped World History*. New York: Bluewood Books, 1993.

Internal Combustion Engine

Year of Invention: 1878

> **What Is It?** An engine to burn fossil fuel to create mechanical motion.
>
> **Who Invented It?** Nikolaus Otto (in Germany)

Why Is *This* Invention One of the 100 Greatest?

The steam engine powered the industrial revolution of the eighteenth and nineteenth centuries. The internal combustion engine made possible the industrial and transportation revolution of the twentieth century. Automobiles, trucks, airplanes, engines for factories and for pumping—it seems that internal combustion engines powered every facet of the twentieth century.

The internal combustion engine reshaped the way we live, the way we organize cities and the nation, the way we work, the way we move and transport raw and manufactured goods. It made suburban sprawl possible, spawned freeways and highways, and created the smog that has plagued our cities.

History of the Invention

What Did People Do Before?

James Watt invented the steam engine. But visionary inventors had long dreamed of other means of creating mechanical power. Dutch scientist Christian Huygens in the seventeenth century experimented with piston engines powered by gunpowder. The experiment didn't work. It, literally, blew up in his face. In 1824, French physicist Sadi Carnot described the principles of an internal combustion engine in a paper but did not attempt to build one.

Then the world's first oil well was dug in 1859 in Titusville, Pennsylvania. They called the black goo that gurgled out of the ground "rock oil." The men who drilled those first wells separated two valuable products from rock oil: lubricants and kerosene for lamps. The rest (principally gasoline) they considered useless and dangerous. They burned it as waste.

How Was the Internal Combustion Engine Invented?

Steam engines used pistons and cylinders. Quite naturally, those who sought to find a better engine design still thought of using pistons to turn a crankshaft to produce mechanical work. Many ideas were attempted before one finally worked. In 1859 Belgian inventor Etienne Lenoir decided to convert a steam engine to fire on coal gas and air (an explosive mixture). He took the idea from a coal mine explosion in Germany. If that mixture could blow up a mine, it should certainly be able to explode in a cylinder and drive a piston.

Lenoir removed the boiler and steam fittings, added a pump to pressurize the coal gas, and added valves to open and close the entrance and exit ports to the two cylinders of his engine. Lenoir's engine produced little power. It barely produced enough power to run itself. But it ran—the world's first two-stroke internal combustion engine. A few were installed in England for pumping water.

(The strokes count how many times each piston moves up or down through its cylinder for each time gasoline is injected and exploded in that cylinder. In a two-stroke engine, the piston moves down and then back up—two strokes—each time gasoline is ignited.)

In 1862, Alfonse de Rochas published a paper providing the practical design and theoretical rules for a four-stroke engine, but he never built one. It wasn't until 1876 that someone decided to build an engine using de Rochas's design. That somebody was German grocery salesman Nikolaus Otto. In his spare time Otto had already built a steam engine and a two-stroke internal combustion engine. Now he wanted to build a more efficient four-stroke engine.

In a four-stroke engine, each piston rode up and down within its cylinder twice for each time it fired. During stroke one, the piston slid down, sucking in fuel and air. Next it slid up, compressing this mixture (stroke two). During maximum compression, an electric spark caused this mixture to explode, forcing the piston back down (stroke three) and powering the engine's crankshaft. Finally, in stroke four, the piston slid back up, pushing the exhaust gasses out of the cylinder.

Otto decided to build a four-cylinder engine so that one piston and cylinder would always be in the combustion stroke, providing power to the engine's crankshaft. He drilled separate intake and exhaust ports into each cylinder and installed metal valve covers with powerful springs to cover each port. Finally, he added a timing belt and a timing crankshaft to lift the valve covers and to send an electric spark into each cylinder at the correct time.

Otto decided to use gasoline (then a new product on the market from the growing petroleum industry) instead of coal gas and so added a liquid fuel tank and fuel pump. Otto's engine, completed in 1878, ran exactly as it was supposed to—powerful and efficient. One hundred twenty-five years and 100 million cars later, cars still use the same basic engine design that Otto created in his carriage workshop.

What's Happened Since Then?

Otto sold 35,000 of his engines over the next 10 years—all for factory use and for water pumping. In 1885, Carl Benz designed a more efficient engine and the entire carriage for an automobile, giving birth to the motor car. The basic design of an automobile engine remained unchanged until the 1980s when pollution control, electronic ignition, and computer control were added.

The only real alternative to Otto's design for an internal combustion engine was the diesel engine invented by Rudolf Diesel in 1892. Diesel's engine didn't need spark plugs and an electric spark to start fuel combustion inside each cylinder. However, diesels require a richer fuel than gasoline, require larger (and noisier) cylinders and pistons, and produce far more soot and smoke than do internal combustion engines.

 Fun Fact: The longest reported traffic jam stretched for 109 miles, from Lyon toward Paris, France, on February 16, 1980. The record number of cars caught in a traffic jam is 18 million, as they crawled bumper-to-bumper along the East–West German border on April 12, 1990.

More to Explore

Bird, Anthony. *Gottlieb Daimler: Inventor of the Motor Engine*. San Francisco: Dufour Editions, 1998.

Dyson, James. *A History of Great Inventions*. New York: Carroll & Graf Publishers, 2001.

McNeil, Ian. *An Encyclopedia of the History of Technology*. New York: Routledge, 1996.

Olney, Ross. *Internal Combustion Engines*. New York: HarperCollins Children's Books, 1998.

Roth, Alfred. *Small Gas Engines*. New York: Goodheart-Wilcox Publishers, 1997.

Suplee, Curt. *Milestones of Science*. Washington, DC: National Geographic Society, 2000.

Yenne, Bill. *100 Inventions That Shaped World History*. New York: Bluewood Books, 1993.

Electric Lightbulb

Year of Invention: 1879

> **What Is It?** A device to create light by passing an electric current through a filament that glows when heated.
>
> **Who Invented It?** There are two competing claims: Thomas Edison (in Menlo Park, New Jersey) and Joseph Swan (in London)

Why Is *This* Invention One of the 100 Greatest?

Electric light has illuminated the world—literally. Night pictures from space shuttle flights show spider webs of white dots connecting every populated area. The dots are electric lights. We build our buildings, design our communities, and plan our lives around electric light.

History of the Invention

What Did People Do Before?

For centuries, humans lived by sunlight and fire light. They adjusted the pattern of their lives to the rhythm of the sun.

Gas lamps were invented in the 1830s. But they were smoky, their light wavered, and gas supplies were irregular at best in most of the United States.

English scientist Humphrey Davy first demonstrated in 1801 that a strip of platinum would glow brightly when an electric current passed through it. But the strips burned out in a few seconds.

Many scientists tried to create a practical lightbulb. Three problems stopped them all. First, no one found a filament that would withstand being heated white hot without disintegrating. Second, their glass bulbs tended to crack from the heat stress. Third, no one could create a vacuum inside the bulb to keep the filament from burning up.

How Was the Electric Lightbulb Invented?

Two men, one working in America, the other in England, independently created electric lightbulbs. Their finished lightbulbs were almost identical. They finished their creations in the same month (October 1879). However, they were unaware of each other's work.

Englishman Joseph Swan apprenticed as a druggist and then started a business with a friend as a chemist. In his free time, Swan dabbled with electricity.

In 1856, he took a stab at creating an electric lightbulb and focused on finding a suitable filament. At the end of six-months of research and experimentation, he brushed strips of paper with a dilute (mild) sulfuric acid to create an extremely smooth surface. He coated this "parchmentized" paper with tar and baked it for hours to drive out all oxygen. What remained was a blackened strip of carbon.

Swan asked glassblower Fred Topham to make bulbs to fit his filaments and attached a base with electric wires dangling out the bottom that Swan connected to a battery. The base also housed a rubber gasket. Swan attached a hand pump to this gasket and pumped out the air from inside his bulb.

When he attached the light to a battery, the light glowed bright white—for two seconds—and then burned out. Swan's filament seemed to work, but try as he might, he couldn't create a vacuum to keep it from burning. Disappointed and frustrated, he dropped the project.

Twenty years later (in 1877), the Sprengel air pump was invented. Because this more powerful pump could create a better vacuum, Swan decided to give his electric light another try.

In that same year (1877), Thomas Edison visited a Connecticut arc light factory and became fascinated with electric lights. Edison was already America's greatest inventor, with over 1,000 patents. By 1877 Edison's inventions had brought him fame and wealth. In October 1877, he set aside his other projects and turned all the resources of his Menlo Park, New Jersey, lab and staff to the problem of finding the best filament material and of creating a practical lightbulb.

As was Edison's habit, he dove headlong into this project, working 18 to 20 hours a day on round-the-clock tests and experiments. In October 1878, Edison built a lightbulb with a platinum filament that burned for 40 minutes. Headlines raced across the world that "the wizard of Menlo Park" had created a working lightbulb. Edison borrowed $300,000 to start the Edison Electric Light Company.

Two months later (in January 1879) Swan, still working alone in his spare time, demonstrated his lightbulb to the British scientific societies. Using the improved Sprengel pump, Swan's electric light burned but did not burn up. However, the filament quickly began to smoke. The smoke collected on the inside of the glass and painted it black. Swan's failure confirmed for scientists around the world that a practical electric light would never be possible.

In October 1879 Edison, having tried more than 300 materials in over 1,400 experiments searching for the proper filament, settled on "carbonized cotton." He started with cotton thread, smoothed it with acid, coated it with lampblack (a common carbon-based sealer), and baked it in a furnace. On its first trial run, this filament burned for 40 hours.

That same month, Joseph Swan cured his smoking filament problem and proudly announced his lightbulb to the world. Only a few English papers mentioned Swan's lightbulb. Newspapers around the world hailed Edison as the inventor genius who created the electric light.

What's Happened Since Then?

Early lightbulb sales were slow, for two reasons. First, there were no electric utilities to deliver electricity to individual houses, stores, and offices. Buyers of lightbulbs also had to buy either a noisy electric generator or a supply of batteries. Second, people were afraid of this new technology. Each Edison lightbulb came with the following warning.

"Do not attempt to light with a match. Simply turn the key. . . . The use of electricity is in no way harmful to health, nor does it affect the soundness of your sleep."

In 1907, Edison discovered that tungsten filaments lasted longer than carbonized cotton. By this time, electric utilities had spread electric lines across the country, and offices, stores, and houses were being wired for electric light as fast as possible.

In 1913, Edison discovered that, if he filled his light bulbs with nitrogen, the filament wouldn't burn up, and he wouldn't have to create a vacuum inside each bulb. Nitrogen-filled tungsten light bulbs are still the standard bulbs we buy and use 90 years later.

In 1927, Edmund Germer invented the fluorescent light. In 1936, two General Electric scientists, George Inman and Richard Thayer, patented the form of fluorescent light that is still common in stores, schools, malls, and offices today.

Research continues, and new lightbulb substitutes dribble onto the market every few years. Watch for some new invention during this new century to bury the lightbulb in the annals of history. It's 130-year run as the light of the world may soon dim.

 Fun Fact: Scientists at the Sandia Laboratory in New Mexico have created a new lightbulb filament to replace the tungsten filaments we have used for 90 years. The new "matrix" filament will use less energy and produce far less heat than current bulbs while increasing the bulb's efficiency from 5 percent (current) to over 60 percent.

More to Explore

Clark, Donald. *Encyclopedia of Great Inventors and Discoveries*. London: Marshall Cavendish Books, 1991.

Dyson, James. *A History of Great Inventions*. New York: Carroll & Graf Publishers, 2001.

Gomer, Rebecca. *Thomas Edison*. New York: ABDO Publishing, 2003.

Haven, Kendall. *Marvels of Science*. Englewood, CO: Libraries Unlimited, 1994.

Jeffries, Michael and Gary Lewis. *Inventors and Inventions*. New York: Smithmark, 1997.

Raatma, Lucia. *Thomas Edison*. Deerfield Beach, FL: Compass Point Books, 2004.

Sprouk, Anna. *Thomas Alva Edison*. New York: Thomas Gale, 2000.

Yenne, Bill. *100 Inventions That Shaped World History*. New York: Bluewood Books, 1993.

Measuring Cup, Tablespoon, and Teaspoon

Year of Invention: 1879

What Is It? Standardized measuring devices to make cooking recipes precise and repeatable.

Who Invented It? Fannie Farmer (in Boston)

Why Is *This* Invention One of the 100 Greatest?

All modern cooking, as well as our understanding of food's nutritional content, is based on precise, standardized scientific measurements using cups, tablespoons, and teaspoons—measures that Fannie Farmer created.

Fannie Farmer created the first precise cooking recipes, brought the scientific revolution into the home, and changed housework into "home science" and "home economics." She revolutionized the mindset of American family cooking.

History of the Invention

What Did People Do Before?

There were no measurements available for cooking. Cooks improvised as best they could. They measured flour in "fists." Sticky ingredients (like butter) were measured in lumps—sometimes with a modifier such as "a lump the size of an egg," or "a lump the size of a walnut." Many recipes listed the quantity of ingredients as "some," "a bit," "a pinch," or "a little."

Most recipes directed the cook to " bake until done," or simply "cook until done." No one had thought to put a thermometer inside a stove. The temperature of wood-fired stoves tended to vary from minute to minute.

How Were Recipe Measures Invented?

Fannie Farmer contracted polio at age 16. It left her with a limp. By the standards of the day she wasn't eligible for college, and the limp that meant she wasn't attractive enough for marriage. She had to work to support herself and, in early 1879 at the age of 22, she took a job as a "mother's helper" in Boston. Cooking for the Shaw family was her primary job.

However, Fannie was not a gifted cook, and Mrs. Shaw was displeased with her dishes. Fannie blamed the "fists," "lumps," and "bits" in her recipes. Her mother reassured her that recipes had always been written that way and that Fannie would get better with time and practice. But this was the era of the industrial and scientific revolution. Fanny hated the idea of quietly accepting such nonscientific instructions.

One Saturday, Fannie Farmer attended a lecture by famed female intellectual Catherine Beecher, who talked about the need to "professionalize work in the home" and to "make it scientific" just as men had professionalized work in the factory and made it scientific. Fannie felt that Beecher spoke directly to her.

Farmer spent two afternoons in the Boston library learning about the physical units scientists used to measure solids and liquids (ounces, pounds, pints, etc.) and the techniques they used for making measurements (balance scales, standardized weights and volumes). Then she spent one afternoon in a chemist's shop purchasing beakers, weights, a balance scale, and one-ounce liquid containers.

Over the next months she carefully changed each of her recipe cards into scientific measurements. She dropped a fist of flour into each of eight bowls and then used a one-ounce beaker to measure how much flour was in each bowl. Amazed at how much variation there was from fistful to fistful, she averaged them to decide how many ounces of flour should be in one fistful.

She prepared a dozen "lumps" of butter and carefully stuffed each into one-ounce vials to decide how many ounces were in one lump. Along the way she discovered that many of the common scientific units were awkward for recipe measurements.

Measuring sugar or flour by volume one ounce at a time was too slow, yet a pint was too big. She decided to create a new measure between an ounce and a pint. She searched through the Shaw's rows of different-sized cups until she found one that held exactly eight ounces of liquid and wrote on a card: eight ounces equals one cup. She set that cup aside as her new standard measure.

Farmer found that a pinch of salt was too small to be accurately measured in ounces. She lined up the Shaw's spoons, from largest serving spoon to tiniest teaspoon, on the counter and found that a pinch of salt just filled one of the teaspoons and that six of these teaspoons just filled the one ounce beaker. She called this new measure a teaspoon. By the fall of 1879, Fannie Farmer had not only created three new standard measurements (cup, teaspoon, and tablespoon), she had also converted several hundred recipes into precise scientific lists of ingredients.

Fannie next tackled oven baking. Some gas stoves existed in 1879, but most people still cooked on wood-fired. No one had actually measured the temperature of a cooking oven. The cook opened the door, felt the heat, and either added wood or raked the wood embers to adjust the temperature up or down.

Fannie began a series of experiments. She measured oven temperature while she cooked and recorded the temperature and cooking time that produced the best results for each of her dishes.

She added these cooking times and temperatures to her recipes and invented the world's first scientifically measured cooking instructions.

What's Happened Since Then?

Fannie's standard measuring spoons and cups began to appear in Boston markets in 1894 in response to a series of magazine articles and recipes Fannie had published. Cups, teaspoons, tablespoons, and home oven thermometers appeared nationwide after release of the *Fannie Farmer Cookbook* in 1896.

Remarkably, no one has altered or improved upon any of Fannie Farmer's units of measure in over 125 years. They are still the basis for all of our cooking and for our calculation of serving sizes and nutritional content.

 Fun Fact: The publisher Little, Brown thought Fanny's cookbook would lose money and so required her to pay for the first printing with her own money. Before her death in 1914, they had sold 360,000 copies of the book. By the year 2000, over 6.8 million copies had been sold in 10 languages, making it the most purchased cookbook in the world.

More to Explore

Ashby, Ruth. *Herstory.* New York: Penguine Books, 1995.

Buehner, Carolyn. *Fanny's Dream.* New York: Dial Books, 1996.

Cunningham, Marian, ed. *The Fannie Farmer Cookbook,* 14th ed. New York: Knopf, 1999.

Haven, Kendall. *Amazing American Women.* Englewood, CO: Libraries Unlimited, 1996.

Hopkinson, Deborah. *Fannie in the Kitchen.* New York: Simon & Schuster Children's Books, 2004.

Jeffries, Michael, and Gary Lewis. *Inventors and Inventions.* New York: Smithmark, 1997.

Ptacek, Greg, and Ethlie Ann Vare. *Women Inventors and Their Discoveries.* 2d ed. Minneapolis, MN: The Oliver Press, 1998.

Vare, Ethlie Ann, and Greg Ptacek. *Mothers of Invention.* New York: William Morrow, 1989.

Bicycle

Year of Invention: 1885

> **What Is It?** A two-wheeled personal transportation system powered by the rider by means of foot pedals and gears.
>
> **Who Invented It?** John Starley (in Coventry, England)

Why Is *This* Invention One of the 100 Greatest?

Bicycles were the first transportation system that provided personal mobility and speed for common folk. Bikes were cheaper than a horse and almost as fast as a train (in the late 1800s). Certainly bicycles were much faster and more convenient than walking. In many parts of the world, bicycles are still the primary mode of urban transportation.

Bicycles were also instruments of sweeping social change. Bikes promoted emancipation of middle- and upper-class women. Women riders had to abandon the corsets, hooped underskirts, and voluminous top skirts previously mandated as the only acceptable fashion.

Finally, bicycles led the way for many aspects of automobile design. Bicycle makers of the 1880s and 1890s became the early automakers at the turn of the century: Peugeot in France, and Humber, Morris, and Rover in Britain. What they learned building bicycles, they applied to early cars.

History of the Invention

What Did People Do Before?

Ordinary people had always walked. Walking was the only available way to get anywhere. Most people experienced all travel at walking speeds—generally two to three mph. The rich rode horses (or horse-pulled carriages) and could cover the countryside at a sustained speed of around 8 mph. Trains (through the mid-1800s) averaged 18 to 20 mph.

How Was the Bicycle Invented?

The bicycle was not created in one brilliant invention. Rather it arrived piecemeal, one idea at a time, until, in 1885, John Starley added the final ideas and created a functioning bicycle.

The first step occurred in 1817 when German inventor Baron von Drais introduced his two-wheeled creation in Paris. The baron's bicycle did not catch on in France, but it became popular as a plaything in England during the 1820s and 1830s, where it was commonly called the *hobbyhorse*. A hobbyhorse had two wheels of equal size and steering handlebars attached to the front wheel. However, there were no pedals. Riders simply sat astride the bike and pushed along the ground with their feet. It was faster and more fun than walking, but it was not a functioning bicycle.

In 1842, Scottish blacksmith Kirkpatrik MacMillan created the first foot-powered bicycle. A rider's feet pumped up and down on stationary pedals like a sewing machine's treadles. These were connected by a complicated set of rods, pins, and gears to the back wheel. Those rods and pins tended to break far too often, and MacMillan's bike never gained popularity.

In 1861 Frenchman Pierre Michaux invented the *velocipede*, the first bicycle to gain international popularity. Known in England as "the boneshaker," the velocipede was the first bike with pedals directly attached to a wheel—the front wheel. That front wheel was built much larger than the back wheel.

People didn't understand how to ride a bicycle with both feet off the ground. Most people crashed and fell regularly. Bicycle rinks sprouted across France and England at which people took lessons. Because of its low top speed (around 8 mph) and its awkward turning mechanism, the velocipede's popularity quickly faded.

In 1870, James Starley (uncle of John) decided that the velocipede could be improved if its front wheel was made even *bigger* to give the bike more power. Working in Coventry, England, James invented the famed Ordinary. This is the bike depicted in many pictures with the monstrous, six-foot-high front wheel and tiny back wheel. The Ordinary featured two important firsts: wire spokes (previous bikes had used wooden spokes) and shock absorbers on the front wheel. Ordinaries were commonly clocked at over 20 mph, and racers topped 30 mph to outrun trains and horses.

However, getting up onto an Ordinary was as tricky as mounting a modern unicycle. Dismounting was worse, often resulting in serious injury and embarrassing and comically unglamorous tumbles onto the road. Soon only daredevils road Ordinaries.

Europeans demanded a "safety first" bicycle. In 1885, John Starley, nephew of the Ordinary's inventor, hit upon the four keys to a successful bicycle. First, he returned to two wheels of the same size, both covered in solid rubber tires. Second, he created the still-used diamond-shaped, four-sided frame for his bike.

Third, Starley moved power to the rear wheel so that the front wheel could be dedicated to steering without having a biker's feet have to awkwardly turn with the wheel as it rotated. Fourth, in order to drive the rear wheel, Starley invented the bicycle chain to link the pedals with the back wheel.

What's Happened Since Then?

Scottish veterinarian John Dunlop invented inflatable bicycle tires in 1888. They had become standard issue equipment on all bikes by 1900. Multiple gears were first added to bikes in 1908. Brake pads to provide faster and more stable breaking were invented in the 1920s.

Since then there have been many advances in materials and bicycle streamlining. However, the basic bicycle has not changed since John Starley first introduced it.

Fun Fact: There are over a billion bicycles in the world, over twice as many as there are cars. Almost 400 million bikes are in China alone.

More to Explore

Beyer, Mark. *Bicycles of the Past*. New York: Rosen Publishing Group, 2003.

Dyson, James. *A History of Great Inventions*. New York: Carroll & Graf Publishers, 2001.

Gibbons, Gail. *Bicycle Book*. New York: Holiday House, 1999.

Hills, Larry. *Bicycle*. Mankato, MN: Capstone Press, 2004.

Ierley, Merritt. *Wondrous Contrivances*. New York: Clarkson Potter, 2002.

McNeil, Ian. *An Encyclopedia of the History of Technology*. New York: Routledge, 1996.

Murphy, Jim. *Two Hundred Years of Bicycles*. New York: HarperCollins Children's Books, 1994.

Pinchuk, Amy. *The Best Book of Bikes*. Burlington, VT: Maple Tree Press, 2003.

Automobile

Year of Invention: 1887

What Is It? A self-propelled vehicle using an internal combustion engine for power.

Who Invented It? Karl Benz (in Manheim, Germany)

Why Is *This* Invention One of the 100 Greatest?

Our modern world is built around the automobile. Our roads were constructed for cars and trucks. We drive cars for pleasure. We drive for work. We drive for vacations. We drive to shop. Suburbs exist because we have cars to get us where we want to go. Interstates were created to accommodate cars. The automobile industry has been one of America's greatest and most powerful industries throughout the twentieth century.

History of the Invention

What Did People Do Before?

Goods were traditionally moved by wagon, by animal (horse, camel, ox, etc.), or by foot. In the late 1700s, steam power arrived. Trains followed shortly thereafter. Bicycles wobbled into existence in 1885. Until the creation of cars, that was all there was for land transportation.

That is not to say that no one had thought of the idea of self-propelled vehicles. Leonardo da Vinci sketched a self-propelled car in the early sixteenth century. Frenchman Nicholas Cugnot built the first steam-powered wagon in 1770. On its second day of use, he crashed the car into a wall of the Paris Arsenal, the first recorded automobile accident.

How Was the Automobile Invented?

Karl Benz was born in 1844, the son of a railroad worker who died when Karl was two. Karl studied engineering but dropped it at the age of 20 to work as a locksmith. As a hobby, he designed "horseless carriages" in his spare time.

In 1875, he began to build an engine for his automobile based on the work of Belgian inventor Etienne Lenoir. Benz discovered that his engine would produce more power if the liquid fuel had time to vaporize and mix with air before it ignited.

Benz made his first great automotive invention in 1876. He invented the carburetor, a separate chamber where liquid fuel mixed with air and vaporized before it was forced into the engine's cylinder.

In 1877, Benz switched to an electric spark to ignite the fuel in each cylinder. It took him four months of experiments to invent spark plugs. Within another three months, he had invented the distributor cap, a rotor with wire brushes to send the spark to each cylinder at the correct time.

He installed batteries but found that he needed to develop a bigger, faster charge than batteries alone would provide in order to start the engine. For four months, Benz hooked his wife's sewing machine to the engine and she pedaled the sewing machine foot pedals to build up a charge when Karl wanted to start his engine. By that time, his wife wanted her sewing machine back. Benz invented an *accumulator*—what we call a capacitor—to store a big enough electric charge to start the engine. The Benz engine worked so well that he opened a factory in 1879 to build engines to run machinery in other factories.

In 1885, Benz decided it was time to use one of his engines to build his first automobile— a three-wheeled beauty with a single bench for two riders. Handlebars connected to the lone front wheel for steering. The rear-mounted engine connected to the two rear wheels by a chain (like a bicycle chain). The wheels looked like bicycle wheels.

Benz was dissatisfied. This auto was too small to carry more than two people. In 1886, he shifted to four wheels and moved the engine to the front so that cargo could be loaded in back.

Over the next year, Benz made four major improvements to this model. He developed a rack and pinion steering system to smooth turning. He invented a *differential* for the rear axle so that the rear wheels would no longer skid and bounce around each turn. He invented a gearbox so that the car had three forward speeds. Finally, he built a jacket of cooling water for the engine. To keep the water from boiling, Benz invented a radiator and water pump to circulate the water and continuously cool his car's engine.

Benz proudly debuted this car at the Paris Exposition. He drove it along Parisian boulevards at its top speed of 10 mph, waving to astounded crowds of pedestrians and frightening the city horses.

What's Happened Since Then?

Orders for motor cars did not flow into Benz's factory as he expected following his Paris demonstration. It took Benz's wife, Bertha, to make sales take off. In 1888, she and their two teenage sons drove the latest Benz model from Mannheim to Pforzheim and back—a round trip of over 120 miles! No automobile had driven for more than two or three miles around town. This long-distance, cross-country drive electrified Europeans. Orders for that model (the first to be called a Benz) began to flow in.

In 1901, Ransome Olds built the first American car, the Oldsmobile, in Detroit. Detroit became the heart of automobile manufacturing. In 1913, Henry Ford invented the assembly line for his Detroit auto factory that built his famous Model T cars. Every automobile builder used a gasoline-powered internal combustion engine except one. The Stanley Steamer—a steam-powered car built by Harold Stanley—enjoyed a brief life from 1907 to 1912.

Garrett Morgan invented the traffic light in 1922 (one of eight major inventions for Morgan). Frederick Jones invented car air conditioning in Minneapolis in 1938. In 1938,

General Motors developed the first automatic transmission ("Hydra-Matic Drive") for the Oldsmobile.

In 1951 (only 50 years after the first American automobile plant was opened) Elma Wischmeir became the millionth American to die in a highway crash. By 1965, all major cities in the Western world were choked by car-produced smog. By 1970, traffic reports and traffic congestion occupied major shares of both radio and television news coverage. By 2000, over 500 million cars were on the world's roads. In that one year (2000), the world's carmakers employed nearly four million people to produce and sell 35,801,618 cars.

Eventually cars will have to change to alternative fuels (hybrid engines, ethanol, and electricity). The world's supply of oil is limited. However, no system or plan now exists to replace the car itself.

 Fun Fact: May Anderson invented the windshield wiper in Alabama in 1902 to make trolley cars safer. They were adapted for cars three years later.

More to Explore

Bankston, John. *Karl Benz and the Single Cylinder Engine*. New York: Mitchell Lane Publishers, 2004.

Barker, Theo. *Rise and Rise of Road Transport, 1700–1900*. New York: Cambridge University Press, 1996.

Conley, Robyn. *The Automobile*. New York: Franklin Watts, 2005.

Haven, Kendall. *Marvels of Science*. Englewood, CO: Libraries Unlimited, 1994.

Ierley, Merritt. *Wondrous Contrivances*. New York: Clarkson Potter, 2002.

Italia, Robert. *Great Auto Makers and Their Cars*. Minneapolis, MN: Oliver Press, 1994.

Lomask, Milton. *Invention and Technology Great Lives*. New York: Charles Scribner's Sons, 1994.

McNeil, Ian. *An Encyclopedia of the History of Technology*. New York: Routledge, 1996.

Rose, Sharon. *How Things Are Made: From Automobiles to Zippers*. New York: DK Publishing, 2003.

Sinclair, Julie. *Automobile*. Mankato, MN: Capstone Press, 2003.

Williams, Brian. *Karl Benz*. New York: Franklin Watts, 1994.

Electric Alternating Current (AC)

Year of Invention: 1888

What Is It? A system for transmitting electricity in which the electric current regularly reverses direction, shifting back and forth 60 times a second.

Who Invented It? Nikola Tesla (in New York City)

Why Is *This* Invention One of the 100 Greatest?

Electric alternating current (AC) made long-distance electrical transmission possible. Electricity is often transmitted for hundreds of miles over long-distance power lines. Without AC, that could never happen.

AC made electric utilities and a national electric grid possible. The greater efficiency of AC electrical transmission allowed the twentieth century explosion of electric motors, electric appliances, and electric lighting to happen.

History of the Invention

What Did People Do Before?

In 1800, Volta invented the electric battery. Michael Faraday invented the electric motor in 1831. Because batteries provided direct current (DC), and because that was all that was available, Faraday created motors that used DC. In America, Thomas Edison developed new DC motors and batteries.

How Was Alternating Current Invented?

Nikola Tesla was born in a poor, Serbian mountain village. By the age of seven, he was especially drawn to the new force of electricity that his mother, a skillful inventor of farm and home implements, feared as a force of evil and refused to use.

In 1881, 25-year-old Tesla graduated from college and took a job with the new telephone company in Budapest. During his year there he made his first important invention. As he strolled through a Budapest park with a friend one day while reciting a passage from a book, "the idea came in a single flash. In an instant I saw it all, and accurately drew the diagrams in the sand with a stick" (*Tesla: Master of Lightning* and *Wizard: The Life and Times of Nikola Tesla*).

What Nikola envisioned that summer day was an entirely new kind of electric motor. Electric motors worked because an electric current created a magnetic field that could make the motor turn. Tesla envisioned a *rotating* magnetic field that would more efficiently drive the motor. He would cause the magnetic field to rotate by changing the direction of the flow of electric current, back and forth through the motor's wires.

Nothing like Tesla's motor existed or had even been thought of in the world until that day. There was not even a name for what he envisioned that day. (The label "multi-phase induction motor" wasn't used until 1910.) Yet Tesla's inspired creation is the very electric motor design we still use today in thousands of electric appliances and equipment.

Tesla's problem was that no electrical power system existed to drive his new motor. So (in 1881) he set the idea aside.

In 1884, Tesla immigrated to the United States to work with famed American inventor Thomas Edison. Within months they began a fight that turned into a lifelong feud.

Edison was a committed supporter of DC transmission. But problems arose with DC transmission. Electrical wires resisted DC flow. Electrical energy could only be transmitted a short distance before it lost most of the power. The loss was called "transmission loss."

Tesla argued that transmission loss was unacceptable and that they had to create alternatives. Edison refused to consider it.

Tesla soon identified the other problem with DC systems. DC electric motors were too inefficient. They produced very little power for the amount of electricity they used. Tesla wanted to do away with DC electrical systems. Edison refused to even discuss it.

In 1885, Tesla recalled his inspired motor design from 1881. Instead of a steady, direct electrical current, this motor needed a current that reversed its direction many times each second. Tesla called such a current an *alternating current* (AC) since it regularly alternated its direction.

Tesla's AC motor consisted of coils of wire and a magnetized iron rod. One end of this rod acted as the magnet's north pole, the other as the south pole. When electricity flowed through the coils, they set up their own magnetic field with its own north and south poles. The iron rod and the coil's magnetic field then tried to align themselves (north pole to south, and south pole to north). Opposite poles attract each other; like poles repel. The iron rod spun in order to align itself with the coil's magnetic field.

At this instant, Tesla's motor alternated the current flow, reversing the field's north and south poles. The iron rod had to spin again to align with this new field direction. If the current alternated many times each second, the iron rod would continuously spin and create continuous rotational motion to turn the motor.

Tesla presented this AC motor to Edison. Edison refused to pay for it. So Tesla quit and sold the idea of AC transmission and AC motors to young industrialist George Westinghouse.

But Tesla soon quit Westinghouse to form his own company to develop AC equipment. The first of these inventions was an *alternator* to convert DC battery power into AC.

Through experiments, Tesla found that transmission loss dropped very low when he ran extremely high voltage AC currents through the wire. In order to convert an electric current up to high voltage and then back down to the low voltage current most motors and lights needed, he had to invent a series of AC *transformers*. Tesla then created the first AC electrical *generators,* and his AC system was complete.

Backed by Westinghouse money, Tesla demonstrated his AC transmission system by sending AC current 186 miles with only a 22 percent loss of power. It was unimaginable efficiency for the time. In 1892 he built an AC power plant at Niagara Falls, New York, which lighted the Chicago World Exposition over 500 miles away. That demonstration converted world thinking to alternating current. Nikola Tesla was the master of electricity, and AC was what the world wanted.

What's Happened Since Then?

The 1912 Nobel Prize committee wanted to jointly award Tesla and Edison for their contributions to electrical development. Tesla refused to do anything jointly with Edison. The prize went to someone else. Embittered, Tesla grew into a total recluse, refusing most human contact, and raised pigeons in a New York apartment until he died in 1943.

But it was Nikola Tesla who single-handedly built over 700 significant electrical inventions and created the energy distribution system we use today. Tesla, more than any other individual (Benjamin Franklin and Thomas Edison included), shaped the way we create and use electricity, our most fundamental energy source.

 Fun Fact: The electricity in your house is AC (alternating current). The electrons in that flow of electricity change directions 60 times every second. However, electrons travel at light speed and so, in that $\frac{1}{60}$ of a second, travel over 3,000 miles.

More to Explore

Aldrich, Lisa J. *Nikola Tesla and the Taming of Electricity.* Greensboro, NC: Reynolds, Morgan Incorporated, 2005.

Cheney, Margaret. *Tesla: Master of Lightning.* New York: Barnes & Noble Books, 1999.

Dommermuth-Costa, Carol. *Nikola Tesla: A Spark of Genius.* Minneapolis, MN: Lerner Group, 1997.

Haven, Kendall, and Donna Clark. *100 Most Popular Scientists for Young Adults.* Englewood, CO: Libraries Unlimited, 1999.

Hunter, Richard. *Basic Electricity and Electronics: Alternating Current.* Toronto: Thomson Delmar Learning, 1996.

Jeffries, Michael, and Gary Lewis. *Inventors and Inventions.* New York: Smithmark, 1997.

Jonnes, Jill. *Empires of Light: Edison, Tesla, Westinghouse, and the Race to Electrify the World.* New York: Random House, 2003.

McNeil, Ian. *An Encyclopedia of the History of Technology.* New York: Routledge, 1996.

Seifer, Marc J. *Wizard: The Life and Times of Nikola Tesla.* Minneapolis, MN: Carol Publishing Group, 1998.

Fast Fasteners
(Zipper and Velcro)

Year of Invention: 1893 (and 1913 and 1957)

> **What Is It?** A mechanism for rapidly fastening two pieces of cloth, fabric, leather, or other material.
>
> **Who Invented It?** Zipper: Whitcomb Judson and Gideon Sundback (in Chicago). Velcro: George de Mestral (in Switzerland)

Why Is *This* Invention One of the 100 Greatest?

Zippers and Velcro® have revolutionized boots, pants, sandals, dresses, jackets, backpacks, luggage, and a thousand other items that must be quickly fastened and unfastened. They have changed the way we design and manufacture consumer products. Virtually every person uses these fast, cheap, reliable fasteners every day. These two fasteners have woven themselves into the very fabric of our lives.

History of the Invention

What Did People Do Before?

People always needed some way to clasp and secure their clothing. The button first appeared around 4,000 B.C. in India. Cultures from Egypt to China used every imaginable gadget to hold their clothes together—broaches, clasps, ties, buckles, catches, clamps, and clasps, as well as loops and buttons.

How Were Zippers and Velcro Invented?

In 1889 chubby Whitcomb Judson worked as a mechanical engineer in Chicago. He grew tired of having to bend over to hook each of the eight metal clasps on each of his boots. He decided to do something about it.

Judson studied metal boot clamps for a year before he got an idea—partly based on 1851 work by Elias Howe (the inventor of the sewing machine). Judson imagined a metal device that would slide from clamp to clamp and hook each one as it went.

Within six months Judson had created a drawing of his "clasp locker"—the world's first zipper. It featured round knobs (slots) on one side and curved metal hooks (teeth) on the other. As the metal slide passed each pair, it forced the hook over the knob. Downward pressure from the pair above it would keep the hook from sliding off.

Judson wanted to display his invention at the 1893 Chicago Worlds Fair and frantically hunted for a metal shop that could manufacture each hook and knob to his exact design. Judson got his moment to shine at the fair, but was a dismal flop. His zipper's teeth were too bulky to flex with a soft material. They had a nasty habit of jamming and splitting apart. Judson sold a grand total of 200 sets over the next five years—all to the U.S. Mail Service for their large mailbags.

In 1909, Swedish engineer Gideon Sundback volunteered to fix Judson's failed clasp. By 1913, Sundback had tripled the number of clasps per inch so that he could make the line of clasps more flexible.

Sundback also redesigned Judson's teeth. He used identical teeth on each side of the clasp. Each tooth was a small metal bar with a rounded knob on top and a matching bowl-shaped depression on the bottom. When the zipper closed, each knob fit into a bowl to lock the fabric together. Even though modern zippers still use Sundback's tooth design, his "toothless fastener" didn't sell well.

In 1923 the BF Goodrich Company decided to build Sundback's "hookless fasteners" into their new rubber boots. It was the Goodrich marketing people who named them *zippers*. The rubber boots (and zippers) were a smash hit. Zippers became a fashion rage. By 1930, millions of zippers each year were being sewn into pants, dresses, jackets, boots, and coats.

However, the zipper still wasn't perfect. It still tended to jam and to split apart. One night in 1948, 44-year-old Swiss engineer and inventor George de Mestral was frustrated trying to free a stuck zipper on his wife's dress before they went out to dinner. He swore that "even I" could invent a better fastener.

Two weeks later, after walking his dog through the woods, de Mestral paused to remove burrs from his pants and from his dog's fur and noticed how marvelously efficient burrs were at hooking onto anything they touched.

De Mestral examined burrs under his workshop microscope and found that they were covered with miniscule hooks that locked into any loops or snags in material they touched. In minutes de Mestral sketched what he called "locking tape." One side of a backing tape would be covered in tiny fabric loops, the other side in miniature hooks.

It took six years of experiments to make this simple idea work. Some tries locked too strongly and couldn't be pried apart. Some weren't strong enough. Some of the materials de Mestral tried for his loops were too soft and wouldn't stand up. Some were too stiff and wouldn't flex with the fabric they were sewn into. Some hooks broke too easily so that the fastener couldn't be reused. Some were too soft to lock solidly when closed.

De Mestral finally settled on 300 loops-per-inch of a soft material that had to be stiffened with infrared light. He opened his first factory in 1957 and named the stuff Velcro: *Vel* from velvet and *cro* from the French word *crochet*, meaning "small hook."

What's Happened Since Then?

Buttons, zippers, and Velcro still dominate the fastener industry—buttons for shirts, blouses, and suit coats; Velcro for sandals, shoes, sports equipment, and baby clothes; and zippers for pants, dresses, jackets, and luggage.

 Fun Fact: Velcro can be separated and reclosed 10,000 times before wearing out and can hold up to nine pounds per square inch of Velcro.

More to Explore

Driscoll, Dan. *The Inventor's Times.* New York: Scholastic, Inc., 2003.

Editors of Time-Life Books. *Inventive Genius.* Alexandria, VA: Time-Life Books, 1998.

McGough, Roger. *Dotty Inventions: And Some Real Ones, Too.* New York: American Natural Hygiene Society, 2004.

McNeil, Ian. *An Encyclopedia of the History of Technology.* New York: Routledge, 1996.

van Dulken, Stephen. *Inventing the 20th century.* New York: New York University Press, 2000.

Wulffson, Don. *Extraordinary Stories Behind the Invention of Ordinary Things.* New York: Lothrop, Lee & Shepard Books, 1996.

———. *The Kid Who Invented the Popsicle and Other Surprising Stories About Inventions.* New York: Puffin Books, 1999.

Yenne, Bill. *100 Inventions That Shaped World History.* New York: Bluewood Books, 1993.

Radio

Year of Invention: 1895

> **What Is It?** An electronic device that sends signals and information through the air on radio-frequency waves.
>
> **Who Invented It?** Guglielmo Marconi (in Bologna, Italy)

Why Is *This* Invention One of the 100 Greatest?

Every car, boat, airplane and house has a radio. Police, fire, and all emergency communications funnel over radio. For all of the twentieth century, important news was always flashed over the radio. Telegraphs and telephones required wires to be strung from sender to receiver. Radio allowed the receiver to travel anywhere and for one transmitter to simultaneously reach millions of listeners.

Radio opened the door to mass communications and to instant worldwide communications. Radio redefined the way countries and governments communicate as well as the way people sought news, music, and entertainment.

History of the Invention

What Did People Do Before?

In 1834, Samuel Morse invented the telegraph. In 1876, Alexander Graham Bell invented the telephone. But both systems only worked along wires that had to be strung across the countryside.

James Maxwell (in 1864) mathematically predicted that radio waves must exist—invisible waves that pulsed with electrical and magnetic properties and sped through the air. In 1887, German physicist Heinrich Hertz actually created radio waves in his Berlin classroom. But even Hertz said that he couldn't see any useful purpose for radio waves.

How Was Radio Invented?

Twenty-year-old Guglielmo Marconi lived at the Marconi family compound in Bologna, Italy. By 1894 he had become fascinated—obsessed—with electronics and converted a small third-floor guestroom into a laboratory. He poured over scientific papers describing work by electrical geniuses Heinrich Hertz and American Michael Faraday. Both had shown that an electric current flowing through one wire could force an electric current to flow through a nearby wire even if the two wires never touched!

In mid-1894, it occurred to Marconi that if a simple electric current could leap through the air from wire to wire, why couldn't he also make a *useful* signal—a message—do the same?

Over the next eight weeks he purchased and tested batteries, wires, oscillator tubes, and circuits. By early fall he could make a signal from his battery-powered transmitter leap across the room to a receiving wire and cause the needle of a magnetic compass there to shift away from north and twitch.

No one was impressed. Marconi tried to explain that he had a problem. The electric current in the receiving wire was too weak to do anything more than shift a compass needle.

For a month Marconi searched for scientific papers that mentioned electric current. Unfortunately, as of 1894, very little work had been done in the area, and he decided he would have to rely on his own intuition and experiments.

One day he found that a large glass jar packed with iron filings could "catch," or receive, a signal better than a plain wire. With this iron-filled tube wired into his receiver, Marconi could move the "receiver" farther away from the "transmitter" and still detect the electric signal he transmitted.

Marconi moved his receiver to the first floor and wired it so that he could make the front doorbell buzz from his third-floor lab.

His father called it a silly party game.

Another month of testing produced two improvements. First, Marconi replaced the iron filings with nickel and silver filings. He called this jar a "signal condenser." Second, he held a metal plate horizontally just below this signal condenser to reflect the extra signal up into the condenser and to block any signal from leaking out of the condenser and down to the ground.

On his next demonstration Marconi was able to send a signal to the house next door. His family was *still* not impressed.

He found that larger metal plates meant better signal reception. With his new giant metal plate he sent a signal 200 meters to the top of a hill behind the Marconi estate. Of course, it did take four strong men to lift, and a horse cart to carry, the receiver's metal plate. But it worked.

During another two months of testing (now March 1895) Marconi again made two important advances. First, he found a way to greatly increase the power flowing through the transmitting wire. Second, he discovered that thin, copper tubes placed eight to ten centimeters apart worked just as well as a heavy metal plate for his receiver. He also found that this receiver design worked best if raised up off the ground.

Marconi welded eight of these eight- or nine-meter-long copper tubes onto thin metal spacer bars and raised the whole assembly on a wooden pole. As he did, Guglielmo Marconi raised the world's first antenna.

He mounted the antenna and receiver on a cart to see how far he could travel and still detect a signal transmitted from his third floor lab. By mid afternoon, he had received a signal over two kilometers (1.6 miles) away in the next village!

With this demonstration even Marconi's father was impressed.

What's Happened Since Then?

In 1899, Marconi made the first international radio transmission—from France to England—a distance of almost 30 miles. Two years later, he had improved his transmitter and antenna technology to the point where he was able to make the first transatlantic radio transmission between England and Newfoundland, Canada—over 2,400 miles! In 1904 the Cunnard Ship Company built radio rooms into their steamships and made the first ship-to-shore radio transmission.

All of these radio systems sent Morse code signals of dots and dashes over the radio. Canadian Reginald Fessenden invented the first radio voice transmitter in 1905. The first public radio station broadcasts occurred in California and Illinois in 1910. Now radio signals beam into space, and pocket-sized radios receive hundreds of broadcast channels. Radio is still a vital part of entertainment, news, and public safety.

 Fun Fact: When Orson Welles broadcast his fictional story, *War of the Worlds*, over radio in 1938, so many people thought it was real that police lines were flooded with horrified callers. People fled their homes in terror to escape Martian invaders. The program created mass hysteria and a national panic that took weeks to dispel.

More to Explore

Dyson, James. *A History of Great Inventions*. New York: Carroll & Graf Publishers, 2001.

Goldsmith, Mike. *Guglielmo Marconi*. New York: Raintree Publishing, 2003.

Haven, Kendall. *Marvels of Science*. Englewood, CO: Libraries Unlimited, 1994.

Lomask, Milton. *Invention and Technology Great Lives*. New York: Charles Scribner's Sons, 1994.

Sherrow, Victoria. *Guglielmo Marconi: The Inventor of the Radio*. Berkeley Heights, NJ: Enslow Publishers, 2004.

Tarrant, Donald. *Marconi's Miracle*. New York: BRP Publishers, 2001.

Worland, Gayle. *Radio*. Mankato, MN: Capstone Press, 2003.

Yenne, Bill. *100 Inventions That Shaped World History*. New York: Bluewood Books, 1993.

Zamos, Susan. *Guglielmo Marconi and Radio Waves*. Bear, DE: Mitchell Lane Publishers, 2004.

Moving Pictures

What Is It? A system of rapidly changing still pictures that simulates motion, projected onto a large screen.

Who Invented It? Antoine Lumière (in Lyon, France)

Why Is *This* Invention One of the 100 Greatest?

Motion pictures record and preserve history. They are a portal to places and times we cannot otherwise reach. Movies bring the world to us—with all its color, sound, and motion.

Motion pictures entertain, teach, and inform and have reshaped human attitudes and values. Many have called motion pictures the greatest entertainment medium ever invented.

History of the Invention

What Did People Do Before?

The idea of motion pictures was not new. In 1504, Leonardo da Vinci described the process and how the human mind would merge sequential images into a smooth motion. Photography developed throughout the 1820s and 1830s and blossomed in America when it was used to record the tragedy and horror of the Civil War. But slow shutter speeds (one to two seconds or longer) limited the usefulness of photography to record live events. In 1873, George Eastman (Eastman Kodak) invented long strips of cellulose film.

How Were Motion Pictures Invented?

It started with a bet—an angry, shouting bet—in 1877. California railroad tycoon Leland Stanford got into an argument over horses. He argued that there was a moment when all four of a running horse's hooves were off the ground. Others said he was crazy. The argument grew heated and turned into a bet for $25,000 (the equivalent of half a million dollars today). Stanford and others watched race horses speed down the track. But the horses' legs moved too fast for watchers to be sure. The bet couldn't be settled.

Stanford hired English photographer Edwin Muybridge to resolve the dispute. Muybridge watched horses at the racetrack for several days before he envisioned a way to accomplish his mission.

He decided to take pictures of a running horse with multiple cameras—each triggered a fraction of a second after the last—to be sure to record every movement in a horse's stride. He mounted 16 cameras side-by-side along the rail of a racetrack and hooked each camera's shutter release to a long string. He ran each waist-high string across the track. As a horse galloped past, it would crash through each of the 16 shutter-releasing strings, capturing pictures of the horse in 16 different postures during the course of one stride.

Muybridge mounted the pictures from his 16 cameras on a rotating disk and shone a light through the gaps between images. The flickering images proved that Stanford was right.

More important, Muybridge created the world's first moving picture. Only one person at a time could peer through the view slot to watch. But viewers left astonished and delighted. They had seen a horse gallop on film. Most swore they actually watched a horse run.

In 1885, Thomas Edison heard about these "moving pictures" and instantly recognized that movies could be huge moneymakers. He ordered his assistant, William Dickson, to devise a suitable moving picture camera and a means for projecting the results. After eight years of struggle, Dickson and Edison revealed their "kinetograph" camera. This camera captured images at 40 frames each second and played them back on the "kinescope" as a "peep show" allowing one individual at a time to watch the film.

The first kinescope booths opened for business in 1894. Interest was strong. Business was steady. One of the first to view a 20-second kinescope show in a downtown New York booth was Frenchman Antione Lumière, a manufacturer of photographic materials in Lyon, France.

Impressed with the idea of moving pictures, Lumière also saw the great flaw in Edison's system. Only one person at a time could view the movie. Lumière returned to France and ordered his two sons, Auguste and Louis, to develop a lightweight camera and a projection system that could be viewed by a large audience.

In less than a year, the Lumières had developed both their own movie camera and a playback system that projected the images onto a white-painted wall for a room full of viewers.

On March 22, 1895, the Lumières showed the world's first projected motion picture. (They called their system a *cinematographie*—the source of our word *cinema.*) They chose the Grand Café in Paris for their debut and played to a standing-room-only crowd. Their debut film was a one-minute movie of workers emerging from the Lumière photographic factory in Lyon, France, smiling and waving.

What's Happened Since Then?

Edison made major improvements to his kinescope in 1896, renamed it the Vitascope, and re-released it in the United States to cheering crowds of viewers. Movie production studios developed first in New York (1898) and then in California as movie houses were slowly built across the country to show movies.

Early movies were silent films. They contained no sound track. Western Electric developed motors that allowed picture and sound to be played back at the same speeds and time. Warner Brothers bought the system in 1925 and named it Vitaphone. The world's first "talking" movie, *The Jazz Singer*, hit the screens in 1927. Few theaters aired the film because few had built-in sound systems on which to play the sound track.

Richard Hollingshead, son of a Camden, New Jersey, auto dealer, invented the drive-in theater in 1930 as a promotional gimmick to help his father's car sales. The first color picture, *The Wizard of Oz*, premiered to mixed reviews in 1939. In 1940, Walt Disney's *Fantasia* was as the first animated, full-length motion picture. The IMAX giant screen format debuted at the 1967 Montreal Expo. George Lucas premiered his advanced movie sound system, THX, in 1983 with his movie, *Return of the Jedi*.

 Fun Fact: Mickey Mouse's official birthday is November 18. On that date in 1928 his first film, *Steamboat Willie*, debuted. It was also the first-ever animated film.

More to Explore

Adler, David. *Picture Book of Thomas Edison*. New York: Holiday House, 1999.

Dyson, James. *A History of Great Inventions*. New York: Carroll & Graf Publishers, 2001.

Editors of Time-Life Books. *Inventive Genius*. Alexandria, VA: Time-Life Books, 1998.

McNeil, Ian. *An Encyclopedia of the History of Technology*. New York: Routledge, 1996.

Middleton, Haydon. *Thomas Edison*. New York: Oxford University Press, 1998.

Yenne, Bill. *100 Inventions That Shaped World History*. New York: Bluewood Books, 1993.

Zemilicha, Shannon. *Thomas Edison*. New York: Barnes & Noble Books, 2003.

Air Conditioning

Year of Invention: 1902

> **What Is It?** A machine that cools and dehumidifies (removes moisture from) the air in a room or building.
>
> **Who Invented It?** Willis Carrier (in Buffalo, New York)

Why Is *This* Invention One of the 100 Greatest?

Air conditioning has revolutionized industrial plant design and operation, commercial building design (especially skyscraper design), and residential building design. Affordable residential air conditioning made possible the population explosion in Florida and across the American Southwest beginning in the 1950s. Automobiles, restaurants, airplanes, houses, schools, and every other facet of our lives are now designed around air conditioning. We live, work, play, eat, and sleep in air-conditioned spaces.

History of the Invention

What Did People Do Before?

People used to design buildings to take advantage of prevailing breezes or to create their own air currents and circulation. They built thick exterior walls to help block out the heat.

Ancient Romans knew that water vapor cooled a person. The rich sprayed fine mists to keep themselves comfortable. They also built underground cellars that stayed far cooler than the scorching surface. Greeks brought ice down from the mountains in winter and stacked it in underground rooms that were insulated with a thick padding of straw. The rooms stayed comfortably cool through most of the summer.

How Was Air Conditioning Invented?

Born and raised in upstate New York, Willis Carrier trained as a mechanical engineer. Carrier was 26 years old and working for the Buffalo Forge Company when, in 1902, John Sackett-Williams, a Brooklyn print shop owner, came to him with a problem. Sackett-Williams's color printing (a new process for printers) wasn't working. Each page had to pass through a printing press four times for a color print. However, changes in shop temperature—and especially in humidity—made his paper expand or contract between runs. As a result, the pages didn't line up correctly. One of the colors would print a tiny bit off and ruin the printing. He asked Carrier to figure out a way to reduce humidity inside his print shop. Reducing blistering summer temperatures would also be nice.

One day Carrier noticed that water droplets formed on cold surfaces when air next to that surface cooled below the dew point. (All air contains water vapor—evaporated water. Warm air can hold more water vapor than can cold air. As air cools, it will reach some temperature at which it can no longer hold all of its water as invisible water vapor. The excess water begins to form tiny droplets on any available surface. That temperature is called the dew point.)

Carrier reasoned that if he cooled air below its dew point, water would be squeezed out as droplets (called *condensation*). With less water in it, the air would be dryer.

Carrier knew about the work on refrigeration begun in the 1840s. As compressed gases expanded, they cooled whatever was around them. That idea was being used to freeze water and create ice. Carrier suspected he could use the same approach to cool air enough to wring water out of it.

Ferdinand Carre (the inventor of refrigeration) used compressed ammonia gas for his refrigerator. Carrier decided to do the same. Compressed ammonia gas would expand through a nozzle into thin metal tubes. The tubes would turn freezing cold and cool the air around them.

As the air cooled, Carrier had to make sure that it lost as much water as possible. Condensation happened on some surface—a glass, a blade of grass, a window. That meant that he would have to build enough surface area inside his machine on which water droplets could form as warm room air was cooled.

He designed a maze of wafer-thin, vertical metal fins (called *baffles*) that extended out from each tube ammonia would pass through. Expanding ammonia would cool the metal tube and attached metal fins. Warm room air would blow through the maze of paper-thin fins. The sub-freezing fins would cool the air. Soon, the air would cool enough to reach its dew point and condensation would form on the baffles. Carrier installed troughs to collect the condensation water as it dribbled down the baffles.

Carrier faced one more challenge. He couldn't simply release ammonia into the atmosphere after it absorbed heat. Ammonia was too expensive. He had to find a way to re-cool, re-pressurize, and re-liquefy the ammonia so that it could be recycled through the system over and over again.

He decided to build a second set of pumps, baffles, and cooling tubes. But this set would be located *outside* the room he was trying to cool. This set of pumps would re-pressurize and re-liquefy the ammonia and then pass that hot liquid ammonia through thin metal tubes, each with more paper-thin metal fins. Hot ammonia would heat these metal fins, which would be cooled by outside air being blown past by strong fans.

Carrier's first air conditioner weighed 30 tons and was itself the size of a small room. Still, Sackett-Williams was thrilled with the results. His printing plant stayed cool and dry and his color prints looked magnificent.

What's Happened Since Then?

Carrier's air conditioner was popular with industrial plants but was too big and expensive for other uses. Within months, Carrier had orders for units to be installed in cotton mills, textile plants, iron works, and a dozen other industries.

Through the 1920s, 1930s, and early 1940s, air conditioners stayed in hot demand for industrial, commercial, and retail buildings. In 1947, Carrier invented a small, inexpensive home air-conditioning unit. This affordable air conditioning, as much as any other force, fuelled the population boom into Florida and the desert Southwest.

 Fun Fact: As of 1990, over 84 percent of American homes and over 96 percent of American businesses had installed air conditioning of some kind. In 2000, 98 percent of all new American construction included built-in air conditioning.

More to Explore

Ackerman, Marsha. *Cool Comfort*. Washington, DC: Smithsonian Institution Press, 2002.

Cooper, Gail. *Air Conditioning America: Engineers and the Controlled Environment, 1900–1960*. Baltimore: Johns Hopkins University Press, 2002.

Dyson, James. *A History of Great Inventions*. New York: Carroll & Graf Publishers, 2001.

Ford, Barbara. *Keeping Things Cool*. New York: Walker & Co., 1996.

Miller, Rex. *Refrigeration and Air Conditioning Technology*. New York: Glencoe/McGraw-Hill, 1997.

Stwertka, Eve. *How Things Cool*. New York: Silver Burdette Press, 2000.

van Dulken, Stephen. *Inventing the 20th Century*. New York: New York University Press, 2000.

Electric Utilities

Year of Invention: 1903

What Is It? A combination of electric generating power plants, electric transmission lines, and transformers to serve the electrical needs of a large area.

Who Invented It? Samuel Insul (in Chicago)

Why Is *This* Invention One of the 100 Greatest?

Our modern world is structured around electric utilities' ability to distribute electric power to every address, building, and place. Cities are organized around the utilities, which provide any amount of current and any voltage to any and every customer. Each new structure simply connects to the electrical power grid, and the electric utility makes sure that electricity magically arrives. Giant central power plants and their spider webs of lines to distribute the power helped make modern cities possible.

History of the Invention

What Did People Do Before?

Electricity was not new in the late nineteenth century. Volta invented the electric battery in 1800. Faraday invented the electric motor and electric generator in 1831.

In 1879, Edison invented the electric lightbulb. However, users of one of these motors or lights had to supply their own noisy, bulky electric generator.

How Were Electric Utilities Invented?

The idea of creating central electric utilities did not spring forward as a single, complete concept. Samuel Insul in Chicago was the one to finally put all the pieces together and invent a working utility.

The first thing an electric utility needed was electric generating power stations. In 1879, Charles Brush, in San Francisco, built the first electric generator with the intent of producing electricity that he would sell to nearby customers.

Initially, Brush's plant supplied DC (direct current) electricity to new street lighting over an eight-block stretch of Market Street. In 1880, he added two small manufacturing plants along the street as customers. Technically, this was the country's first electric utility.

But it was small, never grew, and died out two years before the great San Francisco Earthquake (in 1906) because the country was converting to AC (alternating current) electric power.

In 1882, Thomas Edison built the first East Coast power plant, his Pearl Street Station in lower New York City. Industrialist J. P. Morgan financed the power plant so that it could provide power to one of his nearby factories. Like the San Francisco plant, the Pearl Street Station created DC electric current. By 1885, Pearl Street Station powered 8,000 nearby lightbulbs.

Industrialist and inventor George Westinghouse favored the AC electricity invented by two of his employees, William Stanley and Nikola Tesla. AC had one great advantage over DC. High voltage AC current could travel long distances without losing power, while DC could not. That meant that a power plant didn't have to be located right next to its customers (as did DC generators).

Tesla's AC system included *generators* (power plants), *transformers* to convert the current into high voltage current, *transmission lines* to carry the electricity to where it was needed, and more transformers to convert the electricity back into "regular" low-voltage current that was used in houses and factories. "Regular" current had been set at 110 to 120 volts because that's what Edison's incandescent lights needed. By 1888 Tesla had discovered that AC electric generators had to operate at rates of at least 60 cycles per second to keep Edison's electric house lights from flickering.

Westinghouse opened his first AC power plant in 1892 at Niagara Falls, New York. Quigley's flourmill was his first customer. The city of Niagara Falls was his second, for their streetlights. By 1896, he had installed the giant transformers for a 100,000-volt transmission line to connect his plant with Buffalo, New York—over 20 miles away! At the time it seemed astounding that electricity could travel that far.

Westinghouse also built the transmission lines to connect his Niagara Falls plant with the Chicago World's Exposition, which opened two years later. That line stretched over 500 miles! Westinghouse provided over 25,000 lights to light the entire fair "like a wondrous fairy land." Crowds were bigger at night than they were during the day, as everyone wanted to gawk at the electric wonders.

In 1880, 38-year-old Insul moved to Chicago from New Jersey, where he had briefly served as a secretary to Thomas Edison. Insul began his Chicago electrical empire by providing electric power to the Palmer House Hotel in 1883. Nine years later, he formed the Chicago Edison Company. By 1893, Insul had become a supporter of AC power and built three small AC generating power plants.

Within a decade, Insul had gobbled up over 50 small utility companies to get their transmission lines, and he built the first big (10 megawatt) power plant at his Fisk Street Station facility. This monster power plant was America's first steam turbine power plant. (High-pressure steam from a boiler blew across turbine blades to turn the shaft of the electric generator.)

AC allowed Insul to construct mammoth central power plants and a vast network of transmission lines to distribute power to users all over the greater Chicago area. Insul's Chicago Edison was the first effective electric utility in the country and established the "bigger is better" mentality for power plant design.

What's Happened Since Then?

In 1900, more than 4,000 electric utilities operated in the United States. By 1925, fewer than 800 remained, as some had failed and others merged to form regional utilities. By 1930, giant plants dotted American waterways and rail lines (which provided essential cooling water and fuel).

Ironically, most of our modern computers and consumer electronics require DC. Much of their space and weight are taken up by devices to convert AC back to DC. The Electric Power Research Institute (EPRI) recently predicted the development of local DC grids for computers and consumer electronics in the near future. It may turn out that AC was the power model for the twenty-first century, and that Edison's vision for DC electricity will serve us better in the future.

 Fun Fact: As of January 2004, the electric utilities in the United States had a combined capacity of 948 gigawatts. U.S. electrical capacity is rising at twice the rate that the population is increasing.

More to Explore

Boltz, C. W. *How Electricity Is Made*. New York: Facts on File, 1999.

Hirsch, Richard. *Technology in the American Electric Utility Industry*. New York: Cambridge University Press, 1999.

Plachno, Larry, ed. *Memoirs of Samuel Insul*. Chicago: Transportation Trails, 1992.

Platt, Harold. *The Electric City: Energy and the Growth of the Chicago Area, 1880–1930*. Chicago: University of Chicago Press, 1993.

Seuling, Barbara. *Flick a Switch*. New York: Holiday House, 2003.

Warkentin, Denise. *The Electric Power Industry*. Philadelphia: Pennwell Corp., 1998.

Wyborny, Sheila. *Electricity*. New York: Thomson Gale, 2003.

Airplane

Year of Invention: 1903

What Is It? A heavier-than-air, motor-driven flying machine.

Who Invented It? Wilbur and Orville Wright (in Kitty Hawk, North Carolina)

Why Is *This* Invention One of the 100 Greatest?

Airplanes have changed human life, altered our perceptions, and collapsed our concept of distance. Places that were separated by months of ocean sailing are now no more distant than a few hours' flight. The airplane helped create the expectation of instant worldwide news and interchange. It has made the world a single global community and a single global economy. Airplanes opened the door to the space age.

History of the Invention

What Did People Do Before?

Early myths often involved flight. Greek, Roman, Norse, and Asian gods could fly. Flight was a part of what made them gods. Leonardo da Vinci was the first human to take the next step. Between 1505 and 1510, he designed a series of flying machines. He built several small-scale models.

The first person to intentionally lift off the ground did so in a hot air balloon in France in 1783. In 1843, Englishman William Herson applied for, and received, a patent for a steam-powered, winged aeroplane. But his plane never flew.

The late 1800s saw a host of men building a series of fixed-wing gliders. Prussian Otto Lilienthal was the leader in glider research and experimentation. His work between 1891 and his death during a glider crash in 1896 defined the wing design that the Wright brothers would use in their gliders and motorized planes.

How Was the Airplane Invented?

Successful flight required three things: lift, power, and control. Otto Lilienthal made over 2,500 glider flights and discovered the principles of lift and wing design. Engines (mostly steam) existed to create power. Control was the missing ingredient—as proven by the large number of crashes and deaths of flying enthusiasts.

Through the 1890s the leading American flyer was Alexander Graham Bell, who conducted over 1,200 aviation experiments. In 1896, Bell teamed with Samuel Langley, secretary of the Smithsonian Institution, to build a 14-foot steam-powered aerodrome. That unmanned plane flew over 3,000 feet before it lost steam and gently glided back to earth. Bell wrote that "without a doubt, the practicality of heavier than air flight has been demonstrated."

The death of German aviator Otto Lilienthal that fall shocked Bell. Bell decided not to build a larger, manned version of his plane. He set flight aside and turned to other projects.

Lilienthal's death stopped Bell. However, it sparked the interest in flight of two brothers from Dayton, Ohio, who owned a bicycle shop—Orville and Wilbur Wright.

The Wright brothers made two great discoveries that gave them control over the flight of an airplane and made their success in December 1903 possible. Their first discovery resulted from experiments in their bicycle shop—before they built their first glider.

In the spring of 1899, Orville watched buzzards drift through the clear spring sky and noticed that a buzzard's left wing tipped up when the right wing tipped down. When one wing curled forward, the other curled back. The bird's wings moved in opposition to each other. He realized that he could do the same to an aeroplane's wings—warp the wings in opposite directions to create control of turns and flight.

Wing warp put the Wright brothers years ahead of their competition for successful flight. The Wright brothers' second discovery was made near the end of their two years of glider testing in the sand dunes of Kill Devil Hills just south of Kitty Hawk, North Carolina.

In late September 1902, Orville was flying their glider when he nosed up too steeply and almost stalled. His right wing dipped. He threw the wing warp hard left to compensate. The glider shuddered. Then the tail kicked around. The glider nosed into a spiraling dive and crashed, splintering on the beach.

That night, Orville realized what had happened. The tail had momentarily gotten lift. That was the brothers' second great discovery. Under some conditions the vertical tail section could act like a wing and produce lift—only it was lift to the side instead of up and down. To prevent that, they hooked the tail to the wing warp controls.

Those two discoveries gave Orville and Wilber Wright control of flying for their first motorized aeroplane flight on December 17, 1903. That plane weighed 605 pounds and flew for 12 seconds.

What's Happened Since Then?

The Wright brothers first flew their *Flyer 2* on May 13, 1904. It housed a bigger, 16 hp motor. However, like their first plane, it still tended to stall in turns. *Flyer 3*, debuted on October 5, 1905, flew 34 miles on its first flight (38 minutes in the air). But still the Wright brothers allowed no public viewing of their plane or its flights.

In 1907 Bell formed the Aerial Experiment Association (AEA) to "successfully demonstrate manned motorized flight." The test flight of AEA's first plane (*Red Wing*) in 1907 was the first-ever publicly viewed flight of a heavier-than-air flying machine. AEA's second plane (*White Wing*) was the first aeroplane to incorporate two key Bell innovations: a three-wheel undercarriage for landings and take-offs, and ailerons for stability and maneuvering control.

AEA's next plane, *June Bug*, flew over 150 flights in 1908 without a single problem (a record) and won the *Scientific American* trophy for being the first airplane to fly over a kilometer in a public demonstration. (It actually flew over 5,000 feet, just 120 feet shy of a mile.) The AEA's final design, *Silver Dart*, set 10 speed, endurance, and altitude records during January and February 1909.

Airmail service began in 1918. The first air passenger service didn't start until 1926; a number of small carriers all started at the same time. These eventually merged into TWA, United, American, and PanAm.

The first "modern" airliner was the Boeing 247, first flown in 1933—all metal construction, retractable landing gear, upholstered seats, and onboard flight attendants. The 247 cruised at the staggering speed of 155 mph.

It is possible that some other transport system will eventually replace airplanes. But nothing has emerged beyond the artist's sketchpad.

 Fun Fact: The first flight stewardess flew in 1930 on a Boeing Transport plane for United Air Lines. Early stewardesses had to be registered nurses and be no more than five feet, four inches in height.

More to Explore

Aaseng, Nathan. *Twentieth-Century Inventors.* New York: Facts on File, 1996.

Freedman, Russell. *The Wright Brothers: How They Invented the Airplane.* New York: Holiday House, 1993.

Hallion, Richard. *Taking Flight.* New York: Oxford University Press, 2003.

Haven, Kendall. *Alexander Graham Bell: Visionary and Inventor.* New York: Franklin Watts, 2003.

———. *Marvels of Science.* Englewood, CO: Libraries Unlimited, 1994.

Ierley, Merritt. *Wondrous Contrivances.* New York: Clarkson Potter, 2002.

Lomask, Milton. *Invention and Technology Great Lives.* New York: Charles Scribner's Sons, 1994.

Nakun, Andrew. *Flying Machines.* New York: DK Publishing, 2004.

Washing Machine

Year of Invention: 1906

> **What Is It?** An electric machine to wash and spin-dry clothes.
>
> **Who Invented It?** Alva Fisher (in Chicago)

Why Is *This* Invention One of the 100 Greatest?

Americans do many *millions* of loads of laundry every day. With electric washing machines, each load consumes less water, creates less pollution, and saves several hours of human labor compared to a hand-washed load.

The washing machine was the first of the great electrical household convenience machines. In effect, the washing machine ushered in the domestic mechanical age in which we live.

History of the Invention

What Did People Do Before?

For centuries, people beat clothes on flat rocks at the edge of a stream or lake. By the height of the Roman Empire, most wealthy people had graduated to tubs, whose sudsy water was dumped into a stream or alleyway by servants after the wash. That basic wash tub didn't change for almost 2,000 years.

To do a load of wash, a woman heated water over a fire and carried the hot water inside to her washtub. The tub was hand filled and later hand emptied. She had to heat the wash water in order to melt the soap that would clean her load of clothes. She would flake the soap from a large soap block by hand. She would have to agitate the clothes by hand, wring out the clothes by hand, haul the soapy water out and bring in the rinse water by hand, rinse her load of clothes by hand, and finally wring the clothes to a damp dry by hand.

If clothes were especially grimy or greasy, she would have to add a step where she treated them with lye and beat on the clothes (usually stomped on them in her bare feet) to work the lye in and the grease out. Washing clothes was time consuming, hard work and hard on the material in the clothes.

In the seventeenth century many washtubs added a washing dolly, a pole attached to small paddles that the user pumped up and down to agitate the clothes and soap. The washboard appeared in England sometime before 1800 and spread quickly to America, where it gained popularity.

How Was the Washing Machine Invented?

Early attempts at inventing a washing machine during the early- to mid-nineteenth century mimicked the action and process of hand washing. Each machine used a wooden tub (sometimes lead lined) with a hand-powered rod for the dolly stick (several rocked back and forth like a crib with a foot pedal). The machine provided better agitation and a built-in wringer to wring the clothes to a damp dry after washing. A hand crank operated the wringer.

In 1870, the first tub with a drain plug appeared on the market. The owner was, however, responsible for building a trough or drain line from the tub to a safe outdoor dump spot. In 1880, several American companies offered washing machines that included a built-in firebox to heat the water right in the washer! The first of these burned coal. In 1882, the first machine designed with gas jets to replace coal appeared in a New York company catalog.

Alva Fisher was born and raised in Chicago in the late 1800s. His father owned a dry goods store. His mother helped in the store and ran the house. After completing high school, Alva completed felt at loose ends. He helped in his father's store but didn't want to make the store his career.

Fisher wanted to invent something but had no inspiration about *what* to invent. His mother suggested that he invent something to help her around the house. Alva settled on inventing a better washing machine.

He first hooked an electric motor to his mother's existing wash tub and, over the course of 18 months, slowly hooked every function of the tub to his motor. He attached electric pumps to bring water in and to pump it out. He attached the agitator to his motor through a series of gears so that the agitator paddles automatically turned and pumped up and down. Finally, he hooked the wringer to his motor so that clothes could be hand fed through the wringer without his mother having to provide any cranking effort.

Fisher unveiled his first model in 1905—a vertical, wooden-sided tub on four legs, with all action, motion, pumps, and wringer electrically driven. All his mother had to do was to hook the washer to a pair of hoses and load in the dirty clothes and soap. Fisher mounted the motor underneath the tub and used belts and gears to run the various features of the washer.

However, the tub leaked, shorted out the motor, and started a small electrical fire.

It took Fisher four months to successfully move his motor to the side of the tub and shield it from water splashes. This 1906 model still tended to suffer occasional electrical shorts, but worked well enough for Fisher to sell the design to Westinghouse Corporation.

What's Happened Since Then?

In 1924, the Savage Arms Corporation redesigned its washing machine to take full advantage of electricity. This machine featured an all-metal tub enclosed in an enameled cabinet, an agitator with plastic fins to stir the clothes, and a rotating perforated (colander-like) cylinder within the washtub. Electric pumps pumped water in and out through separate water lines. The perforated basket whirred to spin the clothes damp dry after the wash. This was the first washing machine that resembled modern washers.

Since then, new washer designs have improved efficiency and cycle options. Tumble dryers have been added to avoid having to hang out the wash. But the basic washer design and function have not changed since the 1924 design.

Very recently several "high tech" alternatives to the washing machine have been developed. These use blasts of high-energy sonic and ultrasonic energy to remove dirt and to kill germs and bacteria on skin and clothes. These washing systems use no water and are good for space or for desert enclosures. However, they are far too expensive for common usage. Nothing else threatens to diminish our dependence on the common electric washing machine.

 Fun Fact: The Guney Rotary Club of Adana, Turkey, set a record on May 16, 2004, when they hung out 42,300 pieces of laundry to dry. The line stretched over 20.5 *miles* in length!

More to Explore

Cohen, Daniel. *The Last Hundred Years: Household Technology*. New York: M. Evans, 1995.

Ierley, Merritt . *The Comforts of Home: The American House and the Evolution of Modern Convenience*. New York: Crown Publishing Group, 1999.

Jeffries, Michael, and Gary Lewis. *Inventors and Inventions*. New York: Smithmark, 1997.

McNeil, Ian. *An Encyclopedia of the History of Technology*. New York: Routledge, 1996.

Parker, Steve. *Everyday Things and How They Work*. New York: Random House Books for Young Readers, 1997.

Sayer, Jon. *Everyday Things*. New York: DK Publishing, 1998.

Weaver, Rebecca. *Machines in the Home*. New York: Oxford University Press, 1997.

Plastic

Year of Invention: 1909

> **What Is It?** A man-made substance of polymer chain molecules that changes shape when heated and then retains the new shape once cooled.
>
> **Who Invented It?** Leo Hendrik Baekeland (in New York City)

Why Is *This* Invention One of the 100 Greatest?

No material has changed our lives in the past 100 years as much as plastic and its many derivative forms—Formica, PVC, Plexiglas, nylon, etc. We live in a plastic world: plastic credit cards; plastic computers; plastic phones; plastic car parts; plastic radios and televisions; plastic cameras and clocks; plastic pipe, furniture, and clothes; plastic bins, jars, tableware, plates, and cases. Plastic seems to be everywhere. Plastic has invaded every facet of our lives.

History of the Invention

What Did People Do Before?

Plastic is a new kind of material. Nothing like it existed before. People used ceramics, glass, stone, wood, and metal. Windows were made of glass. Cabinets, furniture, and counters were made of metal or wood.

How Was Plastic Invented?

Plastic was invented in 1909. But 40 years earlier, John Hyatt came close. In 1869, Hyatt invented celluloid, a plastic-like substance made from paper (or wood) fiber that was the forerunner of plastic. The New York firm Phelan and Collender offered a $10,000 prize to anyone who could invent a satisfactory replacement for the ivory they used to make billiard balls. Hyatt decided to win that prize.

Hyatt conducted a long series of experiments in his New York City apartment, mixing whatever chemicals he could afford with anything that offered him carbon chain molecules to work with. One of the substances he often started with was paper. Paper was cheap. Paper came from wood. And wood was built from carbon chain molecules.

One afternoon in late 1869, Hyatt tried dunking paper in a bath of sulfuric acid and nitric acid. The dark liquid bubbled. Fumes rose to sting his eyes. The rank smell made him

cover his nose and turn away. At the bottom of his glass tray lay a lump of cellulose nitrate—what the paper had turned into. But it was not strong enough to substitute for ivory.

Rather than abandon his creation, Hyatt began to experiment with cellulose nitrate to
see if another additive or process could harden it. In one of these tests, he added camphor
and then baked it at high temperatures. This produced a material he named *celluloid*. Celluloid dried hard, cool, reflective, and smooth. It looked like ivory or tortoise shell. Hyatt won
the $10,000 prize. In addition to billiard balls, his celluloid was used for piano keys and
utensils.

Plastic was invented 40 years later (in 1909) as the result of idle play. Belgian-born
chemist Leo Hendrik Baekeland had made his fortune in 1898 by selling his formula for the
first commercially successful photographic paper to George Eastman. A curious experi-
menter by nature, Baekeland was now free to pursue any whim that attracted him.

Baekeland set up a private chem lab in his spacious New York apartment and began to
experiment. In 1908 (at age 45), he was playing with formaldehyde and phenol (two common organic substances) and created a fizzing, foaming reaction that produced billows of
foul smelling, dense yellow smoke. He didn't know what to expect. He was simply trying as
many different experiments as he could, hoping to create synthetic shellac (a substance
much needed for the new electronics industry).

This particular experiment produced a resinous material—hard and amber colored. At
first Baekeland thought it was just trash—another failed experiment. Some urge kept him
from throwing this amber-colored lump away.

Weeks later he began to experiment with the amber lump, adding other chemicals (and
combinations of chemicals) to it to see what he would produce. He played with over 1,000
combinations. One proved to be surprisingly heat resistant and still moldable. He named it
Bakelite and found that it would soften under extreme heat and be moldable to any shape or
form and that it would then hold this new shape when it cooled. Bakelite was waterproof,
corrosion proof, a good electrical insulator, and yet easy to cut and to shape. Baekeland had
invented plastic.

What's Happened Since Then?

New uses for plastic seemed to materialize every day. It became the wonder material of
the early twentieth century. In addition, new forms of plastic were soon invented. PVC
(polyvinyl chloride) was invented in Germany in 1913 but did not come into major worldwide use until after World War II.

Polystyrene was also created in Germany (in 1929), but didn't gain much notice or
popularity until it began to be used as a packing material in the 1960s. It is now also used as
insulation in refrigerators, dishwashers, etc. Polyethylene was invented in 1933 in England
by Imperial Chemicals Industries and was used to create Teflon®, synthetic fabrics, etc.
Plexiglas was invented in 1932 by Julius Nieuwland, a Catholic priest in Montreal, and has
been used for everything from aircraft cockpit windows to decorative tabletops and contact
lenses.

Fun Fact: A tower built of plastic LEGO® blocks in 1998 used 391,478 blocks to reach a height of 82 feet. It holds the record for the tallest LEGO building ever built.

More to Explore

Aaseng, Nathan. *Twentieth-Century Inventors.* New York: Facts on File, 1996.

Clark, Allison. *Tupperware: The Promise of Plastic.* Washington, DC: Smithsonian Institution Press, 1999.

Cobb, Cathy. *Creations of Fire.* New York: Perseus Publications, 2001.

Dyson, James. *A History of Great Inventions.* New York: Carroll & Graf Publishers, 2001.

Lambert, Mark. *Plastics.* New York: Rourke Enterprises, 1995.

McNeil, Ian. *An Encyclopedia of the History of Technology.* New York: Routledge, 1996.

Meikle, Jeffrey. *American Plastic.* Piscataway, NJ: Rutgers University Press, 1997.

Yenne, Bill. *100 Inventions That Shaped World History.* New York: Bluewood Books, 1993.

Assembly Line

Year of Invention: 1913

> **What Is It?** A systematic approach to manufacturing in which a product moves through the assembly line while stationary workers add one piece per station to it as it passes.
>
> **Who Invented It?** Henry Ford (in Detroit, Michigan)

Why Is *This* Invention One of the 100 Greatest?

Henry Ford's assembly line production made cars affordable. It also greatly increased worker productivity and acted as a model that was quickly adopted by virtually every manufacturing process in the Western world. Before Ford's assembly line, most automobile workers were skilled mechanics and craftsmen. On the assembly line, workers needed little training or skill since they performed menial, specific, repetitive tasks. The assembly line redefined the workplace and the expectations of workers and employees.

History of the Invention

What Did People Do Before?

Karl Benz invented the automobile in the 1880s. Within a decade, hundreds of small companies were building cars in America and Europe.

However, each car was hand-made. Many of the pieces and parts (especially the body—or "coach"—work) were hand crafted for each individual car. Car manufacturing plants hired skilled mechanics and metal workers to fit each car together. The process required many hours of labor. Cars were expensive—too expensive for average people to afford. As the twentieth century rolled in, automobiles were playthings of the wealthy—like yachts are today.

How Was the Assembly Line Invented?

At age 16 (in 1874), Henry Ford left the family Michigan farm, quit school, and moved to Detroit to apprentice in a machine shop. There he learned to use specialized tools to make metal parts from fire hydrants to valves. In 1891 (and after a 10-year stint back on the farm), the Edison Illuminating (Light) Company of Detroit offered Ford a job because of his machine shop experience.

Ford still worked for Edison in 1896 when one of the district engineers showed him a magazine article "How to Build a Gasoline Engine." Ford was fascinated and began to build a series of his own cars and, between 1898 and 1902, he helped to start two auto companies that both quickly failed.

Ford also raced his cars and, by setting a speed record during a 1905 race, he gained enough backing to start his own car company—one of literally hundreds of garage-size car companies struggling to build and sell enough cars to stay alive.

Ford believed that there existed a vast market for moderately priced, better-engineered cars. However, that meant drastically cutting the labor cost to build each car.

In 1906, Ford (now 41) began to search for ways to improve manufacturing efficiency. First, he redesigned the Model T's cylinder block so that it could be cast in a single piece. Next he converted to electronic ignition. Finally, he enclosed the body of the car, the first enclosed car model—all for $825!

Ford sold 19,000 Model T cars in 1908, the car's first year of production. He sold 78,400 the second. Rather than being pleased, Ford felt bitter frustration because he knew that he could sell more if he could only produce more.

He divided car production into steps—engine, chassis, body, and electrical ignition. He assigned different workers to specialize in each area instead of working on a car start to finish.

In 1911, he decided to revamp the entire production system. He ordered that every *part* must be exactly the same for every car. Next, he ordered that his factory would make every *car* exactly the same. Customers would not be able to custom design Ford cars.

Finally, Ford hired efficiency expert Frederick Taylor to watch how Ford's employees worked and to suggest more efficient ways of doing things. One worker built (for example) the entire ignition system magneto, moving about the plant to collect individual parts. Workers wasted too much time moving (walking).

In 1912, Ford visited a slaughter house and was impressed by the continuously moving line of carcasses. He decided to use this model for his factory.

In 1913, Ford created his first assembly line following the slaughterhouse model. This line would build only the electrical ignition magneto for each car. Workers stood in one spot. The magneto moved from station to station down a conveyor belt. Each station had bins of the specific parts, screws, bolts, and tools that person would need. No man performed more than three steps at his station, and then he put the assembly back on the conveyor belt to advance to the next station.

This assembly line cut production time from over an hour to less than 13 minutes for each magneto. Ford added a second assembly line for the Model T engine. Then he added a third for the chassis—a 300-foot long overhead drive belt. Each identical chassis hung by chains from this overhead conveyor. Workers welded or bolted parts to it as it inched forward. Chassis construction was cut from 13.5 hours to 1.3 hours. Late that year, Ford installed his final assembly line. This one was for the actual assembly of the finished cars. Ford's factory could now build a car in 93 minutes!

What's Happened Since Then?

In 1915 Ford was able to cut the price of a model T to as low as $290. People lined up at his showroom to buy Model Ts. Ford quickly became one of the richest men in the world. In 1916, he doubled his workers' pay to $5.00 a day—so all his workers could afford the cars they built. By 1920, every automaker in America had followed Ford's lead and created production assembly lines. By 1930, an assembly line was built into every new and revamped factory in the Western world.

Interestingly, there is a modern trend away from the crushing monotony and boredom of automaton-like assembly line work and back toward pre-Ford construction concepts that bolster worker pride and worker involvement. Several automakers are using the fact that their workers stay with a car from start to finish as a major selling point. It is clear that Ford's production model has serious drawbacks that affect worker satisfaction and productivity.

 Fun Fact: Assembly lines use over 95 percent of all robots. The most popular assembly line robot is the PUMA (Programmable Universal Machine for Assembly), invented by Vic Scheinman in 1953.

More to Explore

Aird, Hazel B. *Henry Ford: Young Man with Idea*s. New York: Aladdin Books, 1995.

Brown, David. *Inventing Modern America*. Cambridge, MA: The MIT Press, 2002.

Jeffries, Michael, and Gary Lewis. *Inventors and Inventions.* New York: Smithmark, 1997.

Lacey, Robert. *Ford: The Men and the Machine*. Boston: Little Brown, 1996.

McNeil, Ian. *An Encyclopedia of the History of Technology.* New York: Routledge, 1996.

Pollard, Michael. *Henry Ford*. New York: Thomson Gale, 2003.

Schaefer, Lola M. *Henry Ford*. Mankato, MN: Capstone Press, 2000.

Wyborny, Sheila. *Henry Ford*. New York: Thomson Gale, 2002.

Zarzycki, Daryl. *Henry Ford and the Assembly Line*. London: Mitchell Lane Publishers, 2004.

Sonar

Year of Invention: 1916

> **What Is It?** A system that uses sound waves transmitted through the water to detect underwater objects.
>
> **Who Invented It?** Paul Langevin (in Portsmouth, England)

Why Is *This* Invention One of the 100 Greatest?

Sonar saved hundreds of ships and tens of thousands of lives from attacks by German submarines during World War I and many times that number during World War II. After the wars, active sonar systems made long-range submarine navigation possible. Sonar has made ocean transportation safe and has provided a way for fishing fleets to actively seek out and find schools of fish to catch.

History of the Invention

What Did People Do Before?

Whales have used active sonar for tens of millions of years to guide their underwater path. They broadcast sprays of low-frequency sound waves and read the returning echoes to create a mental image of the water in front of them.

As World War I started, German submarine fleets prowled the North Atlantic like packs of wolves preying on British and French shipping. Surface ships couldn't spot the subs until it was too late.

How Was Sonar Invented?

Sonar was developed because of a desperate need in World War I. The German sub fleet sank thousands of tons of British cargo during the early years of the war. There seemed to be no way for the British Navy to stop them.

The problem reached its climax when a German sub torpedoed the passenger ship *Lusitania* in the spring of 1915 off the coast of Ireland. The *Lusitania* sank in 18 minutes, and 1,198 civilian passengers drowned or froze before help arrived.

In response, the British War Department created the Board of Invention and Research. One of the groups within that organization was the Section on Submarine Detection and Telegraphy. That section was given a massive budget and ordered to get results NOW.

The Sub Detection Section tried everything they could think of. They confined merchant shipping to escorted convoys. That helped, but German subs still roamed the British and Irish coastlines and attacked ships after they left a convoy to head for port or before they rendezvoused with their assigned convoy.

The Section experimented with dowsing rods (often used to find water on land), trying to find a way to make them respond to underwater metal objects. It didn't work. They tried to train sea gulls to patrol the coast as sub-spotting scouts. It didn't work. They tried to train sea lions and seals to search for subs. They discussed equipping porpoises with metal detectors and training them to swim along assigned patrol routes.

Nothing worked.

American physicist Paul Langevin volunteered to help the British war effort and sailed to England in 1915. By November of that year he had joined the Sub Detection Section. Langevin knew from acoustic studies that low frequency sound waves travel for great distances underwater. He recorded the sounds of British naval ship propellers and engines and found that they contained low-frequency, rhythmic beats that should travel for many miles underwater.

However, in 1915 no electrical recording devices existed that could be placed underwater. In early 1916, Langevin read that American researchers had found that some crystals (quartz in this case) created a different electrical charge on opposite sides of the crystal when subjected to physical pressure. They called it the *piezo-electric* effect. Langevin conducted tests to see if the pressure wave of low-frequency underwater sound waves would be sufficient to create this effect in quartz crystals.

When this test worked, Langevin suggested that new piezo-electric microphones could be mounted in underwater housings to detect the sound of a passing ship—or submarine. He spent several weeks redesigning the microphone to make it highly directional (able to detect sounds from only one direction at a time) so that operators could identify the direction of a sub as well as its presence.

Langevin called the device a *hydrophone*. He named the whole system *Sound Navigation and Ranging*.

The Navy tested Langevin's hydrophone by trailing it below a Navy ship. It accurately "heard" and located the engines and propellers of two other nearby surface ships.

In early April 1916, a line of hydrophones was deployed, each dangling from the stern of a British Navy ship. These 20 initial hydrophones were spread along major shipping routes near the English coast.

On April 23, two weeks after deployment, two of Langevin's hydrophones detected their first target. A pair of cruisers converged, opened fire, and sank the German sub. Langevin's system was immediately hailed as a turning point in the Atlantic war.

What's Happened Since Then?

In 1917, the British shortened the name **SO**und **NA**vigation and **R**anging to sonar. By mid-1918, they had developed *active sonar*. Passive sonar systems (like Langevin's) waited quietly to detect a sound made by an enemy ship. Active systems broadcast "pings" (strong single sounds) and listened for a returning echo off solid objects in the ocean. Active sonar could detect a sub that had submerged and shut off its engines in an attempt to hide. Active sonar was used extensively during World War II.

In the mid-1960s the U.S. Navy deployed its SOSUS net across the north Atlantic and Pacific Oceans. This net contained lines of stationary sonar stations capable of detecting and tracking any motorized vessel within 500 miles of the American coast.

In the late 1980s, marine biologists proved that the Navy's sonar tests were responsible for hundreds of whale deaths. The future of active sonar seems limited because of the severe damage it causes to whales' ears.

 Fun Fact: Military sonar gives whales the bends, causing them to strand themselves on the beach.

More to Explore

Cooper, Christopher. *Sound: From Doppler to Sonar.* Portsmouth, NH: Heinemann Publishing, 2003.

Cox, Albert W. *Sonar and Underwater Sound.* New York: Simon & Schuster, 1994.

Dyson, James. *A History of Great Inventions.* New York: Carroll & Graf Publishers, 2001.

Hartcup, Guy. *The Effects of Science on the Second World War.* New York: Palgrave Macmillan, 2003.

Price-Hossell, Karen. *Sonar.* Portsmouth, NH: Heinemann Library Publishing, 2003.

Williams, Kathleen. *Secret Weapon: U. S. High-Frequency Direction Finding in the Battle of the Atlantic.* Annapolis, MD: Naval Institute Press, 1996.

Frozen Food

Year of Invention: 1927

> **What Is It?** Food frozen so that it may be later thawed and eaten without loss of flavor or texture.
>
> **Who Invented It?** Charles Birdseye (in Brooklyn, New York)

Why Is *This* Invention One of the 100 Greatest?

How much of what you eat comes out of the freezer? Frozen food is one of the most important advances in food technology in a thousand years.

Freezing prevents spoilage, rot, and putrefaction. Freezing prevents the spread of disease and preserves food's nutrition, flavor, and texture. Frozen foods have expanded the geographic range of food distribution and the seasons in which important seasonal foods are available. Frozen foods have also made meal preparation faster and more convenient.

History of the Invention

What Did People Do Before?

Historically, people ate what was available locally in season. They caught and ate the game that migrated through. They ate fruits and roots when they matured. Once produced, food had to be eaten quickly (within days) before rot and disease-causing bacteria destroyed it. Drying and salting were two food preservation systems people had developed by 4000 B.C.. Cold became popular as a way to preserve food by 1500 B.C.

Early humans knew that refrigeration and freezing delayed putrefaction and preserved foods. Ice cellars were in use by the Chinese and Greeks by 1000 B.C.. However, food once frozen usually thawed mushy and tasteless.

In 1795, Frenchman Nicolas Appert invented food canning in order to win the 12,000-franc award offered by Napoleon for a new food preservation system. Canning expanded to four the list of available food preservation technologies (joining drying, salting, and refrigeration).

How Was Frozen Food Invented?

Born in upstate New York in 1886, Charles Birdseye was a biology major at Amherst College (in Massachusetts) when he was forced to quit school to earn money. He took a job as a naturalist for the U.S. government and was assigned to work on several Arctic population studies from 1909 to 1911. During this period, Birdseye became acquainted with fur traders. In 1912 and again in 1916 he made yearlong trips to Labrador (in northeast Canada) to study fur trading.

During these trips, Birdseye often froze his catch after a day of fishing. During his 1916 trip, he noticed that fish caught and frozen during the bitter cold of January and February tasted better when thawed and cooked than did fish frozen in April or in the fall. Trappers and fur traders said that they had observed the same thing.

Birdseye suspected that it had something to do with how the fish were frozen. Extending his 1916 trip, he studied native food freezing habits (duck, caribou, bear, fish, etc.) and concluded that food preserved better if it had been frozen quickly. But he had no idea why that should be the case.

Back in the United States, Birdseye borrowed lab space in his home town of Brooklyn, New York. He froze various foods and then watched through a powerful microscope as they thawed. He found that most frozen food contained jagged ice crystals. As the food began to thaw and individual cells softened, these ice crystals tore through the cell walls of the meat or vegetables. Cell fluid—including the food's nutrients—drained away. The thawed food turned into a mushy and tasteless mess.

However, when foods were fast frozen (frozen at extremely low temperatures and frozen quickly) ice crystals didn't have time to form. The food thawed as crisp and tasty as when it had been fresh. After more study, Birdseye found that ice crystals formed over a very narrow temperature range. If the food cooled through that narrow temperature range quickly enough, ice crystals wouldn't form.

From 1920 through 1924, Birdseye experimented with different techniques for fast freezing foods through the dangerous ice-crystal-forming temperature range. In 1924, he settled on a process he called "flash freezing" and formed the General Seafoods Company to market waxed cartons of flash frozen fish and rabbit. Birdseye's flash freezing process used double conveyor belts to pass food between two super-cold metal plates. By 1925, Birdseye had expanded into a variety of meat, fish, and vegetables.

What's Happened Since Then?

Sales were slow for Birdseye's frozen food. Few stores had freezers in which to display frozen food. Further, the public was suspicious of Birdseye's claim that his frozen food tasted as good as fresh. In 1934, Birdseye began to manufacture freezer display cases and leased them to stores well below cost so that the stores would be more interested in carrying Birdseye's frozen food. In 1938 he leased a fleet of refrigerated rail cars to distribute his frozen foods across the country.

Still, frozen food didn't become popular until World War II, when rationing restricted the availability of canned foods. By 1948, frozen foods were a staple of every store and home. In 1952, Betty Cronin invented TV dinners for Swanson Brother's Food. Frozen pizza first entered store freezer cases in 1958. Our reliance on frozen foods is steadily increasing as microwave cooking becomes the mainstay of American meal preparation.

Fun Fact: The Army now issues freeze-dried, packaged meals to troops in the field. Just add water and it rehydrates the food and activates a chemical heating pad that heats the meal piping hot with no flame.

More to Explore

Cole, David. *Encyclopedia of Modern Everyday Inventions*. Westport, CT: Greenwood Group, 2003.

Dyson, James. *A History of Great Inventions*. New York: Carroll & Graf Publishers, 2001.

Editors of Time-Life Books. *Inventive Genius*. Alexandria, VA: Time-Life Books, 2001.

Shepard, Sue. *Pickled, Potted, and Canned*. New York: Simon & Schuster, 2001.

St. George, Judith. *So You Want to Be an Inventor*. New York: Philomel Books, 2002.

Vare, Ethlie Ann, and Greg Ptacek. *Patently Female: Stories of Women Inventors*. New York: John Wiley & Sons, 2002.

Wulffson, Don. *Extraordinary Stories Behind the Invention of Ordinary Things*. London: Lothrop, Lee & Shepard Books, 1996.

Television

Year of Invention: 1927

What Is It? An electronic system for recording, instantly transmitting, and displaying moving images.

Who Invented It? Philo Farnsworth (in San Francisco)

Why Is *This* Invention One of the 100 Greatest?

Television radically changed the way we market ideas and products; the way we seek news, information, education and entertainment; and the way we use and allocate free time. Television has connected the world in a way neither still pictures nor radio could do. It has shown us what the rest of world looks like and how other peoples live and act.

On the down side, television has contributed to a sedentary life style. The term "couch potato" was created to describe those who watch large amounts of TV. Many studies have linked television to an increased prevalence of eating disorders, indifference to violence, fear of the outside world, and reduced self-image. For good and for bad, television has changed modern lives, attitudes, and values.

History of the Invention

What Did People Do Before?

From earliest times, traveling minstrels and storytellers delivered news and entertainment. By 1500, masses of books existed thanks to the printing press. Newspapers followed in the seventeenth century.

In the late 1800s, publishers added magazines to their offerings to meet the information and entertainment needs of the public. By the first years of the twentieth century, commercial radio had come of age. Movies joined the popular entertainment choices in the 1920s with the advent of sound.

How Was Television Invented?

Three men claimed to be the father of television. Two worked in America, one in England. The Englishman, John Baird, technically was the first to build a working television. However, his system was a mechanical system that depended on two synchronized spinning disks, similar in concept to the picture produced by flipping through pages of cartoon drawings to create motion. It was a dead-end technology, completely abandoned by 1936.

One of the other two men was Russian American Vladimir Zworykin, who worked as an engineer at the Westinghouse Corporation. In early 1924 he invented what he called an *iconoscope*, an electronic forerunner of the picture tube.

The industry had high hopes for Zworykin's research. But his progress stalled. The iconoscope was a huge and important step forward, but it was not a complete television system. Zworykin didn't complete his design until 1933. By that time, Philo Farnsworth's electronic television system had existed for five years. Zworykin was also accused of stealing ideas from Farnsworth.

Born in rural Utah in 1906, Philo Farnsworth spent his early years occasionally attending school and more often working on the family farm. However, even as a boy, he was passionately fascinated by electricity and read everything he could about research to merge electricity and light into television.

In 1923, while working in a United Way office to make ends meet, Philo (still a thin, frail-looking teenager) met two professional fund-raisers, George Everson and Leslie Gorell. They agreed to finance the development of Farnsworth's television design if he would move his work to California.

First in Los Angeles and then in San Francisco, Philo worked nonstop in his rented apartment lab. Always intense and high-strung, Farnsworth worked with the shades drawn both for secrecy and to control light in his "studio." The work was made more difficult because he worked alone on new technologies. Most of the pieces of equipment he needed did not exist and had to be scrounged or fabricated from what parts he could find.

Vacuum tubes were a constant expense. In one afternoon, Philo burned up over 50 of them when he forgot to connect the surge protector on his power grid. The giant cathode ray tubes and image dissector tubes (his version of a picture tube) had to be made of specially ordered handblown glass. He had to design electric preheating ovens for several circuits. He had to construct his own magnetic lenses to control the picture tube's electron beams.

A constant procession of odd-looking boxes and jars of supplies flowed into the lab. On one occasion, the strange deliveries and Farnsworth's secretive behavior led to a police raid. This was during Prohibition (a national ban on the production or sale of alcohol), and they expected to find him making alcohol. They found nothing illegal, but refused to believe Farnsworth's story that he was inventing television and grilled him for hours before reluctantly leaving.

In May 1927, Farnsworth was ready to show his system. Eight men stood in his rented living room staring—some expectantly, some skeptically—at a small screen that glowed with hissing static.

In rolled-up shirt sleeves and bow tie, 22-year-old Philo Farnsworth flipped the power switches on the camera, amplifiers, and transmitter. Wavy lines rolled across the screen and slowly resolved into the image of a dollar bill, which faded into a short clip of a boxing match, and then to a clip of movie star Mary Pickford combing her hair. One amazed observer claimed that the images, "jumped out at us from the screen."

In 1928, after another year of system improvements, Farnsworth held press conferences in his laboratory and displayed television images of movie stars and famous scientists to declare his success to the world.

What's Happened Since Then?

Philco, General Electric, and Radio Corporation of American (RCA) were working on their own systems. By late 1928 they had all acknowledged the advantages of Farnsworth's system and offered to purchase his invention. Farnsworth signed a deal with Philco in 1931, quit in 1934, and signed with RCA in 1939.

However, it wasn't until 1947 that GE developed the first cheap, practical television sets. By 1949, so many families owned a television that companies lined up to sponsor shows.

Color TV (Trinitron) was invented by the Japanese Sony Corporation in 1968. The first cable TV system was introduced in the early 1980s. Now private satellite dishes have replaced rabbit ears, and families expect to have access to a wide range of specialty channels never dreamed of 30 years ago.

Over the past five years, personal computers have developed to the point where they are now capable of replacing televisions. It may be that the days of the television set are numbered.

 Fun Fact: The average American school-age child watches 19.8 hours of television every week. That makes TV a half-time job for American youth!

More to Explore

Aaseng, Nathan. *American Profiles: Twentieth-Century Inventors.* New York: Facts on File, 1991.

Barnouw, Erik. *Tube of Plenty: The Evolution of American Television.* New York: Oxford University Press, 1990.

Everson, George. *The Story of Television: The Life of Philo T. Farnsworth.* New York: Arno Press, 1974.

Farnsworth, Philo. "Electron Multiplier Tubes and Their Uses." *Journal of the Franklin Institute* 218 (1934).

Hofer, Stephen. *Philo Farnsworth: The Quiet Contributor to Television.* Bowling Green, KY: Bowling Green University Press, 1977.

McPherson, Stephanie Sammartino. *TV's Forgotten Hero: The Story of Philo Farnsworth.* Minneapolis, MN: Carolrhoda Books, 1996.

Schwartz, Evan. "Who Really Invented Television?" *Technology Review* (September–October 2000): 26–34.

Cyclotron

Year of Invention: 1931

What Is It? An electromagnetic machine that accelerates atomic and subatomic particles to near light speed.

Who Invented It? Ernest Lawrence (Berkeley, California)

Why Is *This* Invention One of the 100 Greatest?

Every discovery in subatomic physics after 1930 depended on a cyclotron or its offspring. The cyclotron, the original "atom smasher," has been called the greatest subatomic research tool ever created and opened the world of subatomic (smaller than an atom) physics to detailed, systematic research. Our understanding of the subatomic world comes from what was learned on the cyclotron. This invention stands as one of the major tuning points for physics research.

History of the Invention

What Did People Do Before?

Marie Curie cracked open the door to the subatomic world. Before 1900 scientists believed that the atom was the smallest possible particle, the basic building block of all matter.

Then Marie, with her husband Pierre Curie, discovered that tiny particles (radioactivity) flew out of some atoms. That meant that the atom could not be the smallest particle of matter. Something—possibly many somethings—must exist inside every atom!

Over the next 25 years, hundreds of scientists struggled to peer inside the atom and discover the new basic building blocks of all matter. They struggled to understand what structures made up an atom.

However, there was no way for scientists to intentionally smash open an atom. They had to wait for atoms (most commonly radium atoms) to naturally disintegrate.

How Was the Cyclotron Invented?

Twenty-seven-year-old Ernest Lawrence abandoned his undergraduate and early postgraduate studies in photoelectric research once he arrived at the University of California, Berkeley, campus in 1928. Instead, he jumped into the exciting new on-campus department studying nuclear physics. Berkeley theorists were hard at work deducing the inner workings of atoms from the scant clues they had been able to gather.

Lawrence realized that theorists were making little more than educated guesses. They needed to crash protons and electrons into other particles because these collisions would provide the data they needed to finally understand subatomic structure. However, those pesky particles flew in uncontrolled and random directions and rarely went where the scientists needed them to go. Scientists needed a way to control the movement of subatomic particles so that they always hit their targets and produced useful experimental data.

In 1929, Lawrence read an article about a failed attempt by a Norwegian physicist to use massive electric currents to accelerate a proton to near light speed. Lawrence realized that this approach had a huge problem: high electrical energy meant high danger. Two researchers had already been electrocuted while trying to operate the Norwegian system.

However, the article brought an idea into Lawrence's mind. He could avoid such high voltages if he boosted the particle's energy with regular *small* hits of electric energy. He envisioned his particles like children on a swing. Those children swung as high as they wanted, not because someone gave them one mighty shove, but because the pusher gave them many small pushes, each adding just a tiny bit of extra energy.

Lawrence decided that the easiest way to control protons and electrons long enough to slowly accelerate them to near light speed was with a magnetic field. It would have to be a powerful magnetic field in order to keep high-speed particles from escaping.

Now Lawrence had to build the hardware to make his idea work. It was an ordinary snail's shell that gave Lawrence the idea to design his particle accelerator as a spiral. Protons would be captured at the center and slowly spiral outward along a path defined by a magnetic field. With each lap, a jolt of electricity would add extra speed to the particle's travels. In this way, Lawrence could force a particle to accelerate through thousands of spiral orbits in a very small space.

It took over a year to design the alternating electric field and magnetic field to work in unison and to accurately guide a charged particle along its spiral path. Equipment shattered during high-stress tests. Parts failed under these new kinds of high-energy loads. Improved parts had to be designed and built.

On January 2, 1931, Lawrence completed the first successful cyclotron test. It used a tiny 4½-inch chamber and accelerated particles to 80,000 electronvolts (a measure of particle energy). It was far short of the atom-smashing power he needed, but it was a start. Two years later, with a 34-inch cyclotron and an 85-ton high-energy magnet, Lawrence accelerated particles to over one million electronvolts, at which point they approached the speed of light.

What's Happened Since Then?

The cyclotron was a turning point in physics and medical research. One of the first applications of cyclotron technology was for cancer research and for the creation of radiation therapy. One of the first test patients of this revolutionary therapy was Lawrence's own mother, successfully treated for cancer in 1937.

In the ensuing years, Lawrence conducted countless experiments on larger and larger cyclotrons. He created new, man-made elements. He isolated the specific isotope of uranium (U^{235}) used for research and development of America's atomic bomb. He studied and revealed the inner workings of the atoms of dozens of elements. He created never-before-available opportunities to study new subatomic particles.

Two improvements to Lawrence's cyclotron were created in the 1950s and 1960s. The first was the Betatron, an accelerator that kept particles traveling in a perfect circle instead of a fixed spiral. Circling allowed greater flexibility in designing research parameters for the experiment being created. The second was a linear accelerator. Often many miles in length, linear accelerators allowed researchers to achieve particle speeds closer to light speed than was possible in a spiral or circular accelerator.

 Fun Fact: The European science research facility, CERN, houses the world's largest accelerator. It is an underground circular accelerator 17 *miles* in diameter!

More to Explore

Childs, Herbert. *An American Genius: The Life of Ernest Lawrence*. New York: Sutton, 1988.

Davis, Nuel. *Lawrence and Oppenheimer*. New York: Da Capo Press, 1996.

Haven, Kendall, and Donna Clark. *100 Most Popular Scientists for Young Adults*. Englewood, CO: Libraries Unlimited, 1999.

Heilbron, J. L. *Lawrence and His Laboratory*. Berkeley: University of California Press, 1993.

Lomask, Milton. *Invention and Technology Great Lives*. New York: Charles Scribner's Sons, 1994.

National Geographic Society. *Those Inventive Americans*. Washington, DC: National Geographic Society, 1991.

Radar

Year of Invention: 1935

> **What Is It?** A device that uses the reflections of pulses of high-energy radio waves to detect and locate moving metal objects.
>
> **Who Invented It?** Robert Watson-Watt (in England)

Why Is *This* Invention One of the 100 Greatest?

Radar is a lifesaver. During World War II, radar stations warned England of approaching German air raids. Airborne radar detected German submarines and made Atlantic and Mediterranean shipping safer for thousands of sailors.

Radar is the essential heart of all air traffic control and has made commercial air travel safe. Marine radar systems have reduced ship collisions and deaths by over 90 percent. Since the early 1950s, improved weather prediction has been based on radar systems.

History of the Invention

What Did People Do Before?

Bats have used radar to locate both food and obstacles for millions of years. There are even moths that have developed "stealth" technology using thick, powdery coatings to absorb a bat's radar beams and avoid creating the reflective echoes that guide a hungry bat to dinner.

In 1888, Heinrich Hertz discovered radio waves. In 1900, Nikola Tesla described a system for using Hertz's radio waves to identify and locate moving objects. However, few paid any attention to this seemingly wild idea.

In 1918 a detection system similar to radar (active sonar) was invented and tested. Sonar uses sound waves and is used underwater where low-frequency sound waves can travel for thousands of miles.

How Was Radar Invented?

The equipment needed to build a successful radar unit existed in 1915. However, no one thought of building one for another 20 years.

In 1924, Sir Edward Appleton bounced radio waves off the upper atmospheric ionosphere (part of his experiments to prove that the ionosphere actually existed). These experiments reminded researchers in the United States, France, Germany, the United Kingdom,

Russia, and Switzerland that their radio waves could bounce off a variety of surfaces. Guglielmo Marconi (inventor of the radio) lectured about the potential of radio waves to detect nearby ships and prevent collisions at sea.

In Great Britain, the push for developing radio wave weapons stemmed from one disastrous test in the fall of 1934. In an attempt to provide a system to warn defenders of approaching enemy aircraft, the British army experimented with massive concrete acoustical mirrors with sensitive microphones at their focal point. On the morning of the system demonstration for generals and dignitaries, a Royal Air Force bomber approached the coast as scheduled. However, at the same time, a milk truck rattled past the site, overwhelming the microphone with its own noise. The plane roared past without being detected by the system's operator.

Alarmed by this failure, British military leaders ordered all departments to search for advanced weapon and detection systems. In early 1935, 43-year-old British National Physics Lab physicist Robert Watson-Watt was ordered to investigate the possibility of using a beam of radio waves as a death-ray weapon. Watson-Watt set up a secret lab at Bawetsey Manor on England's east coast.

It took Watson-Watt less than a weak to confirm what he already believed. Radio waves could not kill.

However, as part of his report, Watson-Watt needed to document his findings and measure the exact power of the radio frequency energy waves he sprayed into the atmosphere. He set up receivers to record the energy levels of his waves. While making recordings he noticed occasional blips (higher energy spikes) on the oscilloscope he used to monitor his tests.

He watched more closely and discovered that the odd blips were reflections of his own radio waves off passing aircraft. He contacted a nearby air base to schedule flybys and found that his radio waves could detect passing planes at ranges up to 75 miles.

He presented his findings in a report titled "Radio Detection and Ranging" (which became the official name of the system), and he arranged a demonstration for army top brass in March 1935. During the test, a British bomber flew back and forth just off the coast. Watson-Watt hooked his receiver to an oscilloscope for the generals to watch. The round oscilloscope screen showed a flat green line across its middle. But when the transmitter rotated to point at the distant, unseen plane, a strong vertical blip jumped onto the screen and a "beep" sounded through the system speakers. A technician read the direction and distance of the plane. These readings were confirmed by radio contact with the pilot.

By early 1939, 20 radar stations had been constructed to guard the approaches up the Thames River estuary toward London. (It was American scientists who shortened **Ra**dio **D**etection **a**nd **R**anging to *radar* in late 1940.)

What's Happened Since Then?

In 1940, John Randall and Henry Boot at Birmingham University invented the cavity magnetron, a device that produced a compact, powerful burst of short-wave, extremely high-frequency radio waves—perfect for generating larger radar echoes. Using a magnetron generator, English radar units could accurately detect airplanes up to 200 miles away.

One of the first U.S. radar units was installed in Hawaii, northwest of Honolulu, in late November 1941 for testing. Early on the morning of December 7, 1941, that radar detected a great mass of approaching aircraft. Army commanders assumed the system was malfunctioning and ignored the readings. That mass was the Japanese force arriving to attack Pearl Harbor.

Radar-defeating *stealth* technology was first developed in 1945 by German scientists to protect their submarines. They painted a mixture of graphite and rubber over the sub's skin to absorb radar signals. Beginning in the 1970s, stealth technology was applied to aircraft. Coatings were sprayed onto airplane wings that could absorb microwave energy and prevent a telltale echo from developing.

Radar units rapidly developed and improved during the postwar years and became the backbone of air traffic control and weather warning systems. There is no system or technology in development that will replace radar's central role in these critical functions.

 Fun Fact: Venus is the hottest planet—hot enough to melt lead. It is also covered by dense clouds that prevented scientists from studying its surface. Radar telescopes have made it possible to see through the clouds and study Venus's surface.

More to Explore

Brown, Louis. *A Radar History of World War II: Technical and Military Imperatives*. New York: Institute of Physics Publishing, 1999.

Dyson, James. *A History of Great Inventions*. New York: Carroll & Graf Publishers, 2001.

McNeil, Ian. *An Encyclopedia of the History of Technology*. New York: Routledge, 1996.

Swords, Seán, ed. *Technical History of the Beginnings of Radar*. London: P. Peregrinus on behalf of the Institution of Electrical Engineers, 1986.

Taylor, Mike. *Weapons of World War II*. New York: ABDO Publishing Company, 1998.

van Dulken, Stephen. *Inventing the 20th Century*. New York: New York University Press, 2000.

Von Kroge, H., ed. *Gema: Birthplace of German Radar and Sonar*. New York: Institute of Physics Publishing, 2000.

Wiley, Richard G. *Electronic Intelligence: The Interception of Radar Signals*. New York: Artech House, Inc, 1995.

Yenne, Bill. *100 Inventions That Shaped World History*. New York: Bluewood Books, 1993.

Nylon (Synthetic Fabrics)

Year of Invention: 1937

> **What Is It?** The first man-made, synthetic fabric produced in a chemistry lab.
>
> **Who Invented It?** Wallace Carothers (in Wilmington, Delaware)

Why Is *This* Invention One of the 100 Greatest?

By the early twentieth century, demand for natural fibers had begun to outstrip their supply. Science turned to the idea of creating artificial (synthetic) fibers to reduce the pressure on these plants and animal herds. The three most successful of these synthetic fabrics—nylon, rayon, and polyester—have accounted for almost 20 percent of total clothing sales over the past 30 years. If not for these synthetic fabrics, cotton and wool would likely be five to ten times as expensive as they now are.

History of the Invention

What Did People Do Before?

Charles Goodyear's vulcanized rubber (1839) counts as the first man-made clothing material, because raw rubber had to be mixed with chemical additives (magnesium, sulfur, and lime) and then fired in a furnace.

Throughout the second half of the nineteenth century, silk was a popular and fashionable material. Limited silk supplies meant that it was also expensive. Researchers in Europe and America sough a way to create "artificial silk."

British researchers C. F. Cross and E. J. Bevan and French scientist Louis de Chardonnet independently developed the same idea for "artificial silk." They washed a wood pulp (cellulose) fiber in caustic soda and treated it with a sulfur-carbon compound to create something called xanthate. Xanthate could be liquefied and then forced at high pressure through tiny spinneret holes to produce long, fine fibers. For 20 years these fibers were simply called artificial silk. In 1924, a British manufacturing company, Courtlaulds, renamed them rayon.

How Was Nylon Invented?

Life was never easy for Wallace Carothers. But the story of how he invented nylon is a tragedy of Shakespearean proportions. Shy, withdrawn, and uncomfortable with people, Carothers enrolled in a Missouri college in 1915 to become a teacher. After graduation he took a teaching job, but he developed a facial tick and insomnia from the stress of teaching. Unable to continue, he retreated to the university to study for his doctorate in chemistry.

In 1928, the DuPont Company offered Carothers a chance to lead an experimental research team at its Wilmington, Delaware, facility. The company gave him a lab, a budget, and a support staff and told him to create new synthetic fibers and materials.

Carothers decided to start his search for a new synthetic silk by using recent research into the structure of rubber. Other researchers had discovered that vulcanized rubber was made up of long chains of molecules called polymers. So Carothers built long carbon chain polymers in his lab. Then he and his team did everything they could think of to these polymers to see what would happen and what they could produce. They dumped them in acids and in bases. They added copper, magnesium, and every other metal and alloy they could find. They boiled them and froze them.

Carothers grew disillusioned and decided to search elsewhere. He issued the order to stop this line of research just as his team was conducting a new experiment in which they mixed hydrochloric acid with a kind of vinyl acetate derived from the original polymers. This combination produced a spongy, elastic material—interesting, but certainly not a suitable substitute for silk. Carothers decided not to pursue it. Others at DuPont picked up the research on this elastic compound and saw its potential. Dupont liked it, named it *neoprene,* and began to market the stuff.

The success of this product he had created—but had not been able to recognize— haunted Carothers. He withdrew more and more into his lab and away from people.

Beginning in 1933, he turned his attention to heavier, longer polymer chain molecules. Again the team produced thousands of new compounds that had to be individually tested. Virtually all proved worthless. One of these compounds, however, drew Carothers's attention. It looked like silk and was at least as strong as silk. However, he couldn't spin it into thread-like fibers because it melted too easily, and heat was required for the spinning process. Again, he set the compound aside.

In early 1935, Julian Hill, one of Carothers's team members, began working with polyester (a type of plastic). That spring he developed a new method for pulling strands of polyester from a liquid beaker-full of the stuff. His new method did not require heat and was called "cold-drawing."

Carothers took no notice. Another of his team members suggested that they try cold drawing on that synthetic polymer Carothers had set aside back in 1933. Carothers wasn't interested.

Others in his research team decided to try it. It worked.

DuPont named the substance *nylon* and was thrilled by its look, feel, and strength. After another 18 months of testing the company filed for a patent and began to market nylon in 1939.

Carothers did not live to see his miracle fiber become the wonder and rage of the 1940s and 1950s and the most successful synthetic fiber ever created. Depressed over his repeated failure to recognize the value of his creations, he took his own life in the same month that DuPont filed for the patent on his nylon.

What's Happened Since Then?

In 1941, James T. Dickson and John R. Whinfield (working in London under contract to DuPont) used Carothers's methods to invent Dacron. In the late 1940s various researchers invented five additional synthetics, including Orlon (1945) and Acrilon (1952).

In 1938 Roy Plunkett, working in a DuPont research lab, invented PTFE, another long-chain polymer (like nylon). DuPont marketed PTFE under the name Teflon. In 1956, electrical engineer Bill Gore turned to PTFE's as a possible way to create an improved insulation for electrical wire. A decade later (1969) Bill's son, chemist Bob Gore, discovered that PTFE fibers could be pulled into a porous, flexible material, and he named it Goretex.

 Fun Fact: U.S. mills now produce over 1.4 billion pounds of nylon every year. That's enough nylon for 500 pairs of stockings for every man, woman, and child in America.

More to Explore

Gaines, Ann. *Wallace Carothers and the Story of DuPont Nylon.* London: Mitchell Lane Publishing, 2001.

Haven, Kendall, and Donna Clark. *100 Most Popular Scientists for Young Adults.* Englewood, CO: Libraries Unlimited, 1999.

Hermes, Mathew, ed. *Enough for One Lifetime.* New York: American Chemical Society, 1996.

McNeil, Ian. *An Encyclopedia of the History of Technology.* New York: Routledge, 1996.

O'Reilly, Sue. *Textiles.* New York: Franklin Watts, 1997.

van Dulken, Stephen. *Inventing the 20th Century.* New York: New York University Press, 2000.

Yenne, Bill. *100 Inventions That Shaped World History.* New York: Bluewood Books, 1993.

Ballpoint Pen

Year of Invention: 1938

> **What Is It?** A writing device that dispenses ink with a small, rolling ball locked into the tip of an ink cartridge.
>
> **Who Invented It?** Ladislas and Georg Biro (in Hungary)

Why Is *This* Invention One of the 100 Greatest?

Ballpoint pens are the most recent invention in the string of four principal writing devices. Collectively, these inventions have made writing possible. You can't write without something to write with. Without a writing implement, there can be no mass literacy and no education system. No child ever learned to write without a pencil or crayon in hand. No business or store functions without a supply of pens. A pen is now the most basic and personal means to record and share any idea, emotion, thought, opinion, note, request, or information. A literate and democratic society relies on an open and constant exchange of ideas, and that still requires pens.

History of the Invention

What Did People Do Before?

The ballpoint pen follows three other notable writing inventions—quill pens, fountain pens, and pencils. Quill pens made from the tail feathers of birds date back to the dawn of humanity. Dip the quill tip in ink and it will carry enough ink for a few words before you have to dip again. However, quill pens were fragile, didn't last long, and tended to leave blobs of ink to smear across the page. Writers switched to metal tips (called nibs) for pens as early as the sixteenth century. However, available ink tended to quickly corrode most metal nibs, and quills still dominated writing until steel, corrosive-resistant nibs appeared in 1829.

In 1832, American John Parker invented the first "self-filling" (fountain) pen. An eye dropper squirted ink into the hollow barrel of the pen, and gravity pulled ink through a tiny hole and onto the nib. Thus began the Parker Pen Company. American inventor Lewis Waterman improved on Parker's design and, in 1884, was the first to use the term "fountain pen" with the claim that his pen held "a fountain of ink."

Fountain pens still suffered from the messy problems of frequent blotting and ink spills. The hands and clothes of writers grew black with ink.

Pencils started much later than pens. High-quality graphite (called black lead) was discovered in Cumberland, England, in the sixteenth century. Locals soon discovered that graphite made an excellent writing medium. They packed graphite into thin, barrel-shaped molds, and baked it. To keep the pencil leads from breaking, writers surrounded them with tubes of wood. The pencil was born.

In 1795, Frenchman Nicholas Conte in Paris made the only significant advance in pencil design since its original invention. Conte mixed low-quality French graphite with sulfur, clay, and water. He stuffed this paste into stick-shaped molds and baked it to remove all moisture. The resulting sticks were named *leads*. Conte found he could make these lead sticks harder or softer by adding or subtracting clay. Number 1, 2, 3, and 4 pencil leads were born. Conte also designed the process still used to manufacture the wood part of wood pencils.

How Were Ballpoint Pens Invented?

In 1937, Hungarian brothers Georg and Ladislas Biro decided to try their luck at creating a better pen. Ladislas was a newspaper editor and hated filling fountain pens and cleaning ink smudges. Georg was a chemist and wanted to create improved inks for Ladislas's new pen. By 1938, they had created a working ballpoint pen. While on a seaside vacation, they demonstrated their pen to an elderly gentleman staying at the same hotel. That gentleman turned out to be Augustine Justo, president of Argentina. He was impressed and invited the brothers to set up their pen factory in his country.

When World War II broke out, the brothers fled Hungary and took up Justo's offer. By 1943, the Biro Pen Company of Argentina was cranking out ballpoint pens. But there was a problem. The pens relied on gravity to pull ink down to the roller ball tip. That meant that the pens only worked when held upright and only when more than half full.

Sales fell. Georg and Ladislas scrambled back to the drawing board. They used a microscope to study the movement of ink and the action of their roller ball. Georg discovered that he could change the liquid base of his ink and increase a property called *viscosity* (the property that makes water climb up a piece of paper). If he also redesigned the ink tube, he could use what was called *capillary action* to make the ink climb up, down, or any way it needed to go to reach the pen's roller ball.

The brothers also redesigned their roller ball so that it would act more like a sponge and draw up just enough ink as it rolled to make the paper wet. Their ballpoint pen would now write upside down as well as right-side up—and always without skipping.

What's Happened Since Then?

The Biros' original ballpoint sold for $5.00 in the United States and was too expensive to generate much interest since pencils only cost a few cents. Ladislas Biro had a brilliant marketing idea. As a former newspaper editor, he wormed his way onto U.S. Secretary of State John Foster Dulles's 1945 and 1946 tour through Europe after World War II. Ladislas passed free ballpoint pen samples to every reporter and government official he met. They were universally thrilled and called ballpoints "wondrous." By 1947 Americans and Europeans clamored for ballpoints.

However, interest in Biro pens faded in America and the Biros' went broke. But an enterprising 54-year-old Chicago salesman, Milton Reynolds, who used and like Biro pens, decided to set up his own ballpoint pen factory in the United States. His pens sold well for a short while but tended to clog and smudge. Reynolds went broke, too.

Two of Reynolds's employees, however, fared better. Fran Seech, a Los Angeles chemist, was one. He went into the pen-making business for himself, starting by designing better inks than Reynolds had used. With his new, no-smear ink, Seech named his pens Paper Mates; they have sold over 800 million.

The other Reynolds employee who found success was Marcel Bich. In 1952, he took his ideas back to France. He experimented and studied for two years before producing a clear-barrel, smooth writing, nonleaking, and—above all else—amazingly inexpensive ballpoint pen. He named it by using the first three letters of his own last name: Bic. Bics are the only pen that have outsold Paper Mates over the past 50 years. By 1975 fountain pens were rare in the United States and ballpoints, roller balls, and felt tips dominated the market for pens.

With the rise of personal computers, e-mail, and printers, most people expect the use of pens and pencils to diminish. However, major U.S. pen and pencil manufacturers have not yet noticed a drop in sales. Over two billion pencils are made and sold per year in the United States. That's an average of seven pencils per person and enough pencils to write 900 million novels of 100,000 words each.

While we in America have forgotten the Biro brothers and their wondrous invention that started the ballpoint revolution, the English have not. There a ballpoint is still commonly called a biro.

 Fun Fact: Paul Fisher (Fisher Pen Company) has invented a pen designed to work best in space. The pen will write in the absence of gravity and in temperature extremes ranging from -50 degrees F to +400 degrees F. Fisher space pens have flown with both American and Russian astronauts.

More to Explore

Editors of Time-Life Books. *Inventive Genius.* Alexandria, VA: Time-Life Books, 1998.

Gostong, Henry. *The Incredible Ball Point Pen.* New York: Schiffer Publishing, 1998.

Jeffries, Michael, and Gary Lewis. *Inventors and Inventions.* New York: Smithmark, 1997.

McGough, Roger. *Dotty Inventions and Some Real Ones, Too.* New York: American Natural Hygiene Society, 2004.

McNeil, Ian. *An Encyclopedia of the History of Technology.* New York: Routledge, 1996.

Nickell, Joe. *Pen, Ink, and Evidence.* New Castle, DE: Oak Knoll Press, 2000.

van Dulken, Stephen. *Inventing the 20th century.* New York: New York University Press, 2000.

Photocopier

Year of Invention: 1938

> **What Is It?** A machine that creates an exact copy of an original document or picture.
>
> **Who Invented It?** Chester Carlson (in Queens, New York)

Why Is *This* Invention One of the 100 Greatest?

The typewriter (1867) and the telephone (1876) changed business practices in America. The next machine to revolutionize business was the copier (xerography), 60 years later. The copier quickly became an indispensable service of modern life. We make hundreds of millions of copies of tens of thousands of pages every day. Copy rooms, copy centers, and copy shops abound.

History of the Invention

What Did People Do Before?

For thousands of years, copies were made by hand. Monks were famous for laboring for long months and even years to copy a single book. Two problems existed with hand copying: it was slow, and errors tended to creep into hand-copied documents.

The printing press (1454) made it possible to create multiple originals, but not to make a copy of an existing document. Early in the eighteenth century, copy-like machines and processes existed. President Thomas Jefferson owned one—even though it was smelly, time consuming, and created poor-quality copies on a tissue-thin paper that had to be read from the back (otherwise it appeared backwards). In 1887 Thomas Edison invented the mimeograph, a smelly duplication process that was used extensively in schools.

How Was Photocopying Invented?

Even though he was a university graduate with a degree in physics, the only job 26-year-old Chester Carlson could find in the depression year of 1933 was as a clerk for an electrical company, P. R. Mallory, analyzing patent forms and papers. Carlson's work involved making copies of masses of technical diagrams and documents—always by hand.

Carlson decided there had to be a better way—both to earn a living and to make copies. He had always wanted to be an inventor and decided that a better copying system would be his great invention. He conducted extensive research at the New York Public Library and read about European work with electrostatic charging.

Having no money for equipment or a lab, Carlson began experimenting with chemicals in his apartment kitchen to see if and how they would hold an electrostatic charge. He also began to play with the process of using intense light to remove that static charge.

After several months, he found that sulfur easily held an electrostatic charge in the dark and, when blasted with an intense light, lost that charge. Unfortunately, the light's heat also made the sulfur waft its intense rotten egg smell into the room.

Carlson learned to ignore the smell. Other tenants in the building did not. The landlady's daughter knocked on Carlson's door to complain. However, she quickly became intrigued by his work. She began to help in his experiments. They became friends and were married in 1934.

By 1935, Carlson was close to creating a working copying system. He coated a metal plate with sulfur in his darkened room and charged the plate by rubbing it with silk. He wrote with grease pencil on a slab of plate glass and placed the glass on top of his metal plate. Next, he shone an intense light through the glass. Sulfur exposed to the light lost its static charge. However, sulfur grains protected by the grease pencil writing were not hit by light and held their charge.

Carlson removed the glass plate and dusted the metal plate with powdered ink that stuck to any electrically charged sulfur grains. Finally, he pressed a piece of paper to the metal plate, transferring ink onto the page.

It was messy. It was smelly. It was time consuming. Worst of all, it only worked when the original document was written on a plate of glass. Real documents arrived at the copier on paper.

Carlson tried to reflect light off a written page, but the light scattered too much before it reached his charged metal plate to record any of the original words. In early 1938, Carlson realized that photographers managed to focus reflected light in their cameras. What he needed were focusing lenses. Bright lights would bombard an original document with light that would reflect off that page, through focusing lenses, and onto the sulfur on his charged metal plate.

Carlson decided to call his process *xerography* from the Greek words meaning "dry writing." On October 22, 1938, he completed construction of the table that held the lights and focusing lenses for his new design. The top of this table was a glass plate on which he would lay the original document. He wrote the date and location on a piece of paper (10-22-38, Astoria) and laid it on his tabletop.

Less than one minute later he held the copy page. It was identical to the original. The process was still messy (because of the powdered ink) and smelly (he still used sulfur). But it worked.

What's Happened Since Then?

Carlson couldn't find anyone interested in his invention until 1944, when he signed a development contract with the Battelle Memorial Institute in Columbus, Ohio, a small science research firm.

Battelle licensed Carlson's copier to a small local firm, Haloid (who later changed its name to Xerox). Haloid dumped smelly sulfur for odorless selenium, which its scientists found worked just as well. Haloid also enclosed the entire process in a metal box so that ink dust would no longer escape into the room.

In 1959, Haloid introduced the Xerox 914. Over a half-million machines were sold during its first decade on the market. By 1969, Xerox copiers were making over 75 billion copies a year.

 Fun Fact: In 1988, the Xerox Corporation made over 20 million copies on just four machines as a test—just to see if its copiers could hold up for that many copies.

More to Explore

Aaseng, Nathan. *Twentieth-Century Inventors.* New York: Facts on File, 1996.

Clark, Donald. *Encyclopedia of Great Inventors and Discoveries.* London: Marshall Cavendish Books, 1991.

Editors of Time-Life Books. *Inventive Genius.* Alexandria, VA: Time-Life Books, 2001.

Ierley, Merritt. *Wondrous Contrivances.* New York: Clarkson Potter, 2002.

Liu, Catherine. *Copying Machines: Taking Notes for the Automaton.* St Paul: University of Minnesota Press, 2000.

Owen, David. *Copies in Seconds: Chester Carlson and the Birth of the Xerox Machine.* New York: Simon & Schuster, 2004.

Schein, Lawrence B. *Electrophotography and Development Physics.* New York: Laplacian Press, 1996.

Wentzell, Timothy H. *Machine Design.* Toronto: Thomson Delmar Learning, 2003.

Zannos, Susan. *Chester Carlson and the Development of Xerography.* London: Mitchell Lane Publishers, 2002.

Jet Engine

Year of Invention: 1939

> **What Is It?** An engine that produces motion through backward discharge of a jet of fluid.
>
> **Who Invented It?** Frank Whittle (in England) and Hans von Ohain (in Germany)

Why Is *This* Invention One of the 100 Greatest?

The jet engine revolutionized air travel and aircraft design. Jets were also the starting point for rocket flight and rocket design, and thus for space travel. The speed of jet engines is an essential aspect of how we plan our travel, work, and leisure. Jets support larger aircraft and carry greater loads.

History of the Invention

What Did People Do Before?

Propeller planes reached speeds of 200 mph by the 1930s. By 1920, two-engine prop planes had the range to fly passengers around the world. However, flight was still a luxury for the rich. Engineers knew that propeller planes would soon reach their upper limit for speed and range.

How Was the Jet Engine Invented?

Two men, each totally unaware of the other's work, developed a jet engine. One, Frank Whittle, worked in London. The other, Hans von Ohain, worked in secrecy for the German military. Whittle was the first to develop a working jet engine, but Ohain's was the first to fly.

In 1926, 21-year-old airplane mechanic Frank Whittle began to study the idea of airplane propulsion without propellers. In 1928, he decided that a gas turbine could create a jet of hot exhaust gas capable of propelling a plane.

Gas turbine engines were well known by this time, being used to create mechanical action (e.g., turning a motor shaft or driving a pump). Fierce plumes of exhaust gas jetted out of the rear of these turbines. Whittle calculated that a supercharged burner would exhaust a greater volume and velocity of gas than the volume that entered. This differential would create forward motion for a plane.

225

Whittle got the idea to create *two* turbines—a front turbine to ram air back into the main chamber, and the main one where air would be mixed with fuel and burned. He designed a nozzle to funnel a jet of exhaust out of the back with the greatest power.

During Whittle's engineering design studies, he calculated that a jet would fly better as it went faster. (Forward speed would help to ram air into the combustion chamber.) This was the opposite of every flyer's experience in prop planes. No one took Whittle, his work, or his engine seriously.

When Whittle first proposed his jet engine to the British Air Ministry in 1929, they refused to even review his proposal.

In 1936, Whittle and several private backers formed PowerJets to build jet aircraft based on Whittle's designs. For 15 months they faced nothing but problems. Turbine blades broke under the extreme conditions of the jet engine. The engines overheated. Uncontrolled engine surges destroyed the turbines and wiring.

In late March they completed construction of their first full engine. Whittle tested it on April 12 of that year in a bolted-down test bed. Waves of heat, screeching thunder, and hurricane force winds spewed out the back of the jet. The jet engine produced power beyond Whittle's wildest imagining.

However, Whittle found that several turbine blades had cracked during the short full-power test. The power output had been uneven and not responsive to his controls. He deemed his engine promising but "not flight worthy." He needed better materials and a better system to control the engine's explosive combustion.

He increased the number of turbine blades to reduce the stress on each. However, Whittle found that this altered airflow through the turbine. In despair, he felt that he had to redesign the entire engine.

Despite the problems Whittle experienced in his first test, the British Air Ministry decided to support the project and ordered Whittle to develop his engine under government contract. By March 1939, his redesigned engine was complete, and he began to work with aircraft designers on the plane that would fly with it.

Meanwhile, Hans von Ohain filed a German patent for his engine design in 1935. He was immediately recruited by Heinkle Company (plane builders) and by the German military air corps. With unlimited funding, Ohain's jet engine was developed in total secrecy. On August 27, 1939, his jet engine flew, mounted in a Heinkle He 178 airplane. This was the world's first jet aircraft flight. Hitler himself watched, but was unimpressed and saw no need for such speed. No jets were ordered.

Two jet engines had been developed by 1939. But neither was put into production until 1944—too late to be a decisive factor in World War II (1939 to 1945).

What's Happened Since Then?

Whittle's first jet plane (the Gloster E.28/29) made its maiden flight on May 15, 1941, but it was not put into production for another three years. The first twin-jet plane, the Heinkle He 280 using Ohain's engines, was launched in late 1942 and reached speeds of almost 500 miles an hour. The first American jet was the Bell XP-59 Airacomet, which debuted on October 3, 1942 (powered by a Whittle engine). Both Whittle and Ohain immigrated to the United States after the war (Ohain in 1945, Whittle in 1950) and helped with American jet aircraft design.

The first jet airliner (British Airways) flew on July 27, 1949. The commercial jet flights were only marginally successful, and the plane was quickly retired. The first successful jet airliner was the legendary Boeing 707, launched in 1954. It was still in active service 30 years later.

Chuck Yeager made the first supersonic flight in the Bell X-1 Rocket Plane, on October 14, 1947. That is, he was the first to fly faster than the speed of sound. Up to the day he did it, many believed it was impossible. The only supersonic airliner ever to fly was the Concord, introduced in 1976 by Air France and British Airways. The Concord was (at best) marginally successful and never economical. In 2004 it was finally retired from service.

 Fun Fact: The world's fastest jet, the SR-71 Blackbird, flies so high that the crew has to wear space suits—the same suits worn by astronauts.

More to Explore

Clark, Donald. *Encyclopedia of Great Inventors and Discoveries*. London: Marshall Cavendish Books, 1991.

Golley, John. *Genesis of the Jet*. London: Aulife Publicatins, 1997.

———. *Whittle: The True Story*. Washington, DC: Smithsonian Institute Press, 1996.

Jeffries, Michael, and Gary Lewis. *Inventors and Inventions*. New York: Smithmark, 1997.

Jeffris, David. *Jet Age*. New York: Franklin Watts, 1998.

McNeil, Ian. *An Encyclopedia of the History of Technology*. New York: Routledge, 1996.

Parker, Steve. *53½ Things That Changed the World—And Some That Didn't*. Minneapolis, MN: Lerner Publications, 1997.

van Dulken, Stephen. *Inventing the 20th Century*. New York: New York University Press, 2000.

Yenne, Bill. *100 Inventions That Shaped World History*. New York: Bluewood Books, 1993.

Nuclear Reactor

Year of Invention: 1942

> **What Is It?** A machine that converts the heat energy of natural nuclear decay into electrical energy.
>
> **Who Invented It?** Enrico Fermi (in Chicago)

Why Is *This* Invention One of the 100 Greatest?

With Enrico Fermi's nuclear reactor, the world entered the nuclear age. The nuclear reactor unleashed a vast new source of electrical energy—a source that didn't depend on limited fossil fuels. More important for science, however, Fermi's reactor proved the mathematical models scientists used for the structure and action of electrons, neutrons, protons, and the Beta decay process. Finally, nuclear reactors set the stage for the creation of the atomic bomb in 1945.

History of the Invention

What Did People Do Before?

In 1940, over 90 percent of the world's electrical supply was produced from fossil fuels. Scientists sought renewable—or inexhaustible—fuel alternatives. Some researchers focused on renewable energy resources (wind, water, and biomass). Some turned to the sun, a virtually inexhaustible energy source. Some turned to the power of the atom.

How Was the Nuclear Reactor Invented?

At 2:20 P.M. on December 2, 1942, Enrico Fermi flipped the switch that raised hundreds of neutron-absorbing cadmium control rods out of his reactor core. Fermi had stacked 42,000 graphite blocks laced with several tons of uranium oxide pellets in an underground squash court situated 20 feet under the west bleachers of Stagg's field, the University of Chicago football field. No one on campus knew what was happening in that squash court.

Theory said that a nuclear reaction in that water-filled tank would become a controlled and self-sustaining nuclear reactor once the rods were removed. (The cadmium rods absorbed too many neutrons to allow the reaction to develop.) But theories were often wrong. Students 20 feet above hurried past in the bitter-cold winter wind without being aware that their lives depended on the theories and calculations of one man, 35-year-old Enrico Fermi.

He had built the world's first nuclear reactor. As the cadmium rods withdrew he would become (1) an international hero and usher in the nuclear age, (2) a failure, or (3) vaporized in a blinding nuclear explosion that would destroy half of Chicago.

By the age of 23, Fermi had already established a solid international reputation as an atomic physicist and was asked to create Italy's first modern school of physics at the University of Rome.

The discovery in 1932 of neutrons (particles with no electrical charge that existed in an atom's nucleus and were about the same mass as protons) shifted Fermi's focus. Fermi recognized that neutrons could solve a problem of subatomic physics. Physicists had been trying to smash both electrons and protons into the nucleus of an atom to see if the collision would reveal new secrets of atomic structure. But electrons and protons both held an electrical charge and had to be accelerated to near light speed to overpower the electrical force of an atom. Accelerators were giant, expensive pieces of equipment.

Fermi realized that if he bombarded atoms with uncharged neutrons, he wouldn't need a massive accelerator, since neutrons wouldn't be repulsed by the target atoms. Fermi hoped the target nuclei would capture these neutrons and transform the target substance into a new, radioactive isotope that would then spontaneously decay (split apart) so that scientists could study the process of nuclear decay. Fermi bombarded every element on the periodic table with streams of neutrons and created over a hundred new, radioactive substances (called *isotopes*, or new versions of an existing element).

In 1940, Fermi, along with other leading physicists, turned to the potential of fission (the splitting apart of an atom's nucleus). If a uranium atom could be persuaded both to split apart when it was struck by a free neutron *and* to release several free neutrons of its own at the same time, then those new neutrons could strike other uranium atoms, forcing them, in turn, to split apart. A chain reaction could be created, releasing incredible amounts of energy.

But a world of questions and incredible dangers stood between that "could" and the reality of a controlled nuclear chain reaction. In 1938 Fermi moved to the United States, where, during World War II, he was given responsibility for the U.S. government's program to create a nuclear chain reaction.

The year 1942 saw a string of frantic experiments and discoveries. First Fermi learned that starting a chain reaction was harder than he originally thought. Then he discovered that a new isotope of uranium, U^{235}, fissioned (split apart) better than U^{238}. But U^{235} was rare, unstable, and hard to isolate. Worse, any impurities in a sample of U^{235} tended to absorb too many free neutrons and stop the chain reaction. Months were consumed with experiments to learn how to create pure U^{235}.

Fermi experimented with bricks, lead, concrete, etc., and found that graphite blocks successfully slowed neutrons to a speed ideal for U^{235} fission reaction.

Next he discovered that cadmium (a metallic element) readily absorbed neutrons and would be a good control substance, allowing him to slow or stop the reaction at will. Each new finding meant weeks of grueling effort.

Before research was consolidated at the University of Chicago in November 1942, Fermi ran smaller, specialized projects in Massachusetts and New York. His task in Chicago was to build the world's first working nuclear reactor. He had only one month to do it.

Fermi was given the use of an underground squash court. His plan was simple: stack blocks of graphite in a tank of water. Each block was to be laced with pellets of U^{235} oxide. A forest of slender cadmium rods dangled from an overhead frame and reached down between the graphite blocks. As long as the cadmium control rods stood in place like a forest of telephone poles, they would absorb enough neutrons to prevent a chain reaction from forming and mushrooming into an explosion.

One month later, at 2:20 P.M. on December 2, the world entered a new era. Fermi switched on the motor that lifted the cadmium rods toward the squash court's ceiling—still with only untested theory protecting him from instant incineration. The world's first self-sustained nuclear reaction boiled the cooling water around it for 28 minutes before being shut down by the reinserted cadmium rods.

What's Happened Since Then?

Based in part on Fermi's work, the first atomic bomb was built and used in 1945. Nuclear electric power plants began to dot the American landscape by the mid-1960s. However, nuclear plants failed to produce the reliable, cheap power their backers promised. In 1980, the United States placed a moratorium on new nuclear plant construction that continues today. The biggest current users of nuclear power are surface ships and submarines for many of the world's navies.

It is unclear if nuclear energy—without some major new invention or discovery—will play any part in our commercial energy future. Its danger and environmental risks loom large, and its shiny promise has dimmed.

 Fun Fact: There are now 440 commercial nuclear power reactors operating in 31 countries. Fifty-six countries operate a total of 284 research reactors, and another 220 reactors power ships and submarines at sea.

More to Explore

Clark, Donald. *Encyclopedia of Great Inventors and Discoveries*. London: Marshall Cavendish Books, 1991.

Daintith, John, et al., eds. *Biographical Encyclopedia of Scientists, Second Edition*, Volume 1. Philadelphia: Institute of Physics Publishing, 1994.

Dear, Pamela, ed. *Contemporary Authors,* Volume 157. Detroit: Gale Research, 1995.

Haven, Kendall, and Donna Clark. *100 Most Popular Scientists for Young Adults*. Englewood, CO: Libraries Unlimited, 1999.

Lomask, Milton. *Invention and Technology Great Lives*. New York: Charles Scribner's Sons, 1994.

Serge, Emilio. *Enrico Fermi: Physicist*. Chicago: University of Chicago Press, 1990.

Tanor, Joseph, ed. *McGraw-Hill Modern Men of Science*. New York: McGraw-Hill, 1996.

Wasson, R. Gordon, ed. *Nobel Prize Winners*. New York: H. W. Wilson, 1997.

Yenne, Bill. *100 Inventions That Shaped World History*. New York: Bluewood Books, 1993.

Digital Computer

Year of Invention: 1943

What Is It? An electronic machine capable of rapid, repetitive calculations, of user interface, and of branching logic decisions.

Who Invented It? Howard Aiken (in Cambridge, Massachusetts)

Why Is *This* Invention One of the 100 Greatest?

Programmable computers govern and control how we do much of what we do. Computers do for information what DNA does for life. They will define it and provide organization, direction, and control for information and information sharing. Virtually all of our activity, development, knowledge, and scheduling are now keyed to a computer. Education, production, and vital decision making are linked to the computer. Every facet of modern life depends on, or is linked to, the programmable computer.

History of the Invention

What Did People Do Before?

The first mechanical device developed to perform math was the abacus, an early adding machine that used beads for counters. Devices like an abacus were drawn in the sand for individual computations by early Babylonians. Some clever, unknown Egyptian was the first to build a wood and metal abacus. About the same time, a similar abacus appeared in China.

In the early part of the seventeenth century the Scotsman John Napier created an early version of a slide rule, called "Napier's Bones." Made of ivory or wood, these strips could slide next to each other to perform multiplication. By the end of that century, formal slide rules were in use throughout Europe.

The first step toward a true computing machine came in the mid-nineteenth century, when Englishman Charles Babbage envisioned a machine capable of performing complex calculations. Babbage could draw his machine on paper, but he could not build it because factories of the day could not produce the precision parts he needed.

Babbage's assistant, Ida Lovelace, recognized the need to create simple, repetitive groups of commands to make the machine run efficiently. She created the first computer language.

How Was the Computer Invented?

In 1936, German mathematician Konrad Zues built the Z1. This was not yet a computer, but it incorporated three features that all computers eventually would use: binary operation (an entire system built on ones and zeros), a floating decimal point so that a calculation could use any number of digits on either side of the decimal point, and memory.

Howard Aiken studied math and physics at the University of Chicago and at Harvard, where, in 1937, he read detailed papers describing Babbage's and Zues's work. Aiken decided that he could merge the two into a working computer and wrote a proposal for an "Automated Calculating Machine" guaranteeing error-free, fully automated calculation of any mathematical problem.

Government and university experts laughed at Aiken's proposal. Then IBM president Thomas Watson read it and liked it. He assigned a team of IBM engineers to the project. For the next 10 months, Aiken led this team in trying to envision what his computer might actually look like and how it would function.

In 1939 Aiken was inducted into the Navy Reserve, and the Navy became interested in his project. The Navy provided lab space in the basement of a building on the Harvard campus. IBM provided the money.

Driven, often working 24 hours straight, Aiken dragged his team through the process of inventing each component and relay of the Mark I—the name given to this first-ever computer. Problems were a daily occurrence. Each solution had to be invented by the team since there was no previous work to use as a design model.

Slowly the Mark I took shape: 8 feet high and over 50 feet long, 530 miles of wire, 175,000 electrical connections, 750,000 parts, 1,200 ball bearings, a weight of 35 tons.

From the front, the Mark I looked like an endless bank of black metal boxes in gray metal frames with columns of floor-to-ceiling lights. Each panel was enclosed in a glass case that could be opened for access and maintenance.

The Mark I used mechanical relays that opened and closed the thousands of electrical connections and therefore was an electro-mechanical computer—part electronic, part mechanical. A four horsepower motor drove the 50-foot-long main driveshaft.

With 4,000 mechanical relays clicking open and closed, the Mark I sounded like an auditorium full of people quietly knitting. But that massive, whirring, clicking monster machine could make calculations at the undreamed-of speed of three computations per second! (Modern computers can make millions—even billions—of calculations per second.)

The Mark I's control panel was modeled after a telephone switchboard. It offered the operator an array of 1,440 dials and 72 separate registers to accumulate calculations. Operators prepared a deck of punch cards that told each register in the computer what to do with the numbers indicated on its input dials.

In Aiken's rush to create his computing machine, neither he nor anyone else on his team thought much about how they would communicate with this mechanical marvel. Grace Hopper, a mathematics teacher and Navy ensign, was brought in. She created the computer language and programs that directed the Mark I.

Much of the operators' time was spent fixing relays that jammed, stuck, or shorted. More often than not, the problem was caused by bugs that flew into the machine and were pounded to death by the mechanical relays. Soon everyone called the process of cleaning them out "debugging" the computer.

In early 1943, Aiken declared the Mark I operational. However, it was not publicly announced since the Mark I only worked on secret navy projects.

What's Happened Since Then?

The Mark I was serviceable for less than two years before it was retired, being declared too slow and bulky to be worth using.

In 1945, Alan Turing completed construction of the first all-electronic computer, the Colossus I, at the University of Manchester, England. In 1946, John Mauchly at the University of Pennsylvania completed the Electronic Numerical Integrator and Computer (ENIAC). This first well-known computer ran a thousand times faster than the Mark I. The ENIAC weighed 30 tons and contained 18,000 vacuum tubes. These tubes produced so much heat that the computer room had to be air conditioned even on bitter-cold winter days.

In 1951, the Sperry Corporation released its new computer, the Universal Automatic Computer (UNIVAC). The UNIVAC became the first commercially successful computer in the world. In 1959, IBM unveiled its 1401 computer, the first computer to successfully replace mechanical business machines.

In 1958, Seymour Cray built his first computer model for Control Data Corp, the first computer to replace bulky vacuum tubes with transistors. Cray also built the first super computer, the Cray I, in 1975. That computer completed 100 million operations per second. Most people at the time didn't believe that such speeds were possible. For comparison, the CM 200 supercomputer built in 1991 performs 9.03 billion operations per second.

In less than 50 years, computers have advanced from bulky toddlers to the central and integral part of every car, airplane, microwave, municipal fire and police system, and virtually every company and store in the developed world. Most agree that computers have only begun to define their full role in our lives.

 Fun Fact: In this age of microcomputers, the world's biggest computer is a cluster of supercomputers in Yokohama, Japan. This monster is the size of four tennis courts and is used to model and predict climate changes.

More to Explore

Adler, Robert. *Science Firsts.* New York: John Wiley & Sons, 2002.

Chapman, Neil. *Charles Babbage.* Portsmouth, NH: Heinemann Library Publishing, 2000.

Coker, I. Bernard. *Howard Aiken.* Cambridge, MA: MIT Press, 1999.

Lomask, Milton. *Invention and Technology Great Lives.* New York: Charles Scribner's Sons, 1994.

Mallern, Joanne. *Passport to the Digital Age.* Chicago: Power Kids Press, 2003.

Randekk, Brian. *Origins of the Digital Computer.* New York: Springer-Verlag, 2001.

Strathern, Paul. *The Big Idea: Turing and the Computer.* New York: Anchor Books, 1997.

Vare, Ethlie Ann, and Greg Ptacek. *Patently Female: Stories of Women Inventors.* New York: John Wiley & Sons, 2002.

Williams, Bruce. *Computers.* Portsmouth, NH: Heinemann Library Publishing, 2001.

Kidney Dialysis

Year of Invention: 1944

What Is It? A mechanical filtration system to replace the function of defective kidneys and remove impurities from human blood.

Who Invented It? Willem Kolff (in Kampen, Holland)

Why Is *This* Invention One of the 100 Greatest?

The human kidney is a biological marvel. Kidneys purify the blood, maintain blood pH balance, regulate the production of various hormones and vitamins, and remove a wide variety of life-threatening toxins.

Kidney dialysis has saved and prolonged the lives of millions worldwide. Dialysis helped set the stage for kidney transplant and the transplanting of other organs. Kidney dialysis was the first procedure that allowed medical scientists to use machines to artificially perform the function of an organ.

History of the Invention

What Did People Do Before?

Even Roman doctors understood that many people died because their blood became toxic. However, no one knew what to do about it. Bloodletting (draining cups or pints of blood from a patient) and leaching (using leaches to suck out toxins from a patient's blood) were popular therapies, but did nothing to attack the real problem.

Beginning in the 1600s European doctors suspected that kidney failure was the cause of the "toxic blood" that killed so many patients. They searched for ways to either cure a failing kidney or perform its function outside of the body. However, through the nineteenth and into the twentieth centuries, no real progress was made on either goal.

How Was Kidney Dialysis Invented?

Late in 1940, Dutch physician Willem Kolff, who was working for Germany, was assigned to work in the municipal hospital in Kampen, Holland. World War II was in full swing. Germany had occupied lowland countries and had taken over the management of most governmental functions.

Kolff had previously invented the idea of a blood bank—a formal storage system for typed blood—and had spent 20 years studying blood composition and function within the body. By 1941 he had become part of the worldwide research effort on the function of the kidney. Kolff was given permission by the German high command to conduct any experiments on prisoners and on Resistance members that he deemed valuable for his research.

It occurred to Kolff that the best way to understand kidney function was to try to duplicate the kidney outside the human body. He collected filters, screens, pumps, wooden drums, cellophane tubing, and laundry tubs and designed a system to pump blood through a series of screens and filters before returning it into the body.

He began his experiments on animals. He hooked them up to his machine, bypassing the animal's own kidneys, and carefully monitored their blood chemistry as, over the course of days, he pumped their blood through his artificial setup. He found that his artificial kidney failed to remove many toxins and realized that they would have to be removed chemically. He added several stages of chemical baths and one stage to balance blood pH. With this improved system, he was able to keep test animals alive for over a week.

In the spring of 1944, Kolff decided to try his apparatus on human patients. He chose 15 men and women who were near death because of kidney failure. Once every other day, he hooked each patient up to his artificial kidney and pumped his or her blood through it and back into the body. In this experiment, Kolff prolonged his patients' lives for three to eighteen days.

Kolff's report drew only minor interest from the German medical community. In this fifth year of the war, they were far more interested in treatments that would save the lives of soldiers. Kolff was ordered to focus his research on treatments that would help in the war effort.

In early 1945, a woman Nazi collaborator suffering from near total kidney failure was brought to Kolff for treatment. Most locals wanted her dead and protested the idea of trying to save her. Kolff hooked her to his machine. In just one treatment he restored her vital signs and blood chemistry. Because of this success, Kolff's work jumped back into the medical headlines. He was able to continue developing his system.

By mid-summer 1945, Kolff had completed the design and construction of the first three complete blood dialysis machines. As the war ground to an end and the German regime collapsed, Kolff shipped his machines and knowledge for free to England and America in exchange for immunity from prosecution as a Nazi doctor.

What's Happened Since Then?

American and British doctors examined and tested Kolff's machine and found that it worked amazingly well. However, although it worked wonders for many kidney patients, it failed to help some, and often caused catastrophic side effects. Another 20 years of research, testing, and refinement were required before Kolff's process—now renamed kidney dialysis—became a "routine" outpatient process.

Fun Fact: Imagine how much more stirring music we would have today if dialysis had existed back in 1790. Wolfgang Amadeus Mozart, one of the world's greatest composers, died of kidney failure in 1791 at age 35. He produced an entire new symphony each year (in addition to other works) for the last six years of his life. With dialysis, we might have another 20 Mozart symphonies to enjoy.

More to Explore

Cameron, J. Stewart. *The History of Dialysis*. New York: Oxford University Press, 2002.

Dyson, James. *A History of Great Inventions*. New York: Carroll & Graf Publishers, 2001.

Kent, Deborah. *Why Me?* New York: Scholastic, Inc., 1996.

Miller, Martha. *Kidney Disorders*. New York: Chelsea House Publishing, 1998.

Tracy, Kathleen. *Willem Kolff and the Invention of the Dialysis Machine*. London: Mitchell Lane Publishers, 2002.

Microwave Oven

Year of Invention: 1946

> **What Is It?** A device that uses microwaves instead of external heat to cook food.
>
> **Who Invented It?** Percy Spencer (in Boston)

Why Is *This* Invention One of the 100 Greatest?

The microwave oven revolutionized American cooking. Publishers have had to re-write their cookbooks to provide microwave directions. Restaurants and homebuilders have redesigned their kitchens and kitchen concepts. Microwaves save energy and space. They cut cooking time by up to 80 percent and are the first great leap forward in cooking technology in a thousand years.

History of the Invention

What Did People Do Before?

Always humans have cooked by using a fire or stove to apply heat from outside the thing being cooked and heating it slowly through to the middle. All cooking development focused on controlling the flame, evening its heat, and controlling the way heat worked its way into food. No one was looking for an entirely new approach to cooking.

How Was the Microwave Invented?

Percy Spencer had every reason to be a troubled failure in life. He was born in a small town in Maine, and his father died before Spencer turned two. His mother left home shortly thereafter. Spencer was raised by an aunt and uncle. When Spencer was seven, that uncle died. In order to help support the family, Spencer dropped out of school as a 12-year-old and took a job in a local factory.

In 1910, a paper mill hired 16-year-old Spencer to help install their first electrical system. Two years later, Spencer, fascinated by electronics and especially by the newly invented radio, joined the navy to be a radio operator. After his tour, he joined a company making radio tubes for the army. In 1928 (still with no formal education beyond sixth grade) he was hired by Raytheon to design and build better radio tubes.

When World War II broke out, Raytheon shifted Spencer to a new military technology: radar, the new British invention to detect distant ships and planes. Spencer was to search for more efficient and effective radar designs.

Radars shot out microwave pulses of energy that reflected off metal objects. A receiver detected the reflected signal and used it to locate the object (a plane or ship). Inside the radar, a device called a magnetron generated the microwave pulses that were sprayed into the air. By 1945, Spencer had completely redesigned the magnetron, making it simpler and more reliable.

In early 1946, something seemingly ordinary and uneventful happened that changed the world. A chocolate peanut butter bar melted in the pocket of Percy Spencer's white lab coat. Another person might have blamed the heat of the day or assumed that the candy bar was too close to Spencer's body.

Not Percy Spencer. He suspected it had something to do with the high frequency microwave beams created by his magnetron. He was not the first researcher to note the heating effect of microwave energy. But he was the first to think about what that effect meant.

He sent an assistant to the store for a bag of popping corn. Each kernel he placed near the nozzle of the magnetron exploded into fluffy popcorn. Next morning he cut a hole in an old teakettle and mounted the magnetron so its nozzle aimed into the hole. He placed an egg inside the kettle and switched on the power. When a curious coworker peered into the kettle, the steaming egg exploded in his face and scattered shell, yoke, and egg white across the lab.

Raytheon recognized the value of Spencer's discovery. The company assigned a team to assist Spencer in discovering how microwaves cooked and how to build a microwave oven. Within five months, the team had completed the first microwave.

What's Happened Since Then?

Raytheon's first Radarange (so named because the magnetron came from radar) went on the market in 1947 and cost $4,800. It weighed almost 1,000 pounds, was the size of a refrigerator, and required cold water to cool its magnetron. The only customers were restaurants, trains, and the military.

In 1965 Amana released the first domestic microwave oven, priced just under $500. It wasn't until the late 1970s that sales began to climb. As of 2000, over 93 percent percent of the kitchens in America have a microwave oven, and tens of thousands of microwaves are used in lunchrooms, offices, dorms, etc. Four times as many meals are now prepared in microwaves as in conventional ovens in American homes. If the current trend continues, microwaves could replace space-wasting, energy-wasting, time-wasting, waste-heat-producing conventional ovens within this century.

Fun Fact: Microwave cooking isn't just fast. It's also healthy. More vitamins and minerals are retained with microwave cooking than with most other methods of cooking.

More to Explore

Brown, David. *Inventing Modern America*. Cambridge, MA: The MIT Press, 2002.

Gallawa, J. Carlton. "Who Invented Microwaves?" In *The Complete Microwave Oven Service Handbook*. Upper Saddle River, NJ: Prentice Hall, 2000.

Jeffries, Michael, and Gary Lewis. *Inventors and Inventions*. New York: Smithmark, 1997.

McNeil, Ian. *An Encyclopedia of the History of Technology*. New York: Routledge, 1996.

van Dulken, Stephen. *Inventing the 20th Century*. New York: New York University Press, 2000.

Yenne, Bill. *100 Inventions That Shaped World History*. New York: Bluewood Books, 1993.

Transistor

> **What Is It?** An electronic device that uses solid chips of semiconductor material to replace the functions of bulky vacuum tubes.
>
> **Who Invented It?** John Bardeen and William Shockley (in New Jersey)

Why Is *This* Invention One of the 100 Greatest?

Transistors made it possible to squeeze more electronic components and electronic logic power into a single cell phone than existed in the whole of England at the end of World War II. Transistors made thousands of other products and inventions possible. Calculators, personal computers, televisions, iPods®, Walkmans®, car ignition and control, robots, satellites—every electronic device in production uses transistors.

History of the Invention

What Did People Do Before?

The field of electronics emerged in the early twentieth century with military advances (sonar and radar) and commercial advances (radio and television). By the early 1940s, digital computers had crept into existence. However, those early electronic devices depended on vacuum tubes—bulky, heat-producing, expensive, energy-guzzling vacuum tubes. Old-style radios and televisions used dozens of them. Early computers used thousands.

How Was the Transistor Invented?

John Bardeen taught theoretical physics at the University of Minnesota from 1938 to 1941. There, as a 30-year-old assistant professor, he found the first research question that stirred both his intellectual curiosity and his passion. He discovered the mystery of superconductivity. Superconductivity, discovered by Kammerlingh Onnes, is the state where, at temperatures a few degrees above absolute zero, many metals lose all resistance to the flow of electricity. A current, once started, will flow forever.

When, in mid-1947, Bell Laboratories (a high-tech communications and electronics research plant) hired Bardeen, he hoped to pursue superconductivity. However, he was asked to join forces with William Shockley and Walter Brattain, who were studying the possible use of semiconductor materials in electronics.

Semiconductors are materials that can't be classified as either electrical conductors or resistors. At times they seemed to impede electrical flow like a resistor. At others, they seemed to act more like conductors. Thus they were given the name *semiconductors*. Shockley and Brattain were studying the properties of two of these semiconductors—the elements germanium and silicon—and their experiments had failed to produce any useful results.

If semiconductors were to replace vacuum tubes, Shockley had to make semiconductor material both amplify (increase) and rectify electric signals (convert them from DC to AC or vice versa). All of his attempts had failed. He couldn't understand why. Bardeen set aside his desire to study *super*conductors to rescue Shockley's work on *semi*conductors.

Bardeen first confirmed that Shockley's mathematics were correct and that his approach was consistent with accepted theory. Shockley's experiments should work. But the results they found using germanium didn't match the theory.

Bardeen suspected that some unidentified surface interference on the germanium must be blocking electric currents. The three men set about testing the responses of semiconductor surfaces to light, heat, cold, liquids, and the deposit of metallic films. On wide lab benches they tried to force electric current to flow into the germanium through liquid metals and then through soldered wire contact points.

Then Bardeen noticed something odd and unexpected. He accidentally misconnected his electrical leads, sending a micro-current to the germanium contact point (a current less than $\frac{1}{1,000}$ of the strength he meant to connect to that lead). When this very weak current was trickled through the germanium from solder point to metal base, it created a "hole" in the germanium's resistance to current flow. A weak current converted the semiconductor into a superconductor. The signal arrived at the base many times stronger than when it first entered the germanium chip.

Bardeen had to repeatedly demonstrate the phenomenon to convince both himself and his teammates that his amazing results weren't fluke occurrences. Time after time the results were the same with any semiconductor material they tried: high current, high resistance; low current, virtually no resistance.

Bardeen named the phenomenon "transfer resistor." A co-worker at the lab and science fiction writer, John Pierce, shortened the name to *transistor*.

On Christmas Eve, 1947, the team invited their managers to a demonstration. With only a single germanium transistor, they amplified an electrical signal. For the invention of transistors, the three men shared the 1956 Nobel Prize for Physics.

What's Happened Since Then?

The first commercial products to use transistors were electronic hearing aids, which first appeared in the marketplace in 1953. The Sony Corporation produced the first transistor radio in 1955. In 1956, Shockley and Bardeen switched from germanium to silicon. Silicone became the standard material for transistor and microchips, giving rise to the name "Silicon Valley" for the area south of San Francisco that produced more computer chips than any other area on Earth.

In 1958, Jack Kilby invented the microchip—an entire circuit of many transistors and other electronic components—on a single chip of silicon. In 1969, Ted Hoff invented the microprocessor—not just a single circuit, but an entire computer processor on a single chip using thousands of transistors.

Fun Fact: The newest generation of microscopic transistors can process 600 *billion* operations a second.

More to Explore

Aaseng, Nathan. *Twentieth-Century Inventors.* New York: Facts on File, 1996.

Eckert, Michael. *Crystals, Electrons and Transistors.* New York: Springer-Verlag, 1995.

Haven, Kendall, and Donna Clark. *100 Most Popular Scientists for Young Adults.* Englewood, CO: Libraries Unlimited, 1999.

Hays, Scott. *The Story of Sony.* New York: Smart Apple Media, 2000.

Hoddeson, Lillian. *True Genius: The Life and Science of John Bardeen.* Washington, DC: National Academy Press, 2002.

Riordan, Michael. *Crystal Fire: The Invention of the Transistor and the Birth of the Information Age.* New York: W. W. Norton Company, 1998.

van Dulken, Stephen. *Inventing the 20th Century.* New York: New York University Press, 2000.

Warno-Blewett, J., ed. *Guide to Sources for History of Solid State Physics.* New York: Springer-Verlag, 1995.

Yenne, Bill. *100 Inventions That Shaped World History.* New York: Bluewood Books, 1993.

Nystatin

Year of Invention: 1948

> **What Is It?** The first artificially created antibiotic capable of killing a wide variety of fungi.
>
> **Who Invented It?** Rachel Fuller Brown and Elizabeth Hazen (in Albany, New York)

Why Is *This* Invention One of the 100 Greatest?

The war against bacteria and viruses was slowly won during the nineteenth and the early twentieth centuries. However, the same was not true for fungal diseases. These maladies were actually on a rapid rise in the middle of the twentieth century as bacterial diseases were in decline.

Rachel Fuller Brown and Elizabeth Hazen created the first fungal killer that was gentle enough to not harm human patients. Nystatin, the commercial name of their invention, has saved literally millions of lives.

History of the Invention

What Did People Do Before?

Throughout the first half of the twentieth century, medical sciences made a concentrated effort to create antibiotic germ killers. Their success created a new problem. Many common antibiotics killed the bacteria that controlled the spread of harmful fungi. Fungal diseases such as ringworm and moniliasis (a fungus-produced soreness of the mouth) rose sharply.

How Was Nystatin Invented?

In the fall of 1948, Drs. Elizabeth Hazen and Rachel Brown accepted the mission of finding an effective antifungal agent. In concept it was a simple assignment. They would grow fungi and test them against various antibiotics. Any successful antibiotics would later be tested in laboratory animals. What made it hard was that there existed over 250,000 kinds of fungi and hundreds of potential antibiotics to test on each.

Fungi are plants that do not contain green matter (chlorophyll) and so cannot use photosynthesis to produce their own nutrients. Ranging from mushrooms to molds, most are harmless, but a number can cause serious illness, and a few are deadly.

Within a week virtually ever surface of Dr. Brown's lab was covered in metal trays. On each tray sat rows of glass petri dishes containing fortified mulch growth medium. On the front of each Brown taped a label card. Like a careful gardener, she and her assistants then planted a few spores of different fungi in each dish.

They grew 50 dishes of each fungus at a time so they could test each fungus against 50 different antibiotics. They grew 300 different fungi in this first batch, each in its own tray. Brown's lab team tended these 15,000 cup-sized dishes of fungus like farmers.

A week later, Brown and Hazen conducted the first round of tests. The team wore masks, long rubber gloves, and protective lab coats. Using eyedroppers, they dripped one drop of an antibiotic solution into each petri dish. By the end of the day they had tested 30 antibiotics on over 200 species of fungus—without success.

It took three more weeks for Dr. Hazen to identify a dozen new potential antifungal agents. Four she found through a search of medical literature. The rest she got from botanists from the Department of Forestry and from tribal healers from two local tribes of Native Americans.

For these tests, the women added goggles to their protective wear, not knowing what kind of reaction they might get. When these new killers were dropped into the petri dishes of mold, many of the fungi sizzled and withered. In several dishes the fuzz of growing mold almost instantly vanished.

One agent, especially, was able to destroy almost all of the fungal samples it touched—the streptomycetes group of bacteria. Hazen had isolated this compound from dirt samples provided by a chief of the Seneca tribe.

Next day, Dr. Brown and her team began to grow the next batch of 300 fungi for testing. A rhythm and routine settled over the lab as they turned it into a factory for growing, nurturing, testing, and killing their trays of fungi.

Three months later they concluded their testing. Some 214 potential fungicides had been tested on over 25,000 fungi. The streptomycetes had clearly been the most effective fungal killer.

Dr. Brown chemically dissected this streptomycetes fungicide. Over the period of several weeks, she isolated the one bacterium that attacked and destroyed the fungal cells. The women named this organism *Streptomycetes noursei*.

The women began tests on lab animals. They started with lab mice, giving each a daily dose of *Streptomycetes noursei* while charting their weight and growth against a control group that didn't receive the fungal antibiotic. After three months it was clear that the antibiotic did not harm the mice.

Hazen infected 32 mice with eight dangerous fungal molds. Four mice received injections of each mold. Two of those four would be treated with *Streptomycetes noursei*. Two would not. Every mouse treated with *Streptomycetes noursei* recovered. Only one of the control group recovered. Dr. Hazen repeated the experiment using monkeys and achieved the same impressive results.

During this same two-month period, Brown isolated the specific protein created by *Streptomycetes noursei* that destroyed fungal cell walls. Next, she developed a process to manufacture an artificial version of it in the lab.

Finally the two women scientists repeated the live tests on mice and monkeys with Dr. Brown's synthetic protein. It worked as well as the naturally grown *Streptomycetes noursei*.

What's Happened Since Then?

Dr. Brown's and Dr. Hazen's program consumed over two years of work. It involved over 3 million individual tests and experiments, required them to grow almost 1.5 million dishes of fungi, and used over 60,000 person-hours of work. The two women named their protein Nystatin, after New York State, the funder of their research.

Since its introduction in 1950, Nystatin has been the most successful and widely prescribed antifungal agent ever developed. It has saved countless lives and opened the door for other researchers to explore for additional medicines in the natural environment.

 Fun Fact: Scientists have recently found a way to prevent fungus-caused athlete's foot with an antifungal sock fabric that prevents the growth of microorganisms.

More to Explore

Coldrey, Jennifer. *Discovering Fungi.* Harrisburg, PA: Bookwrights Press, 1991.

Haber, Louis. *Women Pioneers of Science.* New York: Harcourt Brace, 1991.

Haven, Kendall. *Women at the Edge of Discovery.* Westport, CT: Libraries Unlimited, 2003.

Hudler, George. *Magical Mushrooms, Mischievous Molds.* Princeton, NJ: Princeton University Press, 1998.

Silverstein, Alvin. *Fungi.* New York: 21st Century Books, 1996.

Souza, Dorothy. *What Is a fungus?* New York: Franklin Watts, 2002.

Vare, Ethlie Ann, and Greg Ptacek. *Mothers of Invention.* New York: William Morrow, 1992.

———. *Patently Female: Stories of Women Inventors.* New York: John Wiley & Sons, 2002.

Product Bar Codes

> **What Is It?** A simple, machine-readable line code used to inventory and iden-
> tify items or products.
>
> **Who Invented It?** Joseph Woodland and Bernard Silver (in Philadelphia)

Why Is *This* Invention One of the 100 Greatest?

Tracking and inventorying parts and products on stores shelve and in warehouses became a serious problem in the first half of the twentieth century. The problem hurt business,
government, and every aspect of the economy.

Bar codes solved the problem and have saved billions of employee hours and company
dollars. Virtually every part and product has a bar code used to track and inventory it. Bar
codes have quickly become the one and only, universally accepted way to track sales, inventory, production, and product movement. Bar codes have changed the way manufacturing, transportation, and sales are organized and managed.

History of the Invention

What Did People Do Before?

Periodic "inventories" meant that each item had to be physically counted by some person. Arriving shipments were often delayed days at the loading dock, waiting to be invento-
ried. Grocery stores had to close and bring in teams of clerks to count every item on every
shelf. Countless millions of dollars' worth of time and material were wasted each year because there was no easy way to track parts and products as they flowed through manufacturing, distribution, and retail centers.

How Were Bar Codes Invented?

In 1948 Bernard Silver was a graduate student at the Drexel Institute of Technology in
Philadelphia. He overheard the president of a local grocery store chain pleading with the
school's dean to create a way to automatically record product information at the checkout.
The dean said it couldn't be done. But Silver and his friend and fellow grad student, Joseph
Woodland, decided that they *could* do it and believed they'd make a fortune when they did.

Silver's first idea was to use patterns of ink that glowed under ultraviolet light. The paints were expensive, unstable, and tended to smear. Next he tried a raised Braille system of markings. These were difficult to install and often damaged the product.

After several months of work, Silver decided to try Morse code (the system of dots and dashes invented by Samuel Morse). Silver soon got the idea to extend the Morse code dashes and dots downward to make fat and skinny lines. This idea remains the basis for all bar coding.

Woodland tried to design a machine to read and record the bar codes. He thought of using the system invented by Hollywood's Lee DeForest for early movie sound tracks. DeForest printed patterns of light and dark on the edge of movie film. The projector shined a light through these patterns. A special receiver transformed the light beam into an electrical current that could be turned back into sound. It was a grand idea, but it didn't work for Woodland. His lights weren't powerful enough. The light reflected off a bar code didn't affect the receiver as did light transmitted through a piece of translucent film.

In 1951 the two decided that they needed to build a demonstration bar code reader in Woodland's house in Binghamton, New York. They created a machine that was the size of a desk, had to be wrapped in black cloth to block outside light, and used a 500-watt bulb. The light had to be that bright in order to reflect enough light off a bar code to be detected by the movie sound receiver. The first two pieces of paper they marked with bar codes and tried to read burned up from the intense heat of the 500-watt bulb.

With a better cooling fan, the system worked—though it was frightfully noisy and bulky. But Woodland and Silver still didn't know what to do with the wavy lines their reader produced and displayed on an oscilloscope. They could now create and read bar codes, but couldn't provide any useful information from what they read. The technology didn't exist to make it work.

Two developments in the 1960s changed that. First, lasers were invented. A milli-watt laser could easily produce as much focused light as did Woodland's 500-watt monster bulb. Second, computer technology advanced to the point where a computer could easily read, store, and process the information on a bar code.

In 1972, the grocery industry adopted the Uniform Product Code (UPC), which assigned a number code to each product and manufacturer. By early 1974, most manufacturers were printing these numbers as bar codes on their packages—even though scanners and readers did not yet exist.

The first bar code scanner, using Silver and Woodland's new laser beam design, was installed in June 1974 in Marsh's supermarket in Troy, Ohio. On June 26, the system went operational with four scanners (one at each checkout counter) linked to a simple counting computer in the store office. The first product ever scanned was a ten-pack of Wrigley's Juicy Fruit chewing gum. Today, that pack of gum is on display at the Smithsonian Institution Museum of American History.

What's Happened Since Then?

Grocery stores were the first to use bar codes and scanners. Next came food distributors and wholesalers. Auto manufacturers soon followed and slapped bar codes on every part that flowed along each of their auto assembly lines.

Now scanners exist at virtually every checkout in every kind of retail store. Airline lost luggage claims are down by 95 percent percent because airlines use bar codes to track bags.

Although the first president Bush awarded Woodland the 1992 National Medal of Technology for inventing bar codes, neither Woodland nor Silver made much money from their idea, which started a billion-dollar business and has saved the grocery industry alone over $500 million each year.

 Fun Fact: Companies now make bar code scanners small enough to fit on your key chain. Carry one and you can scan any product to check prices while you shop.

More to Explore

Aaseng, Nathan. *Twentieth-Century Inventors.* New York: Facts on File, 1996.

Adams, Russ. *The Black and White Solution.* Philadelphia: Helmers Publishing, 1997.

Bushnell, Richard. *Getting Started with Bar Codes.* Denver, CO: Cutter Information Corp., 1998.

Dyson, James. *A History of Great Inventions.* New York: Carroll & Graf Publishers, 2001.

Palmer, Roger. *The Bar Code Book.* Philadelphia: Helmers Publishing, 2001.

Romanek, Trudee. *The Technology Book for Girls and Other Advanced Beings.* Chicago: Kids Can Press, 2001.

Truvey, Peter. *Everyday Things and How They Work.* New York: Scholastic Library Publishing, 1996.

van Dulken, Stephen. *Inventing the 20th Century.* New York: New York University Press, 2000.

Chemotherapy

Year of Invention: 1950

> **What Is It?** Chemical compounds able to selectively target and destroy cancer cells within the body.
>
> **Who Invented It?** Gertrude Elion (in New York City)

Why Is *This* Invention One of the 100 Greatest?

The chemical compounds Gertrude Elion created were the first weapons given to doctors that successfully fought the death sentence of cancer. Her chemical compounds attacked cancerous cells while leaving most normal cells unaffected. Millions of people are alive today because of her invention.

Her approach to the development of chemotherapy drugs also led to the discovery of a new family of drugs that have saved millions of lives and have led to miracle cures for diseases, from cancers, to herpes, to gout, to AIDS.

History of the Invention

What Did People Do Before?

Cancer had always been a death sentence. From the moment of diagnosis, there was virtually nothing doctors could do to either slow or to defeat this disease.

Medical science didn't understand how cancer cells worked, how they grew so fast and so powerfully, why cancer happened, what triggered a cancer to start, or even how to detect and prevent it before the disease took hold of a person's body. The only drugs in a doctors' arsenal were used to ease cancer's pain and to make patients comfortable.

How Was Chemotherapy Invented?

In 1933, when Gertrude Elion was 15, her beloved grandfather lay shriveled and pasty-white, dying of stomach cancer. He had lived with Gertrude's family since she was three and had been her companion while growing up. To Gertrude, it was a stranger lying in the bed. His skin was almost translucent and so fragile looking she barely dared touch him. The robust laughter she loved had been replaced by raspy whispers and a face etched in pain. The body had shrunk in on the bones, looking more like a corpse than a vital being.

The terrible sight of what cancer had done to her grandfather, more than anything else, made Gertrude choose her career. It made her a woman with an unstoppable mission.

Gertrude Elion graduated with honors from Hunters College in 1937. Then she ran smack into two big obstacles: the Great Depression and sex discrimination. The Depression meant that precious few jobs existed. Sex discrimination meant that no one would consider giving one of them to a woman.

For seven years, Gertrude Elion worked at temporary jobs, studying for her master's degree at night and on weekends at the NYU lab. When the United States entered World War II, everything changed and positions were suddenly available to women. Elion landed a research position with Johnson & Johnson's chemical research division. That unit closed six months later, and she contacted the Burroughs Wellcome Company, whose research laboratory was hiring.

Senior chemist George Hitchings hired her to investigate the chemistry of purines and pyrimidines, the building blocks of RNA and DNA. Scientists had just discovered that DNA was the carrier of genetic information. No one yet understood how these "nucleic acid" chains stored and transmitted their genetic blueprint and operating instructions for a living body.

Hitchings was trying to develop drugs by imitating natural compounds. In the past, drugs had been developed using slow, trial-and-error methods. Hitchings felt it should be possible to develop a more scientific approach based on a knowledge of cell growth. He hoped to fool harmful cells into taking in a synthetic compound that was similar to a natural compound the cell needed for growth. This, then, would kill the harmful or defective cell. He was hoping to create false building blocks that cancerous cells would absorb and that would kill the cancerous cells without harming normal cells.

Gertrude Elion went to work in the lab, conducting experiments that would help her understand the cell growth process that was stored in the coding of DNA's purines and pyrimidines. Five years after she began her work (in 1950), Elion made her first breakthrough. She uncovered a specific chemical process essential to cell growth that is mutated and accelerated in cancerous cells. Within months of this discovery, she invented not one but two anticancer drugs, thioguanine and 6-MP. 6-MP, taken with other anticancer drugs, cured childhood leukemia. Now 80 percent of children with leukemia survive, thanks mostly to Elion's research. These drugs were the first effective therapy capable of defeating a specific form of cancer.

What's Happened Since Then?

In 1957, Elion discovered that her anticancer drug, 6-MP, could also suppress the body's immune system, thereby allowing organ transplants. Up until that time, organ transplants never worked because the body's immune system attacked any foreign (transplanted) organ. Elion discovered that with a relative of 6-MP called Imuran, doctors could suppress the immune system long enough so that the organ transplant would be successful.

Gertrude Elion's research methods revolutionized drug-making and medicine. Now an army of cancer-specific drugs is at doctor's disposal to attack and destroy almost any specific form of cancer. While the war on cancer is far from won, patients now stand a much better than average chance of survival.

Fun Fact: More than 90 medications developed for humans are also used for pets. The same chemotherapy drugs used in humans are used in animal chemotherapy.

More to Explore

Bardhan-Quallen, Sudipta. *Chemotherapy*. New York: Thomson/Gale, 2003.

Camp, Carole Ann. *American Women of Science*. Berkeley Heights, NJ: Enslow Publishers, 2002.

Haven, Kendall, and Donna Clark. *100 Most Popular Scientists for Young Adults*. Englewood, CO: Libraries Unlimited, 1999.

Mattern, Joanne. *Gertrude Elion and the Development of Revolutionary Medications*. New York: Mitchell Lane Publishers, 2004.

McGrayne, Sharon. *Nobel Prize Women in Science: Their Lives, Struggles, and Momentous Discoveries*. New York: Carol Publishing, 1998.

McPartland, Scott. *Gertrude Elion: Master Chemist*. New York: Rourke Enterprises, 1995.

Stille, Darlene. *Extraordinary Women Scientists*. Chicago: Children's Press, 1995.

Vare, Ethlie Ann, and Greg Ptacek. *Patently Female: Stories of Women Inventors*. New York: John Wiley & Sons, 2002.

Zach, Kim. *Hidden from History: The Lives of Eight American Women Scientists*. Greensboro, NC: Avisson Press, 2002.

Birth Control Pill

Year of Invention: 1954

What Is It? An oral pill to prevent unwanted pregnancy.

Who Invented It? Gregory Pincus (in Shrewsbury, Massachusetts)

Why Is *This* Invention One of the 100 Greatest?

Couples have forever sought safe, reliable contraception. The oral birth control pill was the first such product. This pill is so important, so widely used, it's simply called "The Pill."

The birth control pill meant freedom for countless women and has changed our culture by allowing more women to enter the kinds of positions, careers, and roles where their ideas and beliefs can affect the direction and policies of organizations, corporations, and governmental agencies. The pill was also a turning point for science. It represented the first time science was able to demonstrate that it understood a biological process well enough to successfully tinker with it.

History of the Invention

What Did People Do Before?

Birth control has been an important social issue since the days of the Roman Empire. Dozens of methods have been tried. Some worked reasonably well. Some didn't. Unplanned and unwanted pregnancies were common. No method was truly reliable.

How Was the Birth Control Pill Invented?

The invention of the birth control pill is a story of one hormone, four men, and one woman. Research into the hormones that seemed to dominate the process of human pregnancy began in the 1920s. Within a few years, that effort centered on one hormone, *progesterone*. Pregnant women were found to have much higher levels of that hormone than non-pregnant women.

Researchers soon suspected that progesterone blocked the normal activity of the menstrual cycle. It was as if a high concentration of progesterone announced "we're pregnant!" to the body and instructed the brain not to request the release of a monthly egg. But natural progesterone was difficult to isolate and frightfully expensive.

Enter man number one. Russell Marker was a chemist and professor at Penn State University. In 1938 he discovered an alternative source of progesterone in one variety of Mexican yams. In 1940, he quit his job to study these yams. He wanted to find a way to artificially manufacture his substitute progesterone, but could not do it and gave up in 1947.

Enter men numbers two and three. Carl Djerassi and Frank Colton were both born in 1923. Djerassi, a novelist and chemist, had already become wealthy from his first major invention: antihistamines. In 1946, he read of Marker's work and focused his research on progesterone.

In 1947 he created a chemical compound that mimicked progesterone inside the body of laboratory animals. Djerassi wanted to use this synthetic version of the hormone to treat menstrual discomfort and side effects, believing there would be a big market for such a product.

Djerassi's compound worked when given as a shot. However, he knew the drug would have to be administered orally—as a pill—if it was to enjoy sales success. Djerassi spent a year modifying his compound to survive being taken orally. He patented the final version in 1951.

Frank Colton of Chicago worked for the G.D. Searle chemical company. Without knowing anything about Djerassi's work, Colton began the same search in 1946, also beginning with Marker's yam work. Colton created a similar compound than Djerassi's and brought his to the marketplace in early 1952 to relieve the discomfort, cramps, and other side effects of a woman's monthly period.

Gregory Pincus, man number four in this story, was a medical doctor and research director of the Worcester Foundation of Experimental Biology in Shrewsbury, Massachusetts. The foundation had been studying female infertility since the early 1930s. In the late 1940s, Pincus discovered that a woman's monthly egg release stopped if she was given shots of progesterone to raise her progesterone level to that of a pregnant woman.

In 1953, Pincus was approached by Katherine McCormick, heiress to the McCormick harvester fortune and the one woman in the story. She was searching for a worthwhile cause to support. Margaret Sanger, famed birth control advocate, suggested that work to create a safe, reliable contraceptive was the greatest need facing women of the day. McCormick asked Pincus to develop this product and backed her request with $2 million for research support.

Pincus believed that his research proved that progesterone could block the release of an egg and thus provide effective contraception. However, he had administered his progesterone as shots. When Pincus read about the work by Colton and Djerassi, he realized that, while they were focused on easing menstrual discomfort, they had each also created a birth control pill.

He studied the compounds of each inventor and their dose levels. Finally, Pincus selected Colton's formula. In 1954, Pincus began trials in Puerto Rico of Colton's formula as an oral contraceptive pill and obtained remarkable success over a five-year study. The Pill was ready for the market.

What's Happened Since Then?

Federal regulators approved Pincus's pill in 1960. Searle named it Enovid. Novelist Aldous Huxley coined the name "The Pill" in his 1958 book *Brave New World Revisited.*

The modern birth control pill is considerably different than Pincus's. Modern dose levels have been lowered to about 5 percent percent of the original level, and manufacturers now include a combination of hormones instead of just progesterone.

 Fun Fact: Doctors predict that a male birth control pill will be available within the next few years.

More to Explore

Djerassi, Carl. *This Man's Pill: Reflections on the 50th Birthday of the Pill.* New York: Oxford University Press, 2004.

Dyson, James. *A History of Great Inventions.* New York: Carroll & Graf Publishers, 2001.

Jeffries, Michael, and Gary Lewis. *Inventors and Inventions.* New York: Smithmark, 1997.

Riddle, John. *Eve's Herbs: A History of Contraception and Abortion in the West.* Cambridge, MA: Harvard University Press, 1999.

van Dulken, Stephen. *Inventing the 20th Century.* New York: New York University Press, 2000.

Watkins, Elizabeth. *On the Pill: A Social History of Oral Contraceptives, 1950–1970.* Baltimore: Johns Hopkins University Press, 2001.

Solar Cells

Year of Invention: 1954

What Is It? A chemical process to convert the sun's radiation into electricity.

Who Invented It? David Chapin and Carl Fuller (in New Jersey)

Why Is *This* Invention One of the 100 Greatest?

Electricity is our most important energy source. Yet most of our electricity comes from nonrenewable resources—coal, oil, and gas—that also create millions of tons of pollutants and contribute to the greenhouse gasses that spawn global warming.

The only permanent solution is to shift our energy dependence to renewable, nonpolluting sources. Of these, the sun offers the greatest potential. Solar cells convert sunlight directly into electricity and represent our best hope for a "permanent" supply of essential electricity.

History of the Invention

What Did People Do Before?

Solar energy has been used as a heat source for thousands of years. Archimedes reflected concentrated solar light off polished shields onto the sails of attacking Roman ships in 240 B.C. and "reduced the Roman Navy to ashes."

Clothes are dried in the sun. Water is heated by focusing solar radiation on it. In 1768, French scientist Antoine Lavoisier built a series of curved mirrors to focus solar energy in a concentrated spot to run a solar furnace that could reach 3,300°F. He also built a steam engine driven by concentrated solar energy.

How Were Solar Cells Invented?

French physicist Edmond Becquerel was the first to discover that sunlight could induce an electrical current. In 1839, Becquerel submerged the ends of two metal strips in an acid bath. He connected the exposed ends of the strips through a light bulb and a meter to measure electrical flow.

Over the course of months, Becquerel tested different metals and combinations of metals for the two strips he used. One day he realized that the amount of electricity his metal strips produced often increased when the two metal strips were placed in direct sunlight. It depended on the metals he used, but he often noticed a marked increase in electrical current when he slid his experiment's container into the light. Becquerel named this phenomenon the *photovoltaic effect.*

In 1873, American scientist Willoughby Smith discovered that selenium was particularly light sensitive and produced the photovoltaic effect Becquerel had discovered.

In 1888, American inventor Charles Fritz capitalized on Willoughby Smith's discovery and constructed the world's first photovoltaic cells. He covered strips of selenium with a thin film of gold, letting an electrical circuit flow from the selenium side of his photovoltaic wafer to the gold side.

Unfortunately, Fritz's photovoltaic cell only converted 1 percent percent of the incoming solar radiation into electricity. Because selenium and gold were expensive, the electricity he produced was outrageously expensive.

In 1941, American inventor Russell Ohl discovered that silicon, a semiconductor, could be used as the material in a photovoltaic cell to generate an electric current. Silicon was much cheaper than selenium and gold. While his use of silicon rekindled some interest in photovoltaics, Ohl's cells didn't produce enough electricity to be of any real value.

In 1954, a team working at AT&T's Bell Labs in New Jersey (headed by David Chapin and Carl Fuller) devised a way to use Ohl's silicon in a more efficient way. When they formed silicon into a crystalline matrix and added other elements to it, they found that they could change its electrical properties. If they added phosphorous, the matrix became negatively charged. They called this structure an n-type semiconductor ("n" for negative). If they added boron, the crystal lattice gained a positive charge. They called this a p-type semiconductor ("p" for positive).

When the team sandwiched layers of n-type and p-type silicon semiconductors together, they increased the cell's solar efficiency to over 7 percent percent. These photovoltaic cells were still more expensive than commercial power. But they were efficient enough for commercial production.

What's Happened Since Then?

By 1956 the Bell Labs team had increased cell efficiency to over 9 percent. The Massachusetts Institute of Technology (MIT) built the first solar-powered building on its Cambridge, Massachusetts, campus in 1958. Also in 1958, both the United States and the USSR designed solar cell panels to power their first generations of communications satellites. Every vehicle and satellite launched into space has relied on banks of solar cells for electrical power.

The first solar power plant (a 1.5 megawatt plant) was built at the Volcano Observatory in Hawaii in 1980. Since then, larger photovoltaic plants have been built in the California desert, in Arizona, and across Africa.

The efficiency of modern cells hovers around 15 percent. However, new experimental gallium-arsenic photovoltaic cells are proving to be cheaper than silicon, with efficiencies up to 22 percent. Electricity from these cells is almost as cheap as commercial electricity. The future appears bright for this still-emerging energy technology.

Fun Fact: In 2000, the space shuttle *Endeavor's* crew installed new solar panels on the International Space Station. These panels are so big and so reflective that they are clearly visible from Earth and are outshined only by the planets and brightest stars.

More to Explore

Asimov, Isaac. *How Did We Find Out About Solar Power?* New York: William Morrow & Co., 1986.

Brooke, Bob. *Solar Energy.* New York: Chelsea House, 1995.

Graham, Ian. *Solar Power,* Volume 4. New York: Raintree Publishers, 1999.

Jones, Susan. *Solar Power of the Future.* New York: The Rosen Publishing Group, 2003.

Sherman, Josepha. *Energy at Work: Solar Energy.* Mankato, MN: Capstone Press, 2004.

Yenne, Bill. *100 Inventions That Shaped World History.* New York: Bluewood Books, 1993.

Radioimmunoassay

Year of Invention: 1955

What Is It? A blood test that measures trace amounts of blood components.

Who Invented It? Rosalyn Yalow (in New York)

Why Is *This* Invention One of the 100 Greatest?

The 1977 Nobel Prize committee wrote that Rosalyn Yalow's radioimmunoassay (RIA) "brought a revolution in biological and medical research." They said that it was "more important than the discovery of X-rays."

RIA is used to measure hormones, vitamins, enzymes, toxins, and other trace elements too minute to be otherwise detected. For the first time in history, doctors could accurately diagnose conditions associated with minute changes in hormones—some cancers, hypertension, diabetes, thyroid disease, and sterility. Criminologists use RIA to detect the minute presence of lethal drugs in corpses. The versatility and dependability of this procedure have made it one of the most effective diagnostic tools ever invented.

History of the Invention

What Did People Do Before?

Doctors struggled to make accurate diagnoses of many diseases through the mid-twentieth century, often having to base a diagnosis on indirect information and indirect clues. Far too often a firm diagnosis required specific chemical information that doctors had no way to obtain. Diagnosis was more art than precise science.

How Was Radioimmunoassay Invented?

By age eight (in 1930), Rosalyn Sussman (her married name was Yalow) decided that she wanted to be a "big-deal scientist." She liked knowing things; she liked logic.

When the United States entered World War II, the draft quickly depleted graduate programs of their male students. For a few short years, graduate programs opened their doors to women. Rosalyn received her Ph.D. in nuclear physics in 1945 and moved back to New York City. Radioisotopes (artificially produced radioactive substances) were just coming into use in medicine, and in 1947, Yalow began her work in nuclear medicine for the Veterans Affairs Medical Center in the Bronx.

Rosalyn began a series of radioisotope studies on VA patients. She converted a janitor's closet into a makeshift laboratory for her work—one of the first radioisotopes labs in the United States. Commercial equipment designed for radioisotope work was not yet available. Rosalyn had to design and build most of her own equipment.

At the VA Center she met Soloman Berson, a young physician. They formed a research partnership that would last 22 years. Berson knew physiology, anatomy, and clinical medicine. Yalow knew physics, mathematics, chemistry, and engineering.

The pair focused their work on insulin research by injecting patients with radioactively tagged insulin and taking frequent blood samples to measure how fast the insulin disappeared from the patient's system. Surprisingly, the tagged insulin took *longer* to disappear from diabetics than from non-diabetics.

Intuitively, their results seemed backwards. The problem with diabetics was that insulin drained out of their system too quickly and their bodies couldn't replace it. The tagged insulin should have left their bodies sooner.

After repeated studies, Yalow reasoned that the immune system of the diabetics must produce antibodies to fight the foreign insulin. Those antibodies must have attached to some of the radioactively tagged insulin and held it in the blood stream longer.

The conventional wisdom of the day said that an insulin molecule was too small to produce antibodies. Still, Yalow and Berson had their data. They felt confident of their results.

Then Yalow realized something startling: their technique was actually detecting and measuring the *antibodies* to a hormone—something no one had ever done before. However, that also meant that the inverse of their procedure would measure the hormone itself—something else no one had ever been able to do. They called this method radioimmunoassay (RIA) because it used radioactive substances to measure (assay) antibodies produced by the immune system.

This test worked by placing a patient's blood sample (which included the hormone they wished to measure) into a test tube. They added the hormone's antibody and mixed in a small amount of the radioactive form of the hormone. Then they waited. It could take a few hours to a few days, but eventually the natural hormone and the radioactive hormone would fight to combine with the antibody molecule. By measuring how much of the radioactive hormone actually bonded with the antibody, they could calculate how much of the natural hormone had been present in the patient's body.

Their technique had several powerful advantages. First, it was astoundingly sensitive. It could detect a spoonful of sugar in a body of water 62 miles long, 62 miles wide, and 30 feet deep. Second, it was a test-tube operation, so no radiation entered a patient's body. Third, the test only required tiny amounts of blood for each test. Fourth, it worked for nearly every hormone. Finally, different substances could be tested simultaneously. It was a major breakthrough!

What's Happened Since Then?

It took 10 years for the scientific community to realize the value of what Yalow and Berson had invented. RIA soon became a standard diagnostic tool in every hospital and medical center.

Yalow and Berson didn't patent RIA. If they had, it would have made them rich. Instead, they released their invention to the world. In 1977 (two years after Dr. Berson's death) Rosalyn Yalow was awarded the Nobel Prize for their invention, only the second female to win a Nobel prize in science.

 Fun Fact: Even though there were no books in the house when Rosalyn Yalow was young, still she learned to read before kindergarten. She made twice-weekly trips to the library for books, beginning at the age of three.

More to Explore

Brown, David. *Inventing Modern America.* Cambridge, MA: The MIT Press, 2002.

Dash, Joan. *Triumph of Discovery: Women Scientists Who Won the Nobel Prize.* New York: Silver Burdett Press, 1995.

Freeman, Leonard, ed. *Radioimmunoassay.* New York: W. B. Saunders Co., 1993.

Garell, Dale C., ed. *Nuclear Medicine.* New York: Chelsea House Publishers, 1995.

Haven, Kendall, and Donna Clark. *100 Most Popular Scientists for Young Adults.* Englewood, CO: Libraries Unlimited, 1999.

McGrayne, Sharon Bertsch. *Nobel Prize Women in Science: Their Lives, Struggles, and Momentous Discoveries.* New York: Carol Publishing Group, A Birch Lane Press Book, 1993.

Mould, Richard. *A Century of X-Rays and Radioactivity in Medicine: With Emphasis on Photographic Records of the Early Years.* New York: Institute of Physics Publishing, 1995.

Murphy, Wendy. *Nuclear Medicine.* New York: Chelsea House Publishers, 1997.

Stille, Darlene R. *Extraordinary Women Scientists.* Chicago: Children's Press, 1995.

Vare, Ethlie Ann, and Greg Ptacek. *Mothers of Invention.* New York: William Morrow, 1989.

Robots

Year of Invention: 1956

> **What Is It?** A machine guided by automatic controls or programming that performs complicated and often repetitive tasks.
>
> **Who Invented It?** Joe Engelberger and George Devol (in Stamford, Connecticut)

Why Is *This* Invention One of the 100 Greatest?

Over 1.4 million robots are currently on the job in industrial plants, performing the most dangerous, backbreaking jobs 24 hours a day without complaint. Robots have already vastly multiplied the productivity of every human worker. Even though their full potential and importance lie in the future, robots have already redesigned and redefined the workplace and may soon do the same for the home.

History of the Invention

What Did People Do Before?

In a 1921 play, Czech playwright Karel Capek invented the word *robot* from the Czech word for "compulsory labor." But the idea of robots—machines that do specific, preprogrammed work—started centuries earlier. In 1350, German clockmakers built a mechanical rooster on top of a Strasbourg, Germany, cathedral that automatically flapped its wings and crowed exactly at noon. In 1497 Italian clockmakers built two bell-ringing giants atop the clock tower in Piazza San Marco, Venice, Italy.

In 1942, American science writer Isaac Asimov created the word *robotics* in his collection of stories, *I Robot*. In the same year, the Johns Hopkins Engineering Department built "the Beast," a four-legged walking vehicle. In 1943, Doug Ross at MIT created MPT (Machine Programming Tools), a language to instruct mill machines.

By 1945, the Ford Motor Company had converted its Detroit plants to use automatons, single-purpose machines built to do specific jobs along the assembly line. But automatons were still machines, not thinking robots.

How Were Robots Invented?

Initially, researchers thought that the great challenge in building a robot would be devising ways to mimic human motion. Hands and arms reach, grasp, pick up, turn over, and rotate. Humans can carry, bend, stoop, etc. It seemed that a bewildering maze of servomotors and hydraulics would be required.

By 1945, however, researchers realized that the real challenge would be to control and program a robot. In 1946, George Devol invented a system that provided recorded instructions to a robot. He based his directions on MIT's Machine Programming Tools (MPT) language. A series of commands (reach six inches forward, grab, lift, turn 120 degrees to the left, etc.) could be recorded on tape and replayed to direct a robot through that same specific series of actions over and over again.

Also in 1946, the first commercial electronic computer, ENIAC, came on line. In 1948 Americans Bardeen and Shockley invented the transistor, giving birth to the age of micro-electronics, microchips, and logic circuits.

In 1953 American engineer Victor Scheinman created the first truly flexible mechanical arm, the Programmable Universal Manipulator Arm, or PUMA.

In early 1956, George Devol and mechanical engineer Joe Engelberger met over cocktails to discuss Isaac Asimov's fictional ideas about robots. The two engineers decided that they could bring Asimov's concepts out of fiction and into reality. They formed the Universal Automation company and then shortened the name to Unimation.

First on paper, and then physically, they assembled the available robot technology and realized that the pieces existed to build a programmable, general purpose robotic arm—one that could be reprogrammed over and over again to do different jobs.

However, in order to make it truly useful, the arm would need some sort of sensory and feedback system. How would it *know* if a part sat in exactly the right place to be picked up, or that it had turned and positioned a thing correctly for the next step? What would it do if it saw something it didn't expect?

Certainly, they could build pressure sensors into their arm and mount cameras on it. But how could they teach their robotic arm to use the information received from these sensors? Suddenly, their robot's program became much more complicated.

They ruled out camera sensors since video information was too complex for the computer technology available in the mid-1950s. Simple pressure sensors seemed more appropriate. Now their robot could execute a motion and then read each sensor to see if it felt the pressure it was supposed to feel. If it didn't, an adjustment program could direct the robot to move or turn in specified ways to see if that fixed the problem. Slowly, they taught their robot to grope in order to make things right.

In late 1959, Devol and Engelberger completed their first general purpose, programmable robotic arm and named it Unimate. In 1960, General Motors bought the idea. The first Unimates started work in General Motors automobile assembly lines. Some Unimates lifted hot pieces from die casting machines and delivered them to other workstations. The other Unimates performed spot welding on auto bodies. All Unimates performed exactly as programmed and were easy to reprogram for the next year's models and specific pieces.

What's Happened Since Then?

In the 1960s engineers first developed the CAD-CAM (Computer Aided Design-Computer Aided Manufacturing) computer programs and wove them into robot technology.

In 1968 Hughes aircraft created Mobots (audio remote controlled camera systems) to inspect in hazardous and dangerous areas. In 1970 AI (artificial intelligence) computer electronics first appeared and were built into Stanford Research Institute's robot, Shakey. In 1983, Mobile Robotics built Odetics, a six-legged vehicle capable of climbing over objects.

By 1995, more than 700,000 robots worked full-time in the industrial world—500,000 in Japan, 120,000 in Western Europe, and 60,000 in the United States. That number more than doubled by 2000. Robots are being designed to entertain, to explore, and to perform jobs considered dangerous, repetitive, awkward, or hazardous.

Modern robots still look like machines—even those so small that they consist of only a few atoms. The real potential of robots has not yet even been dreamed of. Many think that robots will be as essential and natural a part of future generations' lives as electricity and telephones are in ours.

 Fun Fact: NASA's Robonaut is a prototype mechanical astronaut. Anticipated to first fly within the next several years, the first Robonauts have a striking resemblance to Boba Fett, the interstellar bounty hunter in the *Star Wars* movie series.

More to Explore

Billard, Mary. *All About Robots.* New York: Penguin Books, 1995.

Dyson, James. *A History of Great Inventions.* New York: Carroll & Graf Publishers, 2001.

Green, Carol. *Robots.* New York: Scholastic Library Publishing, 1998.

Lockman, Darcy. *Robots.* New York: Marshall Cavendish, 2000.

Marrs, Texe. *The Great Robot Book.* New York: Silver Burdett Press, 1995.

McNeil, Ian. *An Encyclopedia of the History of Technology.* New York: Routledge, 1996.

Perry, Robert. *Artificial Intelligence.* New York: Scholastic Library Publishing, 2000.

Storrs, Graham. *Robot Age.* New York: Franklin Watts, 1996.

Endoscope
(Arthroscopic Surgery)

Year of Invention: 1957

> **What Is It?** A device that allows doctors to see and work inside body cavities without making large incisions.
>
> **Who Invented It?** Basil Hirschowitz (in Ann Arbor, Michigan)

Why Is *This* Invention One of the 100 Greatest?

Arthroscopic surgeries featuring fiber optic endoscopes are minimally invasive, create fewer complications, are faster and less expensive, and allow for speedier recovery. Arthroscopic surgery patients stay in the hospital for hours instead of weeks. They leave patients with minimal pain and risk of infection or complication. Endoscopy comes from Greek words meaning "to look inside." Arthroscopic means *microsurgery*.

Arthroscopic surgery revolutionized orthopedic medicine and has been hailed as a great cost cutter for diagnosis and surgery. This process radically changed many areas of body observation and diagnosis, as well as surgery.

History of the Invention

What Did People Do Before?

Before arthroscopic surgery, repairing joint damage meant long half-moon scars and months of painful rehabilitation and therapy. Valuable exploratory surgeries were rare because their long, open gashes created more problems than the information was worth.

Early attempts to peer inside the body used microscope and telescope technology. The tubes were rigid and often several inches across. Worse, when a viewing tube was able to penetrate into a body cavity, there was no light, so the physician still could not see.

The first scope with attached lights was constructed in 1853. However, it was so big and bulky that major surgery was required to open a pathway for the scope.

How Was Arthroscopic Surgery Invented?

Forty-four-year-old Basil Hirschowitz accepted a teaching and research position in the School of Medicine at the University of Michigan at Ann Arbor in 1954, moving there from Belgium. In his work as a doctor, a medical researcher, and a teacher, Hirschowitz was regularly confounded by the inability of doctors to see inside joints and body cavities to assess damage and make accurate diagnoses. It felt like groping in the dark for hints and clues when exact information lay right in front of him, if only he could turn on the lights and see.

In 1955, Hirschowitz visited researchers in the United Kingdom who were sending light signals through long strands of glass fiber. Hirschowitz realized that light traveling down a flexible glass fiber might make the perfect scope and should be able to transmit light into a body cavity. If he could also find a miniature camera that could be inserted along with the light, then detailed pictures could be transmitted back to a viewing screen.

However, Hirschowitz faced several major problems. First, a glass tube could break, scattering shards of glass through the patient's body. Second, no existing camera was small enough to work as part of the flexible probe he envisioned inserting into patients.

Hirschowitz hired graduate student Larry Curtiss to work on the problem. After six months of research and a series of preliminary experiments, Curtiss concluded that too much light diffused out of the glass to make a single glass rod useful for their purposes. After another round of research into the characteristics of different types of glass fibers, Curtiss suggested that melting a tube of glass fibers onto the outside of a higher-quality glass rod would produce a channel capable of sustaining a focused light beam.

In late 1956 they tried it. The core glass rod carried a strong light image, as bright as a good flashlight. The outer coat (called the cladding) locked the light signal inside the inner fiber. It worked—but it was still glass, and Hirschowitz was uncomfortable using a glass probe. Hirschowitz soon hit upon silicon dioxide, a compound telephone communications companies were experimenting with for fiber optic voice channels.

Hirschowitz and Curtiss found that long fibers of silicon dioxide worked as well as glass and remained plastic-like and bendable. Moreover, this new fiber transmitted light so well that it eliminated the need to send a camera into the body. They would attach a light source to one fiber that would shine light into the body while a visual image of whatever was illuminated would travel back up a second fiber that they would connect to a video monitor.

The first test of Hirschowitz's scope occurred in February 1957. Doctors at the university hospital used it on a knee repair operation. Hirschowitz assisted in the operation and operated the scope. It worked flawlessly, having opened the joint to detailed study with only a tiny (1.5-inch) incision that required no more than three stitches.

What's Happened Since Then?

The use of Hirschowitz's endoscope for other diagnoses and surgical procedures expanded rapidly once doctors saw it in operation. By 1980, tissue biopsies as well as visualization of virtually every organ and major blood vessel were routinely conducted with Hirschowitz's endoscope.

By 1970, it was clear that Hirschowitz's fiber optic cable was better than the fibers being used by the telecommunications industry. They switched to Hirschowitz's design.

In 2001, a pill-size, remote-controlled, self-powered camera was invented that could be swallowed by a patient and then, directed by a doctor, make a tiny incision to enter the blood stream and travel to any desired corner of the body. This may become the new version of an endoscope and completely eliminate any surface incision.

 Fun Fact: Endoscopic sympathectomy requires the world's smallest endoscope. The fiber bundle in this scope measures only three millimeters wide (one-tenth of an inch) and is used to locate nerves that run behind the lungs and through the chest.

More to Explore

Asimov, Isaac. *Asimov's Chronology of Science and Discovery*. New York: Harper & Row, 1989.

Eyewitness Books. *Technology*. New York: DK Publishing, 2000.

Koos, Wolfgang T. *Color Atlas of Microsurgery of Acoustic Neurinomas: Endoscope-Assisted Techniques, Neuronavigational Techniques, Radiosurgery*. Baltimore: Thieme Medical Publishers, 2002.

McGinty, Joh. *Operative Arthroscopy*. New York: Lippincott Williams & Wilkins, 2002.

Perneczky, Axel. *Keyhole Concept in Neurosurgery: With Endoscope-Assisted Microsurgery and Case Studies*. Baltimore: Thieme Medical Publishers, 1999.

Wilbur, Keith. *Antique Medical Instruments*. New York: Schiffer Publishing, 2000.

Laser

Year of Invention: 1957

> **What Is It?** A machine that produces a high-energy light beam at the same exact frequency.
>
> **Who Invented It?** Gordon Gould (in Long Island, New York)

Why Is *This* Invention One of the 100 Greatest?

Supermarket checkouts rely on laser beams to scan your purchases. So do almost all retail stores in the Western world. Many eye surgeries are routinely performed using lasers. Communication systems pack thousands of voice channels on laser beam carriers. Engineers and construction crews make extensive use of lasers. Lasers read compact disks. They manufacture surgical cutting tools. There are few aspects of modern life that are not touched by lasers.

History of the Invention

What Did People Do Before?

Lasers were not a direct replacement for any previously existing technology. People managed without. Checkout clerks punched codes and amounts into cash registers by hand. Levels and lines of sight were checked with light scopes and human eyes. Knives held by human hands performed cutting.

How Was the Laser Invented?

Charles Townes first created the theory and idea that led to lasers. He was struck with a powerful vision during a midnight stroll in the spring of 1951 while attending a Washington, D.C., conference called by the Office of Naval Intelligence. Conference attendees were searching for a way to generate higher frequency (shorter wavelength) radio signals. He couldn't sleep and decided a midnight wander might clear his head. Sitting on a park bench, he realized that, if they were ever going to produce signals with microscopically small wavelengths, then instead of using bulky vacuum tubes, they would have to use *atoms* (the smallest device known) to produce those wavelengths. That idea led to lasers.

In 1917 Albert Einstein predicted that stimulated atoms would emit photons—particles of light energy. Townes decided to use blasts of microwave radiation to stimulate atoms into emitting streams of photons. Townes called his 1953 creation a *maser* (Microwave

267

Amplification by Stimulated Emission of Radiation). Four years later, Gordon Gould invented a way to use light instead of microwaves and invented *lasers*.

By the time he reached high school, Gould knew he wanted to be an inventor. He was fascinated by physics and felt that it was a good starting point for his inventions. At the University of Columbia in the early 1950s, Gould hoped to show that light energy could stimulate atoms and force them to give off concentrated beams similar to those Townes had created with microwaves. But through three years of study Gould couldn't figure out how to do it.

On the night of November 11, 1957, as Gould lay in bed, unable to sleep, the answer popped into his head. He saw how to build a laser. He was "electrified." He spent the next day writing down all his thoughts, ideas, and sketches about his new invention, which he called a laser (**L**ight **A**mplification by **S**timulated **E**mission of **R**adiation). The following day, he had his notebooks notarized to prevent anyone from stealing his discovery. Gould had just invented a working laser.

Then he received some bad legal advice. He was told that he couldn't file a patent until he had built a working model of his laser. Since he knew that his professors at Columbia wouldn't fund a wild gamble on the invention of a laser, he left college in 1958 to build his laser.

While Gould was working on his invention, University of Columbia professors Townes and Schawlow beat him to the patent office. They filed their laser patent in late 1958. Gould did not enter his until the next year. Gould's application was rejected— deemed as having too much overlap with the Townes and Schawlow patent.

What's Happened Since Then?

Bitterly disappointed, Gould sought funding to continue his development. Recognizing the implications of laser as a weapon, Gould prepared a proposal for the U.S. Department of Defense. The armed forces not only accepted the proposal, they tripled the funding!

Unfortunately, however, Gould did not pass the intense security check and was not allowed to work on classified Department of Defense programs. Since all of his research, papers, notebooks, and notes *were* an important part of the project, *they* were marked as classified documents. Military police seized them from Gould's home and office and took them to a military base. Gould was never again allowed to see his own research notes or results.

In 1973, 16 years after Gould had invented the laser, a court ruled that the Townes-Schawlow laser patents did not contain enough information to show how to build a laser. Four years later Gould was granted his first laser patent for his laser optic pump. But his legal battles continued until, in 1986, the U.S. Patent Office Appeals Board overruled all previous objections to Gould's patents. It took 28 years, but Gould had finally won. Gould benefited in one more way from his invention. He had two laser eye operations that saved his sight.

Lasers were first commercially used as precision cutters for metal parts. Next came their use in scanners and bar code readers and for scientific measurements and medical applications.

The first ruby laser was built in 1960 by Theodore Maiman for Hughes Research in California. Ruby lasers, however, emit pulses of energy. By 1968, gas lasers existed that emitted a continuous, powerful beam.

Fun Fact: The MacDonald Laser Ringer Station near Fort Davis, Texas, uses a laser to measure the distance between the earth and the moon to an accuracy of ± 1 centimeter. It bounces laser beams off special reflector plates left on the moon by the three Apollo missions that reached the lunar surface. These laser readings have shown that the moon is drifting away from the earth at a rate of 1.5 inches a year.

More to Explore

Aaseng, Nathan. *Twentieth-Century Inventors.* New York: Facts on File, 1996.

Flatow, Ira. *They All Laughed.* New York: HarperCollins, 1999.

Haven, Kendall, and Donna Clark. *100 Most Popular Scientists for Young Adults.* Englewood, CO: Libraries Unlimited, 1999.

Taylor, Nick. *Laser.* New York: Simon & Schuster, 2000.

Tomecek, Stephen. *What a Great Idea*! New York: Scholastic, Inc. 2003.

Townes, Charles. *How the Laser Happened.* New York: Oxford University Press, 1999.

Yenne, Bill. *100 Inventions That Shaped World History.* New York: Bluewood Books, 1993.

Microchip

> **What Is It?** A block of semiconductor material constructed into various layers that form the components of a complete electronic circuit.
>
> **Who Invented It?** Jack Kilby (in Dallas, Texas)

Why Is *This* Invention One of the 100 Greatest?

Considered by many to be more impressive than the ancient alchemists' trick of turning lead into gold, modern electronic wizards turn ordinary sand into working electronic brains—microchips. Computers, video games, car electronics, smart rockets, space shuttles, jet airplanes, stereo systems, microwaves, mail sorting equipment, wrist watches, bar codes and scanners, Game Boys®, telephone routing systems, manufacturing, medical technology, smart toasters, dolls that talk, and a thousand other products that affect our daily lives owe their operation to the microchip.

History of the Invention

What Did People Do Before?

Early computers worked on banks of hundreds of vacuum tubes. As a result, they were bulky, cabinet-size (or room-size) machines that required high-powered air conditioners just to keep them from overheating.

The invention of the transistor (Bardeen and Shockley in 1947) helped. Transistors were miniature, low-heat devices that replaced vacuum tubes. Computers shrank to a tenth of their former size.

How Was the Microchip Invented?

In 1952, 29-year-old Jack Kilby worked at Centralab, a small Michigan company manufacturing miniature circuits for hearing aids, radios, and TVs. The work frustrated and disappointed Kilby. Designing hearing aid circuits seemed unimportant. Kilby felt that he would miss the great electronics revolution happening around him.

But this was also a frightfully frustrating period for electrical engineers. The complex transistorized circuits they designed often required hundreds of thousands of separate, tiny components: resistors, capacitors, transistors, and diodes. Manufacturing lines could not produce the continual perfection required of these complex circuits. There were too many components and solder points. Some would always fail and the circuit would crash.

Jack Kilby realized that Centralab was too small to make any real contribution to this struggle. He landed a job at Texas Instruments (TI) in Dallas in May 1958.

Two weeks after Kilby arrived, the TI operations virtually closed for mandatory summer vacations. Since Kilby hadn't worked long enough to earn a vacation, he reported—alone—to the vast TI lab everyday. TI was already a powerhouse in transistors and semiconductors. Vast stores of raw materials and momentarily abandoned sophisticated lab facilities were at his disposal. Kilby had two weeks to putter in that lab and to follow any whim—with one proviso: either come up with some new and important idea or be ready to work in one of the minor production divisions for years to come.

During those two weeks of tinkering and pondering, a general concept crept into Kilby's mind and onto his notebook pages: replace separate components with a single chip of silicon, minute sections and layers of which could be altered to mimic any of the standard electronic components.

Kilby presented his concept in mid-July. Management was impressed but skeptical. Kilby was given two months to prove that his idea was reliable and inexpensive.

On September 12, 1958, Jack Kilby threw the power switch on the first integrated circuit ever built. While TI executives watched, the green, waving line of a sine wave rolled across an oscilloscope. All that first microchip could do was convert a direct current signal into an alternating current in the shape of a sine wave.

But it did it. Built purely out of shaved slivers of silicon glued together and insulated in a plastic coating, Jack Kilby had proved that microchips were possible.

Within a year TI was employing photographic etching processes similar to those used in silk screening and lithography to implant hundreds of thousands of electronic components onto a chip the size of a baby's fingernail.

What's Happened Since Then?

In 1969, Ted Hoff stumbled onto the next great invention in the electronic revolution. He discovered a way to compress not just a single circuit, but an entire logic-processing unit onto one tiny chip. Hoff created the *microprocessor*—the computer-in-a-chip. Hoff's first complete microprocessor, the Intel 4004, was not much larger than a pencil point. It was smaller, smarter, more powerful, and much cheaper than the large circuit boards from the generation before it.

Microchips and microprocessors are now standard components of virtually every manufacturing process and control thousands of manufactured goods. However, the next generation of computer processors is already on the drawing boards. This next generation will—again—be smaller, faster, and more powerful. To do that, they will have to work on the scale of atoms and on subatomic particles. When that happens, the microchip will become an outdated dinosaur, like the vacuum tube before it.

Fun Fact: A microchip small enough to fit through a hypodermic needle can be injected into your pet so that it can be identified throughout its life by a one-of-a-kind number.

More to Explore

Braunn, Ernest, and Stuart McDonald. *Revolution in Miniature.* Cambridge: Cambridge University Press, 1993.

Desmond, Kevin. *A Timetable of Inventions and Discoveries.* New York: M. Evans & Company, 1997.

Haggerty, Patrick. "Electronics Evolution." *Research Management* XII (September 1989): 317–30.

Haven, Kendall, and Donna Clark. *100 Most Popular Scientists for Young Adults.* Englewood, CO: Libraries Unlimited, 1999.

Kilby, Jack. "Invention of the Integrated Circuit." *IEEE Transactions on Electronic Devices.* ED-23 (July 1991): 648–54.

Reid, T. R. *Chip.* New York: Random House, 2001.

———. *The Chip: How Two Americans Invented the Microchip and Launched a Revolution.* New York: Simon & Schuster, 1996.

Texas Instruments Incorporated. *25th Anniversary Observance, Transistor Radio and Silicon Transistor.* Dallas: Texas Instruments Incorporated, 1994.

Zygmont, Jeffrey. *Microchip.* New York: Perseus Publishing, 2002.

Heart Pacemaker

Year of Invention: 1960

> **What Is It?** A battery-powered device to stimulate the heart to beat at a regular and normal rate.
>
> **Who Invented It?** Wilson Greatbatch (in Buffalo, New York)

Why Is *This* Invention One of the 100 Greatest?

Within seconds of heart failure comes death. If the heart fails to beat regularly and rhythmically, the body's ability to function grinds to a halt.

The invention of the pacemaker prolonged life. An amazingly simple device, no more complex than an electrical flasher, the implanted heart pacemaker has quietly transformed the lives of millions of people.

History of the Invention

What Did People Do Before?

In the mid-twentieth century, hospital researchers invented machines that could stimulate the heart to beat regularly if its rhythm faltered. These early cardiac machines were cumbersome devices about the same size as a television set. These machines kept a patient alive, but meant that he or she could never be mobile again. As a result, these machines only existed in hospitals for use in extreme cases.

How Was the Pacemaker Invented?

Born in 1919 and raised in Buffalo, New York, Wilson Greatbatch had always been fascinated by electronics. He built a shortwave radio as a teenager and, because of this experience, was trained in radio repair by the navy.

After the war, Greatbatch earned a degree in medical engineering from Cornell University. During this period, he worked as an assistant on the Psychology Department's Animal Behavior Farm. Greatbatch was in charge of maintaining instrument packs on about 100 goats and sheep to monitor their vital functions (heart rate, blood pressure, etc.).

During the summer of 1953, two Boston surgeons visited the farm to practice experimental brain surgery techniques on goats. Over brown-bag lunches, Greatbatch and these surgeons discussed various medical topics. One of those conversations focused on what they called "heart block," an affliction in which heart rate can zoom up to hundreds of beats a minute for no reason and then drop to almost zero—also for no reason.

The doctors described a section of the heart called the *sinus node*. They called it the heart's pacemaker since it generated the tiny electrochemical signals that caused the heart muscle to contract. In heart block, that signal was either not generated or failed to get through to the muscle. When that happened, a backup system took over that sent a flurry of random signals to the heart muscle, causing the heart to flutter wildly.

From his work on the farm, Greatbatch knew that an electrical jolt would make the heart contract, and it seemed to him that it should be simple to make a machine to replace a faulty *sinus node*.

Greatbatch, however, didn't pursue the idea until 1956. Then 37-year-old Greatbatch began to play with the newly invented transistors in the small barn behind his house that he had converted into a lab. He was attempting to build a transistorized, battery-powered device to record animal heart sounds for his work at the university. While building an oscillator (a device that generates an alternating electrical current from the direct current from a battery) that would be part of his recording device, Greatbatch reached into his parts drawer and pulled out a resistor (a small electrical piece that resists the flow of electricity). But he misread the color-coding and used the wrong resistor.

By the time he realized his mistake, he had already completed the oscillator circuit. Before ripping it apart to fix his mistake, he connected the circuit to a power source to "see what would happen."

To Greatbatch's surprise, the circuit began to "chirp," sending out electrical pulses at a rate of one per second. In a flash, he recognized that this tiny, transistorized device would serve wonderfully well as the heart pacemaker he had envisioned in 1953. The first device he built was 2.5 inches long and 0.5 inch wide, with two wire leads trailing from one end that would be attached to the heart muscle.

Greatbatch approached Dr. William Chardack, chief of surgery at the Buffalo Veterans Hospital, with his device. Chardack scheduled an operating amphitheater for Greatbatch to use to demonstrate his device on a dog. Greatbatch stitched off the nerve from the dog's *sinus node* to create heart block. Then he connected his pacemaker, implanted the machine inside the dog's chest cavity, and sewed the animal up. Monitors showed that the dog's heart immediately began to beat in strong, regular beats.

However, the pacemaker only worked for four hours. During an autopsy, Greatbatch realized that the interior of a living body is a far more hostile environment than he had imagined. Moisture, heat, and body salts had corroded his electrical components. The dog's body seemed to have systematically attacked the pacemaker as a foreign invader.

In 1959, he encased the device in a block of epoxy plastic and increased survival time to over four months. By mid-1960, one dog survived for nine months. Chardack agreed to use Greatbatch's implant pacemaker on a human—if an appropriate patient appeared. Four months later a 70-year-old man who suffered from severe heart block was referred to Chardack. He was not expected to live much longer. Chardack implanted a pacemaker. It functioned perfectly for 20 months.

What's Happened Since Then?

By 1970, pacemakers listened to the heart and only created a pulse when one was needed. The pulse rate adjusted automatically in response to a person's activity level. Surgical steel casing caused fewer reactions in patients than had epoxy. New lithium batteries extended the pacemaker's life to more than five years.

By 1982, more than 650,000 people in the United States were walking the streets with hearts controlled by implanted pacemakers. By 1990, doctors were implanting more than 300,000 a year.

 Fun Fact: In 1967, a dog received the first pacemaker permanently placed in an animal. Its battery lasted for five years. Today, hundreds of dogs each year receive pacemakers.

More to Explore

Aaseng, Nathan. *Twentieth-Century Inventors.* New York: Facts on File, 1996.

Brown, Kenneth. *Inventors at Work.* Redmond, WA: Microsoft Press, 1998.

Dyson, James. *A History of Great Inventions.* New York: Carroll & Graf Publishers, 2001.

Hardie, Jackie. *Blood and Circulation.* Portsmouth, NH: Heinemann, 1998.

Ierley, Merritt. *Wondrous Contrivances.* New York: Clarkson Potter, 2002.

Jeffrey, Kirk. *Machines in Our Hearts.* Baltimore: Johns Hopkins University Press, 2001.

Lindsay, Judy. *The Story of Medicine from Papyri to Pacemakers.* New York: Oxford University Press, 2003.

Space Flight

Year of Invention: 1961

> **What Is It?** Human crewed ships blasted beyond the earth's atmosphere into open space.
>
> **Who Invented It?** Wernher von Braun (in Huntsville, Alabama)

Why Is *This* Invention One of the 100 Greatest?

Space flights are the first human steps beyond our own planet and represent one of the great expansions of human horizons. Space flights over the past 40 years have gathered a wealth of information about our own planet and about the cosmos. Major physics, biology, medicine, and astronomy theories have been reshaped and rebuilt based on data collected by these manned space flights. Our views of ourselves, our planet, our galaxy, and our universe have been vastly improved by flights into space.

History of the Invention

What Did People Do Before?

Space flights need rocket power. (Rockets and jets use the same type of combustion engine. Jets, however, suck in the oxygen they need from the air they fly through and therefore only carry fuel. Rockets carry their own supply of oxygen as well as fuel and therefore can fly where there is no atmosphere.)

Solid fuel rockets date back to 1100 in China. However, solid fuels could never develop the immense power needed to break free of Earth's gravity.

In 1903 (the same year that the Wright brothers first flew), Russian physicist Konstantin Tsiolkovsky wrote in detail about rocket theory, rocket propulsion, space suits, satellites, and space rockets. No one gave his work serious consideration for another 30 years.

How Was Space Flight Invented?

Rocket development started in the United States before 1920, and its eventual success hinged on the work of two men.

Robert Goddard had toyed with ideas, theories, and equations for rocket flight for years. In 1913, 31-one-year-old Goddard organized his rocket research data and ideas into patent applications—one for a multistage rocket and one for using two tanks filled with combustible material, such as gasoline and liquefied nitrous oxide, that would mix and burn to produce power.

In 1917, he received a $5,000 grant from the Smithsonian Institution to build a rocket to reach "extreme altitudes." The U.S. Army Signal Corps added $20,000 to help fund Goddard's work.

Goddard developed a rocket motor that would run on gasoline and liquid oxygen. When the pumps caused difficulty, he switched to pressurized gas to force fuel and compressed oxygen into the combustion chamber.

On March 16, 1926, Goddard achieved the world's first liquid-fuel rocket flight, launched from a farm near Auburn, Massachusetts. The rocket only flew for 2.5 seconds, rising 41 feet. Two years later, he repeated the experiment with a larger model that reached twice the 1926 altitude before crashing in flames. That modest beginning laid the foundation for every subsequent rocket.

Wernher von Braun, the second of the two men, was a rocket man. In the heyday of Germany's rocket program in the 1930s, von Braun designed the A-1, A-2, and A-4 rockets, the first supersonic rocket, and the first ICBM (InterContinental Ballistic Missile) for the German military. He also drew detailed plans for a German space station and shuttle system 40 years before any other country considered such a concept.

When Germany collapsed at the end of World War II, von Braun delivered his entire team of engineers and scientists to the advancing U.S. Army. Still only 33 years old, he negotiated a deal whereby the United States got all of his technical data and the existing stock of V-2 rockets in exchange for allowing von Braun and his team to continue their work on rocket development in the United States.

After von Braun's team relocated to the Redstone Arsenal in Huntsville, Alabama (later renamed the Marshall Space Flight Center), von Braun split his time between design for the new Saturn series of rockets (used to launch manned capsules) and working to review and assist commercial contractors for the new U.S. space program. The Saturn I, IB, and V rockets were all von Braun designs. His Saturn rockets were rushed into production in order to carry the first American astronauts into space.

The first class of American astronauts was recruited in 1959. That small group was selected from military officers with jet flight experience. NASA assumed that it was best to pick pilots because spacecraft would fly.

NASA raced toward a planned May 1961 date for the first launch. However, the Soviet Union launched its cosmonaut first. Yuri Gagarin spent 89 minutes in space on April 12, 1961, aboard the *Vostok 1*. He completed one orbit of Earth before his capsule reentered the atmosphere and parachuted to the ground in Siberia. Three weeks later (May 5, 1961) Alan Shepard became the first American in space, even though his brief ride did not last through a complete orbit.

What's Happened Since Then?

Von Braun's Jupiter C rocket powered the first American rocket launch into space. His Juno and Redstone rockets provided 30 years of reliable service for commercial and communications satellite launches as well as serving as the backbone of America's ICBMs. His Saturn I, IB, and V powered America's manned space program.

Before 1961 ended, four more astronauts safely reached space—two Americans and two Soviets. Within five years after Gagarin's first flight, the Soviets had launched eight manned space flights and the United States had flown twelve.

The first craft and crew to leave Earth orbit was the *Apollo 8* mission with Berman, Lovell, and Anders on board when they circled the moon. The first woman in space was Russian Valentina Tereshkova, who flew for 48 orbits in 1963. No American woman flew until Sally Ride flew a shuttle mission in 1983.

The first human to leave footprints on the moon was Neil Armstrong, on July 20, 1969. America sent the first interplanetary launches skyward—*Pioneer 10* and *11* in 1972, and *Voyager 1* and *2* in 1977. The two *Voyager* crafts were also the first man-made objects to leave the solar system, in late 1992, traveling at a speed of 300 million miles a year (almost 35,000 mph). In 70,000 years they will reach Alpha Centuri, the nearest star. The first space shuttle launched on April 12, 1981, the first-ever reusable space vehicle.

Spacecraft and space flights today are reminiscent of the airplanes of 1906 and 1907. By 1907 everyone knew that the rickety bi-wings were definitely here to stay. But from watching those planes, it was impossible to envision where flight would be in another 80 years. The same is true of space flight today.

 Fun Fact: What do astronauts do with dirty laundry? One future option might be to feed them to bacteria.

More to Explore

Couper, Heather. *DK Space Encyclopedia*. New York: DK Publishing, 1999.

Haven, Kendall, and Donna Clark. *100 Most Popular Scientists for Young Adults*. Englewood, CO: Libraries Unlimited, 1999.

Lomask, Milton. *Invention and Technology Great Lives*. New York: Charles Scribner's Sons, 1994.

McNeil, Ian. *An Encyclopedia of the History of Technology*. New York: Routledge, 1996.

Moskal, Greg. *The History of Space Exploration: Sequencing Events Chronologically on a Timeline*. New York: PowerKids Press, 2004.

Owen, David. *Final Frontier: Voyages into Outer Space*. Orlando, FL: Firefly Books, 2004.

Rinard, Judith. *The Story of Flight*. Orlando, FL: Firefly Books, 2002.

Scot, Carole. *Space Exploration*. New York: DK Publishing, 2004.

Wellington, Jerry. *The History of Space*. New York: Steck-Vaughn, 1996.

Yenne, Bill. *100 Inventions That Shaped World History*. New York: Bluewood Books, 1993.

Communications Satellite

Year of Invention: 1962

What Is It? Communications device launched into space to relay data, voice, and visual information.

Who Invented It? Jerry R. Pierce (in Bell Labs, New Jersey)

Why Is *This* Invention One of the 100 Greatest?

Communications satellites are humans' most successful venture in space. They have also been critical to both the development of an effective world wide communications system and the development of a sense of global community.

Communications satellites were the first device to extend daily human activity beyond the surface of the earth. They were the first practical use humans made of space.

History of the Invention

What Did People Do Before?

In 1865, as the American Civil War ground to a bitter end, Jules Verne delighted the world by describing space flight to the moon in his novel *From the Earth to the Moon.* In 1924, German scientist Herman Oberth described satellites and space stations in a more scientific way in *Ways to Spaceflight.*

The jet engine became a reality in the late 1930s. The first rocket engines were built in late 1943. By 1948, rockets had edged to the top of Earth's atmosphere and touched the edge of space.

Multichannel microwave systems carried hundreds of voice, data, and television channels beginning in the 1940s. However, relay towers had to be built every 40 or 50 miles.

On December 18, 1958, the U.S. Army launched a secret Signal Communications by Orbiting Relay Equipment (SCORE) satellite. This military satellite contained the electronics to receive and retransmit a few voice and data channels. In 1960, AT&T launched *Echo 1*, a giant reflective balloon tucked inside a 26-inch magnesium sphere. Once in orbit, the sphere broke open and the reflective balloon deployed and inflated. It literally reflected radio signals back to Earth. However, the reflected signals were too weak at ground level to be of much value and were often lost in static.

How Was the Communications Satellite Invented?

Three kinds of problems plagued Jerry Pierce and his associates at AT&T's Bell Labs in New Jersey as they began to design and build the first generation of communications satellites (named Telstar) in 1958. The first was the design of onboard circuitry. Transistors (invented in 1947) would be ideal because of their tiny size, weight, and power requirements. However, existing transistors couldn't handle the three-watt power loads that Pierce calculated the transmitter circuits would have to carry if the satellite's signal was to be detectable back on Earth.

Pierce decided to use TWT amplifiers instead. However, these amplifiers were heavier and bigger, and demanded more power. Pierce also had to build redundant (backup) circuits since the satellite would have to operate maintenance free for its whole life.

The second problem was satellite transmitter power. The satellite's signals would have to be powerful enough to be reliably detected. The closer a satellite could come to the 23,000-mile height of a geosynchronous orbit, the better. However, greater height meant that the satellite had to transmit with greater power in order for its signal to be received by ground stations. Every extra 1,000 miles of altitude meant heavier wiring, bigger amplifiers, and more solar panels to generate electricity.

These first two problems were made critical and nightmarish by the third (and biggest) problem: weight limits. The maximum payload of a liquid-fuelled Delta rocket was 180 pounds. Solutions to either of the first two problems added weight to Telstar—weight they were not allowed to add if the satellite was to be successfully launched. Pierce and his team found themselves playing with ounces—with fractions of an ounce—in their effort to stay under 180 pounds.

The answer had to be compromise. They would use lower orbits so that less onboard transmitter power was required. They would not include the redundant circuitry they had originally planned even though it meant that there would be no backup if some of the satellite's circuits failed. Instead of using readily available antennas, ground stations would build giant dish antennas to receive the faint signal from Telstar.

Pierce planned to build a complete system of between 50 and 60 Telstar satellites in orbits around 7,000 miles high. On July 10, 1962, a Delta rocket lifted *Telstar 1* into a low elliptical orbit that varied between 514 and 3,051 miles in height. The spacecraft weighed 171 pounds and carried electronics for 1,064 channels. The satellite had a tiny 34-inch diameter. Onboard solar cells provided just under 15 watts of power. Later that same day, *Telstar 1* relayed the first live transatlantic television transmission from France to America.

After four months of successful operation, some transistors in *Telstar 1's* command system succumbed to radiation. *Telstar 1* limped on for two more months before it finally fell silent.

What's Happened Since Then?

Telstar 1 only transmitted for six months. Still, in those short six months it revolutionized long-distance communications. In late 1962, the U.S. government created COMSAT (the corporation to develop commercial satellites) and gave that agency the rights to develop and launch all communications satellites.

In 1963 COMSAT launched *Syncom*, the first geosynchronous satellite. With more onboard power, *Syncom* successfully circled 23,000 miles above the earth and beamed down video, voice, facsimile, and data channels. Syncom was followed in 1965 by *Early Bird*, the first in an eventual global network of communications satellites launched by COMSAT.

By the late 1980s, satellites dominated the world of long-distance communications. Hundreds of thousands of wideband channels existed to carry pictures, video, and any data stream.

Over 1,300 active satellites now circle the earth (160 of them for commercial communications). Another 7,500 pieces of space junk float in orbit. Shuttle pilots have described many orbital paths as being "freeway crowded." Yet it was only 45 years ago that *Telstar I* launched into an empty sky and ushered in the era of satellite communications.

 Fun Fact: Communications satellites can now be used to track fish through the ocean.

More to Explore

Asimov, Isaac. *Asimov's Chronology of Science and Discovery*. New York: Harper & Row, 1989.

Byers, Ann. *Communication Satellites*. New York: Rosen Publishing Group, 2003.

Dyson, James. *A History of Great Inventions*. New York: Carroll & Graf Publishers, 2001.

Graham, Ian. *Satellites and Communications*. Minneapolis, MN: Raintree Publisher, 2002.

MacLeod, Elizabeth. *Phone Book: Instant Communication from Smoke Signals to Satellites and Beyond*. Chicago: Kids Can Press, 1997.

Mattern, Joanne. *From Radio to the Wireless Web*. Berkeley Heights, NJ: Enslow Publishers, 2002.

Spangenburg, Ray. *Artificial Satellites*. New York: Scholastic Library Publishing, 2001.

Whiting, Jim. *John R. Pierce: Pioneer in Satellite Communication*. London: Mitchell Lane Publishers, 2003.

Yenne, Bill. *100 Inventions That Shaped World History*. New York: Bluewood Books, 1993.

Calculator

Year of Invention: 1968

What Is It? A handheld device that performs basic math functions.

Who Invented It? Jack Kilby and Jerry Merryman (in Dallas, Texas)

Why Is *This* Invention One of the 100 Greatest?

Handheld calculators provide instant and reliable arithmetic, algebraic, and trigonometric calculations. They are as powerful as early room-sized computers—all while being quiet, small, compact, and incredibly cheap. Suddenly, every office, every clerk, every house, virtually every person can stuff their own calculator into a pocket, purse, or backpack and perform any needed calculation. The calculator revolutionized the way we perform math.

History of the Invention

What Did People Do Before?

Math calculation is such an important human function that five of the truly great inventions have been dedicated to it. Four preceded the calculator: the abacus, the adding machine, the slide rule, and the digital computer. The abacus's origins are lost in prehistory. The modern abacus first appeared in Egypt and China around A.D. 190. However, earlier forms of the device were used in ancient Babylonia, appeared in Egypt by 500 B.C., and were used by Roman accountants and scribes.

Abacuses are still popular in China because of their speed. In a 1946 contest, Kiyoshu Matzukai, a Japanese clerk, was pitted against an American with an electric adding machine. The abacus user easily won.

Scotsman John Napier invented the first mechanical multiplication machine in 1606. Napier is best known for inventing the mathematical system of *logarithms* and for inventing the idea of separating a whole number from its fractional part with a dot, or period. Fifty-five year-old John Napier invented a series of tiles, commonly called *Napier's Bones*, that slid against each other to perform multiplication problems.

In 1673, German inventor, mathematician, and philosopher Gottfried Leibniz created a metal adding machine that could multiply by performing repetitive addition and storing each new result in an accumulator.

The first commercially successful adding machine was invented in 1886 by American William Burroughs and became a standard business tool and a part of every company's office before typewriters and telephones (both invented about the same time).

In 1621, English mathematician and cleric William Oughtred used Napier's logarithms to invent the slide rule. Slide rules became an instant hit with scientists and engineers. However, they never gained general acceptance outside of those two professions. In 1972 calculators first appeared on the market. Within five years, slide rules had virtually disappeared from the Western world.

How Was the Electronic Calculator Invented?

Transistors were invented in 1947. Jack Kilby invented the microchip in 1958. From that moment, there was an explosion of activity in the field of microelectronics—logic circuits, memory circuits, central processors. The universal goal of this wild scramble was to build faster, cheaper, and more powerful central computers.

Computers, invented in the 1940s, were still room-sized pieces of equipment in the 1960s that required specially trained operators and programmers. Actual computer users never touched (and usually never saw) the computer. Personal computers had neither been invented nor even dreamed of.

Jack Kilby (already famous for his 1958 invention of the microchip) and Jerry Merryman worked for the Texas Instrument company, one of the companies trying to create a mainframe computer and share in the profit to be made in this rapidly growing market. The pressure was on to develop faster computers with bigger memories, all in smaller boxes and for less money.

While working on annual budgets in the fall of 1966, Kilby sat in the Texas Instruments accounting department where noisy adding machines clicked and clunked. While walking back to his lab, it occurred to Kilby that they had already created microelectronic circuits capable of doing everything those adding machines did. And these chips were smaller than the palm of his hand.

Light-emitting diodes (LED) were already in use for computer display consoles. Kilby and Merryman decided an LED display was perfect for a handheld calculator since it used very little energy and would not drain the calculator's batteries. Using microchips they had already developed, the two men completed the design of the first handheld calculator in less than a year as a side project to their main effort of designing a mainframe computer. Their biggest struggles in its design were the plastic molding to house it and decisions about how many digits to include in the LED display.

That calculator, the TI-2500, was capable of addition, subtraction, multiplication, and division. It was 5.5 inches long and 3 inches wide, weighed three-quarters of a pound, and cost $120 when it was released in 1972.

However, by the middle of that same year, Kilby and Merryman had developed a new model, the TI-2550, that incorporated every ability found on common slide rules. This "scientific" calculator hit the market in 1973 for $256.

What's Happened Since Then?

Within five years, basic calculators cost less than $10 and were in common use by students from junior high through college and by clerks and office workers. Now, calculators capable of performing far more complex calculations and with built-in memory are used as giveaways at stores and malls.

Modern calculators, costing under $20, are able to perform arithmetic, trigonometry, and geometry and to be programmed to solve simple equations, are built with multiple memory slots, and can handle complex calculations—capabilities Kilby and Merryman never dreamed of building in. Calculators have invaded every facet of life, from school, to office work, to construction, to kitchen recipe calculations, to leisure activities.

 Fun Fact: Each year in Hong Kong a race is held to work out the same sums on a calculator and on an abacus. Every year the abacus wins.

More to Explore

Dyson, James. *A History of Great Inventions*. New York: Carroll & Graf Publishers, 2001.

Jortbert, Charles. *First Computers*. New York: ABDO Publishing, 1997.

McNeil, Ian. *An Encyclopedia of the History of Technology*. New York: Routledge, 1996.

Petroski, Henry. *Small Things Considered*. New York: Vintage Books, 2004.

Randekk, Brian. *Origins of the Digital Computer*. New York: Springer-Verlag, 2001.

Reid, T. R. *Chip*. New York: Random House, 2001.

Yenne, Bill. *100 Inventions That Shaped World History*. New York: Bluewood Books, 1993.

Organ Transplant

Year of Invention: 1972

What Is It? The replacement of a defective human organ with one donated from another human.

Who Invented It? Surgical techniques: Norman Shumway (Stanford University). Immunosuppressive drugs: Jean-François Borel (in Geneva, Switzerland)

Why Is *This* Invention One of the 100 Greatest?

The vital organs (heart, lungs, kidney, liver, etc.) must function properly in order for a human to exist. When any of these essential organs wears out and ceases to function, we die. Organ transplants have given thousands of people a second chance at life. Faulty organs are replaced with donated ones. The whole body is no longer held hostage by its weakest organ.

History of the Invention

What Did People Do Before?

Transplanting tissue from one person to another is, surprisingly, not a new concept. Skin grafts are a type of transplant. So are bone grafts and arterial grafts. Each of these operations was attempted over 3,000 years ago—usually with little success. The operations seemed to go well, but the transplanted tissue withered, as did the patient, after surgery. No one knew why.

These transplant operations involved noncritical body parts. No one dared attempt the replacement of vital organs, since the operation to reach the organ usually killed the patient.

How Was Organ Transplantation Invented?

Inventions in two separate areas were needed to make organ transplants possible: surgical procedures and suppressing the recipient's body's natural rejection of the donated organ. Surgical techniques were far easier to develop and were available 20 years before successful suppression drugs existed.

French surgeon Alexis Carrel developed techniques for sewing veins and arteries during his animal experiments in the early twentieth century. These techniques later allowed surgeons to successfully reconnect a donated organ to the recipient's blood vessels.

Beginning in the 1930s, doctors made hundreds of attempts to transplant a kidney from one animal to another. All failed except for a few of the mother-to-child transplants and some sibling transplants. Rejection of the donated organ was almost always the cause of death.

Dr. Frank Mann at the Mayo Clinic in 1934 was the first to attempt a human-to-human kidney transplant. His surgical technique was flawless, but the patient quickly died because of organ rejection. The next attempt was in 1954. A 43-year-old Boston man was in the final stages of kidney failure. But this man had an identical twin who could donate a kidney. Both donor and recipient lived for over 25 years after the operation. But identical twins were a tiny part of the population needing organ transplants.

The heart is a much simpler organ than the kidney. Extensive animal heart transplant experiments also began in the 1930s. In 1946, Soviet Dr. Vladimir Demikhov successfully transplanted the heart and lungs of a dog. The animal lived for 9.5 hours using the transplanted organs.

Stanford University Medical Center became the leader of heart transplant research in America. Beginning his animal experiments in the late 1950s, Dr. Norman Shumway worked to develop a heart/lung machine that could temporarily replace those organs during surgery. He completed work on this machine with its pump, oxygenation system, filters, and flow and pressure regulators in late 1966.

During that same year, he developed a way to "hyper-cool" the heart during heart operations. That allowed surgeons to work on either a patient's heart or on a donor heart without having to keep its blood supply connected during the operation and without causing any damage to the heart itself.

On December 3, 1967, Christian Barnard, a surgeon in Cape Town, South Africa, was the first to use Shumway's techniques and equipment. He replaced the failing heart of a 55-year-old man with the heart of a 22-year-old woman who was the victim of a fatal car accident. The man lived for 18 days before he died of pneumonia. Dr. Shumway performed the first heart replacement in the United States on January 6, 1968. The patient died six days after the operation. Organ rejection was still the stumbling block, the thing surgeons could not overcome.

The first attempt to suppress the body's immune response was made in 1958. A woman scheduled for kidney replacement in a Boston hospital was accidentally irradiated before surgery. She did not reject her new kidney, and it functioned normally. Two surgeons in Paris noted the same phenomenon. However, irradiation caused terrible side effects and was soon abandoned as a way to suppress the human immune system.

In the 1960s doctors tried several corticosteroid drugs, hoping they would stop the organ rejection cycle. Results were marginal. Steroid side effects were often devastating. Then, in 1972, Swiss biochemist Jean-Francois Borel made the discovery that made organ transplants possible. He isolated a compound from a fungus he found in a soil sample that, when tested in animals, successfully suppressed the immune system's response to foreign grafts.

Borel invented a synthetic version of this compound and named it *cyclosporin*. In animal tests, cyclosporin reduced rejection rates by over 90 percent. Human tests began in the 1970s, with the same amazing results. One-year survival rates jumped from around 15 percent to over 80 percent.

What's Happened Since Then?

By 1980, 80 percent of Dr. Shumway's heart transplant patients lived at least one year—thanks to cyclosporin. Kidney transplant patients enjoyed a 90 percent one-year survival rate.

More than 15,000 organ transplant operations were performed annually in the United States as of 2000. The one-year survival rate is 80 percent to 87 percent for heart transplants and 88 percent to 95 percent for kidney transplants. Median survival time for kidney transplants has also risen from 12 years in 1980 to 21 years in 2000. Cyclosporin, more than surgical techniques, is credited with these improvements. However, cyclosporin brings with it serious side effects. The hunt is on for safer immunosuppressive drugs.

 Fun Fact: On August 7, 1997, Sarah Marshall received a triple organ replacement—stomach, liver, and bowel—in London's Children's Hospital. She was only 177 days old on the day of the operation.

More to Explore

Asimov, Isaac. *Asimov's Chronology of Science and Discovery*. New York: Harper & Row, 1989.

Berger, Melvin. *Artificial Heart*. New York: Franklin Watts, 1992.

Bryan, Jenny. *Medical Technology*. New York: Franklin Watts, 1993.

Durrett, Deanne. *Organ Transplants*. New York: Thomson Gale, 1993.

Hoffman, Nancy. *Heart Transplants*. San Diego, CA: Lucent Books, 2003.

McClellan, Marilyn . *Organ and Tissue Transplants: Medical Miracles and Challenge*s. Berkeley Heights, NJ: Enslow Publishers, 2003.

Metos, Thomas, ed. *Artificial Humans: Transplants and Bionics*. New York: Silver Burdett Press, 1994.

MRI

(Magnetic Resonance Imaging)

Year of Invention: 1977

What Is It? A process that uses magnetic fields and radio waves to scan a body and gather detailed information about the cell structure inside.

Who Invented It? Raymond Damadian (in Brooklyn, New York)

Why Is *This* Invention One of the 100 Greatest?

MRI has been called a magic window into the body and has sparked a revolution in medical diagnosis. MRIs produce safe, noninvasive images that detect cancer and other diseases, that guide surgeons, and that reveal body secrets that cannot be learned in any other way without invasive surgery. An MRI scan doesn't just produce a picture, it records a detailed, three-dimensional computer file that doctors can manipulate to view the precise set of images they need. MRI's do all that while creating no adverse side effects.

History of the Invention

What Did People Do Before?

Before MRIs were invented, doctors had only two ways to see inside a body: X-rays and surgery. Neither produced a detailed chemical analysis of an organ or of its individual cells. Both created serious side effects. Doctors often had to rely on circumstantial evidence, on clues, and on patient symptoms for their diagnoses.

How Was MRI Invented?

American physicist Isador Rabi first developed the principles of Nuclear Magnetic Resonance Imaging (NMR) in 1939. In 1941, American physicist Felix Block built the first working machine based on these principles. The size of a breadbox, this NMR machine was a way for physicists to peer inside molecules and into the atomic and subatomic structure of matter.

The NMR concept was simple. Place a small sample of some matter in a strong magnetic field, and some of the atomic nuclei in this matter will behave like compass needles and align themselves with the magnetic field. When the sample is then hit with radio wave energy, the aligned nuclei tend to jump from one energy state to another, absorbing energy as they do. After a short period, the nuclei give off characteristic energy waves as they jump back to their normal energy state.

Scientists can then record how much energy was absorbed and how long it was held, and study the characteristic patterns of how energy was given off. Those data reveal information about the internal structure and composition of the sample matter. Physicists used NMR extensively throughout the 1940s and 1950s to explore the structure of chemical elements and molecular compounds.

Born in New York in 1936, Raymond Damadian trained as a doctor specializing in cancer. He also completed advanced studies in physics. In the mid-1960s, he was plagued by recurring abdominal pain. Doctors poked, prodded, took X-rays, and conducted countless blood tests, but were unable to identify the cause. Damadian swore that there had to be a better way to examine a body, and he began to search for it.

While conducting routine screening of cancerous tissue samples in 1970, Damadian decided to try an experiment. He had seen NMR at work on chemical samples. Maybe NMR could help identify cancer cells as well.

He placed cancerous and non-cancerous tissue samples in a strong magnetic field, blasted them with radio waves, and noticed that cancerous cells took much longer to return to their normal energy levels than did healthy cells.

Over the next two years, Damadian conducted additional NMR tests on healthy and cancerous tissue samples from mice and rats. The NMR machine he built for these tests was just big enough to hold a glass slide with a smear of sample tissue.

In 1972, Damadian realized that he could map cancerous cells throughout a human body without having to resort to exploratory surgery if he could build a big enough NMR machine.

However, his magnetic field generator would have to be enormous to cover an entire human body. He would also have to learn how to focus and refocus the radio wave beam as it traveled the length of a body.

Physicists couldn't help him because they knew nothing about using NMR on living tissue. Medical specialists knew nothing of physics. Damadian's team had to invent each part of the machine as they went, piecing together and adapting available equipment on their shoestring budget.

Damadian's team finished the machine late in the spring of 1977. It featured a giant, plastic-encased magnet (like a five-foot-long donut tube) and a small radio beam transmitter that traveled slowly in a spiral around the body to excite nuclei and record their energy absorption and emissions.

They named it *Indomitable* because the team had overcome countless obstacles over a five-year struggle and had never given up. On July 2, 1977, Damadian's assistant slid into the tube. Five hours later, Damadian had completed the first human NMR scan. Observing doctors were amazed at the detail and precision of his images.

Later that year, Damadian changed the name from NMR to MRI (Magnetic Resonance Imaging) because of the strong negative connotation of all things "nuclear."

What's Happened Since Then?

Scan times dropped quickly from four or five hours to ten or fifteen minutes as physicists assembled better components. Now every hospital and medical center uses multiple MRI machines as a normal part of diagnoses and surgery preparation.

 Fun Fact: Metal objects are dangerous in an MRI room. The strong magnetic field can pull pens, keys, jewelry, etc., out of pockets and send them hurtling at lethal speeds across the room.

More to Explore

Brown, David. *Inventing Modern America*. Cambridge, MA: The MIT Press, 2002.

Davidson, Sue. *DK Revealed: Human Body*. New York: DK Publishing, Inc, 2002.

Dyson, James. *A History of Great Inventions*. New York: Carroll & Graf Publishers, 2001.

Kevles, Bettyann. *Naked to the Bone: Medical Imaging in the Twentieth Century*. New York: Perseus Publishing, 1998.

Mattson, James S. *Pioneers of NMR and Magnetic Resonance in Medicine: The Story of MRI*. Minneapolis, MN: Dean Books, 1996.

Moe, Barbara. *Revolution in Medical Imaging*. New York: Barbara Moe, 2003.

van Dulken, Stephen. *Inventing the 20th Century*. New York: New York University Press, 2000.

Winkler, Kathy. *Radiology*. New York: Marshall Cavendish, 1996.

Personal Computer

Year of Invention: 1977

What Is It? A programmable, interactive computer designed to be operated and owned by an individual.

Who Invented It? Steve Wozniak (in Palo Alto, California)

Why Is *This* Invention One of the 100 Greatest?

The personal computer (PC) redefined how we work, play, and communicate. PCs opened the power of computers to individuals, schools, homes—to the whole population. PCs made the growth and explosion of the World Wide Web and the Internet possible.

PCs have not only replaced all other word processing machines, business management machines, and accounting machines, but have also become a prime method of personal and business communication. PCs have also become a principal source of entertainment (games, music, and movies).

Amazingly, PCs have accomplished all this in less than 25 years! Business, work, study, personal connections, entertainment—all facets of life now seem to revolve around the PC. Personal computers are as much a part of many people's day as is a wristwatch, electric lights, or a car.

History of the Invention

What Did People Do Before?

The first computers were built in the early 1940s. Room-sized monsters that spewed heat from tubes and mechanical relays, they required teams of specially trained operators. These massive central computers were housed in guarded, air-conditioned, and dehumidified rooms on university campuses and in governmental complexes.

The transistor, invented in 1947 by Bardeen and Shockley, eliminated the need for bulky, heat-producing vacuum tubes and shrank the size of central computers to less than one-tenth of their former size. The microchip, a complete electronic circuit built into one tiny slab of silica, invented by Jack Kilby in 1958, sliced the size of the central processors again by 90 percent.

Finally, Ted Hoff's invention of the microprocessor (complete logic central processing computer) in 1969 shrank the central processor cabinet of a central computer to the size of a two-drawer file cabinet.

How Was the Personal Computer Invented?

Technically, the first small, personal computer was the Altair 8000, first released in 1975. Bill Gates (founder of Microsoft) wrote its operating system as his first programming job. However, the Altair 8000 was controlled by throwing toggle switches. A few LED lights acted as the only response from the computer.

In 1974, Intel released the 8080 processor (a microprocessor chip). One of the people who took instant notice of this chip's potential was then 24-year-old Steve Wozniak.

Steve Wozniak was 11 when he got an idea for his first electronic machine. Steve began to build the machine in his room and soon his desk, his bed, and his floor were covered with mounds of resistors, capacitors, and transistors. Miles of colored wire, endless diagrams, and stacks of circuit boards and metal framing strips were heaped in tangled piles.

The project grew too big for his room and sprawled onto the kitchen table and living room floor. What Wozniak thought would be compact bits of circuits became sprawling mazes of wire, board, and components. When he finally finished, the machine weighed more than he did and was bigger than the kitchen stove. But when he turned it on, it worked! He had built a machine that could play tic-tac-toe—at the age of 11.

In high school, Wozniak was elected president of the Electronics Club, and he gave lectures and wrote papers for the club that explained electronics principles he learned on his own. He dropped out of college for money reasons and wound up working at Hewlett-Packard as an engineer. There he taught himself how to write programs incorporating graphics, something that had never been done before on a computer.

His good friend Steve Jobs worked at Atari, and the two of them joined the newly formed Homebrew Computer Club, where members swapped ideas, showed off new designs, raffled off computer parts, and generally had fun. Wozniak wanted to impress these fellow enthusiasts with an improved circuit board he built using new microprocessor chips from Intel and Motorola.

He connected this new control board to a TV (the monitor), a power supply, transformers, and a keyboard. When Wozniak demonstrated his newest invention at the club, Jobs immediately saw its potential. Never before had computers been so small, so affordable, and so easy to use. He knew others would want one. He knew there was a market for Wozniak's creation.

Wozniak built a plastic housing for his invention. Jobs and Wozniak decided to call it the Apple because they were looking for something fresh, a name that reflected a break with tradition. On April Fool's Day, 1976, they officially formed the Apple Computer Company. They sold Jobs's Volkswagen and Wozniak's programmable calculator to raise $1,350 to begin making computers.

They sold a few Apples, but Wozniak clearly saw that this design wasn't meeting the real needs of computer users. He went to work to make the next one more powerful, expandable, easy to use and to program, and capable of displaying high-resolution color graphics. The result of this effort was the Apple II. Within a year, the Apple II computer was the largest-selling computer in the world.

What's Happened Since Then?

Together Jobs and Wozniak founded Apple Computer in a garage in 1977, where they built their first computers. By the time the last Apple II rolled off production lines in 1991, there were millions of Apple computers in homes and classrooms and on office desktops—places no one had previously envisioned a computer occupying.

The mouse was invented in 1964 by Douglas Engelbart but was not introduced as part of a PC until the Apple MacIntosh in 1983. In 1981, the first IBM PC was released. On July 21 of the previous year, Bill Gates of the fledgling Microsoft Corp. was asked by IBM to create the operating system for their new personal computer. Microsoft's Basic and DOS were born. A few years later (1985) Windows followed, and Microsoft mushroomed into one of the biggest companies on Earth.

Personal computers have—in only 25 years—become an integral part of normal work, study, information storage and retrieval, entertainment, communications, and life and work management. Only visionaries can guess what importance these magical machines will have after they have had time to develop their fullest potential.

 Fun Fact: There are now an estimated 50,000 computer viruses in existence, with as many as 10 new ones appearing in cyberspace every day.

More to Explore

Butcher, Lee. *Accidental Millionaire: The Rise and Fall of Steve Jobs at Apple Computer.* New York: Paragon House Publishers, 1998.

Herz, J. C. *Joystick Nation: How Videogames Ate Our Quarters, Won Our Hearts, and Rewired Our Minds.* Boston: Little, Brown, 1997.

Ierley, Merritt. *Wondrous Contrivances.* New York: Clarkson Potter, 2002.

Kendall, Martha E. *Steve Wozniak: Inventor of the Apple Computer.* New York: Walker and Company, 1996.

Moritz, Michael. *The Little Kingdom: The Private Story of Apple Computer.* New York: William Morrow, 1994.

Sherman, Josepha. *History of the Personal Computer.* New York: Franklin Watts, 2003.

Slater, Robert. *Portraits in Silicon.* Cambridge, MA: The MIT Press, 1997.

Artificial Heart

Year of Invention: 1981

What Is It? A mechanical device to replace the human heart.

Who Invented It? Robert Jarvik (in Ogden, Utah)

Why Is *This* Invention One of the 100 Greatest?

We live only so long as our hearts continue to beat. When our hearts stop, we die. Heart disease is the number one killer in this country. Mechanical heart replacements could stop that killer in its tracks.

Heart transplants require a donor. One person dies so that another can live. Not so with a mechanical heart. An endless supply could be manufactured, sitting on hospital shelves, waiting for the need to arise.

History of the Invention

What Did People Do Before?

Open-heart surgery began in the 1950s to repair defective heart valves. These operations were extremely risky, expensive, and used sparingly.

Successful heart transplant operations began in the 1970s. But donors for these operations were few and far between. Far more often, the patient died before a donor appeared.

How Was the Artificial Heart Invented?

In 1952, Soviet doctors implanted a plastic heart in a dog. It survived for 45 minutes. In 1958, Willem Kolff implanted a two-chamber, polyvinyl chloride heart in a dog. That animal survived for 90 minutes. Kolff then developed a silicon and rubber heart pump for a calf in 1965. That animal survived for over six hours.

American surgeon Denton Cooley was the first to implant an artificial heart in a human's body. In 1969 he implanted a plastic heart as a temporary measure while waiting for a donor heart. The patient survived for three days on the plastic heart before heart replacement surgery. Even after so short a time, the artificial heart showed signs of rejection wear and pitting.

By 1975, groups at a dozen university medical centers around the country were working on an artificial heart. One of these centers was at the University of Utah. That team was headed by 29-year-old Dr. Robert Jarvik.

By the time Jarvik celebrated his thirtieth birthday, his team had defined what a mechanical heart had to do. It had to pump at least five liters of blood each minute (the average flow rate for an adult heart). It had to be quiet. It had to produce very little heat. It had to be made of material that the recipient body would not reject. The pump had to run for 10 years without any maintenance. It should mimic the action of a normal heart, creating beats and a pulse rate (instead of a continuous flow as is created by most fluid pumps). Finally, it had to include some internal, rechargeable battery to keep the heart going during showers and other times when it would be disconnected from its primary, external power source.

It was an imposing list. For valves and connectors, Jarvik chose the new plastic materials created to replace damaged arteries and veins. These materials did not produce a strong immune rejection response. Jarvik tested each new concept of his artificial heart on the university's heard of calves that was available for research projects.

After experimenting on a number of calves, Jarvik settled on an air pump design to power his heart. It was lightweight, quiet, and easy to build. A tiny DC electric motor powered the pump, which forced air into two artificial chambers that would replace the two ventricle chambers of the patient's own heart. Flexible diaphragms inside these chambers would bulge in response to air pressure, forcing blood out of the heart—either to the lungs or out into the body. One-way Teflon®-coated plastic valves would connect to the two atrium chambers of the patient's heart and to the major arteries.

An electronic timing unit controlled the pace at which the various valves were opened and closed as well as the pump speed and pressure. By 1981, Jarvik's team had tested, revised, and re-revised the device for five years. He had successfully implanted it in six calves.

The patient had to wear a permanent waist-strap battery pack. Electrical leads traveled from this battery through the air vent tube that penetrated through the patient's skin and into the balloon chambers of the artificial heart. Jarvik added a small, rechargeable lithium battery inside the heart's control unit. This battery supplied approximately 30 minutes of power so the patient could shower.

With animal trials completed, Jarvik teamed with surgeon Willem DeVries to implant his artificial heart. In early 1982, DeVries found the perfect candidate in Seattle dentist Barney Clark. The surgery was completed in eight hours and Clark, resting in the recovery room, was the first human to live with an artificial heart.

What's Happened Since Then?

Barney Clark survived with his Jarvik 7 heart for almost four months. His death was disappointing, but not wholly unexpected for such an experimental treatment. The next three patients to receive the heart, however, fared little better. They were prone to strokes. Several severe infections developed at the point where tubing entered through the skin. The Jarvik 7 experiment was called off.

Several other artificial heart designs followed shortly after Jarvik's. The most successful of these was the Abiocor Artificial Heart. This grapefruit-size design reduced blood clotting and strokes. The power system didn't pierce the skin, but instead transferred power through the skin with a magnetic field. This heart didn't use an air pump and so was quieter—so quiet, a doctor needed a stethoscope to hear its 18,000 rpm motor hum.

Jarvik also improved his heart design. His thumb-size Jarvik 2000 was first implanted on September 12, 2000, by Dr. Stephen Westaby in Peter Houghton, a 61-year-old, facing death from cardiac failure. Mr. Houghton is now walking, traveling, and living a normal life.

The potential for artificial hearts is vast. However, this industry is still in its infancy. The current designs are likely to be viewed in the future in the same way we view Ford's Model T car—awkward, inefficient, rough, but a necessary starting place for the industry.

 Fun Fact: A healthy human heart beats over 100,000 times a day!

More to Explore

Avraham, Regina. *The Circulatory System.* New York: Chelsea House Publishers, 2000.

Bankston, John. *Robert Jarvik and the First Artificial Heart.* New York: Mitchell Lane, 2002.

Berger, Melvin. *Artificial Heart.* New York: Franklin Watts, 1997.

Brown, David. *Inventing Modern America.* Cambridge, MA: The MIT Press, 2002.

McGowen, Tom. *The Circulatory System: From Harvey to the Artificial Heart.* New York: Franklin Watts, 1993.

van Dulken, Stephen. *Inventing the 20th Century.* New York: New York University Press, 2000.

World Wide Web

Year of Invention: 1991

> **What Is It?** A set of software programs designed to allow easier navigation of computer networks through the use of graphical user interfaces and hypertext links.
>
> **Who Invented It?** Tim Berners-Lee (in Geneva, Switzerland)

Why Is *This* Invention One of the 100 Greatest?

The Internet and the World Wide Web have opened the world and its full range of information to our fingertips—the best classes, best products, and best resources. Art, information, maps, phone books—it seems that everything a person could want can be found on the Web.

The World Wide Web has transformed school, education, shopping, the marketing and promotion of products and ideas, and political debate.

Most startling, the Web is still in its infancy. Its impact on our lives is just beginning. There seems to be no limit to how deeply this invention will intrude into our lives and control how we live them.

History of the Invention

What Did People Do Before?

People wrote letters. People talked on the phone. They visited. They used bulky phone books and store catalogs. People had drawers stuffed with folded maps and address books. Schools had no student computers and no computer labs.

How Was the World Wide Web Invented?

There are two parts to this grand invention: the Internet and the World Wide Web. The Internet is primarily hardware. It is the tens of thousands of host computers all linked together so that anyone who can reach any of these computers can, in fact, reach them all.

The Internet grew, almost organically, as individual computer networks that were one-by-one linked over a 35-year period.

The Internet began with the ARPA (Advanced Research Projects Agency) net, first envisioned in 1967 and brought into existence in 1969. ARPA linked government and university research computers. In 1972 Ray Tomlinson invented an e-mail program for the ARPA net and the @ sign for e-mail addresses. In 1975, John Vittal added reply, save, and forward capabilities to ARPA's e-mail programming.

The World Wide Web can be tracked back to the invention of one individual. The idea of the World Wide Web was born in 1980 at CERN (the Central European Science Research Facility). There, 26-year-old physicist Tim Berners-Lee wondered if there was a way to organize the various kinds of information he used every day—phone book, research notes, reports, research papers, experimental data—on the computer. This was before the dissemination of the personal computer. Individual scientists had printers and terminals (card readers and card punches) that connected them to a central computer.

Over the course of a year, Berners-Lee wrote a program that let him store and access these different kinds of documents. At the time, he didn't intend it for general use—even at CERN. During this process Berners-Lee realized that if computers were going to be valuable for storing, sorting, and sharing information, the computers would have to learn how to make connections between a wide variety of types of documents and types of sources. He began to develop programs to enable CERN's computer to perform these functions.

However, by 1983 he had expanded his goal. Now he wanted to create programs that would show computers how to link documents and how to make the results available to many people all at once. He realized that he needed to create an information web—a system that would link (web) all stored information with all other information so that users could cross check for whatever they wanted quickly and efficiently.

First, Berners-Lee needed a standardized way to make documents readable and linkable. He chose HTML (hypertext markup language)—an existing simple computer language. Next, he created the first "server," a dedicated computer that CERN users could access that would search through other CERN computers and "serve up" the documents or information the searcher was looking for. This programming took almost four years of Berners-Lee's time as he slowly expanded the capability of his CERN server and HTML programs.

By the late 1980s, Berners-Lee had decided that he wanted to make this not just a CERN asset, but a worldwide one. That is when he decided to call his information web the World Wide Web. In late 1991, Berners-Lee connected his CERN server computer to the growing Internet and posted information and programming to show people how to access and use it. The World Wide Web was born.

What's Happened Since Then?

Berners-Lee's World Wide Web got an average of 100 hits a day in 1992 and jumped to 10,000 a day in 1993. In 1993, American student Marc Andersen created a new browser, "Mosaic" (the forerunner of Netscape) that could display whole pages from the CERN web (the origin of Web pages) including graphics, fonts, and colors.

By 1991, the Internet included some 5,000 networks with 70,000 host computers and 4,000,000 users. In 2000, over 800,000 host computers serviced 500,000,000 users making tens of billions of hits on the system.

Berners-Lee never patented his World Wide Web or any of the programs he created for it. He believed that access to the Web should be free for all users. In 2002 Berners-Lee was awarded $1.2 million as the recipient of the first Millennium Technology Prize by the Helsinki, Finland, Millennium Prize Committee and was knighted. In one short decade, his invention had grown to dominate the thinking and information activity of the world.

Fun Fact: Google's index of Web pages is the largest in the world, comprising more than eight billion eb pages, which if printed would result in a stack of paper more than 454 miles high. Yet when Google was founded in a Menlo Park, California, garage in 1998, it only had a staff of four people.

More to Explore

Beners-Lee, Tim. *Weaving the Web*. New York: Harpers, 1999.

Brown, David. *Inventing Modern America*. Cambridge, MA: The MIT Press, 2002.

Bullock, Linda. *The World Wide Web*. New York: Steck-Vaughn, 2002.

Christos, J. *The History of the Internet*. New York: ABC-CLIO Publishing, 1999.

Gains, Ann. *Tim Berners-Lee and the Development of the World Wide Web*. London: Mitchell Lane Publications, 2001.

Sherman, Josepha. *History of the Internet*. New York: Franklin Watts, 2003.

Stewart, Melissa. *Tim Berners-Lee*. New York: Ferguson Publishing, 2001.

Wolinski, Art. *The History of the Internet and the World Wide Web*. Berkeley Heights, NJ: Enslow Publishing, 2000.

Cloning

Year of Invention: 1996

> **What Is It?** A descendant produced from a single parent plant or animal that is an exact genetic match of the parent.
>
> **Who Invented It?** Ian Wilmut and Keith Campbell (in Scotland)

Why Is *This* Invention One of the 100 Greatest?

Cloning seems like a science fiction technology. But cloning technology exists today. Its potential benefit is far greater than fiction writers ever imagined.

Cloning technology has the potential to cure a dozen deadly diseases, to stop another dozen debilitating ailments, to reduce world hunger, and to eliminate infant genetic defects. Cloning technology can repair DNA and gene defects and repair damaged spinal tissue so than many wheelchair-bound people could freely walk.

History of the Invention

What Did People Do Before?

The idea of cloning dates back to 1938. German scientist Hans Spellman proposed a "fantastic experiment" to transfer one cell's nucleus into an egg cell that didn't have a nucleus. The idea sparked wild enthusiasm in the global biology community. Cloning seemed like the perfect way to study the process of cell and DNA division and the meaning of life.

In 1962, American researcher John Gruden tried to clone frogs. Gruden used a microscopic pipette to suck the nucleus out of one cell in a frog embryo and implanted that nucleus into a frog egg from a different frog. As that egg began to develop, it was a perfect clone of the donor frog. However, each cloned frog died in the tadpole stage before it began to feed.

Even though Gruden failed, his experiment was a milestone in cloning. He had cloned an animal.

In 1984, Danish scientist Steen Willadsen was the first researcher to successfully clone a mammal. He cloned a sheep by transferring a nucleus from one cell of a sheep embryo to the egg cell from another sheep before that egg had time to divide for the first time.

How Was Cloning Invented?

All early cloning attempts were stopped by the same problem. They could only make the process work when they took the nucleus from a cell of a very young embryo (one that was still smaller than 120 cells).

What farmers and governments wanted was the ability to clone a full-grown prized bull, exceptional sheep, or extinct species. No one could tell if an embryo of only 120 cells was worth cloning. However, cells taken from older embryos (or from live animals) were already too specialized to make the process work. A second problem was that every cloned animal through 1994 mysteriously died in an infantile stage.

Ian Wilmut and Keith Campbell worked on cloning techniques at the Roslin Institute in Scotland. In late 1995, Keith Campbell realized that every attempt to use adult cells for cloning might have failed because the cell cycles of the donor and egg cells were out of rhythm. All cells go through cycles of growth, rest, and division. If the nucleus from the donor cell and the egg cell into which it was planted were in different parts of their cycle, then the egg cell wouldn't accept and develop with the new nucleus.

For months the two men tried to catch a cell at just the right moment. They always failed. Campbell and Wilmut then tried to force the donor cell to slow its cyclical rhythm. Eventually, they realized they needed to put the donor cell into a state of hibernation by depriving it of some key cell nutrients. This created a new problem. They couldn't bring the hibernating nucleus out of hibernation after transplanting it into an egg cell.

Wilmut suggested using electrical shock. In late January 1996, they took cells from the udder of an adult sheep and forced them into hibernation in a glass dish. They used powerful microscopes and a microscopic pipette to break into each cell and remove the sleeping nucleus. Each nucleus was inserted into an egg cell from another sheep and placed in its own glass dish in a nutrient soup. They ran a low-voltage electric charge through the dish for a few thousandths of a second, jolting the egg.

The researchers found that this electric current jump-started both nucleus and egg cell. It resynchronized their rhythms and cued the egg to start the process of cell division.

After each embryo developed sufficiently in the laboratory glass dish, it was implanted into a female sheep. On July 5, 1996, one of these clones was born and was named Dolly, the first true clone made from adult donor tissue.

What's Happened Since Then?

Two hundred fifty-seven sheep clones were created at the same time. Dolly was the only one to survive. Her birth was not announced until 1997 to let patent applications proceed through courts and to make sure that Dolly *did* survive. Dolly not only survived, she gave birth to six normally bred lambs. Suffering from cancer and arthritis, Dolly was put down in February 2003, at the age of 6½.

Dolly's success is remarkable because it proved that the genetic material—the DNA's genetic coding—from a specialized adult cell could be reprogrammed to generate an entire new organism.

Dolly opened the world to the possibility of practical, mass cloning. By 1998, labs in six countries were cloning bulls, cows, monkeys, mice, pigs, goats, and horses. In 1999, three separate companies claimed to have plans to, and to be capable of, cloning a human.

Beginning in 1997, the U.S. government and several other national governments curbed or stopped cloning research along with the related stem cell research. (Cloning is one way to produce stem cells.) Cloning technology has been invented. It remains to be seen if it will be put to uses that allow it to fulfill its promise as one of the greatest of human inventions.

 Fun Fact: In 1995 Japan created the Kagoshima Prefectural Cattle Breeding Development Institute. In January 2000, they successfully cloned six live calves from skin cells of a prized bull's ear.

More to Explore

Asimov, Isaac. *Asimov's Chronology of Science and Discovery*. New York: Harper & Row, 1989.

Cefrey, Holly. *Cloning and Genetic Engineering*. New York: Scholastic Library Publishing, 2000.

Goodnough, David. *The Debate Over Human Cloning*. Berkeley Heights, NJ: Enslow Publishing, 2003.

Jefferies, David. *Cloning*. New York: Crabtree Publishing, 1999.

Nardo, Don. *Cloning*. Toronto: Thompson Educational Publishing, 2003.

Yount, Linda, ed. *Cloning*. New York: Thomas Gale, 2000.

Appendix A: List of Featured Inventors

Following is an alphabetical list of the inventors featured in the discussion of the 100 greatest inventions. Each is listed with his or her invention and its year of invention.

Name	Invention	Year	Page
Howard Aiken	digital computer	1943	231
Muhammad ibn Al-Khwarizmi	zero	810	27
Archimedes	compound pulley	230 B.C.	6
	screw	235 B.C.	6
Thomas Aspdin	Portland cement	1824	24
Charles Babbage	computer	1854	231
Roger Bacon	gunpowder	1261	30
Leo Hendrik Baekeland	plastic	1909	195
John Bardeen	transistor	1947	240
Joseph Bazalgette	city sewers	1875	147
Alexander Graham Bell	telephone	1876	150
	airplane (manned flight)	1906	189
Karl Benz	automobile	1887	168
Tim Berners-Lee	World Wide Web	1991	297
Henry Bessemer	steel	1856	126
Charles Birdseye	frozen food	1927	204
Ladislas and Georg Biro	ballpoint pen	1938	219
James Bogardus	skyscraper	1885	120
Jean-Francois Borel	organ transplant	1972	285
Rachel Brown	Nystatin	1948	243
Hans Busch	electron microscope	1926	54
John Campbell	sextant	1759	69
Keith Campbell	cloning	1996	300
Chester Carlson	photocopier	1938	222
Wallace Carothers	nylon	1937	216
Ferdinand Carre	refrigeration	1859	132
Anders Celsius	temperature scale	1741	66
D. Chapin	solar cells	1954	255
William Chardack	heart pacemaker	1960	273
Jacques Charles	hydrogen balloon	1783	75
Frank Colton	birth control pill	1952	252
Willis Currier	air conditioning	1902	183
Louis Daguerre	photography	1839	111

Name	Invention	Year	Page
Raymond Damadian	MRI	1977	288
George de Mestral	Velcro	1957	174
George Devol	robots	1956	261
Carl Djerassi	birth control pill	1951	252
Edwin Drake	oil well	1859	135
George Eastman	photography	1889	111
Thomas Alva Edison	moving pictures	1894	180
	electric typewriter	1872	141
	phonograph	1877	153
	electric lightbulb	1879	159
Gertrude Elion	chemotherapy	1950	249
Joe Engelberger	robots	1956	261
Daniel Fahrenheit	thermometer/temperature scale	1714	66
Michael Faraday	electric motor	1831	99
Fannie Farmer	measuring devices	1879	162
Philo Farnsworth	television	1927	207
Enrico Fermi	nuclear reactor	1942	228
Alva Fisher	washing machine	1906	192
Henry Ford	assembly line	1913	198
Benjamin Franklin	bifocal eyeglasses	1755	33
C. Fuller	solar cells	1954	255
Robert Fulton	steamship	1807	93
Carl Gerhardt	aspirin	1853	123
Galileo Galilei	telescope	1609	57
	clock pendulum	1594	63
Joseph Glidden	barbed wire	1873	144
Robert Goddard	rocket (space flight)	1926	276
Charles Goodyear	vulcanized rubber	1839	108
Gordon Gould	laser	1957	267
Elisha Gray	telephone	1876	150
Wilson Greatbatch	heart pacemaker	1960	273
Catherine Greene	cotton gin	1793	78
Johannes Gutenberg	printing press	1454	48
James Hargraves	spinning jenny	1764	72
John Harrison	naval clock	1759	69
Elizabeth Hazen	Nystatin	1948	243
Prince Henry of Portugal	caravel	1410	45
Basil Hirschowitz	endoscope	1957	264
Ted Hoff	microprocessor	1969	270
Christian Huygens	mechanical clock	1657	63
Samuel Insul	electric utilities	1903	186
Robert Jarvik	artificial heart	1981	294
Hans and Zacharias Janssen	microscope	1590	54
Edward Jenner	vaccinations	1796	81
Steve Jobs	personal computer	1977	231
Whitcomb Judson	zipper	1893	174

Name	Invention	Year	Page
Jack Kilby	microchip	1958	270
	calculator	1968	282
Willem Kolff	kidney dialysis	1944	234
Rene Laennec	stethoscope	1816	96
Edwin Land	instant photography	1947	111
Paul Langevin	sonar	1916	201
Ernest Lawrence	cyclotron	1931	210
Etienne Lenoir	internal combustion engine	1859	156
Otto Lilienthal	glider design	1891	189
Hans Lippershey	telescope	1608	57
Joseph Lister	antiseptic surgery	1865	117
Crawford Long	anesthesia	1846	114
Antoine Lumière	moving pictures	1895	180
Ts'ai Lun	paper	105	21
Anton Lueewenhoek	microscope	1650	54
Guglielmo Marconi	radio	1895	177
Cyrus McCormick	combine harvester	1831	102
Gerard Mercator	projection maps	1569	51
Jerry Merryman	calculator	1968	282
Joseph Monier	reinforced concrete	1867	24
Lady Mary Wortley Montagu	vaccinations	1796	81
Joseph and Etienne Montgolfier	lighter-than-air flight	1783	75
Samuel Morse	telegraph	1838	105
William Morton	anesthesia	1846	114
John Napier	slide rule	1614	282
	"Napier's Bones" (calculator)	1621	282
Sir Isaac Newton	reflective telescope	1670	57
Albert Nobel	dynamite	1866	138
Robert Noyce	microchip	1958	270
Elisha Otis	elevator	1852	120
Nikolaus Otto	internal combustion engine	1878	156
Louis Pasteur	pasteurization	1858	129
J. R. Pierce	communications satellite	1962	279
Gregory Pincus	birth control pill	1954	252
Ignaz Semmelweiss	antiseptics	1847	117
William Shockley	transistor	1947	240
Christopher Sholes	typewriter	1868	141
Norman Shumway	organ transplant	1968	285
Bernard Silver	bar codes	1949	246
Percy Spencer	microwave oven	1946	237
Alessandro della Spina	eyeglasses	1280	33
John Starley	bicycle	1885	165
Gideon Sundback	zipper	1913	174
Joseph Swan	electric lightbulb	1879	159
William Talbot	photography	1840	111

Name	Invention	Year	Page
Nikola Tesla	alternating current	1888	171
Evangelista Torricelli	barometer	1643	60
Charles Townes	maser	1953	267
Richard Trevithick	railroad	1804	90
Vitruvius	waterwheel	25 B.C.	12
Wernher von Braun	space flight	1961	276
Alessandro Volta	electric battery	1799	87
Hans von Ohain	jet engine	1939	225
Robert Watson-Watt	radar	1935	213
James Watt	steam engine	1798	84
George Westinghouse	electric utility	1892	186
Eli Whitney	cotton gin	1793	78
Frank Whittle	jet engine	1939	225
Ian Wilmut	cloning	1996	300
Joseph Woodland	bar codes	1949	246
Steve Wozniak	personal computer	1977	291
Orville and Wilbur Wright	airplane	1903	189
Rosalyn Yalow	radioimmunoassay	1955	258
Vladimir Zworykin	TV picture tube	1924	207

Appendix B: Inventions by Branch of Science

Following are the 100 greatest science inventions divided into their appropriate categories so that readers can easily identify the individual inventions that relate to the same area of science. Within each category inventions are listed chronologically.

Invention	Inventor	Year	Page
Prehistoric Essentials			
knife	unknown	by 40,000 B.C.	xviii
bow and arrow	unknown	by 30,000 B.C.	xvii
rope	unknown	by 30,000 B.C.	xix
pulley	unknown	by 10,000 B.C.	xix
lever	unknown	by 6000 B.C.	xviii
balance scale	unknown	by 5000 B.C.	xvii
dam	unknown	by 5000 B.C.	xviii
soap	unknown	by 5000 B.C.	xix
wheel	unknown	by 4000 B.C.	xx
Communications			
printing press	Johannes Gutenberg	1454	48
telegraph	Samuel Morse	1838	105
typewriter	Christopher Sholes	1868	141
telephone	Alexander Graham Bell	1876	150
phonograph	Thomas Edison	1877	153
radio	Guglielmo Marconi	1895	177
moving pictures	Antoine Lumière	1895	180
television	Philo Farnsworth	1927	207
photocopier (Xerography)	Chester Carlson	1938	222
communications satellite	J. R. Pierce	1962	279
Electronics			
digital computer	Howard Aiken	1943	231
transistor	John Bardeen and William Shockley	1947	240
microchip	Jack Kilby	1958	270
personal computer	Steve Wozniak	1977	291
World Wide Web	Tim Berners-Lee	1991	297
Personal, Domestic, and Civic			
screw	Archimedes	235 B.C.	6
glass	Syrian glassmakers	100 B.C.	9
paper	Ts'ai Lun	105 A.D.	21
eyeglasses	Alessandro della Spina	1280	33

Invention	Inventor	Year	Page
mirror	Venice, Italy craftsmen	1291	39
photography	William Talbot	1840	111
elevator and skyscraper	Elisha Otis and James Bogardus	1852	120
refrigeration	Ferdinand Carre	1859	132
sewer	Joseph Bazalgette	1875	147
measuring spoons	Fannie Farmer	1879	162
fast fasteners (zipper and Velcro)	Gideon Sundback and George de Mestral	1893	174
air conditioning	Willis Currier	1902	183
washing machine	Alva Fisher	1907	192
plastic	Leo Hendrik Baekeland	1909	195
frozen food	Charles Birdseye	1927	204
nylon	Wallace Carothers	1937	216
ballpoint pen	Ladislas and Georg Biro	1938	219
microwave oven	Percy Spencer	1946	237
bar codes	Joseph Woodland and Bernard Silver	1949	246

Scientific Measurement and Computation

compass	Unknown	83 A.D.	15
zero	Muhammad ibn Al Khwarizmi	810	27
microscope	Hans and Zacharias Janssen	1590	54
telescope	Galileo Galilei	1608	57
barometer	Evangelista Torricelli	1643	60
mechanical clock	Christian Huygens	1657	63
thermometer	Daniel Fahrenheit	1714	66
cyclotron	Ernest Lawrence	1931	210
calculator	Jack Kilby and Jerry Merryman	1968	282

Transportation

roads	Roman engineers	250 B.C.	3
caravel	Prince Henry of Portugal	1410	45
projection maps	Gerard Mercator	1569	51
navigation (longitude)	John Harrison and John Campbell	1759	69
lighter-than-air flight	Joseph and Etienne Montgolfier	1783	75
railroad	Richard Trevithick	1804	90
steamship	Robert Fulton	1807	93
bicycle	John Starley	1885	165
automobile	Karl Benz	1887	168
airplane	Wright brothers	1903	189
jet engine	Frank Whittle and Hans von Ohain	1939	225
space flight	Wernher von Braun	1961	276

Invention	Inventor	Year	Page
Medical Science			
vaccinations	Lady Mary Wortley Montagu and Edward Jenner	1796	81
stethoscope	Rene Laennec	1816	96
anesthesia	William Morton	1846	114
antiseptic	Ignaz Semmelweiss	1847	117
aspirin	Carl Gerhardt	1853	123
pasteurization	Louis Pasteur	1858	129
dialysis	Willem Kolff	1944	234
Nystatin	Rachel Fuller Brown and Elizabeth Hazen	1948	243
chemotherapy	Gertrude Elion	1950	249
birth control	Gregory Pincus	1954	252
radioimmunnoassay	Rosalyn Yalow	1955	258
arthroscopic surgery	Basil Hirschowitz	1957	264
pacemaker	Wilson Greatbatch	1960	273
organ transplant	Jean-Francois Borel and Norman Shumway	1972	285
MRI	Raymond Damadian	1977	288
artificial heart	Robert Jarvik	1982	294
cloning	Ian Wilmut and Keith Campbell	1996	300
Industrial and Agricultural			
plow	Roman farmers	100 A.D.	18
cement	Roman engineers	285	24
blast furnace	Rievaulz Abbey monks	1350	42
spinning jenny	James Hargraves	1764	72
cotton gin	Eli Whitney and Catherine Greene	1793	78
steam engine	James Watt	1798	84
electric motor	Michael Faraday	1831	99
combine harvester	Cyrus McCormick	1831	102
vulcanized rubber	Charles Goodyear	1839	108
steel	Henry Bessemer	1856	126
barbed wire	Joseph Glidden	1873	144
internal combustion engine	Nikolaus Otto	1878	156
assembly line	Henry Ford	1913	198
robots	Joe Engelberger and George Devol	1956	261
laser	Gordon Gould	1957	267
Military			
gunpowder	Roger Bacon	1261	30
dynamite	Alfred Nobel	1866	138
sonar	Paul Langevin	1916	201
radar	Robert Watson-Watt	1935	213

Invention	Inventor	Year	Page
Power and Electricity			
waterwheel	Vitruvius	25 B.C.	12
windmill	Unknown	1280	36
electric battery	Alessandro Volta	1799	87
oil well	Edwin Drake	1859	135
electric lightbulb	Thomas Edison	1879	159
alternating surrent (AC)	Nikola Tesla	1888	171
electric utilities	Samuel Insul	1903	186
nuclear reactor	Enrico Fermi	1942	228
solar cells	D. Chapin and C. Fuller	1954	255

Appendix C: The Next 40 Inventions to Research

Following are 40 great science inventions that almost made the top 100 list, ones that would have been ranked numbers 101 through 140. Certainly the inventions we would rank as numbers 101 and 102 are worthy of mention. Certainly they deserve as much attention as numbers 99 and 100. Some might place some of these next 40 in their versions of the top 100. Let this list of 40 additional great science Inventions serve as launching points for student research—both on the inventions and on their inventors.

Invention	Inventor	Year
scissors	China	1500 B.C.
Euclidean geometry	Euclid	300 B.C.
slide rule	John Napier	1614
vacuum pump	Otto von Guericke	1650
submarine	Cornelius Drebbel	1624
calculus	Isaac Newton	1666
pressure cooker	Denis Papin	1679
match	Robert Boyle	1680
Leyden jar	Pieter van Musschenbroek	1746
eraser	Joseph Priestly	1772
ball bearings	Philip Vaughan	1759
gyroscope	Jean-Bernard Léon Foucault	1852
metal detector	Alexander Graham Bell	1878
first artificial lung machine	Alexander Graham Bell	1878
motorcycle	Gottlieb Daimler	1885
contact lenses	Eugene Frick	1887
escalator	Jesse Reno	1894
oscilloscope	Karl Braun	1897
paper clip	Johan Vaaler	1899
safety pin	Walter Hunt	1899
vacuum cleaner	H. Cecil Booth	1901
electroencephalogram	Willem Einlhoven	1903
neon (lights)	Georges Claude	1910
mass spectrometer	Sir Joseph Thompson	1919
Band Aid™ (sticky plaster)	Earle Dickson	1920
electronic hearing aid	A. Edward Stevens (Marconi Co.)	1923
synthetic insulin	Frederick Banting	1923
Geiger counter	Hans Wilhelm Geiger	1925

Invention	Inventor	Year
iron lung	Philip Drinker	1928
helicopter	Heinrich Foche	1936
walkie-talkie	Al Gross	1937
DDT	Paul Muller	1939
Teflon (PTFE-polytetrafluoroethylene)	Roy Plunkett (DuPont)	1939
synthetic penicillin	Vincent du Vigneaud	1942
aqualung (SCUBA)	Jacques Cousteau	1943
atomic bomb	Robert Oppenheimer	1945
hologram	Dennis Gabor	1947
Scotchguard®	Patsy Sherman	1952
utrasound	Robert Lee Wild	1952
Kevlar™	Stephine Kwolek	1964

Appendix D: Reference Sources

The following books and Internet sources are good general references on inventions, inventing, and groups of inventors.

Books

Aaseng, Nathan. *Twentieth-Century Inventors.* New York: Facts on File, 1996.

Adler, Robert. *Science Firsts.* New York: John Wiley & Sons, 2002.

Ashby, Ruth. *Herstory.* New York: Penguin Books, 1995.

Asimov, Isaac. *Asimov's Chronology of Science and Discovery.* New York: Harper & Row, 1989.

Beshore, George. *Science in Ancient China.* New York: Franklin Watts, 1993.

Bijker, Wiebe. *Of Bicycles, Bakelites, and Bulbs.* Cambridge, MA: The MIT Press, 2001.

Brockman, John. *The Greatest Inventions of the Past 2,000 Years.* New York: Simon & Schuster, 2000.

Brodie, James. *Created Equal: The Lives and Ideas of Black American Inventors.* New York: William Morrow, 1999.

Brown, David. *Inventing Modern America.* Cambridge, MA: The MIT Press, 2002.

Brown, Kenneth. *Inventors at Work.* Redmond, WA: Microsoft Press, 1998.

Chang, Laura, ed. *Scientists at Work.* New York: McGraw-Hill, 2000.

Clark, Donald. *Encyclopedia of Great Inventors and Discoveries.* London: Marshall Cavendish Books, 1991.

Cole, David. *Encyclopedia of Modern Everyday Inventions.* Westport, CT: Greenwood Group, 2003.

Day, Lance, ed. *Biographical Dictionary of the History of Technology.* New York: Routledge, 1996.

Downs, Robert. *Landmarks in Science.* Englewood, CO: Libraries Unlimited, 1993.

Driscoll, Dan. *The Inventor's Times.* New York: Scholastic, Inc., 2003.

Dyson, James. *A History of Great Inventions.* New York: Carroll & Graf Publishers, 2001.

Editors of Time-Life Books. *Inventive Genius*. Alexandria, VA: Time-Life Books, 2001.

Francis, Raymond. *The Illustrated Almanac of Science, Technology, and Invention*. New York: Plenum Trade, 1997.

Gibbs, C. R. *Black Inventors from Africa to America*. Sliver Springs, MD: Three Dimensional Publishing, 1999.

Gratzer, Walter. *Eurekas and Euphorias*. New York: Oxford University Press, 2004.

Haven, Kendall. *Amazing American Women*. Englewood, CO: Libraries Unlimited: 1996.

———. *Marvels of Math*. Englewood, CO: Libraries Unlimited: 1998.

———. *Marvels of Science*. Englewood, CO: Libraries Unlimited, 1994.

———. *Women at the Edge of Discovery*. Englewood, CO: Libraries Unlimited: 2003.

Haven, Kendall, and Donna Clark. *100 Most Popular Scientists for Young Adults*. Englewood, CO: Libraries Unlimited, 1999.

Hayden, Robert. *9 African American Inventors*. New York: Twenty-First Century Books, 1992.

Hornsby, Jeremy. *The Story of Inventions*. New York: Crescent Books, 2002.

Ierley, Merritt. *The Comforts of Home*. New York: C. Potter, 1999.

———. *Wondrous Contrivances*. New York: Clarkson Potter, 2002.

Ives, Patricia. *Creativity and Inventions: The Genius of Afro-Americans and Women in the United States and Their Patents*. Arlington, VA: Research Unlimited, 1997.

Jeffries, Michael, and Gary Lewis. *Inventors and Inventions*. New York: Smithmark, 1997.

Karnes, Francis, and Suzanne Bean. *Girls and Young Women Inventing*. Minneapolis, MN: Free Spirit Publishing, 2001.

Lomask, Milton. *Invention and Technology Great Lives*. New York: Charles Scribner's Sons, 1994.

MacDonald Anne. *Feminine Ingenuity: How Women Inventors Changed America*. New York: Ballantine, 2002.

McGough, Roger. *Dotty Inventions: And Some Real Ones, Too*. New York: American Natural Hygiene Society, 2004.

McKinley, Burt. *Black Inventors of America*. Portland, OR: National Book Company, 2000.

McNeil, Ian. *An Encyclopedia of the History of Technology*. New York: Routledge, 1996.

Messadie, Gerald. *Great Scientific Discoveries*. New York: Chambers, 2001.

National Geographic Society. *Inventors and Discoveries: Changing Our World*. Washington, DC: National Geographic Society, 1998.

Norman, Donald. *The Designs of Everyday Things.* New York: Basic Books, 2002.

Oxlade, Chris. *Inventions.* Dillwyn, VA: Chrysalis Children's Books, 2003.

Petroski, Henry. *The Evolution of Useful Things.* New York: Vintage, 2000.

Ptacek, Greg, and Ethlie Ann Vare. *Women Inventors and Their Discoveries.* 2d ed. Minneapolis, MN: The Oliver Press, 1998.

Rainbow, Jacob. *Inventing for Fun and Profit.* San Francisco: San Francisco Press, 2002.

Richards, Norman. *Dreamers and Doers: Inventors Who Changed the World.* New York: Simon & Schuster Children's Books, 1998.

Rose, Sharon. *How Things Are Made: From Automobiles to Zippers.* New York: DK Publishing, 2003.

Science Museum of London. *Inventing the Modern World: Technology Since 1750.* New York: DK Publications, 2000.

St. George, Judith. *So You Want to Be an Inventor.* New York: Philomel Books, 2002.

Stanley, Autumn. *Mothers and Daughters of Invention.* New Brunswick, NJ: Rutgers University Press, 1998.

Suplee, Curt. *Milestones of Science.* Washington, DC: National Geographic Society, 2000.

Temple, Robert. *The Genius of China: 3,000 Years of Science, Discovery, and Invention.* New York: Simon & Schuster, 2000.

van Dulken, Steven. *Inventing the 19th Century.* New York: New York University Press, 2001.

———. *Inventing the 20th Century.* New York: New York University Press, 2000.

Vare, Ethlie Ann, and Greg Ptacek. *Mothers of Invention.* New York: William Morrow, 1989.

———. *Patently Female: Stories of Women Inventors.* New York: John Wiley & Sons, 2002.

Wulffson, Don. *Extraordinary Stories Behind the Invention of Ordinary Things.* London: Lothrop, Lee & Shepard Books, 1996.

———. *The Kid Who Invented the Popsicle and Other Surprising Stories About Inventions.* New York: Puffin Books, 1999.

Yenne, Bill. *100 Inventions That Shaped World History.* New York: Bluewood Books, 1993.

Internet References

These sites contain good information on, and links to additional information about, inventors, inventing, and inventions.

www.blackinventor.com.
http://inventors.about.com
www.pbs.org/wgbh/theymadeamerica/
www.mainepbs.org/guest/info-inventors-history/
www.invent.org/
www.infoplease.com/ipa/
www.washington.edu/doit/
www.spectrum.ieee.org/publicaccess/inventive/
www.npr.org/templates/story/
www.library.thinkquest/J001490/ProcessofInventing/
www.inventorhelp.com
www.ipl.org/div/subject/browse/hum30.03.80/
www.americanhistory.si.edu/timeline/
www.inventored.org/k-12/inv-hist/
www.invention.smithsonian.org/resources/
www.factsonfile.com/newfacts/
www.iniva.org/library/
www.inventionconvention.com

Index

About the Author

Former research scientist Kendall Haven holds a master's degree in oceanography and spent six years with the Department of Energy before finding his true passion for storytelling. He has now performed for over to four million people in 40 states, and has won numerous awards, including the Storytelling World Silver Award for Best Story Anthology, the 1993 International Festival Association Silver Award for Best Education Program, the 1992 Corporation for Public Broadcasting Silver Award for Best Children's Public Radio Production, and the 1991 Award for Excellence in California Education. He has twice been an American Library Association "Notable Recording Artist" and is the only storyteller in the United States with three entries in ALA's *Best of the Best for Children*. He is also the only West Point graduate to ever become a professional storyteller.

Haven was founder and chair of the International Whole Language Umbrella Storytelling Interest Group and served on the Board of Directors as well as the Educational Advisory Committee of the National Storytelling Association. He was co-director of the Sonoma Storytelling Festival, past chair of the Bay Area Storytelling Festival, and founder of storytelling festivals in Las Vegas, Nevada; Boise, Idaho; and Mariposa, California.

He lives with his wife in the rolling Sonoma County grape vineyards in rural Northern California.